D1752412

Comparative Politics –
Vergleichende Politikwissenschaft

edited by

Prof. Dr. Susanne Pickel, University of Duisburg-Essen
Prof. Dr. Christof Hartmann, University of Duisburg-Essen
Prof. Ingo Rohlfing, PhD, University of Passau

Volume 11

Tanja Walter

Chinese (Non-)Interventions

A Comparative Analysis of Chinese Interventions
in the Middle East and Africa

Nomos

The Deutsche Nationalbibliothek lists this publication in the
Deutsche Nationalbibliografie; detailed bibliographic data
are available on the Internet at http://dnb.d-nb.de

a.t.: Universität Duisburg-Essen, Diss., 2021

ISBN   978-3-8487-7455-5 (Print)
        978-3-7489-3247-5 (ePDF)

British Library Cataloguing-in-Publication Data
A catalogue record for this book is available from the British Library.

ISBN   978-3-8487-7455-5 (Print)
        978-3-7489-3247-5 (ePDF)

Library of Congress Cataloging-in-Publication Data
Walter, Tanja
Chinese (non-) Interventions
A Comparative Analysis of Chinese Interventions
in the Middle East and Africa
Tanja Walter
314 pp.
Includes bibliographic references.

ISBN   978-3-8487-7455-5 (Print)
        978-3-7489-3247-5 (ePDF)

Onlineversion
Nomos eLibrary

1st Edition 2022
© Nomos Verlagsgesellschaft, Baden-Baden, Germany 2022. Overall responsibility for manufacturing (printing and production) lies with Nomos Verlagsgesellschaft mbH & Co. KG.

This work is subject to copyright. All rights reserved. No part of this publication may be reproduced or transmitted in any form or by any means, electronic or mechanical, including photocopying, recording, or any information storage or retrieval system, without prior permission in writing from the publishers. Under § 54 of the German Copyright Law where copies are made for other than private use a fee is payable to "Verwertungsgesellschaft Wort", Munich.

No responsibility for loss caused to any individual or organization acting on or refraining from action as a result of the material in this publication can be accepted by Nomos or the author.

ABSTRACT

China's rise is increasingly covering the military activities of the People's Republic of China (PRC) on the global stage. Beijing's traditional principle of non-intervention seems to be interpreted more flexibly and the presence of Chinese troops in conflict regions in Africa and the Middle East is expanding. This thesis presents a Qualitative Comparative Analysis (QCA) combined with process tracing on drivers underlying China's decision (not) to intervene in areas of conflict in Africa and the Middle East North Africa (MENA) region. In this regard, the study also considers a connection to China's Belt and Road Initiative (BRI). The inquiry shows that Chinese efforts at military diplomacy are largely concentrated on UN peacekeeping missions. Beijing has been focusing on well-established international structures to promote a soft image of China as a guarantor of peace and stability. With the help of an additional analysis of 300 UN Security Council Resolutions, this study finds evidence about changes in the design of UN peacekeeping missions over the last two decades. A Chinese "road map for peace" with particular characteristics is reflected in a new weighting of priorities in multilateral military diplomacy. To understand the implications of Beijing's quest for an indispensable position in the global balance of power, traditional theoretical explanatory approaches need to be expanded. In the framework of foreign policy analysis, this study contributes to a better understanding of the PRC's evolving role in international conflict resolution.

Keywords: China, Conflict Resolution, Military Diplomacy, Peacekeeping Mission, Balance of Power, Belt and Road Initiative

ACKNOWLEDGEMENTS

A journey of a thousand miles begins with a single step[1]. And so did this research project when I first stepped into my professor's office four years ago. I would like to express my sincere gratitude to Professor Nele Noesselt for her great support during my whole PhD process. Her advice and guidance, her commitment to and continuous encouragement of my work made this project possible. I am also thankful to Professor Thomas Demmelhuber, who kindly agreed to be my second supervisor, and whose input was very helpful in finalising this publication. Finally, I would like to thank the auditors, Professor Christof Hartmann and Beate Bernstein, for supporting my publication with this series.

On a personal level, I am deeply grateful to my husband and my family, who have always believed in me. This applies especially to my dear grandmother, who passed away in early 2022, but whose proud eyes I will always remember when I told her I had finished my thesis. This book is for her.

---

1 Proverb by the Chinese philosopher Lao Tzu.

Table of Contents

List of Figures		13
List of Tables		15
ABBREVIATIONS		17
1.	INTRODUCTION	21
	1.1. Outline of the Argumentation	21
	1.2. Setting the Stage: China in Conflict-Affected States	27
	1.3. Peace and Conflict in Africa and the Middle East	32
	1.4. Structure of the Study	35
2.	CONTEXT AND DISCOURSE	38
	2.1. China's (Non-) Intervention Policy	39
	2.2. Understanding State Interventions in Conflicts	45
	2.3. Chinese Peacebuilding Dreams	50
	2.3.1. Beijing's Rhetoric: Between Military Strength and Harmony	51
	2.3.2. Tianxia: A Chinese Concept of World Order	58
	2.4. Summary of Context and Discourse	59
3.	THEORETICAL FRAMEWORK	62
	3.1. Analysing (Chinese) Foreign Policy	63
	3.2. Approaches to Conflict Resolution	69
	3.3. Military Diplomacy and Conflict Mediation	74
	3.4. Power Concepts and Measuring in International Relations	86
	3.4.1. The Concept of Soft Power	88
	3.4.2. Comprehensive National Power	94
	3.5. Formulation of Hypotheses	98
	3.6. Summary of the Theoretical Framework	109

Table of Contents

4.	METHODOLOGY	110
	4.1. Introduction of the Research Design: Qualitative Comparative Analysis	110
	4.2. The Added Value of Process Tracing	113
	4.3. The knowledge gained from a keyword analysis	116
	4.4. Summary of the Methodology	117
5.	OPERATIONALISATION	118
	5.1. Concept Development	118
	5.2. Selection of Cases with and without Chinese Intervention	119
	5.2.1. Further Regional Conflicts since 2013	124
	5.3. Summary of the Operationalisation	127
6.	IDENTIFYING DRIVERS FOR INTERVENTION	129
	6.1. Political Factors and their Influence on Conflict Intervention	131
	6.1.1. Special Relationship	131
	6.1.2. Regime Type	133
	6.1.3. Civil War	134
	6.1.4. Self-Defence	135
	6.2. Economic Factors and their Influence on Conflict Intervention	138
	6.2.1. Resource Wealth of the Conflict-Affected Country	138
	6.2.2. Trade Balance between China and the Conflict-Affected Country	139
	6.2.3. Financial Relations between China and the Conflict-Affected Country	141
	6.2.4. Infrastructural Projects with Chinese Participation in Conflict-Affected Countries	142
	6.3. Sociocultural and Historical Factors and their Influence on Conflict Intervention	143
	6.3.1. Number of Chinese Citizens Abroad	144
	6.3.2. The Question of Taiwan	147

6.4.	Regional and International Factors and their Influence on Conflict Intervention		148
	6.4.1.	Country Location	149
	6.4.2.	Situation in Neighbouring Countries	150
	6.4.3.	Conflict Involvement by Other States or Parties	151
	6.4.4.	Multilateral or International Conflict Intervention	152
	6.4.5.	Chinese Official Development Aid	154
6.5.	Summary of the drivers for intervention		155
7.	**IMPLEMENTATION OF THE QCA**		**157**
7.1.	Results of the QCA		158
	7.1.1.	Evidence from the Synchronic Comparison	160
	7.1.2.	Evidence from the Dyachronic Comparison	161
	7.1.3.	Overall Findings of the QCA	161
7.2.	Summary of the QCA		162
8.	**PROCESS TRACING**		**164**
8.1.	Analysis of Cases during Process Tracing		165
	8.1.1.	Morocco 1991	165
	8.1.2.	DR Congo 2003	168
	8.1.3.	Liberia 2003	173
	8.1.4.	Ivory Coast 2004	176
	8.1.5.	Lebanon 2006	178
	8.1.6.	Sudan 2007	183
	8.1.7.	South Sudan 2013	187
	8.1.8.	Mali 2013	190
	8.1.9.	Israel/Palestine 1990	193
8.2.	Identifying Causal Factors		197
8.3.	Summary of the Process Tracing		203
9.	**KEYWORD ANALYSIS**		**205**
9.1.	Analysis of UN Security Council Resolutions		205
9.2.	Analysis of Security Council Meeting Records		209
10.	**RESULTS AND IMPLICATIONS**		**213**
10.1.	Development of a Causal Model		213

Table of Contents

10.2.	Evidence about Chinese (non-) interventions	216
10.3.	Findings about China's Quest for Power	224
10.4.	Theoretical Implications	232
	10.4.1. China's Placement in International Relations	233
	10.4.2. China's Quest for a Military (Soft) Power Status	238
10.5.	Summary of Results and Implications	241

11. CONCLUSION — 243

11.1.	Empirical Findings: Introducing China's Road Map to Peace	244
11.2.	Filling Methodological Gaps: Identifying China's Drivers	249
11.3.	Theoretical Contributions: Understanding Chinese Soft Power	251
11.4.	Outlook	254

12. ANNEXES — 259

Annex 1: Background Information on Synchronic Control Cases — 259

Annex 2: Background Information on Diachronic Control Cases — 262

REFERENCES — 267

List of Figures

Figure 1: Opening the Black Box with Empirical Narratives 115

Figure 2: Drivers of Chinese Intervention 215

List of Tables

Table 1:	China's vetoes in the UNSC between 1945 and 2020	41
Table 2:	Calculation Elements of CNP by Hu and Men (2002)	96
Table 3:	Purpose of Process Tracing	114
Table 4:	Overview of Cases of Conflict	121
Table 5:	Overview of Synchronic Comparative Cases	122
Table 6:	Overview of Diachronic Comparative Cases	123
Table 7:	Overview of Causal Factors to be tested in the QCA	156
Table 8:	Coding Examples	157
Table 9:	Overview of Chinese Contributions to MINURSO	166
Table 10:	Chinese Contributions to MONUC	170
Table 11:	Chinese Contributions to MONUSCO	170
Table 12:	Chinese Contributions to UNMIL	174
Table 13:	Chinese Contributions to UNOCI	177
Table 14:	Chinese Contributions to UNIFIL	180
Table 15:	Chinese Contributions to UNAMID	185
Table 16:	Chinese Contributions to UNMISS	189
Table 17:	Chinese Contributions to MINUSMA	191
Table 18:	Chinese Contributions to UNTSO	195

List of Tables

Table 19:	Ranking of China's Import Trading Partners	201
Table 20:	Ranking of China's Export Trading Partners	202
Table 21:	Summary of Causal Factors	203
Table 22:	Number of Resolutions adopted by UNSC per year	205
Table 23:	Selection of Keywords	206
Table 24:	Keyword Analysis of UNSC Resolutions 2001–2020	207
Table 25:	Comparison of Keywords in Two Ten-Year Periods	208
Table 26:	Security Council Meeting Records	210
Table 27:	Chinese Drivers of and Priorities in Peacekeeping	235

ABBREVIATIONS

AIIB	Asian Infrastructure Investment Bank
AMIS	African Union Mission in Sudan
AMS	Academy of Military Science (of the PRC)
AU	African Union
BRI	Belt and Road Initiative
BRICS	Brazil, Russia, India, China, South Africa
CAR	Central African Republic
CAD	China–Africa Development Fund
CNP	Comprehensive National Power
COVID-19	Coronavirus Disease 2019
CPC	Communist Party of China
CsQCA	crisp-set Qualitative Comparative Analysis
CWM	Civil War Mediation
DAC	Development Assistance Committee
DDPD	Doha Document for Peace in Darfur
DDR	Disarm, Demobilise, Reintegrate
ECOWAS	Economic Community of West African States
ETIM	East Turkistan Islamic Movement
EU	European Union
FC	Force Commander
FDI	Foreign Direct Investment
FOCAC	Forum on China–African Cooperation
FsQCA	fuzzy-set Qualitative Comparative Analysis
GCC	Gulf Cooperation Council
GDP	Gross Domestic Product
GNP	Gross National Product
ICC	International Criminal Court
ICISS	International Commission on Intervention and State Sovereignty
IGAD	Intergovernmental Authority on Development in East Africa
IMF	International Monetary Fund
IO	International Organisation
IR	International Relations
ISIS	Islamic State of Iraq and Syria
JCPOA	Joint Comprehensive Plan of Action
LAF	Lebanese Armed Forces
M23	Movement of 23rd March (DR Congo)
MENA	Middle East and North Africa
MINURSO	United Nations Mission for the Referendum in Western Sahara

ABBREVIATIONS

MINUSMA	United Nations Multidimensional Integrated Stabilization Mission in Mali
MNLA	Islamist National Movement for the Liberation of Azawad
MONUC	United Nations Mission in the Democratic Republic of Congo
MONUSCO	United Nations Organization Stabilization Mission in the Democratic Republic of the Congo
mvQCA	Multi-Value Qualitative Comparative Analysis
NAM	Non-Aligned Movement
NATO	North Atlantic Treaty Organization
NIF	National Islamic Front (Sudan)
NPFL	National Patriotic Front of Liberia
OAU	Organization of African Unity
OBOR	One Belt One Road
ODA	Official Development Assistance
OECD	Organisation for Economic Cooperation and Development
ONUCA	United Nations Observer Group in Central America
OPEC	Organization of the Petroleum Exporting Countries
PKO	Peacekeeping Operation
PLA	People's Liberation Army
PLO	Popular Front of the Liberation of Palestine
POLISARIO	Frente Popular para la Libération de Seguia el Hamra y de Río de Oro
PPP	Public–Private Partnership
PRC	People's Republic of China
PRIO	Peace Research Institute Oslo
P5	Five permanent members of the UN Security Council (People's Republic of China, France, Russian Federation, the United Kingdom, and the United States of America)
QCA	Qualitative Comparative Analysis
RAID	Rights and Accountability in Development
R&D	Research and Development
RtoP / R2P	Responsibility to Protect
SADR	Sahrawi Arab Democratic Republic
SPLA	Southern People's Liberation Army
SRSG	Special Representative of the Secretary General
ToT	Terms of Trade
UAE	United Arab Emirates
UCDP	Uppsala Conflict Data Program
UN	United Nations
UN DPKO	United Nations Department of Peacekeeping Operations
UN OCHA	United Nations Office for the Coordination of Humanitarian Affairs
UNAMID	African Union/United Nations Hybrid Operation in Darfur
UNGOMAP	United Nations Good Offices Mission in Afghanistan and Pakistan

ABBREVIATIONS

UNIFIL	United Nations Interim Force in Lebanon
UNIIMOG	United Nations Iraq–Iran Military Observer Group
UNIKOM	United Nations Iraq–Kuwait Observation Mission
UNMHA	United Nations Mission to Support the Hudaydah Agreement
UNMIL	United Nations Mission in Liberia
UNMIS	United Nations Mission in Sudan
UNMISS	United Nations Mission in South Sudan
UNOCI	United Nations Operation in Côte d'Ivoire
UNOMIL	United Nations Observer Mission in Liberia
UNRWA	United Nations Relief and Works Agency for Palestine Refugees in the Near East
UNSC	United Nations Security Council
UNTSO	United Nations Truce Supervision Organization
USA	United States of America
US AFRICOM	United States Africa Commands
USSR	Union of Soviet Socialist Republics

1. INTRODUCTION

1.1. Outline of the Argumentation

A famous Chinese proverb says "to know the road ahead, ask those coming back" (unknown author). This saying may be fitting for many different situations, both in the lives of ordinary people and on the global political stage. In terms of the road to world peace, the picture of returning and departing actors can be applied to current developments in conflict-affected countries. While great powers such as the United States of America (USA) have been at the forefront of many international conflict zones for decades, US troops have increasingly withdrawn from global hotspots in the recent past, most prominently during the presidency of former US President Donald Trump, who clearly denied the US role as the "world's policemen"[2] in his speeches. Although Donald Trump's narratives often did not reflect actual US foreign policy during his presidency, the hasty withdrawal of US soldiers from conflicts in Syria (2019), Iraq (2020), Somalia[3] (2020) and Afghanistan (2020/21) has left these countries in a perpetually fragile state with a population at risk of the resurgence of violent atrocities and war. Hence, those "coming back" often paint a disillusioning picture.

Over the last twenty years, academic debate about peacekeeping has covered models of "liberal peace", which promised the achievement of welfare and stability (Newman, 2009; Paris, 2010). The advocates of liberal peace have always been accompanied by critics arguing in favour of alternative, "post-liberal" concepts or the combination of both models (Debiel & Rinck, 2016; Richmond, 2009). However, expectations of sustainable conflict resolution could frequently not be fulfilled and the imposition of standardised (democratisation) concepts have only been partially successful until today (Debiel, Held, & Schneckener, 2016, p. xi). Current conflict zones illustrate that achieving world peace remains an ambitious goal. The number of conflicts worldwide augmented from fewer than twenty

---

[2] Words used by Donald Trump in his commencement address for the United States Military Academy at West Point on 13th June 2020.
[3] Some troops were moved to other African countries such as Kenya and Djibouti.

1. INTRODUCTION

conflicts in 1946 to fifty-four in 2019[4] (Palik, Rustad, & Methi, 2020, p. 8; UCDP&PRIO, 2020). While conflict resolution therefore remains one of the most pressing challenges for the international community, the landscape of major actors is changing. The US presidency of Donald Trump has shown the retreat of US military troops from international conflict zones as well as a reduction of contributions to UN peacekeeping missions, which incrementally illustrated the US' withdrawal from their position as a self-appointed leader of peace[5]. At the same time, the People's Republic of China (PRC) has taken the road towards increased participation in international conflict resolution activities and appears to have abandoned its traditional policy of non-intervention. These opposite movements of the USA and China raise the question of whether China will follow the proverb and metaphorically "ask those coming back" about the way ahead. If yes, it is questionable if China will follow the US' footsteps or if Beijing will use this window of opportunity to present its own "road map for peace". This question is also relevant with regard to China's economic rise. At the opening forum for the Belt and Road Initiative in 2017, Chinese President Xi Jinping indicated a connection between China's giant infrastructural project and Beijing's interest in international conflict zones when he stated that, "we should build the Belt and Road into a road for peace [since the] pursuit of the Belt and Road Initiative requires a peaceful and stable environment" (Xi quoted from Xinhua, 2017). The PRC's aspiration to become a guarantor of peace and stability might thus create both hope and scepticism for some of the most volatile and conflict-affected states. Critical voices have been heard saying that the "[talk] of forthcoming peace and harmony may […] be no more than a smokescreen to counter perceptions that China's attempted mass reorganization of national and regional economies seeks to secure its global dominance" (Bowen, 2017).

Data shows that Chinese troops were active in nine conflict-affected states in the Middle East and Africa in 2013, the official beginning of the BRI with increasing numbers of troop contributions until 2020 (Bowen, 2017; UCDP&PRIO, 2020; UN Peacekeeping, 2020). While Chinese troops have been present in Lebanon and Sudan for several years, however,

---

4 The figures presented here relate to state-based violence only. When adding conflicts involving non-state violence and one-sided violence, the number of conflicts increases to a total of 152 conflicts in 2019 (Uppsala Conflict Data Program, 2020).
5 This observation refers to developments until January 2021, the end of Donald Trump's presidency in the USA.

Beijing has refrained from getting involved in conflicts in Yemen and the Central African Republic (CAR)[6]. Whether President Xi's proposed connection between China's increased activities in conflict resolution practices and the BRI is shaping Beijing's quest to become a guarantor of peace is one of several questions emerging from China's recent activities.

Throughout recent years, the PRC's infrastructural activities particularly in Africa have been confronted with local political instabilities and conflicts that have outlined China's economic vulnerability abroad (Hartmann & Noesselt, 2020, p. 1). Beijing's foreign policy behaviour has therefore increasingly considered questions of security and stability (Hartmann & Noesselt, 2020, p. 4; Noesselt, 2020, p. 18). China's second Africa policy paper of 2015 even states that:

> "China will play a constructive role in maintaining and promoting peace and security in Africa. It will explore means and ways with Chinese characteristics to constructively participate in resolving hot-button issues in Africa and exert a unique impact on and make greater contributions to African peace and security" (China Daily, 2015).

To identify which direction China's road to peace will take and how Beijing's increased international conflict resolution is changing the PRC's power status in the international community, it is necessary to take a closer look at the PRC's peacekeeping efforts. In doing so, this dissertation identifies drivers for Chinese interventions in conflict situations in the MENA region and Africa and examines to what degree they can be considered specifically "Chinese characteristics" in international designs for conflict resolution.

First, this dissertation aims at understanding when, how and why China intervenes in conflicts, either alone or as part of an international mission, thereby abandoning its traditional policy of non-intervention. Second, the thesis provides answers to the question of China's changing role in the international balance of power system. Specifically, the following questions were addressed in the research phase:

---

6 In 2020, China contributed to a UN Peacekeeping mission to the CAR for the first time.

1. INTRODUCTION

> *What variables drive China's interventions in the MENA region and in Africa?*
> *How do China's contributions to conflict resolution affect the PRC's power status?*

To answer these questions, a Qualitative Comparative Analysis (QCA) in combination with process tracing was used. This method allowed a range of empirical conflicts to be analysed and causal factors for China's interventions in conflicts in the MENA region and in Africa to be discovered. Overall, twenty cases were identified and analysed along twenty-six coded criteria in fifteen categories. Whilst previous research has concentrated on conducting case studies of Chinese activities in specific countries such as Mali and Sudan or on the African continent (Seesaghur & Ansong, 2014), this comparative analysis adds knowledge about China's general approach to international conflict resolution. In his regard, previous results of case studies were valuable in order to compare factors such as trade relations or the type of conflicts.

The QCA in this dissertation focused on the year 2013 to investigate a possible connection between Chinese interventions in conflict regions and the beginning of the Belt and Road Initiative. Moreover, in 2013 Xi Jinping presented the strategy of "striving for achievement" for the first time, which indicated a departure from China's previous concept of "keeping a low profile" (see chapter 2.1.) and might have effects on China's behaviour in international conflict resolution, too (Yan, 2014, p. 154). In addition to the comparative analysis of cases in the year 2013, the method of process tracing was added to the study with the aim of gaining a better understanding of the circumstances during the time of intervention. This approach enabled the causal mechanisms of China's decision to be understood better (Beach & Pedersen, 2013, p. 2). When these two methods were combined, the causal factors identified provided evidence concerning the drivers and characteristics of China's international efforts. The question about drivers was broadly defined and intended to find out what temporal, geographic and geopolitical conditions must be met for China to militarily intervene in a conflict. The goal was to understand which conditions must be fulfilled for China to participate in an operation. Clustering the factors identified made it possible to recognise drivers that characterise China's activities in conflict resolution. An additional examination of 300 resolutions adopted by the Security Council between

1.1. Outline of the Argumentation

2001 and 2020[7] hinted at the increasing influence of such drivers on the design of international peacekeeping missions and points to a change in the international balance of power towards a greater weight of Chinese priorities.

The results cast doubt on some widely accepted theories. For example, the assumption that military intervention is only used to increase a country's own wealth cannot be confirmed (Carr, 1939; Mearsheimer, 2001). Instead, the results of this study suggest that China's interventions aim at repositioning the PRC within the international community and the system of UN missions in particular.

The analysis of different cases of conflict-affected states showed that the causal structures underlying Chinese intervention are complex and vary from case to case. The most important condition found in the study was the existence of UN peacekeeping missions, which turned out to be an indispensable factor in conflict intervention by China. However, conflict-affected states' recognition of the One-China principle was also significant[8]. Moreover, other factors tested such as trade relations, the threat of regionalisation and reputational opportunities were identified as coincidentally causal conditions for China's decision to participate in international missions for conflict resolution. The QCA furthermore showed that bilateral military Chinese interventions in conflicting areas in the MENA region and Africa could not be found. However, the focus of China's interventions in the MENA region and Africa is connected to China's need for regional stability and security to realise its giant infrastructural project of the BRI. Chinese interventions in conflict-affected countries in both regions are also determined by the PRC's attempt to increase its soft power image (Arif, 2017; Kurlantzick, 2007). Beijing is thus using the reputation of UN peacekeeping to establish a positive image of China's armed forces. From a theoretical perspective, Joseph Nye's theory about soft power is valuable in explaining China's approach. According to Nye, soft power refers to the ability to shape preferences and co-opt by means of attraction in contrast to coercion (see chapter 3.4.1.) (Nye, 2004). Yet,

---

7 This period was chosen since the results of the QCA showed increased Chinese military contributions to UN peacekeeping since the beginning of the new millennium.
8 The One-China principle insists that both the People's Republic of China (PRC) and Taiwan—also known as the Republic of China (ROC)—are parts of a single state. Since the "1992 Consensus", both the PRC and ROC have agreed about the existence of one China but disagree on which government is the legitimate one to represent and govern it. See also Chapter 6.3.2.

1. INTRODUCTION

to fully understand how the PRC is using its military activities to create the image of China as a guarantor of peace, an extension of Nye's theory is necessary.

The results of this study have also been discussed with renowned Chinese scholars. On the occasion of a two-day workshop on "China's Silkroad Initiative", which took place at the Confucius Institute of the Free University in Berlin in June 2019, Liu Haifang and Tang Xiaoyang were interviewed in English with regard to the research question of this study. Their input provided valuable insights into the Chinese perspective on peacekeeping and the connection of China's military activities to the BRI. Liu Haifang, an Associate Professor at the School of International Studies at Peking University considered that China is still upholding its principles of non-intervention while, at the same time, the PRC is seeking another way of assuming responsibility (Liu, 2019). According to Liu, one such way is the provision of 8,000 blue helmets and a budget of one billion USD to the United Nations (ibid.). Liu furthermore named the Forum on China–African Cooperation (FOCAC) as a major platform for security questions. Yet, she considered that while the BRI is a project that encouraged everyone to join, security aspects were dealt with separately on a case-by-case basis. The participation of China in peacekeeping operations (PKO) was thus not directly related to security challenges on the ground such as robbery, but rather an indicator of China becoming a more responsible power within the international platform (ibid.).

Deputy Director Tang Xiaoyang from the Carnegie-Tsinghua Center for Global Policy shared Liu Haifang's perception that China's participation in UN missions is politically motivated (Tang, 2019). Tang likewise did not see a contradiction between China's principle of non-intervention and its participation in UN missions since China would not intervene in any conflict without the UN. The expert furthermore considered the BRI more important for China than the implementation of UN missions since the BRI covers a whole network and PKOs are usually seen on a case-by-case basis. Within the BRI partner countries, local governments were asked to ensure protection. Tang, nevertheless, admitted that security assumes a high priority in President Xi Jinping's speeches given that the keyword "peace" is frequently mentioned. Tang highlighted that while host countries along the Belt and Road were asked to take care of security, China would promote peace and security through employment and development, which would automatically lead to a more secure environment (ibid.).

Overall, the results of this study confirm the opinions expressed by Liu Haifang and Tang Xiaoyang with regard to the observation that the PRC's activities remain within established international structures of conflict resolution. Whilst the USA, Great Britain, France and Russia (P5) have historically remained reluctant to provide peacekeeping personnel to the UN and the USA has reduced its financial support recently, both China's increasing troop and financial contributions to UN missions as well as the changing patterns of UN Resolutions are evidence of China's growing influence on decisions about peacekeeping in the UN Security Council, an organ that is respected by all 193 UN member states.

Finally, the investigation of both concrete conflict cases and UN Resolutions allowed for the concretisation of Chinese priorities and "characteristics" in the field of peacekeeping. Throughout the research process, it became clear that China does not add new elements to international conflict resolution but rather introduces a new weighting of previously known components in the design of UN peacekeeping missions. "Chinese characteristics", therefore, refer to a new proportioning of elements, which can be considered a new "road map for peace". In this regard, an increased focus on stability can be noted in the design of UN Security Council resolutions on peacekeeping. While traditionally, Western principles such as the protection of human rights, the installation of (liberal) institutions and a system of good governance are still included in the clauses of UN resolutions, topics such as economic development and infrastructure have gained weight during the last two decades. Hence, this study finds that China's contributions to international conflict resolution have gained weight on the international stage and could possibly change the global balance of power in the field of conflict resolution. China has changed the country's policy of (non-) intervention and is promoting reorganisation in the proportions of well-established ingredients on the international road to peace. However, the implementation of this new road map will also depend on other actors' reactions and their efforts in defending Western values in peacekeeping.

1.2. Setting the Stage: China in Conflict-Affected States

This dissertation considers China's (non-) interventions in conflict-affected states and aims at finding drivers that unveil Beijing's approach to conflict resolution and shed light on a possible Chinese "road to peace". Three main reasons underpin this research project's relevance.

1. INTRODUCTION

First, the PRC is increasingly present in conflict-affected world regions, particularly the Middle East and Africa, where Beijing has introduced its own international agenda, challenging the previous US leadership. In recent studies, scholars have explored the integration of both regions into China's BRI and highlighted China's economic interests there (Blanchard, 2021; Farooq, Feroze & Kai, 2019; ZiroMwatela & Zhao, 2016). Indeed, at least some countries in the MENA region are already part of the Silk Road Economic Belt, whereat Eyler noted that the Maritime Silk Road Initiative was "all about Africa" (Eyler, 2014). So far, most analyses have focused on the economic advantages and risks of greater integration of these countries into the BRI. When the BRI—previously announced as One Belt One Road (OBOR)—was first presented in 2013, commentators used to view China as a free rider of US security provision in risky areas, while Beijing was focusing on business relations only (Haenle, 2013; Spegele & Bradley, 2013). In recent years, however, multiple security threats against Chinese citizens and companies in volatile regions were followed by an increase in activities related to security protection by the Chinese government. This also helped Beijing to defend the government's strategy of "going out" domestically (Grieger, 2019, p. 2). As ZiroMwatela & Zhao note: "Whichever powerful state controls the security of [the Horn of Africa region and the Suez Canal], also controls the maritime trade routes between Asia, Europe and Africa" (ZiroMwatela & Zhao, 2016, p. 11). Beijing's recent interest in global security is noteworthy since China's diplomacy has been driven by the People's Republic's Five Principles of Peaceful Coexistence for many decades (Ministry of Foreign Affairs of the PRC, 2014). These principles were laid down by Premier Zhou Enlai at a Peace Conference held in Bandung in 1955 and include respect for the sovereignty of others, non-aggression, peaceful coexistence and non-interference (Dirlik, 2015). Referring to these principles, China mostly kept out of conflicts in the past. The principles thus helped China to refrain from situations that might have challenged its government to take sides in a conflict (Gonzales-Vincente, 2015, p. 208). Yet, considering the increasing numbers of Chinese military in conflict-affected countries during the last two decades, the principles seem to have been interpreted more flexibly, as has Beijing's attitude towards unstable world regions. While China's increased efforts in questions of international security were still welcomed by the US in 2008 and 2009 (see chapter 2.1), the Trump administration[9] broadly judged China's secu-

---

9 The presidency of Donald Trump began on 20th January 2017 and ended on 20th January 2021. He was the 45th president of the United States.

rity behaviour as an attempt to seek world domination (Yang, 2021, p. 144). While Trump outlined China as an existential threat that should be met with confrontation, the 2020 administration of Joe Biden has changed the US approach towards considering China both an economic and a normative challenge that has to be competed with (Chen, Rogers, Moore, & Yankus, 2021, p. 1). In March 2021, Biden presented the first interim national security strategic guidance of his presidency, which stated that "[China] is the only competitor potentially capable of combining its economic, diplomatic, military, and technological power to mount a sustained challenge to a stable and open international system" (The White House, 2021, p. 8). The report continues with Biden's assurance to "position [the USA], diplomatically and militarily, to defend [the US'] allies" (ibid., p. 20). At the same time, however, the report states that the US "will right-size [its] military presence" in the Middle East because "[we] do not believe that military force is the answer to the region's challenges" (ibid., p. 11; 15). Finally, Biden sets the goal of "[shaping] new global norms and agreements that advance our interests and reflect our values", while "[deterring] Chinese aggression and counter[ing] threats to our collective security, prosperity, and democratic way of life" (ibid., p. 20). Hence, the report illustrates the US recognition of China as a serious protagonist on the international stage, with whom cooperation is proposed whenever "national fates are intertwined" (ibid., p. 21). To examine when and where such cooperation might be possible, it is necessary to first assess and understand the underlying motives and capabilities of China's increased military activities in conflict-affected countries. This study attempts to fill this research gap and contributes to a better knowledge of drivers for China's changed behaviour in foreign policy.

Second, China has taken on a proactive role within the United Nations and the instrument of UN peacekeeping in particular. China's mounting contributions to UN peacekeeping missions visualise the PRC's shift in strategy towards a more prominent and assertive position in security-related topics on the multilateral stage. While China was reluctant to make international commitments during the 1980s and 1990s, the PRC has become the top provider of both financial and personnel contributions for this international instrument (UN Peacekeeping, 2020). As Niu pointed out: "China's attitude towards the UN changed from denying and doubting the role of UN to recognizing and valuing it" (Niu, 2018, p. 65). The more Beijing intensified its participation in the UN, the more actively involved China became in multilateral diplomacy (ibid., p. 65). This observation can also be made with regard to different thematic areas dealt

1. INTRODUCTION

with at the UN. Whilst China used to focus on development activities, Beijing's increased contributions to UN peacekeeping illustrate China's interest in the UN's "peace and security work" (Feltman, 2020, p. 1). This shift became particularly apparent in September 2015, when President Xi Jinping announced he would expand China's contributions to the UN and establish a USD 1 billion "China–UN peace and development fund" (Xi, 2015). Xi declared that

> "China will join the new UN peacekeeping capability readiness system, take the lead to set up a permanent peacekeeping police squad and build an 8,000-strong standby peacekeeping force. China has also decided that it will provide 100 million USD of free military assistance to the African Union in the next five years to support the establishment of the African Standby Force and the African Capacity for Immediate Response to Crisis" (ibid.).

In combination with the BRI announced in 2013, Beijing underscored China's ambitions for a more confident international profile. In the following years, Western actors especially experienced the implications of increased Chinese participation in security-related questions. As a recent example, Feltman mentions China's affiliation with Russia in vetoing UN resolutions on the protection of human rights in Syria (see also chapter 2.1) (Feltman, 2020, p. 1). China's powerful negotiating position is strengthened both by its status as the second largest financial donor and by the fact that China—unlike the USA—paid its contributions to the UN on time (Feltman, 2020, p. 4). Whilst former US President Donald Trump introduced cuts to the US contributions to the UN budget, President Joe Biden announced that the US "will re-engage as a full participant [in the United Nations] and work to meet [the USA's] financial obligations, in full and on time" (The White House, 2021, p. 13). It remains to be seen to what extent the new US government will hold to Biden's promise. Whilst the amount of budget available to the UN defines how much the UN can spend and achieve, those spending the funds have traditionally also claimed greater influence on the organisation's orientation and the design of its missions. China's increased financial contributions have thus been accompanied by demands for the greater influence of Chinese substantive and content-related contributions on the design of peace and security policies (Feltman, 2020, p. 1). Pohl wrote, however, that "different religious traditions in China have also led to a specific political culture with other priorities for the common good and living together in society. China and most of the East Asian countries give top priority to social harmony and stability" (Pohl, 2012, p. 99). China's strengthened international position might thus lead to a change in the UN's previous focus on Western priority values, such as human rights and democracy. As Feltman states, "The United States tends to undervalue multilateralism. Europeans usually overvalue multilateralism. And China wishes to change multilateralism" (Feltman, 2020, p. 1). If Western actors and particularly the USA decide to compete and preserve the values on which the United Nations was once founded, it is necessary to have a profound knowledge about the motivations that underly China's increased contributions and if any replacement of Western values can really be observed. This study provides an analysis of China's previous military contributions in the field of peace and security, especially within the UN. Furthermore, the research results provide evidence about what drives Beijing's military activities and how a Chinese "road map for peace" can be met from a Western perspective.

Third, China's ambition to become a major world power is multifaceted. With regard to economics, the People's Republic's massive economic investments in the Belt and Road Initiative outline Beijing's claim to occupy an economic leadership role. To become a responsible great power, however, security and stability are closely connected to China's promise of "win-win cooperation" (Xi quoted from Xinhua, 2017). While other major powers such as the USA have not yet succeeded in bringing peace to a range of countries in the Middle East and Africa, China's approach is worth looking at. The discourse overview in chapter 2.3.1 outlines to what extent military-related topics as well as the field of peace and security have been covered by leading Chinese politicians in recent speeches. In the past, Western leaders barely noticed China when dealing with questions of security and considered global security in the hands of the USA (Zaborowski, 2018, p. 1). This might also have been reasoned by China's policy of keeping a "low profile" (see chapter 2.1.). In 2003, when the EU and China agreed on the importance of a "pluralistic international system" and China subsequently enhanced its presence in the Middle East and Africa and initiated the modernisation of its military, the US and the EU remained silent (ibid., p. 1). Almost twenty years later, Western powers have paid more attention to China's moves. Beijing's increasing efforts in security-related questions and China's contributions to conflict resolution have been acknowledged as part of the PRC's efforts to change the global balance of power. Whilst the European Commission acknowledges Beijing as a cooperation partner in many areas, China is considered "a systemic rival promoting alternative models of governance" that challenges the EU in promoting European "interests and values" (European Commission,

1. INTRODUCTION

2019, p. 1). Moreover, whilst China, the EU and the US are three biggest traders in the world and their economic relationship is closely intertwined, the European Commission considered in their strategic outlook of 2019 that "China's economic power and political influence have grown with unprecedented scale and speed, reflecting its ambitions to become a leading global power" (ibid., p. 1). European concerns regarding China's ambitions as a rising power are shared by the US. In US President Joe Biden's remarks on "America's Place in the World" in February 2021, Biden stated that "American leadership must meet this new moment of advancing authoritarianism, including the growing ambitions of China to rival the United States" (Biden, 2021). At least since Xi Jinping's announcement in 2017, it has become clear, however, that the PRC is striving "to become a "world-class" military by the end of 2049" (US Department of Defense, 2020, p. i). However, Zaborowski outlines that the concerns in the USA and Europe differ with regard to Beijing's military modernisation efforts. Whilst the USA is alarmed by increased spending on China's defence, the EU is concerned about the "lack of transparency in this process" (Zaborowski, 2018, p. 4). Both Western powers have recognised, however, that after the launch of China's BRI, Beijing is also reaching out to the field of peace and security. With the objective of understanding which role Beijing wants to adopt here and if traditionally dominant Western powers need to fear a Chinese threat to the current rules-based international order, this study assesses the extent to which China's approach is changing the current balance of power in international conflict resolution.

1.3. Peace and Conflict in Africa and the Middle East

When one analyses China's increased contributions to conflict intervention, the MENA region and Africa are outstanding. Many countries in these geographical areas are chronically unstable and have experienced numerous conflicts in the past. In the Middle East, long-term civil wars in Syria and Yemen are currently contributing to a volatile security situation in the region (Yang, 2018a, p. 286). What began with political upheavals as part of the Arab Spring in many countries in the MENA region in 2011 challenged the legitimacy of political rule in these countries (Demmelhuber & Zumbrägel, 2017, p. 47). While large parts of the population longed for new configurations of regional order, massive protest movements triggered significant processes of change in the power structures, particularly in Arab republics (ibid., p. 60). At the same time, the protests were accompanied by an increase in state military violence and repression against protestors (Stacher, 2015, p. 260). While new configurations of political order became apparent in some countries, with Tunisia being the most prominent example, this has not been the case in all the Arab states affected. In countries such as Yemen, Syria or Libya, the Arab Spring was the predecessor of subsequent political crises that further undermined these states' integrity (Demmelhuber & Zumbrägel, 2017, p. 47). As Yang outlines, unsuccessful regime changes have resulted in prolonged civil conflicts leaving behind power vacuums that make it easy for extremist groups to infiltrate what has been left of state and societal structures (2018a, p. 286). The hybrid threats to stability and security that emerged after the onset of the Arab Spring combine traditional (Israel–Palestinian conflict) as well as non-traditional (emergence of ISIS) concerns and have had spill-over effects on neighbouring countries and even on Europe (refugee crisis) (ibid., p. 287). Beijing's reliance on resource supplies from Middle Eastern and African countries—albeit diversified—leaves China vulnerable to conflict incidents and sudden interruptions of supplies in those regions (ibid., p. 284f). Beijing is closely monitoring developments on the ground, not least because of its extensive energy and commercial interests. Several countries in the two regions are located along or near the land and maritime routes of the BRI and China has recognised the threat of transborder extremism caused by non-state actors in fragile countries (Noesselt, 2020, p. 18). Large, capital-intensive infrastructural projects along these routes require a secure environment to avoid sabotage or attacks (Yang, 2018a, p. 284). The beginning of turmoil and war in Libya is one of the most prominent examples of China's sudden escape from the country and the associated losses of Chinese state enterprise (ibid., p. 284). Many countries in the Middle East possess large oil reserves which have become crucial to Chinese energy demands (U.S. Energy Information Administration, 2020). Yet, also African countries such as Angola and Gabon have become important for Chinese crude oil imports (ibid.). Oil fields and other energy sources are strategic targets for extremists and terrorists and thus particularly vulnerable to attacks which may harm trade flows (Zhu, 2011).

In addition, many African states are suffering from a failure of governments to ensure fundamental state functions (Acemoğlu & Robinson, 2013). While in the past China focused on a state-centric approach when reaching out to Africa for economic reasons, Beijing has been confronted with local power structures that are often rooted in complex structures of religious and ethnic elites (Noesselt, 2020, p. 18). In many cases, the state plays a rather limited role in delivering services to the population

1. INTRODUCTION

and the system of rivalling groups represents a constant trigger for political violence (Azam, 2001, p. 430). The distribution of power between ethnic divisions in many African countries remains crucial in the provision of basic services for the population such as security (Azam, 2001, p. 429). Continued warfare and conflict have become a source of livelihood and "when war became a business, peace would inevitably mean unemployment or at least a drop in profits and brand recognition" to many factions (Williams, 2011, p. 178). Hence, rebel groups, guerrilla movements and civil wars endanger "China's African dream", as Noesselt (2020) outlines. Moreover, Islamist terrorist groups have increasingly attempted to recruit new members among Muslim minorities living in China, which adds a domestic security perspective to Beijing's interest in conflict resolution (ibid., p. 24). The PRC's initial approach of ignoring local regime types had to be modified in search of a "stabilization policy" since even non-intervention can be supportive for one fraction or another (Hartmann, 2020, p. 83; 95). Supporting the stabilisation of local governance, however, poses challenges depending on the prevailing governance model. Hartmann outlines three different models of governance that result in different perceptions about China by African actors (Hartmann, 2020, p. 95). Neo-patrimonial regimes and democratic and authoritarian models each imply specific expectations from their respective leaders, ranging from short-term benefits to general legitimisation (ibid., p. 95).

In addition to measurable factors such as trade and resource supply, the question of security in the Middle East and Africa is also one of image, prestige and power. Insecurity and instability contradict China's vision of a "harmonious world" as postulated by President Hu Jintao in 2007 (Hao, 2008, p. 29). Will China be the one actor to finally promote peace in these conflict-torn world regions? After the rather moderate successes of other major powers such as the USA, Russia, France or Great Britain, China seems to be making an attempt. With regard to China's increasing engagement in the regions and its higher self-interest in regional security, it makes sense for China to re-evaluate the risks and costs of conflict (non-) intervention. Since military strength is often considered a main element of a country's power status, China's contributions to conflict resolution as part of the PRC's foreign policy are considered here in relation to a possible change in the global balance of power. This provides sufficient reason for a more detailed analysis of China's understanding of its role and power status on Beijing's new road to conflict resolution, peace and stability.

1.4. Structure of the Study

To answer the research questions and contribute to the scholarly debate on China's contributions in the field of international conflict resolution, this study is divided into eleven chapters. The following overview of the chapters clarifies the analytical procedure and the structure of the study.

To understand the context and relevance of the topic of this research project, chapter 2 provides an overview of the history of China's (non-) intervention policy. This is important to understand since it helps us to grasp why Beijing's recent increased contributions to international conflict resolution are a decisive change in the country's traditional position. Chapter 2.2. integrates this new Chinese positioning into the general framework of state interventions and clarifies which type of "intervention" this inquiry focuses on. A clear definition is necessary to set the limits of this research project and concretise the specific contribution of this thesis to political science. Chapter 2 furthermore covers an overview of the discourse used by Chinese politicians with regard to China's changing role in international conflict resolution and highlights that Beijing is announcing a new "road map for peace" with "Chinese characteristics".

Chapter 3 provides a theoretical framework for the study and covers two methods of conflict resolution in foreign policy analysis, namely military diplomacy and mediation. Since a peacebuilding process depends on the distribution of power among the actors involved, concepts of power and measurement tools are presented. This is an important part of the study as it allows a theoretical classification of China's behaviour and leads to the formulation of hypotheses to be tested in this inquiry.

In chapter 4, the methodology used for the investigation is presented. The study is based on a comparison of different cases of conflicts with and without Chinese military intervention. The core of the study is comprised of a QCA. Whilst the results of the QCA provided evidence of the simultaneous occurrence of several different factors, the method did not provide information about causality. To overcome this deficiency, the method of process tracing was added to the study. Moreover, the study was enriched with a keyword analysis.

Chapter 5 focuses on the operationalisation of the study. This includes a presentation of cases that have been selected for the study. The consideration of databanks such as the Uppsala Conflict Data Programme (UCDP) resulted in the identification of nine main cases where China actively participates in military conflict resolution. In addition, four synchronic con-

1. INTRODUCTION

flicts were found without China's involvement. Finally, seven diachronic comparative cases of conflict without China's participation are presented.

Possible drivers for Chinese interventions are collected in chapter 6. These drivers were derived from secondary literature and clustered into four categories: (6.1) political, (6.2) economic, (6.3) sociocultural and historic, and (6.4) regional and international factors. Each category has several sub-categories[10] that are described in the chapter. The choice of categories and factors was developed by analysing literature on research findings on military operations. This presents a crucial element for the development of the causal model of drivers for Chinese state intervention in conflicting regions and the design of a possible Chinese "road map for peace".

The implementation and results of the QCA are covered in chapter 7. Evidence gained from both synchronic and diachronic comparisons is provided and summarised. The synchronic comparison revealed numerous solution terms with different combinations of national, regional and international factors. Remarkably, the prevalence of a UN peacekeeping mission was found in all cases with Chinese participation. Yet, the solution terms were too diverse to discover a single combination of factors necessary for Chinese intervention in conflicts. Therefore, the cases were analysed once again using the method of process tracing.

In chapter 8, an examination of each case is presented in terms of the year when China's contribution started. Accordingly, the context of China's intervention can be examined, including both its relations to the host country as well as international circumstances. While the existence of a UN mission was found to be an adequately causal factor in the QCA, process tracing showed that the host state's consent to military intervention has remained an essential element of China's contributions. The opportunity to increase the reputation of Chinese troops furthermore emerged as an important factor in several cases. Moreover, changes in the importance of trade relations for particular goods with specific countries were found. In addition, the recognition of the One-China principle turned out to be decisive in at least one case. The combination of the results of the QCA and additional knowledge gained by conducting process tracing led to evidence about a correlation of drivers that could be seen as causal factors in Chinese interventions in conflicts.

Chapter 9 outlines the results obtained from the additional keyword analysis of UN Security Council Resolutions. By applying this method, evidence could be found for the visibility of Chinese priorities in interna-

---

10 In total, the four categories consist of 15 sub-categories.

tional peacekeeping. The results outlined changes in the use of terms in Resolutions over the past twenty years and hint at a shift in the design of UN peacekeeping missions.

In chapter 10, a model for Chinese interventions is presented. The results are integrated into the theoretical framework outlined in chapter 3. An extension of previous theoretical approaches is undertaken to explain China's approach to conflict resolution. Whilst the results obtained in chapters 7 and 8 allowed the first research question of this study to be answered, the results of the keyword analysis allowed a comprehensive response to the second research question. On the whole, chapter 10 merges the results attained in the study and provides answers to the hypotheses and the research questions of this thesis.

At the end of each chapter, a summary of that chapter's main findings is provided to help the reader to easily recognise the essential information in each chapter. Chapter 11 concludes this dissertation. It provides a summary of the findings, discusses the implications of this inquiry for future research and proposes future research avenues.

2. CONTEXT AND DISCOURSE

As outlined in chapter 1, this study adds knowledge to the debate about China's (re-) positioning in conflicts by focusing on Africa and the MENA region. In this regard, China's changing attitude towards international conflict resolution is framed by a more general discourse on the PRC's developing role as a responsible power (Butler & Wheeler, 2012, p. 2). Overall, the terms "peace" and "development" have become central elements in Chinese foreign policy discourse. Beijing's additional emphasis on "political stability", however, is connected to the PRC's popular principle of non-interference, which will be presented below (see chapter 2.1). The consideration of this principle is relevant since it has served to characterise Beijing's political positions vis-a-vis conflicts for many decades.

The observation of China's increasing involvement in conflict zones is subject to this study. To identify under which circumstances China has opted for interference, it is important to consider the type of intervention. Chapter 2.2 provides an overview of historical lessons about state intervention and the definition used in this study. Whilst modern 21st century interventions encompass cyber or drone attacks as well as the implementation of sanctions, this study focuses on traditional military means such as employing troops in the territory of another sovereign nation state.

The behavioural change in China's foreign policy is also reflected in the narrative statements of Chinese political leaders. Chapter 2.3.1. therefore includes extracts from various official speeches by President Xi Jinping. His choice of words helps to identify how China considers and positions itself on the international stage and allows us to determine whether Chinese priorities and the possible "characteristics" of a new "road map for peace" can be identified on the rhetoric level. Which image does Xi Jinping create? Which expectations arise thereof? Through careful operationalisation, this study examines whether rhetorical announcements are already being implemented or if a discrepancy between the rhetorical and the empirical level can be observed.

2.1. China's (Non-) Intervention Policy

China's foreign policy has long been characterised by the People's Republic's principle of "non-interference" or "non-intervention" (Chen, 2016, p. 349; Pang, 2009, p. 234). At the domestic level, this implies a strong state with a government that can ensure "regime stability" through top-down power (Butler & Wheeler, 2012, p. 2). The principle, however, also extends to China's bilateral relations. Due to China's increasing presence and engagement in conflict-affected states and Beijing's quest to become a great power, the PRC's non-interference policy has been challenged and a more careful understanding of Chinese concepts and approaches is needed.

The principle of non-intervention is one of China's five principles of peaceful coexistence, which furthermore include respect for the sovereignty of others and territorial integrity, non-aggression, and equality and mutual benefit (Ministry of Foreign Affairs of the PRC, 2014). These characteristics of Chinese diplomacy were first put down in writing and presented in an Agreement on Trade and Intercourse between the Tibet region of China and India in 1954 (Van Eekelen, 1967, p. 38). During an African–Asian Conference in Bandung the following year, they were officially presented by China's former Premier Zhou Enlai (Dirlik, 2015). The conference hosted representatives from twenty-nine countries in Africa and Asia with the aim of discussing their future economic development (Acharya, 2016, p. 343). Many participating countries had just been decolonised and wanted to unite as Third World states that were not aligned to either Russia or the USA during the Cold War (ibid., p. 346). Zhou Enlai stated that "India, Burma and China have affirmed the five principles of peaceful coexistence as the guiding principles in their mutual relations. These principles have received support from more and more countries" (Zhou, 1955). The five principles thus offered a new approach to the organisation of bilateral and multilateral relations and an alternative to the Soviet Union's efforts to internationalise a socialist revolution and the United States' attempts to spread democratic thoughts (Sofer, 2012, p. 2). Zhou Enlai's speech aimed at creating new partnerships with actors from the Non-Aligned Movement (NAM) and was the first conference where "China [was able to] show its independent face in international affairs, rather than as the representative of a monolithic communist bloc" (Acharya, 2016, p. 348). The conference in Bandung demonstrated that uniting emerging nations could have a voice in international politics and was later referred to as the "cornerstone of [the] African–Asian solidarity" (Lumumba-Kasongo, 2015, p. 10). The NAM continued its criticism of both the Soviet Union and the USA until the end of the Cold War whilst China considered both opponents an "equal 'hegemonic' threat to the world" (Shambaugh, 1994, p. 204). In his speech at the Bandung conference, however, Zhou Enlai expressed a moderate line and appeased Western fears of an ideological shift (Lumumba-Kasongo, 2015, p. 11). Moreover, Zhou Enlai used his ability to negotiate to initiate the settlement of several conflicts with South-Eastern countries at the conference[11] (Hinton, 1994, p. 361). In the final "declaration on promotion of world peace and cooperation", which was adopted at the end of the meeting, all participants agreed on ten points, which included the five principles of peaceful cooperation (Asian-African Conference, 1955). In the following years, China referred to the five principles—in particular to the principle of non-intervention—to justify the People's Republic's restraint from commitments on the global stage. This became particularly apparent in abstentions on international conflict resolutions. China concentrated its resources on domestic economic and military growth instead (Sofer, 2012, p. 2). The idea was to minimise its efforts on the external stage and, instead, completely focus on the internal development of the country. China was not the only country to follow these thoughts. Similar approaches were observed in countries such as India, Brazil, South Africa and partly also in Turkey (Sofer, 2012, p. 2). In 1957, India, Yugoslavia and Sweden even prepared a resolution on peaceful coexistence for the United Nations General Assembly, which included the five principles to promote the objectives of the United Nations Charter (A/RES/1236(XII)) (UN General Assembly, 1957).

Chinese leaders favoured the non-interventionist approach as they expected their international partners to likewise refrain from interference in Chinese affairs (Sofer, 2012, p. 2). This became particularly relevant when foreign governments sanctioned China for its reaction to the Tiananmen protests in 1989 and China's leaders strongly rejected any international commenting on the incidents (ibid., p. 2). Similarly, in 2007 and 2011, China warned the US not to honour the Tibetan leader the Dalai Lama and, instead, to refrain from meeting with the spiritual leader. Beijing warned that this would negatively affect Chinese internal affairs and affect Sino-American relations (Fuchs & Klann, 2011). Thus, bilateral relations between China and other states have traditionally been shaped by China's non-interference strategy (Gonzales-Vincente, 2015; Pang, 2009). However,

---

[11] Conflicts mostly related to the question of Chinese citizenship of historical Chinese immigrants in South-East Asian countries.

some scholars have noticed a recent change in China's behaviour with regard to conflict interventions, particularly in Africa (Aidoo & Hess, 2015; Osondu, 2013; Sofer, 2012). For example, a study by Yan Xuetong outlined a shift from China's strategy of "keeping a low profile" towards a more proactive approach of "striving for achievement" since 2013 (2014, p. 153). Yet, on the international stage China has kept referring to its guiding principle of non-interference when abstaining from resolutions in the United Nations Security Council. As China is a permanent member, its veto would lead to a failure of resolutions, which might result in irritation among its proponents. China has, therefore, most commonly abstained from critical resolutions while expressing its objections to any intervention to other countries (Sofer, 2012, p. 3). China's hesitant use of its veto power is illustrated by comparing numbers of all five permanent members of the Security Council. Between 1945 and 2020, the USSR[12]/Russia vetoed 117 resolutions, whereas the United States objected to 82 resolutions. In comparison, the United Kingdom made use of its veto power in 29 cases while both France and China vetoed 16 resolutions (see table 1) (Dag Hammarskjöld Library, 2021). Remarkably, most Chinese vetoes took place in the new millennium, especially after 2011, the beginning of the Syrian civil war.

Table 1: China's vetoes in the UNSC between 1945 and 2020[13]

Year	Name of the Resolution	Resolution Topic
2020	S/2020/667	The situation in the Middle East, Humanitarian access to Syria
2020	S/2020/654	The situation in the Middle East, Humanitarian access to Syria
2019	S/2019/961	The situation in the Middle East, Humanitarian access to Syria (via borders with Iraq and Turkey)
2019	S/2019/756	The situation in the Middle East, northwest Syria offensive
2019	S/2019/186	The situation in the Bolivarian Republic of Venezuela
2017	S/2017/172	Middle East—Syrian Civil War, Condemnation of the use of chemical weapons in Syria
2016	S/2016/1026	Middle East—Syrian Civil War, Condemnation of human rights abuses in Syria
2014	S/2014/348	Middle East—Syrian Civil War, Condemnation of human rights abuses by the Syrian Government

---

12 Union of Soviet Socialist Republics.

2. CONTEXT AND DISCOURSE

Year	Name of the Resolution	Resolution Topic
2012	S/2012/538	Middle East—Syrian Civil War, Condemnation of Syrian human rights abuses
2012	S/2012/77	Middle East—Syrian Civil War, Condemnation of Syrian human rights abuses
2011	S/2011/612	Middle East—Syrian Civil War, sanctions against Syria
2008	S/2008/447	Peace and Security in Africa, sanctions against Zimbabwe
2007	S/2007/14	Myanmar, Military junta rule triggering the Saffron Revolution, Condemnation of human rights abuses in Myanmar
1999	S/1999/201	Extension of UN Peacekeeping Mission in Macedonia, Resolution on the situation in the former Yugoslav Republic of Macedonia. Kosovo War on Macedonia and the subsequent insurgency in the Republic of Macedonia in 2001.
1997	S/1997/18	Central America: efforts towards peace (the Guatemalan Peace Process 1994–1996 ending the Guatemalan Civil War), Establishment of UN Peacekeeping Mission in Guatemala
1972	S/10771	Admission of Bangladesh to the UN

Source: (Dag Hammarskjöld Library, 2021)

China's increased use of its veto power can be seen as part of the PRC's "going out" strategy, which was launched in 2001. Shortly thereafter, China became a member of the World Trade Organisation (WTO, 2018). "Going global" or "going out" thus framed the conditions for Chinese companies to expand globally and focus on resources and foreign sales markets abroad, where they would apply the same business practices that had already worked in China (China Policy, 2017, p. 3). However, especially in the MENA region and Africa, Beijing was confronted with different political and civil circumstances than within the PRC. Chinese business abroad was often hampered by political challenges such as corruption, rent-seeking and uprising local civil societies who revolted against Chinese business practices (China Policy, 2017, p. 4). From 2012 onwards, more attention was paid to local circumstances and also to the image Chinese actors exported abroad. The Communist Party's leader Xi Jinping restructured the strategy of "going out" by establishing a "made in China 2025 plan" as well as five-year plans for particular sectors such as science and technology (China Policy, 2017, p. 4). At that time, the new strategy

---

[13] In 1955, China vetoed UNSC Res. S/3509 on the Admission of new Members Mongolia (Mongolian People's Republic and the end of the Sino-Soviet Treaty of Friendship and Alliance). Until 1971, however, China was represented in the UN Security Council by the Republic of China (ROC)/Taiwan.

was meant to contrast the Mao-era line of thinking and allow China to participate and profit from world trade (China Policy, 2017, p. 3). In retrospect, one can conclude that the decision to "go global" marked the beginning of China's path to becoming an influential global actor. As Yan Xuetong concludes, the strategy of striving for achievement has already led to "more improved relations between China and other countries than to deteriorated ones" (2014, p. 184).

By refusing to take part in international sanctions against economically important states such as Libya, Syria or Sudan, China tried to pragmatically focus on its domestic economic interests (Sofer, 2012, p. 6). Referring to China's non-intervention principle, however, did not prevent protesters in these states from accusing China of having chosen a side in the conflicts by deciding against intervention (ibid., p. 6). In an analysis of the PRC's military strategies from 2008 to 2017, a change in China's foreign military engagements becomes evident. This has also been noticed on the international level, in particular by the USA, which has been closely monitoring China's military rise in annual reports to Congress. Until 2008, reports about "military and security developments involving the People's Republic of China" contained little about Chinese international military contributions. "The international community has limited knowledge of the motivations, decision-making, and key capabilities supporting China's military modernization." (Office of the Secretary of Defense, 2008, p. I). One year later, however, the report highlighted that China has capabilities "that have allowed it to contribute cooperatively to the international community's responsibilities in areas such as peacekeeping, humanitarian assistance and disaster relief, and counter-piracy" (Office of the Secretary of Defense, 2009, p. I). By 2010, these contributions were "recogniz[ed]" and "welcome[d]" by the United States, a formulation that cannot be retrieved in any of the subsequent reports (US Department of Defense, 2010, p. I). In 2010, China published a Defence White Paper which included an acknowledgement of China's connectivity with the international community (Ministry of National Defense, PRC, 2010). From 2012 to 2017, annual reports to the US Congress observed an increase in China's military investments and participation in numerous missions abroad. China is both involved in sea lane security and counter-piracy, peacekeeping missions as well as humanitarian assistance and disaster relief (annual reports to Congress by the US Department of Defense, 2012–2017). The reports show that Chinese efforts and increased influence on the international level are being recognised. Yet, scepticism seemed to have risen too. The annual report of 2016 holds that "China's military modernization is producing capabilities that have the potential to reduce core U.S. military technological advantages." (US Department of Defense, 2016, p. I)

The opening of China's first overseas military base in Djibouti was another step towards a larger presence of Chinese forces abroad (Ashley, Jr, 2019, p. 29). This marine support for the Chinese People's Liberation Army (PLA) signalled unprecedented expansion of the Chinese military presence in the Indian Ocean region and opened a new entry opportunity to the African continent (ibid. p. 29). In addition, by December 2020, the number of personnel China provided to ongoing UN missions was significantly higher than that provided by the United States. While China provided 2,520 experts, troops and police staff, the United States only deployed 30 men and women (UN Peacekeeping, 2020). Since former President Donald Trump assumed power in the United States, Washington has incrementally withdrawn from international cooperation, thereby abandoning its former leadership position in UN peacekeeping (Lanteigne, 2018; Lippert & Perthes, 2020, p. 7). By contrast, China has increased both its personnel and financial contributions to UN peacekeeping during the last few years. Whilst the PRC provided about 10.2 per cent of the UN peacekeeping budget in 2018, this sum increased to 15.2 per cent in 2019 (United Nations Peacekeeping, 2020). By contrast, the United States slightly decreased its budget support from 28.4 per cent in 2018 to 27.9 per cent in 2019. Both figures remained stable in 2020. Overall, the figures illustrate a change in Beijing's international efforts with regard to support for military involvement during recent years and a departure from Beijing's traditional policy of non-intervention. The PRC seems ready to take on greater responsibilities and influence and has already done so in several UN missions. Questions arise about how this development can be explained and whether there is a strategic connection between China's involvement in some conflicts and the BRI.

To gain a better understanding of China's changing attitude towards conflict interventions and its increased efforts on the international level, a profound understanding and definition of state interventions in general is necessary and will be provided in the following. This will help to classify China's choice of involvement in international conflict resolution and hint at a possible Chinese "road map for peace".

2.2. Understanding State Interventions in Conflicts

State intervention in another state's territory can be a means to influence and affect this state's internal affairs. To this end, one party needs to barge into the domestic or foreign politics of another state (Schmidt, 1995, p. 448). The intervening party can either be a single state, a group of states or an international organisation (ibid., p. 448). In this regard, the type of intervention can take various forms, through which the intervening state seeks to influence the society or economy of another nation state. By means of foreign intervention of a lesser or greater extent, a state can try to manipulate the society or economy of another nation state (Department of Defense, 2018).

According to Schmidt, this can be expressed either through the threat or the actual use of political pressure or force (1995, p. 448). This thesis focuses on the actual use of forces in military interventions. Following the definition by Pickering, which is also used by Grimm, military interventions are external interference characterised by the use of foreign military personnel (Grimm, 2015; Pickering, 2002, p. 301). Discussions have been raised about whether or not the government's agreement by the state affected would make the term "intervention" inappropriate (Grimm, 2015). Yet, in many conflicts, especially in developing states, it is not clear which party has enough ruling power to invite another nation to take sides in the dispute. Grimm (2015) and Weiss (2014) furthermore argue that the actual intrusion into the inner affairs of a state does not change with or without a party's permission and is one of the distinctive attributes of intervention. Vincent (1974) adds that "[state intervention] is not necessarily lawful or unlawful, but it does break a conventional pattern of international relations" (Vincent, 1974, p. 13). In their study, Hermann and Kegley stated that interventions have become the most frequent example of using military force today (Hermann & Kegley, 1996, p. 440).

State interventions can have various occasions such as a declaration of war, self-defence or interference in an already existing conflict. Originally, military interventions were undertaken in nearby countries and used to achieve geopolitical goals such as the protection of a state's territory or population or to gain control over natural resources (Pearson, 1974, p. 442). The United States Department of Defense defines military intervention as "a deliberate act of a nation or group to introduce its military forces into the course of an existing controversy" (Department of Defense, 2018). This definition shall be used to determine the cases that are selected for this inquiry.

2. CONTEXT AND DISCOURSE

Military interventions can have a number of forms such as sea blockades, air strikes or the operation of ground forces (Grimm, 2015, p. 625f). Further possibilities are military espionage or the provision of military equipment to one party in the conflict (ibid. p. 625). This thesis considers military interventions in the form of military troops that are sent to a foreign conflict. Hence, the scope of the "intervention" relies on the definition by Schmidt (1995) and the US Department of Defense (2018). The understanding of military intervention is thus a traditional one, considering military troops on the ground. Interventions via modern warfare systems such as drones are not considered here[14].

For many decades, military interventions in foreign countries have been a common feature of international politics and have affected both democratic and autocratic regimes. To analyse and understand foreign military interventions, political scientists have mostly considered individual cases to explain particular situations and events. Some have also focused on military interventions by a state's own army in the political set-up (Riffat, 2016). An overview of motivations for military interventions is, however, by and large still lacking. In 2019, Cho published a paper on China's participation in UN peacekeeping operations in the 2000s, which is a first approach in this direction (Cho, 2019). While Cho's paper compares different UN missions, it neither explains the temporal change in China's attitude to military interventions nor does it elucidate why China intervened in these countries in the first place. In general, it can be said that there is usually not one single factor that causes a country's decision to intervene in a foreign country. Instead, when one is comparing different case studies, a set of combined factors related to structural characteristics within a country as well as the current international setting may explain military interventions (Goethals, Okenda, & Mbaya, 2009; Perez-Des Rosiers, 2019; Seesaghur & Ansong, 2014). While the number of major wars has progressively declined, foreign military interventions have apparently become an alternative to economic sanctions (Pickering & Kisangan, 2006, p. 363). At the same time, military interventions by third parties are not uncontested in political debates, both on the domestic level of intervening in host states and in the international arena (Woo, 2017, p. 2). In 2019, the Uppsala Conflict Data Program (UCDP) identified 54 conflicts with state-based violence, 67 with non-state violence and 31 conflicts with one-sided violence (Uppsala Conflict Data Program, 2020). Both numbers of sate-based

---

14 A comprehensive overview of modern warfare is provided in the book "Understanding modern warfare" by Jordan et al (2016).

violence, non-state violence and one-sided violence have increased over time (Uppsala Conflict Data Program, 2020). Conflicts within countries do not exclude the involvement of other states in the dispute. Conflicts can have various reasons, including disputes over land or natural resources such as water, oil or diamonds (Peace Research Institute Oslo, 2020). Another reason can be political change and instability in both autocratic and democratic regimes (ibid.). Finally, unemployment and poverty can lead to internal conflicts in a state (ibid.).

Once a conflict has broken out, the actors affected can react in various ways: negotiate, use violence or contract a third party (Berekovitch, 1991, p. 17). A third party can, for example, enter a conflict with non-violent support for one or more parties in the conflict. By acting as an arbitrator, a neutral party can help the disputing parties to establish a peace agreement or the like to end the conflict (ibid., p. 17). Thereby, third parties can help to settle disputes and support parties to avoid a loss of face. In addition, they can act as a guarantor in agreements or as an insurance policy which checks that all sides are complying with the agreement, if necessary, by leverage (Brecher & Wilkenfeld, 1997, p. 849f). The involvement of third parties can, however, also include military means of conflict management. In the case of military interference in another state, member states of the United Nations have established strict rules. In general, states may intervene on their own or in coalition with other partners. In either case, a UN mandate provides legitimisation for the intervening parties. During the 20th century, states began to cluster their foreign policy activities in so-called coalitions of the willing (Anderson, Bennis, & Cavanagh, 2003, p. 1). One example of such an alliance was the 2003 US-led Coalition of the Willing, which enabled the invasion of Iraq to remove Saddam Hussein (Anderson, Bennis, & Cavanagh, 2003, p. 1).

Moreover, the concept of the Responsibility to Protect[15] was endorsed by the United Nation's World Summit in 2005. It denotes an approach to prevent war crimes, ethnic cleansing, genocide and other crimes against humanity (ICISS, 2001). The principle is based on the idea that states' sovereignty also implies a responsibility to protect their populations from atrocities and human rights violations. Today, R2P also encompasses protection from environmental disasters such as that in Haiti in January 2010, when an earthquake left the country's nine million population in need

---

15 Abbreviations are both RtoP and R2P.

of humanitarian assistance[16]. This responsibility is furthermore premised on principles of international law and provides a framework for measures such as mediation or economic sanctions (ICISS, 2001). Employing the use of force under the umbrella of the Responsibility to Protect remains under the authority of the United Nations (ibid.). While originally opposing the principle of the Responsibility to Protect, China has recently become more in favour of this multilateral approach, which also includes the use of force in emergency situations (Fung, 2016). It is, however, questionable if China sincerely supports the principle's mandate or if its new advocacy is a result of the PRC's ambitions to reshape global rules of governance (ibid. p. 4). While the application of the RtoP has been discussed for the conflicts in Libya and Syria, an international set of criteria is still lacking.

Until now, four major types of interventions have been categorised on the international level: (1) humanitarian interventions, (2) peacekeeping missions, (3) self-defence and (4) democratic interventions. With regard to humanitarian interventions, collective Security and Peace Support Operations by the United Nations can be named. The United Nations Security Council examines whether a given situation or conflict is a threat to or breach of international peace under Chapter VII of the UN Charter. If such a case is found, Article 41 and 42 of the UN Charter provide the legal foundations for the Security Council to react by means of military action. Article 41 of the UN Charter stipulates the following:

"The Security Council may decide what measures not involving the use of armed force are to be employed to give effect to its decisions, and it may call upon the Members of the United Nations to apply such measures. These may include complete or partial interruption of economic relations and of rail, sea, air, postal, telegraphic, radio, and other means of communication, and the severance of diplomatic relations."

Article 42 of the UN Charter further elaborates:

> "Should the Security Council consider that measures provided for in Article 41 would be inadequate or have proved to be inadequate, it may take such action by air, sea, or land forces as may be necessary to maintain or restore international peace and security. Such action may include demonstrations, blockade, and other operations by air, sea, or land forces of Members of the United Nations."

---

16 On January 19th, 2010, the United Nations Stabilization Mission in Haiti (MINUSTAH) was established by UN Security Council Resolution 1542.

2.2. Understanding State Interventions in Conflicts

Hence, the UN Charter limits the use of military measures to cases of extreme violation of international peace such as serious abuse of human rights or genocide. Yet, in the past, members of the UN Security Council often disagreed on the degree of severity of various conflicts. One recent example is the war in Syria, where the two veto powers Russia and the USA disagreed on if and how the United Nations should interfere in the conflict. Numerous draft resolutions have been provided by both parties, yet only one very short UN mission took place in 2013 (UN Peacekeeping, 2020).

While UN veto powers have frequently prevented military measures in the form of blockades or sea and air forces in the past, the Security Council has increasingly made use of deploying peacekeeping missions to areas of conflict. UN troops, so-called blue helmets, are present as nonpartisan actors and supervise a peace treaty that must be agreed on by the conflicting parties. Since the end of the Cold War, however, the scope of mandates for UN Peacekeepers has been a controversial topic. A comprehensive report by Louise Riis Andersen and Peter Emil Engedal has studied the grey areas of multilateral UN peace operations (Andersen & Engedal, 2013). In general, both humanitarian interventions and peacekeeping missions require a mandate by the United Nations. If the UN cannot ensure the mission itself, other regional organisations or agencies can be used under its authority (UN Charter Article 53). Apart from collective security and peace support operations and UN peacekeeping missions, a third type of intervention considers a military reaction by a state to defend its territory, people or resources immediately or after an attack such as those stated in Article 51 of the UN Charter.

Finally, a military intervention can be called a democratic intervention which aims to support democratic regimes to gain or hold power (Grimm, 2015). This type of intervention, however, has been discussed controversially since a lack of democracy is not considered a serious threat to human rights by many states (ibid.). Yet, the use of force is strictly regulated by the United Nations. Article 2(4) of the UN Charter explicitly states that

> "All Members shall refrain in their international relations from the threat or use of force against the territorial integrity or political independence of any state, or in any other manner inconsistent with the Purposes of the United Nations."

Article 2(7) UN Charter, furthermore, states that

> "Nothing contained in the present Charter shall authorize the United Nations to intervene in matters which are essentially within the

domestic jurisdiction of any state or shall require the Members to submit such matters to settlement under the present Charter; but this principle shall not prejudice the application of enforcement measures under Chapter VII."

Whenever a state intervenes in another state without a mandate by the United Nations and without a reason for self-defence, such intervention is considered a breach of international law. The exception of self-defence in Article 51 and also the possibility of mandating regional organisations under Article 53 consider interstate conflicts. The latter have, however, decreased in number during recent years and non-state violence has appeared more frequently (Uppsala Conflict Data Programm, 2020). The change in type of conflict worldwide has made the unambiguous application of the UN Charter more difficult.

Before continuing with the underlying theoretical assumptions of this study, I introduce the rhetorical narratives of how Chinese political leaders present the PRC's activities. The following chapter presents a discourse overview of how China's foreign military involvement has been portrayed in official speeches by Chinese politicians and President Xi Jinping.

2.3. Chinese Peacebuilding Dreams

An overview of the Chinese discourse helps us to gain insights into the country's self-conception and the image the PRC conveys of its military strength. This rhetorical level is useful to understand which theoretical explanation of international relations best covers China's global actions. First, several statements by China's President Xi Jinping from 2013 and later are presented to identify rhetorical characteristics. The statements were selected randomly and cover the period after the announcement of the BRI. After that, the Chinese concept of *tianxia*[17] is presented to highlight a Chinese attempt to frame the PRC's discourse on its power perception. In this study, the results of this chapter are compared with the empirical results of the QCA to find out if both the rhetorical level and China's actual behaviour can be assigned to the same theoretical framework.

---

17 天下, literally: under heaven.

2.3. Chinese Peacebuilding Dreams

2.3.1. Beijing's Rhetoric: Between Military Strength and Harmony

When one is analysing China's behaviour, it is important to pay attention to the Chinese discourse. This applies both to China's understanding of its global role and to the dimension of peace and security in particular. In 2015, Camilla T.N. SØrensen conducted a study about the significance of Xi Jinping's "Chinese Dream" for Chinese foreign policy, in which she observed a change in China's foreign policy strategy. SØrensen analysed speeches and articles focusing on how Chinese foreign political leaders articulated their strategic direction and, thereby, she determined a shift in China's foreign policy approach (Sørensen, 2015, p. 53). In the 1990s, Deng Xiaoping had introduced the strategy of "Tao Guang Yang Hui", which means "hide capabilities and keep a low profile", that had long been applied by Chinese leaders (Zhu, 2010, p. 51). Yet, in her study, SØrensen noticed a shift towards a new approach called "Fen Fa You Wei", which translates as "striving for achievement" (Sørensen, 2015, p. 53). The first hints at this change were made in speeches by Xi Jinping in 2013, connecting China's new strategy to the Chinese Dream concept. When Chinese President Xi Jinping outlined the Chinese Dream, he described "the great renewal of the Chinese nation" (Xi, 2013). Achieving "the great rejuvenation" has also been stressed by Chinese leaders at conferences with China's neighbouring countries (CCICED, 2013; Ministry of Foreign Affairs PRC, 2013). In 2013, Xi Jinping furthermore called for a new type of international relations by pointing out win-win situations and the mutual benefit of cooperation (Ministry of Foreign Affairs PRC, 2013). SØrensen (2015) considers the PRC's current president Xi Jinping capable and strong enough to introduce a new foreign policy strategy that would replace Deng Xiaoping's approach with a new vision—the Chinese Dream. SØrensen discovers that the great rejuvenation and a national Chinese revival lie at the heart of the concept (Sørensen, 2015, p. 55). Certainly, the realisation of such a new strategy can only be completed by the Communist Party of China (CPC) (ibid., p. 56). As regards the internal Chinese revival, Beijing announced that "Socialism with Chinese characteristics" should be achieved by 2049 (ibid. p. 56). The Chinese Dream, however, is not only an inwardly oriented Chinese process. As early as in 2009, the Chinese colonel Liu Mingfu argued in his book *China Dream: The Great Power Thinking and Strategic Positioning in the Post-American Age* that China was entitled to become the world's leader due to the fact that China has historically proven to be a superior nation (Liu, 2015)[18]. He argued that China was the heir to a millennium-old civilisation which was the world leader in science and technology as well as culture during the 16th century—a time in which China considered itself to be the Middle Kingdom surrounded by barbarians (von Hein, 2018). Liu's concept of the "Chinese Dream" refers to that time but was not greatly regarded at first. It only became popular through Xi Jinping after 2012 (Sørensen, 2015, p. 57).

The Western media has regarded presentations of the "Chinese Dream" rather sceptically, fearing that it would undermine the international order (Brown, 2018). In this regard, a central question is if Beijing's upgrade in armament is actually meant to be used or just a symbolic realisation of the country's new power status (ibid.). In any case, Western academic and political literature has noticed China as a growing military power. While Sørensen (2015) analyses the implications of Xi Jinping's new foreign policy strategy of "striving for achievement", she identifies several elements that demonstrate China's new proactivity. They relate to the newly established security commission and the combination of economic, political, military and non-governmental instruments in foreign policy issues (Sørensen, 2015, p. 66). In doing so, she claims that China aims at influencing and decisively determining developments and acquiring an internationally indispensable status (ibid. p. 66). Sørensen interprets this behaviour as proof of China turning away from Deng Xiaoping's approach. Instead, she argues that China will begin to distinguish friends and enemies by using sanctions and alliances as instruments of diplomacy (ibid., p. 67). This implies the PRC is turning away from its non-intervention policy to ensure its political and economic goals in order to achieve leadership functions within the system (ibid., p. 67f). While Sørensen (2015) conducts a discourse analysis about the Chinese Dream and its implications for Chinese foreign policy more generally, this chapter is especially concerned with statements relating to Chinese military power.

By comparing and analysing speeches and statements by Xi Jinping, we can observe three main lines of argumentation. First, China's president does not tire of emphasising that China's rise has been peaceful and that hegemony is not its objective. Second, it seems that President Xi cares a lot about China's military reputation abroad. Third, China's military activities worldwide are stressed. All of the three lines of argumentation are subsequently discussed here.

---

18 A Chinese version of his book was already published in 2009.

First, President Xi stressed China's interest in a stable environment in 2014, when he outlined that "First, we must read each other's strategic intentions correctly. [...] There is no such thing as the so-called Thucydides trap[19] in the world" (Ministry of Foreign Affairs PRC, 2015). On the 70th anniversary of the end of the Second World War in 2015, Xi Jinping announced that the number of troops in the Chinese army would be cut by 300,000 (Kokoshin, 2016, p. 11). The reduction was, however, part of a larger restructuring of the People's Liberation Army (Defense Intelligent Agency, 2019, p. 6). When presenting the One Belt One Road (OBOR) initiative in 2017, Xi stressed the advantages of the project and underlined that "China will enhance friendship and cooperation with all countries involved in the Belt and Road Initiative on the basis of the Five Principles of Peaceful Coexistence" (Xi, 2017). Similarly, he emphasised that "China remains unchanged in its commitment to uphold[ing] world peace. Amity with neighbors, harmony without uniformity and peace are values cherished in the Chinese culture" (ibid.).

The second and third lines of argumentation in Xi Jinping's speeches focus on the Chinese army's worldwide reputation as well as China's global (military) contributions. When the first troops were sent to China's new military base in Djibouti, President Xi Jinping asked them to establish a favourable image of the Chinese military at the Horn of Africa to enhance peace and stability in the region (Xi cited from Reuters, 2017). China should furthermore become a mighty force leading the world in the fields of politics, economics and the military to realise the nation's rejuvenation (Haas, 2017). At the 19th National Congress of the Communist Party of China in October 2017, Xi explicitly mentioned the development of a powerful military as part of the Chinese Dream (Xi, 2017, p. 5). He said:

> "Building people's forces that obey the Party's command, can fight and win, and maintain excellent conduct is strategically important to achieving the two centenary goals and national rejuvenation. To real-

---

19 The term originates from a historian and military general from Athens named Thucydides, who considered the Peloponnesian War (431–404 BC) between Athens and Sparta inevitable because Sparta was too afraid of Athens' rising power. Based on this historical quote, the term "Thucydides' Trap" emerged and has been used by the American political scientist Graham T. Allison to describe an increasing possibility of war when a new power emerges and a previous power feels threatened it will be replaced as the hegemon. With regard to potential rivalries between the United States and China, the term has frequently been used in literature.

ize the Party's goal of building a powerful military in the new era, we must fully implement the fundamental principles and systems of Party leadership over the military, and see that Party strategy on strengthening military capabilities for the new era guides work to build national defence and the armed forces. We must continue to enhance the political loyalty of the armed forces, strengthen them through reform and technology, and run them in accordance with law. We must place greater focus on combat, encourage innovation, build systems, increase efficacy and efficiency, and further military–civilian integration." (ibid., p. 21).

Xi moreover pointed out that "[a] military is built to fight. Our military must regard combat capability as the criterion to meet in all its work and focus on how to win when it is called on" (ibid., p. 48). During a speech in front of Chinese military personnel in January 2018, Xi, furthermore demanded the soldiers to "[c]reate an elite and powerful force that is always ready for the fight, capable of combat and sure to win in order to fulfil the tasks bestowed by the Party and the people in the new era" (Crabtree, 2018).

In Xi Jinping's 2018 New Year's speech, the PRC's president underlined China's contributions hereto and added a global perspective:

"As a responsible major country, China must speak out. China will staunchly safeguard the authority and status of the United Nations and actively fulfil its due responsibility and duty in international affairs; China will honor its promises in countering global climate change and actively push forward the common construction of the 'Belt and Road'; China will act as a builder of world peace and a contributor to global development, and an upholder of the international order. The Chinese people are willing to join all peoples of the world in creating a beautiful future of greater prosperity and greater peace for mankind" (Xi, 2018).

Xi Jinping thus presents Chinese military forces as the builders of world peace that will act as safeguards of international order and foster development. The development of China's military forces and their modernisation was not greatly discussed or officially presented between 2013 and 2016. Rhetoric changed with the opening of China's overseas naval base and the subsequent 19th National Congress of the Communist Party when the army's readiness to fight became central to the fulfilment of the Chinese Dream. At the same time, Xi Jinping started to highlight Chinese global military contributions as an essential contribution to international peace and stability. On the one hand, SØrensen's (2015) conclusion regarding China's military can be confirmed. "Striving for achievement" has entered Xi's rhetorical narratives, which have been translated into several actions already. On the other hand, Xi's reference to global commitments can be seen as political justification for China's military upgrading. By using the word "commitment" in his speeches, Xi emphasises that China's activities are not limited to the provision of troops. Rather, China's "commitment" is presented as its dedication to the international community, which aims at increasing China's role in and influence on conflict resolution.

The rhetorical analysis shows that Xi Jinping strongly distances himself from a realistic arms race that will inevitably lead to war. He even mentions Thucydides' trap and denies that China's efforts will lead there. At the same time, however, reality shows that China has modernised and upgraded its military to become a global leader and fulfil the "Chinese Dream". Xi's focus on *how* Chinese troops present themselves clearly aims at developing and extending China's soft image. If people in the country they are deployed perceive Chinese soldiers as "peacebuilders", this might foster their acceptance of Chinese armament. Xi Jinping also reaffirms the importance of introducing Chinese characteristics. For example, at the 19th National Congress of the Communist Party of China in October 2017, the PRC's president repeated that China had become the world's second largest economy under this banner. "Socialism with Chinese characteristics", which was first introduced at the 12th Congress of the CPC in 1982, is furthermore intended to be China's leading principle towards modernisation. While a clear definition of Chinese characteristics has not been provided yet, Xi Jinping indicated a series of reference points in this speech at the National Congress in 2017. These do not only shape the country's domestic development but also describe China's new self-conception on the international level. First of all, Xi Jinping stresses the Communist Party's "overall leadership over all areas of endeavour in every part of the country" (Xi, 2017, p. 17). This includes "[people's] thinking, political orientation, and actions" (ibid. p. 17). Hence, a people-centred approach will be pursued with the goal of improving the lives of people. Xi Jinping stressed the need to further open up and reform China in order to develop socialism on a Marxist basis (ibid. p. 37). In doing so, he presented a new vision which includes a focus on "a new vision for development" by promoting economic globalisation and "[continuing] to increase China's economic power and composite strength" (Xi, 2017, p. 18). Xi Jinping stresses the importance of "[u]pholding core socialist values" while promoting Chinese cultural traditions, values and roots in order to "provide a source of cultural and moral guidance" (ibid. p. 19f). On this basis, development will lead to the well-being of people through "social fairness and justice" (ibid. p. 40). The fields of childcare, education and healthcare are highlighted as focal areas through which to address poverty alleviation. Xi Jinping stresses the Chinese government's objective to "continue the peaceful China initiative, strengthen and develop new forms of social governance, and ensure social harmony and stability" (Xi, 2017, p. 13). To achieve these goals, Xi Jinping considers national security of great importance. China needs to be prepared "to protect itself against potential dangers in time of peace" to "ensure both internal and external security, homeland and public security, traditional and non-traditional security, and China's own and common security" (ibid. p. 21). These words especially highlight that China no longer sees itself as a closed country, isolated from the rest of the world. Xi Jinping makes clear that China's security does not only depend on internal circumstances but, to a large extent, also on external threats. President Xi, moreover, mentions "common security" as a goal, which implies that China is not only interested in domestic development but also seeks peace and stability on a global level. Remarkably, Xi Jinping's next point in his speech addresses the Party's leadership over China's armed forces. President Xi stresses the need to "[…] place greater focus on combat, encourage innovation, build systems, increase efficacy and efficiency, and further military–civilian integration" (Xi, 2017, p. 21).

While the main audience of Xi Jinping's speech are members of the Chinese Communist Party, worldwide reporting about the Party's 19th National Congress ensured the spread of President Xi's message abroad. Whilst Xi Jinping began his speech by stating his original goal to achieve "happiness for the Chinese people and rejuvenation for the Chinese nation", the concretisation of Chinese priorities makes clear that an international dimension has been added to China's ambitions (Xi, 2017). Earlier in his speech, President Xi explicitly mentioned international peacekeeping as one of several reforms within the military which should be recognisable among Chinese characteristics as well (ibid., p. 5). By including the readiness of Chinese military forces for international missions in the midst of a paragraph about increasing military training and war preparedness, President Xi rhetorically neglects the fact that upgrading the Chinese military aimed at threatening the outside world. Rather, Chinese forces are presented as guardians of maritime rights, stability and humanitarian assistance (Xi, 2017).

Moreover, in September 2020, China's State Council Information Office published its first White Paper on "China's Armed Forces: 30 Years of UN Peacekeeping Operations", in which China's previous contributions as well as China's vision for the development of peacekeeping were portrayed (State Council PRC, 2020). Remarkably, China seemingly divides the last 30 years of peacekeeping into two eras: firstly, an "old" era, during which China increasingly sent armed forces to peacekeeping operations and became both the overall second largest financial contributor[20] and the largest troop contributor at least among the P5 (ibid.). Yet, the White Paper also outlines China's "ideas on safeguarding world peace in the new era, and to elaborate on the efforts they make" (State Council PRC, 2020). Whilst the exact starting point of this "new era" is not identified, four reasons are mentioned why China will continue to participate in UN peacekeeping missions: First, "the pursuit of peace is in the genes of the Chinese nation", second, "Chinese people care about the well-being of humanity" and third, "serving the people is the fundamental purpose of the people's armed forces". Hence, the paper outlines China's understanding of a "harmonious world where everyone belongs to one and the same family" (ibid.). This suggests that Chinese military forces would fight for all people belonging to such a harmonious unity. The fourth reason states that "China honors its responsibilities as a major country" to build "a community with a shared future for mankind" (ibid.). The PRC clearly presents itself as an integrated part of the international community striving for harmony and peace. To underline China's previous contributions, five key tasks of Chinese peacekeepers are outlined in the paper: ceasefire supervision, stabilising situations, protecting civilians, providing force protection and deploying enabling capabilities such as engineers, transport, medical assistance and helicopter units, and finally restoring livelihoods (ibid.). While post-war reconstruction covers infrastructural elements rather than good governance, the monitoring of elections is mentioned as one task of Chinese peacekeepers. Overall, the Chinese focus on material support and economic development becomes clear and sets China's approach apart from the Western narrative of the importance of individual political and legal human rights (Zürcher, 2019, p. 10). Zürcher (2019) observed that China has started promoting its own narrative of human rights in resolutions for the UN Human Rights Council (ibid., p. 10). In this regard, the notion of

---

20 Financial contributions refer to peacekeeping assessments and UN membership fees here.

2. CONTEXT AND DISCOURSE

"negative peace", as outlined by Johan Galtung in 1967, seems a plausible tool with which to grasp Beijing's approach (Galtung, 1967)[21].

The White Paper on Chinese peacekeeping efforts furthermore provides a review of the fulfilment of President Xi Jinping's 2015 promises to the UN, among them the registration of an 8,000 strong standby battalion of troops as well as training for 1,500 peacekeepers from 60 countries (State Council PRC, 2020). Moreover, the White Paper stresses the importance of continuing support for the African Union as a regional organisation. Finally, the Chinese provision of the UN's first helicopter unit as well as the set-up of a China–UN Peace and Development Fund are highlighted. Having outlined China's previous contributions, the last part of the White Paper covers China's priority areas of building a "community with a shared future for mankind", including a focus on development, stronger cooperation with regional and sub-regional organisations and the safety of peacekeeping troops (State Council PRC, 2020). While the paper does not include any surprises about China's efforts, it is nevertheless another expression of China's military commitment to the international community and the institution of UN peacekeeping in particular that has not been made by other major powers in recent times.

This overview of China's discourse has outlined China's self-perception both with regard to its military strength and its proclaimed status in the international community. The Chinese state media have celebrated the country's efforts in conflict regions, highlighting both their standards and quality. From the rhetorical level, it becomes clear that China aims to assume a guiding role in global governance to participate in formulating international rules (Zaobao, 2018). To fully depict and grasp the Chinese attitude towards intervention, it is important to consider the Chinese concept of *tianxia*, which will be presented in the following.

2.3.2. Tianxia: A Chinese Concept of World Order

China's presentation of itself as a peaceful actor in international relations has also been reflected in Chinese philosophical concepts which frame the Chinese discourse on how the country's power can be reflected. Whilst discussions have long been ongoing about whether or not a Chinese School of international relations exists, political scientists agree that several Chi-

---

21 Galtung (1967) understands negative peace as the absence of violence, which can, for example, be achieved through a ceasefire.

nese concepts are available (Noesselt, 2012). One of them is the Chinese theoretical concept of *tianxia*, also known as the philosophy of "All-under-heaven" (Zhao, 2009). The concept provides input to political discourse and refers to a world perspective that was established by the Zhou Dynasty about 3,000 years ago. It addresses the question of how to control large entities on a global level (ibid., p. 8). The concept stresses the importance of harmony, the inclusion of all peoples and thus opposes the dominance of any particular religion or the hegemony of one state (ibid., p. 11; 17). Zhao thus understands the concept in opposition to current international politics, which are characterised by the dominance of powerful nation states over less powerful ones (Zhao, 2009, p. 6). "An important lesson history teaches us is that peaceful development is the right path, while any attempt to seek domination or hegemony through force is against the historical trend and doomed to failure", China's President Xi Jinping said during a visit to the Seattle (USA) in 2015 (Soper, 2015). Xi's words thus correspond to the theoretical approach of *tianxia*, criticising "American leadership", which is characterised by domination and hegemony (Zhao, 2009, p. 17). Instead, the concept of *tianxia* calls for a world institution based on six ancient principles of the "All-under-heaven" philosophy that need to be adapted contemporarily (ibid., pp. 8–9; 17). The concept was applied by the Zhou dynasty and included a monarchic system which was similarly an open network with several sub-states. The latter decided on their economy, culture and traditions but were governed by a world government which possessed a military force to control the lands (ibid. p. 8). In contrast to the United Nations system, the world government proposed in *tianxia* has the power of political leadership with the principle of cooperation among all sub-states. To preserve its institutional balance, the world government's military forces outnumber those of the sub-states (ibid., p. 8). Whilst the concept dates back several millennia, its application on today's international stage has remained under discussion in China. For the purpose of this study, the ideas of *tianxia* provide indications about China's propositions for global order that may already be reflected in Beijing's foreign policy behaviour.

2.4. Summary of Context and Discourse

As shown in this chapter, the topic of this study deals with the changes observed in China's traditional policy of non-intervention. Chapter 2.1. presented an overview of the roots of this principle, which has shaped

2. CONTEXT AND DISCOURSE

Chinese foreign policy since its introduction in 1954/1955. It was one of the five principles of peaceful coexistence and was established as an alternative approach to the Soviet Union's attempt to internationalise Socialism and the USA's aim of spreading democracy. During more than four decades, the PRC referred to the non-intervention principle to refrain from conflicts and to abstain from UN resolutions in the Security Council. China's strategical change from Deng Xiaoping's "low profile" to Xi Jinping's approach of "going out" has therefore been a remarkable development since the beginning of the new millennium. This shift did not only change China's economic development but was combined with a parallel increase in military interference in conflict-affected countries. The opening of China's military naval base in Djibouti as well as large increases in troop contributions to UN peacekeeping missions are thus notable and highlight a shift in Beijing's attitude towards China's involvement in international conflict resolution. To classify China's recent operations in conflict regions, chapter 2.2. provided an overview of the legal framework for interventions and outlined that any intervention without a mandate by the UN or without reason for self-defence would be classified as a breach of international law. This step was important to identify which instruments China is using to establish a Chinese "road map for peace".

In addition, chapter 2 outlined the Chinese narrative discourse on the topic of (non-) intervention among Chinese experts and in the narratives used by political leaders in China. As shown in the analysis of speeches by Chinese politicians, the technical and personnel improvement of China's military strength has been a major element in Chinese discourse and might be an attempt to combine the narrative of traditional principles and new military practices on the international level. Moreover, chapter 2.3.1. outlined how Chinese President Xi Jinping has promoted China's peaceful rise through his rhetoric, while stressing the PRC's contributions to world peace and the importance of a favourable image of Chinese military forces. With regard to Xi's reference to harmony instead of hegemony, the related Chinese philosophical concept of *tianxia* was presented in chapter 2.3.2. On the whole, the overview of the context and contemporary discourse of the topic under discussion provided in chapter 2 are valuable in order to compare Beijing's rhetoric with the empirical results of this study to find out if the principles that China promotes have already been incorporated on the multilateral level. The results of the rhetorical analysis will later be compared with the empirical results of the QCA presented in this inquiry.

With the aim of making statements about China's role in international relations, the identification of a suitable theoretical approach will be dealt

2.4. Summary of Context and Discourse

with in the following chapter. For many decades, Chinese scholars have been searching for their own Chinese theory of international relations with Chinese characteristics (Liang, 1997). At the beginning of the 21st century, the term Chinese School became more popular (Qin, 2005). Debates, however, continue to focus on traditional indigenous concepts of Chinese ancient philosophers which do not (yet) provide an encompassing framework that is comprehensive enough to serve as a universal theory (Noesselt, 2012). The following chapter summarises different theoretical approaches within foreign policy analysis in which the study can be embedded.

3. THEORETICAL FRAMEWORK

In chapter 2, the context of the topic of this study as well as the respective Chinese discourse wereoutlined. The narratives expressed by Chinese politicians and scientists illustrate a change in China's rhetoric on international conflicts and hint at a changing understanding of the principle of non-intervention. In particular, the promotion of Xi Jinping's "going out" strategy has changed China's attitude towards international conflicts. This study embraces this development and aims at illuminating under which circumstances China opts for a military response to conflicts in the MENA region and sub-Saharan Africa. Previous literature offers various theoretical approaches to the analysis of China's foreign policy. Chapter 3 presents three major streams of theorising to which this study contributes.

First, the study focuses on establishing analytical concepts for Chinese foreign policy. So far, no single model has prevailed out of a multitude of approaches. Rather, historical descriptions can be contrasted with analytical models, such as those summarised by Peters (2007). When one is analysing specific events, external influences, the state itself and individuals are relevant objects of analysis (Hudson & Vore, 1995).

Second, emphasis is placed on the specific foreign policy area of conflict studies. Various research traditions are presented to illustrate the variety of available approaches. An overview of methods from different time epochs and regions facilitates the specification of the theoretical framework on which this study is based.

In this context, the assumption that Chinese military activities aim at purely maximising power could easily be made. Yet, to understand the role of power and power balances for China's foreign policy behaviour in conflict resolution, a detailed analysis of different concepts of power is necessary and will be provided as a third theoretical stream in chapter 3. After a general overview of the academic discussion about power, the concepts of soft power and comprehensive national power are outlined in more detail since both approaches have only been developed in recent decades but have the potential to revolutionise traditional perceptions about power in the case of China.

After outlining theoretical frameworks to approach the topic of Chinese foreign policy behaviour, Chapter 3 furthermore derives hypotheses on China's reactions to conflicts. Overall, four hypotheses are presented to be

3.1. Analysing (Chinese) Foreign Policy

tested in a comparative study. This allows conclusions to be drawn about a possible Chinese approach to peacebuilding. The aim is to understand how Beijing is using the instrument of international conflict resolution in its foreign policy to change its power status on the international level.

3.1. Analysing (Chinese) Foreign Policy

This chapter provides an overview of the theoretical levels at which China's foreign policy approaches are discussed. The different models are helpful for us to understand how Chinese foreign policy can be analysed. Since the different types of analysis have evolved over time, the chapter also stresses the historical development of the various concepts.

The question of how political systems behave towards their environment has been a central subject of research analyses of foreign policy. One of the most prominent contributions has been made by Kenneth N. Waltz (1996), who clearly stated that "any theory of international politics can at best limp along, able to explain some matters of foreign policy while having to leave much of foreign policy aside" (Waltz, 1996, p. 54). With the aim of structuring the various concepts that have been provided, Dirk Peters (2007) provided a valuable example of categorisation in his contribution *Approaches to and Methods of Foreign Policy Analysis*[22] (Peters, 2007). Peters illustrates the differentiation between a historically descriptive approach which focuses on specific phases of a state's foreign policy and an explanatory analytical approach that examines what influences a state's foreign policy (Peters, 2007, p. 815). The author's contribution is based on several primary materials that are summarised into a comprehensive overview. While major schools of thought have emerged in the discipline of international relations, this is not the case in the field of foreign policy analysis. Rather, countless approaches have been developed and appear today as "A Hundred Flowers Bloom", as Hudson and Vore describe this variety of different concepts (Hudson & Vore, 1995, p. 222). To provide some orientation, Peters presents three approaches explaining the content of foreign policy (Peters, 2007, p. 817ff). The categories relate first to influences from the international environment, second to factors within the state and third to impacts at the level of the individual (ibid., p.817ff).

Until the 1950s, influences from the external environment were considered to be of high relevance for a state's position on the international

---

22 Original German title: Ansätze und Methoden der Außenpolitikanalyse.

3. THEORETICAL FRAMEWORK

level (Peters, 2007, p. 817). Foreign policy was mostly understood as a response to external circumstances (Ranke, 1955, p. 42f). Yet, other authors have recognised that external influences always need to be communicated through a state's bureaucracy and individual decision makers in order to result in foreign policy decisions (Singer, 1961, p. 80f). Thus, theories which aim to explain the foreign policy behaviour of a state should not only focus on external factors since "[d]ifferences in behavior arise from differences of internal composition" (Waltz, 1996, p. 54). In particular, the connection between influences from the international environment and a state's foreign policy has been considered regarding the international and political balance of power as well as the role of international institutions (Peters, 2007, p. 817). The latter may influence the foreign policy behaviour of a state in two ways, namely by creating incentives for cooperation and by defining who actually counts as a player in the international arena (Keohane, 1988, p. 380f; Peters, 2007, p. 820). The incentives provided by international institutions, however, can only be effective if actors in the domestic decision-making process can adopt them and translate them into foreign policy (Peters, 2007, p. 820). With regard to the balance of power in the international system, the absence of a superior authority with a monopoly on the use of force would oblige states to take care of their security on their own and thus seek appropriate resources (ibid., p. 818). The most prominent resource would be power (Morgenthau, 1948). In addition, history has shown that the quest for security has also been of major concern to states and was often targeted through territorial expansion (Snyder, 1991, p. 1). Finally, states often seek autonomy to increase their security within the global system of anarchy (Baumann, Rittberger, & Wagner, 1998). A state's scope of activities, however, stays limited due to the international distribution of power, which results in great powers having less trouble achieving their goals (Peters, 2007, p. 818).

An inconsistent picture results from the assumption that economic dependencies were decisive factors in the external environment of a state in shaping its foreign policy behaviour (Peters, 2007, p. 819). Accordingly, it could be supposed that states which depend on other states economically would orient their foreign policy towards the dominating state:

> "If, for example, country A gains more from its trade with B than the other way around, B would appear to have less to lose by interrupting that trade than would A. This situation would therefore seem to provide B with an opportunity to influence the behaviour of A" (Richardson, 1978, p. 5).

3.1. Analysing (Chinese) Foreign Policy

Yet, a relationship between economic dependence and foreign policy compliance could not be verified in further studies (Armstrong, 1981). Rather, external economic influences also need to be considered in combination with domestic circumstances (Peters, 2007, p. 819). With regard to the latter, research literature provides an almost infinite range of approaches. Peters, for instance, outlines a categorisation model of internal factors into three types: general national features, the relation between state and society, and decision processes within the political–administrative system (Peters, 2007, p. 821).

General national features such as the territorial size of a state, its development status and its degree of openness towards the international system, while easy to compare, provided only minor results with regard to their influence on foreign policy decisions (ibid., p. 821). Hence, subsequent research focused on a state's predominant culture and regime type (Hudson, 1997, pp. 1-24; Terhune, 1970). A state's foreign policy behaviour can be shaped by its predominant culture and concept of order when states try to project their views on the international system (Peters, 2007, p. 822). In the relation between state and society, the influence of societal groups highly depends on the subject under consideration in different states (Atkinson & Coleman, 1989). The German Farmers' Association, for example, is characterised by an influential network of financial, political and economic actors and thus significantly influences the German position on European agricultural policy (NABU, 2019, p. 10). Two factors have been identified which enable the influence of domestic networks and society on foreign policy decisions: first, structural variables and conditions in the political system that are independent of specific actors and situations and, second, situation-specific factors (Peters, 2007, p. 823). Finally, decision processes determine foreign policy behaviour. Both the organisation of foreign policy decision-making as well as conflicts and dynamics between stakeholder groups are considered (ibid., p. 824). The way in which both external and domestic factors influence relevant stakeholders strongly depends on how they are perceived (ibid., p. 827). Therefore, the question of how people come to decisions has become subject to foreign policy analyses. In this regard, Kahneman and Tversky (1979) conclude that "[t]he decision weight associated with an event will depend primarily on the perceived likelihood of that event, which could be subject to major bias" (Kahneman & Tversky, 1979, p. 289). As part of the so-called prospect theory proposed by Kahneman and Tversky (1979), the concept of framing describes the way people perceive and classify problems. "A change in frame can [thus] result in a change in preferences (preference reversal) even if the values

3. THEORETICAL FRAMEWORK

and probabilities associated with outcomes remain the same" (Levy, 1997, p. 90). Levy furthermore outlines the relevance of situational factors according to which people seem to be more willing to take risks after having experienced a series of losses in order to eliminate those losses (ibid., p. 91).

In addition, traditional analyses of foreign policy have shown a need to integrate cognitive and psychological perspectives to "produce theories that are realistically grounded in both the realities of cognitive actors and the regularized habits of the human mind" (Rosati, 2000, p. 75). Such a perceptual approach discusses people's perceptions and the connection to international relations (Voss & Dorsey, 1992). The use of cognitive patterns is therefore helpful in outlining the effects of a person's beliefs and knowledge on his or her decisions (Peters, 2007, p. 827). Hence, the examination of individual thinking and world views has become integral to understanding how actors classify information and orientate their actions accordingly (Harnisch, 2003, p. 332). In his work, Yaacov Vertzberger considered cognitive elements and external environmental factors, turning his inquiry into one of the most comprehensive studies on the underlying dynamics of information management in foreign policy decision-making so far (Vertzberger, 1990). Wherever human patterns of perception are examined, it is important to also take into account possible ways of shaping such perceptions. Spontaneous events can influence individual thought patterns as well as targeted advertising campaigns or the use of the film industry.

On the whole, a countless number of approaches to foreign policy analyses can be found in research literature. Until today, a tendency towards ever greater differentiation of particular aspects has existed (Peters, 2007, p. 830). Two of the most prominent attempts to integrate and connect various approaches were made by Robert Putnam (1988) and Andrew Moravcsik (1998). Putnam recognised that "[t]he most portentous development in the fields of comparative politics and international relations in recent years is the dawning recognition among practitioners in each field of the need to take into account entanglements between the two" (Putnam, 1988, p. 459). His metaphor of the two-level game provided an approach to integrating both domestic politics and international relations which has valuable implications for the analyses of foreign policy (Peters, 2007, p. 830). A further attempt to integrate different levels of analysis is made by Andrew Moravcsik, who investigated the domestic formation of foreign policy positions. With regard to the field of economics, Moravcsik found a particular connection between the influence of social actors

3.1. Analysing (Chinese) Foreign Policy

and the international negotiating power of a state (Moravcsik, 1988). In addition, other authors have considered the effect of a state's capacity to mobilise domestic resources and the perception of its power for the formulation of foreign policy decisions (Rose, 1998, p. 147). Christensen (1996), for instance, developed a two-level approach by focusing on how leaders use and manipulate low-level conflicts to persuade the public of long-term security strategies. He applied this approach to US President Truman's policy towards the Chinese Communists and to the beginning of the Taiwan Straits Crisis under Mao in 1958 (ibid., p. 194ff). A central task with regard to all integrative approaches is to consider both connections between different influencing factors and foreign policy decisions as well as the relation of the various factors (Peters, 2007, p. 831). As Peter (2007) concludes, a comprehensive analysis is most likely to be achieved if different perspectives are applied to the subject and their references are presented (ibid., p. 832).

With regard to China, research literature provides broad initiatives to help understand foreign policy decisions in the field of conflict resolution. The past decades have shown China's impressive rise in economics accompanied by a more prominent appearance on the international political stage and growing military strength. China's multifaceted developments have not escaped the attention of researchers and have resulted in a great number of analyses and papers on various aspects of China's foreign policy. In the 1960s and 1970s, a central debate arose around the question of which Chinese traditions seemed unchangeable and which patterns paved the way to changes in China's foreign policy. Notable authors of this time period are Robert Boardman, John K. Fairbank and Samuel S. Kim (Boardman, 1974; Fairbank, 1968; Kim, 1979). Yet, this polarised distinction was softened in the following years, and a broad spectrum of analyses and concepts emerged. Thomas W. Robinson (1982), by way of example, assessed three episodes of Chinese foreign policy between 1957–61, 1965–69 and 1970–80 and found that China's policy orientation changed rapidly from dependence to self-reliance to isolation and finally to diversification (Robinson, 1982, pp. 134-171). In contrast, Harry Harding (1983) notes that "China's foreign policy since 1949, then, has contained elements of both change and continuity". He adds that:

> "At the same time, Chinese leaders continue to view international politics as struggle for hegemony among the superpowers—a view that has persistently impelled Beijing to seek ways of preserving China's security and sovereignty, to treat stronger allies with a good measure

of mistrust and to orient the PRC principally toward the other developing countries" (Harding, 1983, p. 18).

Finally, Michael Ng-Quinn (1983) observes great consistency in Chinese foreign behaviour since the end of the Second World War and identifies external factors as the main cause of Chinese foreign policy (Ng-Quinn, 1983, p. 204). In his book "China and the world"[23], Samuel S. Kim adds four levels of variables he considered necessary to understand China's foreign policy (Kim, 2018). According to Kim's analysis, China's policy structure was composed of

> "the top level, *policies* (most variable); the second level, *principles* (most vocal); the third level, the *basic line* (*jiben luxian*, reaffirmed or revised every five years at the party congress); and the fourth level, *world-view* (*shijie guan*) and *national identity* (most constant)" (ibid., p. 10).

The challenge Kim (2018) described was not to understand the different levels individually, but to understand how they were connected (ibid., p. 10). With the aim of exploring the relationship between these variables and to contribute a structural framework for Chinese foreign policy behaviour, research scholar Samuel S. Kim (1984) developed a behaviour-centred approach that can be integrated "into the larger framework of concepts, theories, and methods in comparative foreign policy and international relations" (Kim, 1984, p. 4). In this regard, Kim outlines two categories of factors that determine Chinese foreign policy behaviour: domestic and societal factors as well as external, systemic factors, and he added linkages between both of them (ibid., pp. 16–24). Kim highlights domestic factors, in particular traditional and cultural aspects, as profound parts of many foreign policy analyses (ibid., p. 16). In this regard, John K. Fairbank notes "tradition provides the base-line for foreign policy and even the most novel of our policies has points of reference in the past" (Fairbank, 1969, p. 450). Kim, however, points out weaknesses when concentrating on traditional political culture solely, since culture may change over time (Kim, 1984, p. 17). Rather, Kim suggests limiting linkages between domestic politics and foreign policy behaviour to a particular period (ibid. p. 17). Moreover, external factors have increasingly been recognised by researchers since the mid-1970s (ibid. p. 18). In this regard, Kim names international values, norms and structures, which may "[...] provide standards of desirable and preferable state behaviour" (Kim, 1984, p. 19). As

---

23 The book was first published in 1998.

a general definition, international norms can be understood as "specific prescriptive or proscriptive rules of state behaviour appropriate to a particular role or situation, elaborated and codified in accordance with the value system of the global society" (ibid., p. 19). Not all international norms have to be codified in treaties or other official documents. Rather, they can also relate to customs and habits and often function as a "socializing agent for state behaviour" (ibid, p. 19). Hence, when states are interacting units, they compose an international structure with defined roles, positions and statuses, while the distribution of power remains the most delicate part of their foreign policy behaviour (Kim, 1984, p. 20). The smaller a state, the more vulnerable it may be to external powers and pressure within the system. Yet, small states are not inferior per se. Kim mentions that the definition of "power" such as was the case with the definition of "culture" changes over time (ibid. p. 20). Thus, the question of how "power" shapes a state's foreign policy behaviour has to be constantly reviewed. This applies as much to China as to all other actors in the system, including non-state actors that have taken a non-neglectable role in international power distribution in recent years (Josselin & Wallace, 2001). Both domestic and external factors can interact in decision makers' perception of interests in foreign policy (Kim, 1984, p. 22). In this regard, mediating variables and continuous feedback processes are decisive for decision makers' perception of the situation (ibid. p. 23). Moreover, with increasing globalisation, it has become increasingly difficult to clearly categorise factors into the two suggested categories of domestic and societal or external and systemic (Kim, 2018, p. 22). Hence, it is necessary to recognise and analyse the interaction between variables and consider both the sources and outcomes of foreign policy decisions (ibid., p. 22).

This chapter has outlined previous approaches to analysing Chinese foreign policy. In the following, the focus lies on the field of conflict resolution.

3.2. Approaches to Conflict Resolution

The previous chapter provided an overview of approaches to understanding Chinese foreign policy. This chapter continues with a summary of international approaches to conflict resolution and China's previous role in this respect. A historical review of developments to date is included.

The more prominently a state acts and develops its power status on the international level, the more their "responsibility for a functioning

3. THEORETICAL FRAMEWORK

international economic system" will be demanded (Claude, 1986, p. 720). This holds particularly true for the resolution of international conflicts, an area that has increasingly become the focus of political analysis in the wake of ever-increasing globalisation. The first considerations of alternative methods of conflict resolution date back to the end of World War I. While the Soviet leader Vladimir Ilych Lenin advanced authoritarianism and Adolf Hitler, the leader of Nazi Germany, glorified the use of violence under fascist rule, contrary developments could also be observed (Neu & Kriesberg, 2019, p. 3). Instead of focusing on violence, some British leaders, for example, concentrated their efforts to establish institutions such as the League of Nations Society in 1915 to prevent wars and strengthen collective security (Cortright, 2008, p. 53). Yet, World War II could not be prevented by this mechanism of settling conflicts internationally and until 1945, scholars such as Pitirim A. Sorokin and Quincy Wright dealt with explanations for the outbreaks of conflicts (Sorokin, 1925; Wright, 1942). Others have considered the role of propaganda and other psychoanalytical elements (Lasswell, 1935). However, in 1942, Mary Parker Follett added negotiation practices instead of domination to the international debate on conflict resolution (Follett, 1942).

During the Second World War as well as at the beginning of the Cold War, the field of conflict analysis and resolution was further developed (Neu & Kriesberg, 2019, p. 4). The use of nuclear weapons was considered a legitimate option in this regard (Brodie, 1959, p. 147). In parallel, contrary developments could be observed again with the building of multinational institutions such as the United Nations but also the European Coal and Steel Community (Neu & Kriesberg, 2019, p. 4). Moreover, Holsti, Brody and North (1964) elaborate on the Cuban missile crisis of 1962, which served as an example of creative negotiations.

> "In the Cuban crisis, both sides (the United States and the Soviet Union) tended to perceive rather accurately the nature of the adversary's actions and then proceeded to act at an appropriate level. Efforts by either party to delay or reverse the escalation toward conflict were generally perceived as such, and responded to in like manner" (Holsti, Brody, & North, 1964, p. 189).

In addition, Neu and Kriesberg (2019) mention the case of India, where Mohandas Gandhi assumed the lead in peaceful conflict resolution (Neu & Kriesberg, 2019, p. 4). Gandhi had developed a new technique to promote social and political change by using non-violent conduct in conflict, named "Gandhian Satyagraha"[24] (Bondurant, 1965). In practice, these new strategies were applied by the public at large during the civil rights movements in the United States and formed the basis for theory building in relation to non-violent control of political power (Sharp, 1973, p. 32ff). In retrospect, this can be considered the beginning of broad acceptance of non-violent means as a valuable alternative method to "[achieve] independence and justice" (Neu & Kriesberg, 2019, p. 5). In fear of a possible nuclear war during the 1950s and 1960s, researchers focused on preventive theories from behavioural science to find ways to avoid a catastrophe (ibid. p. 5). Simultaneously, general peace and conflict studies emerged on both conflict escalation and outcomes. Charles E. Osgood, for example, contributed an analysis of psychological paradoxes in the way humans were thinking in the period of the Cold War and added a plan on how the beginning of unilateral disarmament in America could prevent the outbreak of a war with the Soviet Union (Osgood, 1962). In 1959-Europe, the International Peace and Research Institute (PRIO) was founded, followed by the opening of the Stockholm International Peace Research Institute (SIPRI) in 1966 (Neu & Kriesberg, 2019, p. 6). Later, the Department of Peace and Conflict Research at Uppsala University (1971) was established (ibid., p. 8).

From the 1970s onwards, conflict resolution theories experienced another rise. A prominent example of mediation policies was shown by the successful negotiations and shuttle diplomacy of Henry Kissinger in the Arab–Israeli dispute (ibid., p. 7). Thereafter, the practice of conflict negotiation was categorised as "two track diplomacy", distinguishing between official and unofficial diplomatic efforts to achieve a peace resolution (Davidson & Montville, 1981-1982, p. 153). In general, theories promoted ideas on how to reduce violence and still achieve peace (Neu & Kriesberg, 2019, p. 7). Positive sanctions and persuasion became popular ideas for modern conflict resolution (Sharp, 1973). During this time, conflict mediation

---

24 Satyagraha describes a basic attitude developed by Mohandas Gandhi when he lived in South Africa at the beginning of the 20th century. It is considered a political strategy based on a special form of non-violent or civil resistance. The opponent is met through non-violence and through the willingness to take on pain and suffering. This approach aims to "transform" the opponent into an ally and friend, based on the idea that appealing to the opponent's heart and conscience increases the chances of success, as violence would only lead to counter-violence. According to Gandhi, non-violence would instead enable opponents to break the spiral of violence and pain. Satyagraha is therefore seen as the weapon of the morally strongest party in a conflict.

3. THEORETICAL FRAMEWORK

became a widely discussed topic. Neu and Kriesberg (2019) consider the book by Fisher and Ury to be one of the most influential works in this regard. Fischer and Ury (1981) state:

> "More and more occasions require negotiation; conflict is a growth industry. Everyone wants to participate in decisions that affect them; fewer and fewer people will accept decisions dictated by someone else. People differ, and they use negotiation to handle their differences" (Fischer & Ury, 1981, p. 6).

Universities started to offer courses and degree programmes in the field of conflict mediation, and research centres and NGOs were established (Neu & Kriesberg, 2019, p. 8).

On the whole, these new practices supported managing the Cold War and allowed for agreements and confidence-building. (Neu & Kriesberg, 2019, p. 10). By considering non-violent alternative ideas, both the leaders of the US and the Soviet Union finally adopted "some of the language of the peace researchers" (ibid., p. 10).

The international system profoundly changed after the end of the Cold War in 1989. The newly adopted UN Agenda for Peace emphasised the increased role of the UN in conflict prevention, peacebuilding, peacemaking and peacekeeping (Boutros Ghali, 1992). In light thereof, the UN developed its new role as a third-party mediator to prevent international conflicts in the post-Cold War era (Neu & Kriesberg, 2019, p. 10). Moreover, the agreement on the importance of compliance with international norms such as human rights led to the creation of the International Criminal Court (ICC) in 2002 (ibid., p. 11). The underlying idea was that every human has basic needs which need to be met to avoid conflicts (Burton, 1990).

From then on, increased attention was paid to the traditional practices and rituals of peoples in the most remote places of the world. Emphasis was given to cultural characteristics since "[f]or the greatest part [...] the setting of such conflicts [in Africa] and their resolution must have been predominantly local" (Malan, 1997, p. 14). In the Middle East and North Africa, for instance, "formalised techniques for conflict resolution have a long tradition in Arab and Islamic societies" (MacQueen, 2009, p. 30). Incrementally, new practices of conflict resolution such as dinner diplomacy as well as the use of symbols were of significant importance.

> "In dinner diplomacy, participants do more than simply eat food to nourish their bodies or enjoy the pleasure of dancing. These acts become symbolic because the participants themselves are unusual.

They come from opposing sides of a conflict. Eating and dancing take on new meanings when they are done in the company of enemies" (Schirch, 2005, p. 5).

The spread of culture-specific customs combined with the research and teaching about various methods of conflict resolution received further attention with the spread of the internet (Neu & Kriesberg, 2019, p. 12).

Despite the newly acquired knowledge on methods of conflict resolution, violent suppression, terrorist attacks as well as ethnic and religious tensions returned on the agenda with the 9/11 attacks and the subsequent counterattack by the George W. Bush administration on Iraq (Neu & Kriesberg, 2019, p. 13). In his research, Kriesberg recognises the inevitability of conflicts in some cases but suggests a constructive conflict approach to minimise destruction and increase the benefits for all parties involved (Kriesberg, 2015).

With the new millennium, both the types of conflicts and their frequency have changed. By way of example, intrastate wars have become increasingly numerous, and ethnicity and religion have frequently become the main causes of disputes (Neu & Kriesberg, 2019, p. 13). At the same time, the number of external interventions has become more frequent, which has brought back earlier discussions on greed, grievances and identities. "Ethnic and religious groups use violence to intimidate and destroy other groups, seeking control over resources, a sense of security, and to restore lost honour" (Jenkins & Gottlieb, 2007, p. 1). Indeed, research on rituals and symbols in the context of conflict resolution has shown that the consideration of cultural sensitivities can even exceed the effect of material awards. Atran, Axelrod and Davis (2007) noted:

> "We found that the use of material incentives to promote the peaceful resolution of political and cultural conflicts may backfire when adversaries treat contested issues as sacred values. Symbolic concessions of no apparent material benefit may be key in helping to solve seemingly intractable conflicts" (Atran, Axelrod, & Davis, 2007, p. 1039f).

Additionally, the analysis of conflict resolution increasingly considered different types of interventions and their consequences, such as the work by Anderson and Olsen (2003), which concludes that:

> "peace practice combines personal dedication with hard-headed savvy. Dedication without savvy can result in programs that consume time, energy, and faith but that miss the mark in terms of promoting social change that is necessary for peace. Savvy without personal dedication

3. THEORETICAL FRAMEWORK

can result in actions that lack integrity, feed cynicism, and reinforce the systems that perpetuate war and injustice" (Anderson & Olson, 2003, p. 89).

In addition, a greater focus was given to longer-lasting peace through institution building (Paris, 2004).

Today, new challenges have emerged that require conflict resolution analysis, among them the global threat of climate change but also movements against dictatorship and corruption, as happened during the Arab Spring in many Middle Eastern and North African countries[25] (Neu & Kriesberg, 2019, p. 15f). In response to the rise in terrorism, a Global Terrorism Index was introduced in 2013 (ibid., p. 16). The use of media for and against conflict resolution presents another relevant topic to today's researchers (ibid. p. 16).

To find out if and how China is involved in international conflict resolution and to what extent military contributions may change the PRC's position on the global stage, research literature provides two popular mechanisms, namely military diplomacy and conflict mediation, which are presented in the following chapter.

3.3. Military Diplomacy and Conflict Mediation

In addition to China's economic development and the country's increased participation in global trade, the PRC is also establishing a growing role for itself in international peace and security. In the field of conflict resolution, science differentiates between the two interdisciplinary concepts of military diplomacy and conflict mediation. The following literature review gives an overview of both strands of research and identifies how China's contributions can be categorised.

Historically, mediation diplomacy has been used by international entities, sovereign states or regional actors to participate in global governance (Sun & Zoubir, 2018, p. 224). As a result, political influence was able to be exercised and relations were facilitated towards other nations or powers (ibid. p. 224). In this regard, the MENA region has been a prominent testing area for the most different actors. Since the outbreak of the first Arab–Israeli War in 1948, both US and European actors as well as the

---

25 Most recently, the global fight against infectious diseases can be added. However, this topic was not part of the study.

former Soviet Union and later Russia and Arab and African states have tried to settle a whole series of conflicts in the Middle East by applying mediation policies (ibid. p. 224). While this type of conflict resolution requires patience given that positive outcomes are not self-evident, mediation can increase political influence and improve a country's capabilities in setting the international agenda (ibid. p. 224). One recent example of successful mediation is the Joint Comprehensive Plan of Action (JCPOA), which is better known as the Iran nuclear deal of 2015 that was negotiated between Iran and the P5+Germany[26] (Garver, 2018). While, in the case of Iran, China's role was perceived as particularly constructive, the PRC's general engagement in conflict resolution processes in the MENA region has been developed only recently (Sun & Zoubir, 2018, p. 225; 236). Overall, mediation diplomacy can be understood as intervention by a neutral third party in a conflict with the aim of supporting the management of the conflict by transforming the bilateral relations between the two conflicting parties into a tripartite relationship (Ramsbotham, Woodhouse, & Miall, 2011, p. 180ff; Sun & Zoubir, 2018).

Previous research on mediation diplomacy concentrates on concretising definitions and establishing categories to assort actors' motivations. For instance, Asaf Siniver (2006) looks at conditions which allow for successful mediation using the example of the Arab–Israeli conflict (Siniver, 2006). The authors Kenneth Kressel and Dean G. Pruitt, furthermore, examine in what cases mediation can be used most effectively by comparing a variety of disputes (Kressel & Pruitt, 1989). Finally, Christopher Moore adds a description of different mediator roles such as authoritative and independent mediators as well as social networks, which cannot only be found in policy mediation but also in the fields of psychology and sociology (Moore, 2014).

In addition, existing literature covers historical case studies on examples of mediation applied by specific countries or organisations. Kristian Coates Ulrichsen, for instance, focuses on Qatar, which adopted mediation as a key pillar of its foreign policy in 2003 (Ulrichsen, 2013). In this case, mediation was applied to implement Qatar's regional interests and improve its international profile with regard to conflicts in Yemen, Lebanon and Sudan (ibid., p. 1). The composition of works in the book *Mediation in*

---

26 The USA unilaterally withdrew from the Iran nuclear deal in 2018. In 2021, the USA and Iran started discussions about restoring the deal or parts of it. When this study was finalised in July 2021, the outcome of these negotiations was not clear.

3. THEORETICAL FRAMEWORK

International Relations by Jacob Bercovitch and Jeffrey Z. Rubin adds a whole list of possible mediators such as private individuals, scholars and practitioners, formal mediators, representatives of an international organisation such as the African Union or the United Nations, small countries such as Algeria (which assumed a decisive role in the Iranian hostage crisis), the Pope as a religious mediator, or superpowers such as Russia or the US (Bercovitch & Rubin, 1992). A special view on the UN as a key actor in conflict mediation is provided by Elodie Convergne, who focuses on the UN Mediation Support Unit and its effectiveness (Convergne, 2015). The authors J. Michael Greig and Paul F. Diehl add an overview of when, where and how the tool of mediation has taken place in conflict management since the Second World War (Greig & Diehl, 2012). The authors also examine the view of the countries that have already been subject to mediation and were mostly found in Africa and Europe in the past (ibid., p.41).

Moreover, several authors examine mediation as a means of diplomacy with which to manage crises and even prevent conflicts. Dwight Golann and Jay Folberg outline skills and strategies about how disputes can be resolved effectively (Golann & Folberg, 2011). Rashid Sid adds thoughts on the case of Libya, stating that Canada could have taken on the role of the mediator in the conflict (Sid, 2013). Michael Greig and Patrick M. Regan add an analysis on the question of when both third parties and conflict-affected countries agree to mediation (Greig & Regan, 2008). The authors conclude that willingness in this respect depends predominantly on the third party's interests in the country as well as the historical relation between them (ibid., p. 759). With regard to mediation by third parties as a key to preventing conflicts, Francois Debrix points out the importance of transitional cultural interactions and looks at how cultural practices such as exhibiting art or travelling through airports as sites of mediation influence the success of this type of conflict resolution (Debrix, 2003).

By applying conflict mediation, the international community has found a tool that has the potential to change civil wars (DeRouen Jr, Bercovitch, & Pospieszna, 2011, p. 663). To quantify the use of mediation practices, DeRouen Jr. et al. have collected data on about 460 conflicts and their respective incidences of mediation. As a result, a Civil War Mediation (CWM) data set has been produced that provides information about the wars and the actors involved (ibid., p. 663ff). On the whole, representatives of international organisations make up one quarter (25 per cent) of the mediation actors (DeRouen Jr, Bercovitch, & Pospieszna, 2011, p. 665). Representatives of large governments make up 20 per cent, followed by

3.3. Military Diplomacy and Conflict Mediation

representatives of small governments, who are ranked third with 16 per cent and closely followed by representatives of regional organisations with 15 per cent (ibid., p. 665). The study's result implies that leaders of both small (10 per cent) and large governments (4 per cent) were less active in adopting a mediation role in conflicts between 1946 and 2004 (ibid., p. 665).

The CWM thus shows three categories of main mediation actors, namely institutions or organisations, states and individuals. Bercovitch and Schneider (2000) contribute a characterisation of each category (Bercovitch & Schneider, 2000, p. 146ff). With regard to institutions and organisations, international ones represent collections of states on a regional or international level and are thus bound to the respective obligations of their formal treaties (ibid., p. 148). By contrast, organisations can also be transnational and represent individuals across countries as non-governmental entities (ibid., p. 148). Yet, the latter have shown to take on the role in only three per cent of the mediation cases and, hence, only play a marginal role compared to international organisations (DeRouen Jr, Bercovitch, & Pospieszna, 2011, p. 665). In addition, states can be invited to mediate a conflict, which is usually done by sending state representatives (Bercovitch & Schneider, 2000, p. 147). These can be a state's top decision maker but also other representatives who are provided with a mandate to fulfil a mediatory role (ibid., p.147). The scope of their mediation capabilities is defined by the position they hold, the room for manoeuvring that they are given in their mandate as well as the financial and human resources their country provides (ibid., p.147). Finally, individuals who are not sent by a state or organisation can also take on a mediatory role in conflicts. While this form of mediation implies great flexibility to test out various mediation experiments, the data set by DeRouen et al. (2011) has shown that it is a rather less applied form of mediation which makes up only two per cent of all mediation cases (DeRouen Jr, Bercovitch, & Pospieszna, 2011, p. 665). In the majority of cases, conflict mediation is, therefore, provided by representatives of states or even their leaders (ibid., p. 665). Since the end of the Cold War, however, international organisations and mostly the UN have taken on mediating roles (Bercovitch & Schneider, 2000, p. 157). In terms of the countries that took on a mediatory role in conflicts between 1950 and 1990, the USA was by far the most invited in 84 out of 273 cases with one nation mediation only (Bercovitch & Schneider, 2000, p. 158). Syria and the United Kingdom are ranked second and third with thirty-one and sixteen mediatory roles respectively (ibid., p. 158). France was a mediator in eleven conflicts in the time period under

3. THEORETICAL FRAMEWORK

consideration and the Soviet Union in five cases (ibid., p. 158). Yet, in the list of 55 countries, China cannot be found and is thus the only permanent member of the UN Security Council that had not been a mediator in a conflict by the year 2000 (ibid., p. 161). When different international governmental organisations and their involvement in mediation during the Cold War period from 1950 to 1990 are compared, the UN is outstanding with 158 cases, followed by the Organisation of African Unity (OAU) with thirty-eight cases (ibid., p. 159). On the whole, the studies by DeRouen et al. and Bercovitch and Schneider illustrate that the circle of mediators is volatile and highly dependent on a number of conditions (Bercovitch & Schneider, 2000; DeRouen Jr, Bercovitch, & Pospieszna, 2011). While powerful single states as well as international governmental organisations dominated the number of conflicts with mediatory involvement in the past, their involvement highly depended on their status and influence at the given time and, to a lesser degree, on their mediation record (Bercovitch & Schneider, 2000, p. 162f). Moreover, a common cultural identity increases the probability of a state being invited to be a mediator (ibid., p. 161).

While China has not appeared as a relevant actor in previous studies about major conflict mediators, a group of scholars has concentrated on the development of mediation practices within China's contemporary diplomacy. For example, Chris Alden and Ana Cristina Alves examined Chinese-led forums in developing countries where China's economic power is particularly prevalent and bureaucracies are able to hold such international activities (Alden & Alves, 2017). Although China has proclaimed the norm of mutual benefit, their analysis finds that member states are increasingly challenging China's predominance and structural power in such forums. (ibid.). When considering China's mediation efforts in Africa, research director Dan Large finds that "[m]eaningful participation in African conflict-resolution processes is not an important aspect of China's current Africa relations" (Large, 2008, p. 35). Instead, Beijing considers the UN Security Council as the primary actor in managing peace and security (ibid., p.36f). Consequently, Large finds only few cases of Chinese mediation efforts in African conflicts, such as in the case of Darfur (see chapter 8.1.6). With regard to China's security governance towards the Middle East, Sun (2017) provides an overview of China's use of special envoys and foreign aid as well as its contribution to peacekeeping missions in the region (Sun, 2017). Yitzhak Shichor furthermore outlines China's reluctance to act as a mediator in Middle Eastern conflicts. Instead, Beijing prefers interventions by international or regional organisations or a decision by the UN Security

Council (Shichor, 2013). Hence, the author presents the continuous relevance of China's non-interference policy, which is increasingly becoming contested by international actors with China's economic rising and the PRC's political importance growing (ibid.). A general look at factors that increased the probability of Chinese interference in intrastate wars during and after the Cold War is provided by Mordechai Chaziza and Ogen Shlomo Goldman (2016). It shows that the geographic neighbourhood, the regime type of the adversary as well as China's military capabilities were particularly important in the cases examined (Chaziza & Goldman, 2016).

Finally, a profound overview of China's participation in conflict resolution through the use of mediation is provided by Sun and Zoubir (2018). The authors' comprehensive summary finds that China has not yet engaged in genuine mediation in the MENA region (ibid., p. 229). However, with the announcement of the BRI, the region has become a crucial part of the realisation of this immense infrastructural project. In this regard, the authors claim that China has engaged in "quasi-mediation diplomacy" which "in the MENA in recent years has been driven primarily by necessity, not ideology" (Sun & Zoubir, 2018, p. 229). Four categories of quasi-mediation diplomacy are presented, which cover multifaceted interventions such as special envoys and economic aid, proactive involvement by declaring China's position openly, limited intercession such as symbolic envoys and finally indirect participation such as that within the United Nations (ibid. p. 239f). On the whole, however, quasi-mediation is more concentrated on China's commercial or political interests than actually encouraging mediation. Both in the MENA region and sub-Saharan Africa, the authors emphasise China's quest for natural resources with regard to modernisation projects worldwide and a need to maintain the regional balance to prevent local turmoil (ibid., p. 231). Since up to now none of the traditional mediators such as the US and the EU or emerging powers such as India have succeeded in expanding their sphere of influence to include the MENA region, China has been able to extend its mediation efforts to propose to the region a "new model of great power relations" (Sun & Zoubir, 2018, p. 230). While Chinese mediation efforts are far more developed with regard to Korea given that security interests are more prominent to China, the authors find that the MENA region currently serves as a testing ground for Chinese quasi-mediation efforts (ibid., p. 240). This may be due to limitations in available diplomatic resources and a lack of domestic consensus on the necessity of using capacities in mediation diplomacy (ibid., p. 242). Finally, a stronger engagement in

3. THEORETICAL FRAMEWORK

conflict resolution via mediation could challenge Beijing's zero enemy policy (ibid. p. 242). Nevertheless, China's patiently conducted quasi-mediation diplomacy without the attempt at quick achievements may appear "increasingly more sophisticated and might in fact enhance its image as a responsible state, thus increasing the country's soft power" (ibid., p. 242).

To conclude, primary data on mediatory actors as well as secondary literature provide limited evidence about Chinese contributions to conflict mediation as a one-nation actor. Whilst between 1946–2004, 30 per cent of mediation cases led to a ceasefire, 18 per cent to a partial settlement, 15 per cent to a full settlement and 13 per cent to a process agreement, China's contributions have been rather marginal so far (DeRouen Jr, Bercovitch, & Pospieszna, 2011, p. 666). It is questionable if the low number of China's mediatory contributions is due to little effort or if the PRC has simply not been invited to become a third-party mediator in conflicts. Research literature suggests that China has limited its attempts at quasi-mediation. In general, it is not self-evident that China will become a popular mediator. Numerous authors have already dealt with the question of which characteristics and attributes a successful mediator must have. Kleiboer identifies (im)partiality, leverage and status as the main criteria to increase the chances of mediatory success (Kleiboer, 1996, p. 368). When choosing a mediator or when evaluating the success or failure of a mediation effort, actors are thus assessed on the basis of these factors (Susskind & Babbit, 1992, p. 35). In his book *Conflict Regulation*, Wehr (1979) covers a whole list of necessary skills for a successful mediator. He mentions skills such as empathy, active listening, a sense of timing, communication skills and the creativity to imagine alternative solutions (Wehr, 1979). Young adds the need for persuasiveness as well as the ability to transfer information (1972, p. 56). In addition, conflicting parties mostly trust mediators if they are perceived as neutral by both sides (Jackson, 1952; Northedge & Donelan, 1971; Young, 1967). Apart from neutrality, however, a mediator must also be equipped with leverage and resources that all conflicting parties value such as economic resources or political support. As Zartman and Touval put it: "[l]everage is the ticket to mediation" (Zartman & Touval, 1985, p. 40). Moreover, mediators' cultural backgrounds play a crucial role in their acceptance (Cohen, 1996). In this regard, the "[i]deological position provides a kind of safety net for all participants in conflict" (Bercovitch & Schneider, 2000, p. 150). On the whole, previous research has shown that although the USA has dominated mediation activities in the past, the USA is not the sole actor and power is not the only factor that influences the choice of a mediator (Bercovitch & Schneider, 2000, p. 163). Yet, China remains rather absent from mediation activities.

In research literature, another form of conflict involvement is referred to as military diplomacy. While the use of the military and force was most common in achieving political aims and even led to the description of gunboat diplomacy in the 18th and 19th centuries, military diplomacy based on negotiations, service attachés and (peaceful) support of conflict prevention were not given as much attention in previous literature (Muthanna, 2011, p. 2). This may be due to its close links to military intelligence operations, on which less information and fewer sources are available for research (Pajtinka, 2016, p. 180). Moreover, the understanding of military diplomacy varies among researchers and so far, no single concept has gained widespread acceptance (Muthanna, 2011, p. 2; Pajtinka, 2016, p. 180).

With regard to China, Article 65 of the Law of the People's Republic of China Law on National Defence states:

> "In independently handling its foreign military relations and conducting military exchange and cooperation with other countries, the People's Republic of China adheres to the five principles of mutual respect for sovereignty and territorial integrity, mutual non-aggression, non-interference in each other's internal affairs, equality and mutual benefit and peaceful coexistence" (Law of the PRC on National Defence, 1997).

Furthermore, Article 66 stipulates:

> "The People's Republic of China supports the world community in its military-related actions taken for the benefit of safeguarding world and regional peace, security and stability and supports it in its efforts to impartially and reasonably resolve international disputes and its efforts for arms control and disarmament" (Law of the PRC on National Defence, 1997).

Since the adoption of the Law on National Defence at the 5th Meeting of the 8th National People's Congress on March 14, 1997, China has strengthened its military diplomacy and has constantly increased military exchanges (Matsuda, 2006). The phenomenon of Chinese military diplomacy can be understood as activities by state institutions, mainly led by the defence department, to assert foreign policy interests which are of particular concern regarding security (Pajtinka, 2016, p. 179). The activities are concentrated on negotiations as well as other diplomatic action, which are in contrast to the use of guns or coercive approaches (ibid. p. 179). The functions of military diplomacy can be summarised as, first, collecting security-related information on the receiving state and gaining insights concerning the conditions of its military forces (ibid. p. 179). Second, security cooperation can be strengthened and military exchanges organized. Finally, military diplomacy can facilitate trade in arms and other military equipment between the states and can thus serve as a relevant business tool (ibid. p. 179).

The amount of research on Chinese military diplomacy remains limited. In China, a comprehensive and valuable overview of *Sixty Years of China Foreign Affairs* (1949–2009) has been published by Wang Yizhou and Tan Xiuyin (Wang & Tan, 2009). In addition, several political scientists from outside China have dealt with Chinese military diplomacy; however, they mostly focus on bilateral military exchanges and relations.

David M. Finkelstein, for example, addresses US–China military exchanges and finds that security cooperation between the two countries was not well developed in the past with the exception of the 1980s, when the Soviet Union represented a common threat (Finkelstein, 2010, p. 2f). Yet, after the end of the Cold War and with growing disputes on the status of Taiwan, military diplomatic activities were reduced. They have slowly increased again during the 21st century with emerging new common threats such as those in maritime security (ibid. p. 2). Thomas Christensen finds that military cooperation between China and the US has increased in particular due to North Korea's nuclear weapons programme and due to Islamic fundamentalism, which have overshadowed the Taiwan issue (Christensen, 2003). A summary of military diplomacy between China and the US since Tiananmen is provided by Jong-Dong Yuan, who acknowledges the difficulties in stabilising the relationship and expresses inter alia the need for long-term strategies and an increase in exchanges of officer corps as necessary requirements for an improvement (Yuan, 2003, p. 65). Finally, Kevin Pollpeter finds that China and the US should focus their relations on security management and improve it through lower-level facility visits and exchanges of students to strengthen their bilateral dialogue (Pollpeter, 2004).

With regard to China–Russia (formerly China–Soviet) relations, Ming-Yen Tsai provides a profound overview of the two countries' bilateral military relations since they established a strategic partnership in 1996 (Tsai, 2003). However, Tsai finds that their military ties remain fragile due to a low level of trust, while cooperation has been developed in arms trade and technological exchanges (ibid., p. 117f; 153f). Tsai concludes that both countries' ambitions to become regional great powers have resulted in continuous tensions (ibid., p. 183).

As regards China's military approaches to countries in the Asia-Pacific, Kenneth W. Allen provides a summary on the increasing role of the People's Liberation Army in implementing Chinese foreign policy interests in the region (Allen, 2001). He identifies that China's military relations with countries in the Asia-Pacific region contribute to several key Chinese security objectives such as improving military relations with foreign countries, modernising China's defence industry and gaining knowledge of and training in military operations and administration (ibid.). The author furthermore highlights that these goals are pursued through envoys of military attachés and high-level visits as well as arms purchases (ibid., p. 645).

In addition to the numerous analyses of military diplomacy in China's bilateral relations with particular countries or regions, there is a limited number of reports on China's military diplomacy approach in general. A comprehensive paper is provided by Kenneth Allen, Phillip C. Saunders and John Chen (2017) with a focus on trends and implications between 2003 and 2016 (Allen, Saunders, & Chen, 2017). The authors find that military diplomacy has become a central part of Chinese foreign policy efforts and the PLA seeks to achieve strategic goals by interacting with foreign militaries, in particular with major powers such as Russia, the US and Asian countries (ibid., p. 3f). Simultaneously, Chinese military diplomacy also includes trade in arms and advice on internet censorship and is organised in a top-down approach headed by the Central Committee of the Chinese Communist Party and the Central Military Commission, which defines foreign policy goals (Allen, Saunders, & Chen, 2017, p. 1). Between 2003 and 2016, bilateral meetings were mostly conducted by senior-level military officials, while China increasingly participates in multilateral meetings and contributes to non-traditional security cooperation such as humanitarian assistance (ibid., p. 2). The authors also stress China's increased participation in UN peacekeeping operations (ibid., p. 3).

In addition, a general summary and categorisation of China's military diplomacy after the Cold War was published by Yasuhiro Matsuda (Matsuda, 2006). The author distinguishes between "Bilateral Routine Military Diplomacy" and "Multilateral Routine Military Diplomacy" (Matsuda, 2006, p. 7; 12). Bilateral routine military diplomacy can be exercised in four different ways. First, the mutual exchange of military attachés who are controlled by the Ministry of National Defence (ibid., p.7). Second, mutual visits by military delegations, which strongly increased in the 2000s,

3. THEORETICAL FRAMEWORK

just like the opening of military bases and military exercises (ibid., pp. 8–10). In comparison, China currently operates four military bases abroad, Russia operates nine and the USA operates 56 bases[27]. Finally, China sends students of military studies abroad and provides training for military personnel, mainly in the countries of the Global South[28] (Matsuda, 2006, p. 10f).

With regard to Multilateral Routine Military Diplomacy, Matsuda provides three classifications. They include participation in international arms control and disarmament activities, in which "China puts the UN at the center" and only selectively participates in control activities, has reluctantly joined international treaties and continues to sell missile technologies (Matsuda, 2006, p. 13f). Second, joint exercises targeting non-traditional threats are mentioned, which represents an area China has actively promoted in the past, in particular concerning terrorism, separatism and religious extremism (ibid., p. 15f). Moreover, China's increased efforts in UN peacekeeping missions are mentioned. Since China's first participation in 1989, the PRC has become one of the major supporters of this instrument of international military diplomacy. Matsuda states that "[i]t was probably around this time that China first became aware that UN PKOs could be of benefit in improving the country's international image" (ibid., p.12).

The literature overview in this chapter has shown that both the PRC's military diplomacy and Chinese conflict mediation still seem to be in a testing phase and more research is needed to understand what role both of them play regarding China's intentions in the country's foreign strategy. When one is analysing the Chinese discourse and the image of a peaceful rising power that is conveyed, it might be expected that China would

---

27 *Chinese military bases* are located in Argentina, Djibouti, Myanmar and Tajikistan. *Russian military bases* are located in Armenia, Belarus, Georgia, Kazakhstan, Kyrgyzstan, Moldova, Syria, Tajikistan and Ukraine. Additionally, there have been recent announcements about the opening of further military bases in Egypt, the Central African Republic, Madagascar and Sudan.
US military bases are located in Afghanistan, Akrotiri and Dhekelia, Aruba, Australia, Ascension, Bahamas, Bahrain, Belgium, Bosnia and Herzegovina, Brazil, British Indian Ocean Territory (United Kingdom), Bulgaria, Cuba, Cameroon, Curaçao (Netherlands), Djibouti, Ecuador, Egypt, Estonia, Germany, Greece, Greenland (Denmark), Honduras, Hungary, Iceland, Indonesia, Iraq, Israel, Italy, Japan, Jordan, Kenya, Kosovo, Kuwait, Netherlands, Niger, Norway, Oman, Pakistan, Peru, Philippines, Poland, Portugal, Qatar, Romania, Saudi Arabia, Seychelles, Singapore, South Korea, Spain, Syria, Thailand, Tunisia, Turkey, the United Arab Emirates and the United Kingdom.

28 For a discussion about the term Global South see (Dados & Connell, 2012).

3.3. Military Diplomacy and Conflict Mediation

particularly expand its mediation efforts (see chapter 2.3.1.). However, an analysis of secondary literature does not indicate such an approach. Rather, China is reluctant to meet international demands for more engagement and limits its contributions to quasi-mediation efforts. By contrast, previous research provides evidence that China has become increasingly active in military diplomacy efforts on both the bilateral and multilateral levels.

While the existing body of scholarship shows that China has increased mutual visits by military delegations as well as military student exchanges, the number of military bases abroad still ranks far behind those of Russia or the USA. On the multilateral level, China's increased contributions to the United Nations suggest both an increased emphasis on and possibly also a novel interpretation of military diplomacy in conflict resolution.

This study builds on the current state of research on military diplomacy. It seeks to add findings on when and where China uses military diplomacy for conflict resolution and on how the PRC's foreign policy activities can be classified and compared to other great powers. Hence, evidence shall be provided about drivers that make China intervene militarily in conflicts. In the framework of UN peacekeeping, this contributes to knowledge about when China engages in multilateral military diplomacy as part of international missions, particularly in the MENA region and sub-Saharan Africa. The approach is intended to add findings about the application of military diplomacy and the use of military troops and personnel in Chinese participation in conflict resolution.

In this context, it is assumed that the foreign policy actions of a state are directly correlated with the distribution of power at the international level and the associated balance of power. Hence, the study not only notes an increase in Chinese military contributions, but also offers added value in terms of China's motives that are directly related to the PRC's quest for a great power status. Indeed, the distribution of power is central to states' behaviour. As Gallaroti notes "[t]he global system is in flux, while the power of nations continues to be the principal instrument for determining our collective fate as a planet" (Gallaroti, 2011, p. 4). Guzzini, furthermore adds that "the distribution of power would give us the basic indication of who was responsible for controlling that international system" (Guzzini, 1993, p. 478). Following the assumptions of these two researchers, the concept of power must be considered as soon as international affairs such as global security or peacekeeping and conflict resolution are addressed (Marigat, Nzomo, Kagwanja, & Kiamba, 2017, p. 14). Indeed, the distribution of power as well as the extent to which a state is equipped with instruments of influence have an impact on peacebuilding processes (ibid.,

3. THEORETICAL FRAMEWORK

p. 14). An actor's power status thus needs to be compared relatively to the opposing state or party (ibid., p. 14).

In foreign policy, the balance of power is central to any action taken on the international stage. Actors that are powerful enough to solve conflicts implicitly communicate their ability to control and manage the whole system. Hence, conflicts provide opportunities to show one's ability to appease the conflicting parties and to stand out as a powerful third-party actor. Conflicts may thus lead to changes in the existing power equilibrium and lead to a readjustment of positions (Haas, 1953, p. 444ff). Marigat, Nzomo, Kagwanja and Kiamba assume that powerful states "try and guard the equilibrium that favors them", which implies that less powerful actors might try to influence this equilibrium to their interests (2017, p. 14).

Today, this holds particularly true for emerging countries such as Brazil, Russia, India, China and South Africa[29] (Yang, 2019). With regard to China and the Chinese discourse on the country's great rejuvenation, Chinese foreign policy behaviour in conflict resolution processes could thus aim at increasing the country's power status and, consequently, change the current power equilibrium. This study will provide evidence on the question of to what extent China is increasing its international power status in conflict resolution. To this end, it is relevant to outline how the concept of power is understood in international relations theories. By doing so, the study classifies how China's contributions to conflict resolution translate into a new understanding of the PRC's power status and role in the global arena and which implications can be assumed to result thereof for the structure of the international community.

The theoretical concepts presented create the framework for this study and facilitate theoretical categorisation of Chinese military interventions abroad. This will help to better anticipate Chinese actions in the future under certain circumstances. The QCA conducted in this work conducts a quest for drivers to find empirical evidence to explain China's increased international military activity.

3.4. Power Concepts and Measuring in International Relations

Power is a central element in international politics. At the same time, it is a highly contested concept and scholars have not yet agreed on a single

---

[29] The four states are often referred to as the BRICS.

3.4. Power Concepts and Measuring in International Relations

definition and meaning (Marigat, Nzomo, Kagwanja, & Kiamba, 2017, p. 8). As Dahl put it:

> "Thus we are not likely to produce—certainly not for some considerable time to come—anything like a single, consistent, coherent "Theory of Power". We are much more likely to produce a variety of theories of limited scope, each of which employs some definition of power that is useful in the context of the particular piece of research or theory but different in important respects from the definitions of other studies. Thus, we may never get through the swamp" (Dahl, 1957, p. 202).

In international relations, the concept of power has been crucial in decisions relating to war and peace as well as the associated question of conflict management and resolution (Marigat, Nzomo, Kagwanja, & Kiamba, 2017, p. 8). Most scholars define power as either domination or capacity, although the typologies and forms of power vary in different writings (ibid., p. 8). Bachrach and Baratz, for example, proposed investigating "the dominant values, the myths and the established political procedures and rules of the game" to identify how these are influenced (Bachrach & Baratz, 1962, p. 952). Lukes adds that "one way to capture this is to see the concept of domination as adding to the notion of power over others the further claim that those subject to it are rendered less free" (Lukes, 2004, p. 114). By contrast, Mary Follett, a representative of the feminist movement, considers power to "be defined as simply the ability to make things happen, to be a causal agent, to initiate change" (Follett, 1942, p. 76). Miller agrees with this approach and adds the understanding that power can also mean enabling and empowering others (Miller, 1982).

In addition, one of the most prominent definitions of power is provided by Weber, who states that it is "the probability that one actor within a social relationship will be in a position to carry out his own will despite resistance, regardless of the basis on which the probability exists" (Weber, 1947, p. 52). Weber's assumption is that the actor would do everything to implement his will, regardless of the costs (Neu & Kriesberg, 2019, p. 9). Yet, Weber's definition was further developed by Dahl (1957) and Guzzini (2002). To understand the concept of power, Dahl supposed that "A has power over B to the extent that he can get B to do something that B would not otherwise do" (Dahl, 1957, p. 202f). The Dahlian definition covers three relevant elements of power which have been elaborated by Barnet and Duval (2015). First, A must have an intention to move B in a particular direction. If B changes his or her behaviour only because he thinks that A wants it, we cannot speak of A's power over B. Second, A and B must have conflictive desires and, third, A must be sufficiently equipped with resources to direct B's actions (Barnett & Duval, 2005, p. 49). With regard to the third condition, Guzzini (2005) adds that it is not only enough to possess enough resources but that they also have to be used. Guzzini states that the sole possession of a revolver does not mean that A has power over B but that only the use of the gun would allow A to force B to do what he or she would otherwise not have done (Guzzini, 2005, p. 501f). In contrast, Bachrach and Baratz express that power could also be exerted unintentionally, with A being unaware of the effects of his actions on B (Bachrach & Baratz, 1962, p. 952). In any case, manipulation by A can be shaped as a corrective or persuasive influence (Scot, 2007, p. 26). Power can thus be exercised as "power over" and "power to" (Neu & Kriesberg, 2019, p. 9). In academic debate, realists tend to use the corrective understanding of power, whilst liberals and others prefer a persuasive understanding (ibid., p. 9). The relative distribution of power is particularly focused on in realists' theories due to the assumption that "changes in the distribution of power that are triggered by a rising power have significant implications for the overall stability of the international system" (Schmidt & Roy, 2013, p. 67). By contrast, liberalists are not all that concerned about shifting power relations as long as the rising powers are already part of the global liberal order (ibid., p. 67). Ironically, Ikenberry even concluded that currently "China is more worried that the US will abandon its commitment to the old, Western-oriented global rules and institutions than it is eager to advance a new set of Asian-generated rules and institutions" (Ikenberry, 2008, p. 19). As evidence of China's willingness to accept Western rules, Moravcsik cites China's accession to the World Trade Organization (WTO) in 2001 (Moravcsik, 2010, p. 95). Cheung even argues that China's historical collaboration with Asian partners shows the country's peaceful nature and predicts that the China's development of soft power will even enhance more cordial bilateral relationships with China (Cheung, 2008, p. 11). However, some authors express great anxiety about a change in the balance of power and an American decline in particular since they assume that rising powers destabilise the international order and that it will take time to establish a new equilibrium (Schmidt & Roy, 2013, p. 67).

3.4.1. The Concept of Soft Power

In his works about soft power, political scientist Joseph Samuel Nye (2005) considers the origins of power. He outlines that power is more than commands and pressure since a dictator's instruction to execute a dissident is nullified if the dissident plans to become a martyr (Nye, 2004, p. 2). Nye outlines the importance of the respective context and relationship between the actors with regard to the balance of power among them (ibid., p. 2). Moreover, Nye (2004) states that one actor may have power over another without threatening him (ibid., p. 2). Instead, faith or acceptance of a leader's legitimacy may empower an actor and provide him with power over others (ibid., p. 3). As examples, he refers to religious leaders such as the Pope but also to fundamentalists such as Osama bin Laden (ibid., p. 3). The point Nye (2004) is making here is that the mere possession of capabilities or resources is not sufficient to explain the power status of an actor. In terms of resources, for example, the USA has always been far more powerful than Vietnam and yet it lost the war in 1975 (ibid., p. 3). Similarly, in terms of military power, the USA is still more powerful than the EU, Russia or China in 2020. Yet, the USA cannot achieve its goals in free trade, finance or even anti-terrorism activities without the others (ibid., p. 4).

With regard to transnational power relations, Nye thus outlines the relevance of considering more than just hard power assets like resources and the military. Instead, in the 20th century, neoliberalist Nye noted a change in the meaning of power. Nye does not neglect "the traditional concern for the military balance of power" but finds that power must be defined more broadly (Nye, 1990, p. 156). In this context, Nye stresses modern changes in economics such as the emergence of private actors and also new means of communication (Nye, 1990). Whilst states used to be concerned with their survival in military terms, their national security today also depends on economic and ecological factors (ibid.). The use of force, therefore, refers to organisational structures and communication skills to control economic interdependences and a state's environment. According to Nye, power represents a relationship between actors (Nye, 1990, p. 160). If a country is able to make another country "want what it wants", it means to have power over this country's actions (Nye, 1990, p. 166). In doing so, one country can persuade another country of its ideology or culture without using any military force. Making one's beliefs and ideology attractive will make others follow this path without having to be forced (ibid., p. 167). The main challenge for an actor would thus be to establish values and options for action that others *want* to follow. In this regard, "[the] ability to establish preferences tends to be associated with intangible assets such as an attractive personality, culture, political values and institutions, and policies that are seen as legitimate or having moral

3. THEORETICAL FRAMEWORK

authority" (Nye, 2004, p. 6). Other than hard power, this communicational soft power is less costly and might be more effective. To increase its soft power, an actor thus has to focus on these elements and increase its attraction. The success of such efforts can be measured, for example, by polls (ibid., p. 6). In contrast to coercive hard power, soft power is described by Nye as "the ability of a country to structure a situation so that other countries develop preferences or define their interests in ways consistent with its own" (Nye, 1990, p. 168). In international politics, Nye suggests that the use of soft power reduces the costs of "carrots and sticks", which are needed to increase traditional hard power (Nye, 2004, p. 11). However, at this point Nye underestimates the costs of the personnel and time that are needed to attain soft power results. To persuade parties of the legitimacy of one's objectives and authority to implement them, several meetings and soft interventions are necessary. In view of the sources of such soft power, Nye proposes three elements: culture, political values and foreign policies (Nye, 2004, p. 11). Yet, the promotion of cultural values via brands, movies and logos takes time to change people's attitude even though they may be highly effective in the long run (ibid., p. 12). Moreover, the perception of power elements varies depending on its communication. While Nye (2004) points at the different emotions a T-shirt with an American logo may have in China or Pakistan and thus highlights that the effects of soft power depend on the context, the author does not consider that *how* sources are used will also make a difference to the perception of power. For instance, a knife can both be used to cut bread or to hurt somebody. Providing military assistance to a conflict may both appease the conflicting parties and increase the military's reputation. What is still missing in the concept of soft power so far is that many sources of power can both be used as hard and soft power tools depending on the context. The study at hand will provide findings that seek to fill this gap and contribute to further developing Nye's theoretical approach.

In academic debate, the role of soft power in the case of China's foreign policy has also been addressed (Arif, 2017). In his study, political scientist Arif finds that soft power has largely been developed in China's diplomatic strategy during the last few years. In particular, Arif outlines Chinese Presidents' initiatives such as the aim to form a "harmonious society" and a "harmonious world" using Hu Jintao or Xi Jinping's "Asia-Pacific Dream", the "Chinese Dream" and finally the "Silk Road Economic Belt" to begin a new type of major-country relations[30] (Arif, 2017, p. 97). According to Shambaugh (2005), such slogan diplomacy has been of major importance to Beijing's soft power push (Shambaugh, 2005, p. 99). Both Arif and other authors such as US journalist Joshua Kurlantzick stick to Joseph Nye's original understanding of soft power as being based on cultural attractiveness or ideology and political values (Nye, 1990). Kurlantzick distinguishes between cultural elements such as arts, language or ethnicity and between what he calls business tools such as investments, trading and aid (Kurlantzick, 2007). Remarkably, military-related tools have not been considered instruments to be used with regard to soft power. While much attention has been paid to cultural aspects, foreign policies or political values, political scientists have neglected the impact of China's military troops on its international soft image status. This study illustrates that whilst a central feature of soft power has been the development of power without using economic incentives or military threats, China uses exactly these tools to improve its image. For example, President Xi Jinping stated in his speech *China and the World in the New Era* in September 2019 that "The Chinese military is a resolute defender of world peace", thus using an instrument of hard power to influence how China is perceived internationally (Xi Jinping, 2019). Remarkably, China thus seems to have reinvented the term soft power with a whole new approach. While Nye (1990) contrasted hard and soft power by opposing military and economic means with diplomacy, history and culture, China uses the hard power element of military strength to enforce its soft power impact on the international level. Nye's classification of power can be described as follows. Hard power consists of both military and economic power, which are characterised by coercion and deterrence (Nye, 2004). Threat and force but also investments and money-making are the basic tools to achieve coercive diplomacy, win wars or form alliances (Yavuzaslan & Cetin, 2016). The area of soft power is clearly distanced from this and includes the creation of an agenda by using policies and institutions in order to achieve bilateral and multilateral diplomacy (Nye, 2004; Yavuzaslan & Cetin, 2016). Some economic activities may include both hard and soft power, especially when public institutions such as schools or healthcare facilities are built. According to Nye's definition, soft power covers any chance or alternative a country has apart from military action (Nye, 2004). Nye thus understands soft power in direct contrast to military force. Consequently, the observation

---

30 Additionally, China has recently launched the core module for the PRC's "Heavenly Harmony" space station (June 2021).

3. THEORETICAL FRAMEWORK

of China's new military banner and international military charm initiative requires an extension of Joseph Nye's theory. To understand how Nye's theoretical approach is being used and amended, his original argument needs to be considered and compared to China's current conditions.

As early as in 1990, Nye observed the development of an increasing interest among states in commonly controlling non-state actors. Today, international cooperation has become more important than ever before, with international institutions becoming increasingly significant. "Information becomes power," said Nye (Nye, 1990, p. 164). Technological progress has played its role in the development of satellite technologies, which today are no longer only in the hands of the United States, but available and used by many more states, including Russia and China. Again, power does not emerge from the sole possession of modern technology but from its application. In this regard, Nye proposed two options. First, recognition through the use of hard power, which implies "ordering others to do what [you want]" (Nye, 1990, p. 166). Alternatively, Nye proposes the use of co-optive power or soft power, "which occurs when one country gets other countries to do what it wants" (ibid., p. 166).

In 1990, Joseph Nye commenced his paper with a general definition of power: "an ability to do things and control others, to get others to do what they otherwise would not" (Nye, 1990, p. 154). In this regard, controlling others had usually been related to the possession of resources such as territory, population, natural resources, commercial size, military strength or political stability (ibid. p. 154). The competition between two states for supremacy in these categories was predominantly decided in armed conflicts. Yet, shortly after the end of the Cold War, Nye observed a change in the factors of power with "geography, population, and raw materials [...] becoming somewhat less important" (Nye, 1990, p. 154). Instead, he noted the rising relevance of technological and educational advantages as well as economic growth for the description of a powerful state.

Nye wrote his paper in the historical context of the fall of the Soviet Union, a not yet unified Europe, a weak Japan and a Chinese People's Republic which was still categorised as a less-developed country. Hence, the United States remained the only state with clear superpower status with a "broad range of power resources—military, economic, scientific, cultural, and ideological" (ibid., p. 155). And yet, Joseph Nye anticipated that the sole accumulation of these resources would not be enough for a country to remain a superpower. Rather, he recognised that power was only established and maintained when the available resources were utilized "to change the behaviour of states" (ibid., p. 155). States' competition over superpower status would be decided on the question of who can best control the political environment and make other states do what it wants. The power shift Nye describes is thus a change from power over particular countries to power over outcomes (ibid., p. 156). While the first could be attained by military force, the latter demands much more.

Nye stated that, in the past, states were very concerned about their survival and the way to secure territorial integrity was military force. Yet, threats have become multifaceted with economic and ecological menaces gaining relevance (ibid., p. 157). Since 1990, this trend has developed further and the financial crisis of 2008/2009 as well as the current debate on climate change illustrate states' interdependency in the face of global threats. With regard to military threats, however, recent years have shown a new form of military threat which relates to an increasing threat by non-state actors such as guerrilla groups or terrorist cells. Ever since the devastating events of 9/11, the world has experienced that danger can emerge far away from a country's geographical border. In this regard, costly military force is no longer enough for a state to protect its population and safeguard its integrity. Instead, as observed by Joseph Nye in 1990, "[o]ther instruments such as communications, organizational and institutional skills, and manipulation of interdependence have become important" (ibid., p. 157).

Nye's assumptions in 1990 were based on the theory that military power was a form of bipolar distribution. About 30 years later, the situation has become more complex. On the one hand, non-state actors are gaining ground, especially in fragile environments. On the other hand, international cooperation has led to a rise in UN peacekeeping missions, where states cooperate in safeguarding international peace and security or exercising their responsibility to protect. Nye considered "[...] the direct use of force for economic gain [...] too costly and dangerous for modern great powers" (Nye, 1990, p. 159). With the development of international military cooperation within the United Nations, however, one can say that the shared costs of military intervention may be worth taking for the greater economic gain of regional stability. In particular with China's ambitious Belt and Road Initiative connecting Asia with Europe and Africa, shared costs imply shared benefits for more than just one great power. Nye wrote about power as a relationship (Nye, 1990, p. 160). He believed protected states depended on protective powers to ensure their security. UN peacekeeping missions dissolve this relationship, however, to the extent that many small, presumably less powerful states provide large numbers of

3. THEORETICAL FRAMEWORK

troops. Yet, the final decision about a mission remains with the Security Council, where at least the P5 have veto power. China's quest for power is reflected in the PRC's increased contributions to international conflict resolution within the United Nations. Joseph Nye's approach provides a term that describes and analyses the exercise of power on the international stage based on cultural attractiveness and ideological cornerstones. The concept of soft power is thus relevant in understanding China's evolving role.

While traditional Western theories of international relations have dominated political science for a long time, the rise of non-Western actors from Asia has been accompanied by the introduction of non-Western concepts (Noesselt, 2012, p. 5). In this regard, Asian theoretical approaches and indigenous ideas are shaped by Asian philosophical and traditional experiences and history (Alagappa, 2011, p. 194). Combining emerging new approaches with traditional Western theories and understanding "how the rethinking of concepts in non-core contexts interacts with and influences disciplinary developments at large" is an ongoing task for political scientists in this field (Waever & Tickner, 2009, p. 3). Some authors predict that "Chinese IR theory will serve as one symbol of the growth of Chinese soft power" (Wang, 2009, p. 115). Whilst an official Chinese IR theory is not yet available, frameworks with Chinese characteristics are under construction. In the following, the Chinese concept of comprehensive national power will be presented.

3.4.2. Comprehensive National Power

In the 1970s, China began its strategy of opening up its economy, which has not only increased the country's economic growth but also removed large parts of the population from poverty and allowed for social development (Chuwattananurak, 2016, p. 1). What began with economic reforms turned into a more than thirty years of growth and resulted in the rise of a new global power status for China (ibid., p. 1). Within the global community, China became a permanent member of the UN Security Council in 1971 and signed the Non-Proliferation Treaty as one of five nuclear powers in 1992 (UNODA, 2020). Moreover, with a population of approximately 1.4 billion, China has become home to the world's largest population (World Bank, 2020).

In view of China's growth, Chinese scholars established a scientific method to measure China's status and rank the PRC among other nations (Pillsbury, 2000, p. 203). This concept has become known as *zonghe guoli*, which translates as comprehensive national power (CNP). CNP ranks competing countries, particularly big powers in the process of economic globalisation and integration (Bajwa, 2008, p. 151). As far back as in ancient times, the Chinese military strategic advisor and philosopher Sun Tzu[31] stressed the importance of assessing the level of an enemy's power, strengths and weaknesses to calculate the chances of successful warfare:

"You may advance and be absolutely irresistible, if you make for the enemy's weak points; you may retire and be safe from pursuit if your movements are more rapid than those of the enemy" (Sun Tzu, 2000; Sun Tzu Textproject 2020).

Therefore, one of the objectives of Chinese authors and researchers has been to be able to predict the future distribution of power on the international level (Pillsbury, 2000, p. 203). The Chinese concept of CNP thus allows for a strategic assessment of the status and position of foreign states and results in a ranking of powers (Bajwa, 2008, p. 151). Changes in CNP are associated with a change in a country's strategic resources, which serves as an indicator of its changing power status (ibid., p. 151).

While most Western approaches to measuring political power are not numerical, CNP consists of a number of quantitative elements that can be calculated and result in a numerical value (ibid., p. 151). Remarkably, the indicators consist of both military and economic factors such as military forces, territory or natural resources but also take into account cultural aspects and the domestic government (Pillsbury, 2000, p. 203f). Without roots in either Western theories, Marxism or Leninism, the elements of the Chinese concept can nevertheless be categorised according to hard and soft power indicators (Bajwa, 2008, p. 152). The CNP, furthermore, includes qualitative and quantitative factors which are included in formulas (Pillsbury, 2000, p. 204). Chinese scholars have developed their own index system, neglecting Western measures such as the gross national product (GNP) index (ibid., p. 204). As regards the calculation of CNP, a number of Chinese think tanks are involved and combine different statistical indicators (Golden, 2011, p. 99). Two of the most prominent Chinese scholars in defining and categorising the concrete indicators of CNP are Hu Angang and Men Honghua, who consider CNP to be the

---

31 Sun Tzu lived between 534 BC and 453 BC. His Book *The Art of War* is considered a masterpiece on strategy and has remained one of the most important works on the subject until today. In particular, East Asian theorists and military strategists have cited and referred to the book until today. In 13 chapters, 68 theses deal with different aspects of war and how to best prepare for warfare.

3. THEORETICAL FRAMEWORK

"most important indicator in measuring the basic national conditions and resources of a country, and a comprehensive indicator for the economic, political, military and technical powers of a country" (Hu & Men, 2002, p. 2).

Table 2: Calculation Elements of CNP by Hu and Men (2002)

Category	Indicator
Economic Resources	– GDP in PPP – % of World GDP
Human Capital	– % of 15–64-year-old people of the world's total – Average years of schooling
Natural Resources	– Electricity production – Commercial energy use – Arable land – Freshwater withdrawal
Capital Resources	– Gross Domestic Investment – Capital market value – Net FDI
Knowledge and Technological Resources	– Personal computers – Patent applications filed by residents – Scientific and technical journal articles – Internet hosts – R&D spending
Governmental Resources	– % of central spending in GDP – % of central spending of the world's total
Military Resources	– Armed forces personnel – Military expenditure
International Resources	– Exports and imports and services – Royalty and license fees receipts

Sources: (Hu & Men, 2002, p. 21) and (Golden, 2011, p. 99)

While the authors refer to American economist Michael Porter et al's. (2000) growth competitiveness categories of physical resources, human capital, infrastructure, knowledge resources and capital resources, they present eight categories with respective indicators for the calculation of CNP (Hu & Men, 2002, pp. 4-16; Porter, Sachs, & Warner, 2000). Although Hu and Men (2002) stress the importance of soft power elements for CNP, the resulting categories in their study are rather concentrated on what Western academics would classify as hard power. Sean Golden (2011) summarised Hu and Men's definitions as illustrated in table 2.

In his book, Pillsbury refers to Wang Songfen and states that the CNP framework additionally includes a social development level which covers educational expenditure per person, as well as the proportion of people studying in higher and secondary education (Pillsbury, 2000, p. 221; Wang, 1996). In addition, a cultural level covers the adult literacy rate and the number of people per one thousand who get a daily newspaper (Pillsbury, 2000, p. 221). Moreover, a health case indicator covers healthcare expenditure per person as well as the number of doctors and nurses available (ibid., p. 221). Additionally, a communication indicator covers the number of people who own a phone per 1000 people and, finally, the level of urbanisation is included (ibid., p. 221). Beyond Pillsbury's (2000) contribution, Colonel Huang Shuofeng of the Academy of Military Science of the Chinese People's Liberation Army (AMS) has established detailed mathematical formulations to calculate CNP (Huang, 1992). Huang categorised four subsystems, namely material power (hard power), spirit power (soft power), coordinated power and an environmental index (ibid., pp. 155–172).

Yet even if the choice of variables to be covered by CNP can be agreed on, the weighting of the different variables will be needed to establish a standardised country comparison. On the whole, the Chinese scholar's efforts to establish a holistic index and assess the nation's power displays a holistic approach that covers a wide spectrum of both hard resources and soft components. The concept, however, remains under development and scholars have to agree consistently to carry out valid comparisons. While the concept is still being established, the term comprehensive national power is already being used by political leaders and promoted in official documents such as in China's 2015 military strategy, which states that "China's comprehensive national strength, core competitiveness and risk-resistance capacity are notably increasing, and China enjoys growing international standing and influence" (State Council of the People's Republic of China, 2015). Accordingly, the concept of CNP has already been adopted by foreign analysts and can be found in Western strategy papers such as the annual report to the US Congress on Military and Security Developments Involving the People's Republic of China 2019 (US Department of Defense, 2019). The concept's recognition can thus be considered a first step towards its broader application within international relations. This overview of different understandings of power helps to explain the

3. THEORETICAL FRAMEWORK

increased Chinese involvement in international military interventions and the country's possible approaches to redefining the international power equilibrium.

3.5. Formulation of Hypotheses

So far, chapter 3 has provided the theoretical framework for the operationalisation of this study. Foreign policy approaches were presented to find methods to understand Chinese actions, particularly in international conflict resolution. Concepts of international relations were added with a special focus on different understandings of power. The evidence gained allows us to derive four hypotheses on the two research questions of the study: *What variables drive China's interventions in the MENA region and in Africa?* and *How do China's contributions to conflict resolution affect the PRC's power status?* For the investigation of Chinese military interventions in conflict-affected countries in both regions, the following hypotheses shall be made:

1. China aims at changing the international power equilibrium of states by taking on leading roles in conflict resolution within the UN framework.

The establishment of the United Nations in 1945 was accompanied by the hope of a guarantor of peace having been created. Article 1 of the UN Charter states the first purpose of the UN as follows:

> "To maintain international peace and security, and to that end: to take effective collective measures for the prevention and removal of threats to the peace, and for the suppression of acts of aggression or other breaches of the peace, and to bring about by peaceful means, and in conformity with the principles of justice and international law, adjustment or settlement of international disputes or situations which might lead to a breach of the peace" (UN Charta, 1945).

Chapter VI of the Charter furthermore delegates the main responsibility for a "peaceful settlement of disputes" to the UN Security Council (ibid.). The introduction of peacekeeping forces was not foreseen to begin with. Yet, PKOs have become the main tool for UN military tasks and are valued in view of collective security (Väyryne, 1985, p. 189; 195).

3.5. Formulation of Hypotheses

As Väyryne outlines, peacekeeping operations are "a complement to the diplomatic activities by the Security Council, by the Secretary-General or by the [conflicting] parties themselves" (ibid., p. 195). Since the decision to implement a peacekeeping operation is made on the basis of what Hakimi & Katz Cogan call the "institutional code", which ensures the application of "structured and collective decision-making processes", they are characterised by "substantive norms that strictly limit the use of force" (Hakimi & Katz Cogan, 2016, p. 258). By contrast, the "state code" applied by states outside an institution is characterised by the deregulation of the use of force in the interest of single states with regard to specific conflicts (ibid., p. 258). For decades, controversial discussions have adhered to the question of the unconditional prerequisite of the UN's authorisation with regard to the use of force in severe humanitarian crises (Badescu, 2007, p. 52). This question has been raised on the common use of veto by the P5, which all too often prevents action by the international community. While it is argued that intervention without a prior UN mandate could be justified by applying customary international law, it is still contested and often considered illegal (ibid., p. 52). One of the most prominent cases of the use of force without a UN mandate is the 2003 US intervention in Iraq, which has been criticised by a number of scholars. Slaughter, for instance, considers the intervention both illegal and illegitimate, while Kramer et al. even see a threat to international law in the US-led war (Kramer, Michalowski, & Rothe, 2005, p. 73; Slaughter, 2004, p. 262). Moreover, the intervention has affected the US' reputation as a credible and reliable great power and has opened up the leeway, in particular for Middle Eastern countries to reflect on their assumptions about both US power and leadership (Wehrey, Kaye, Watkins, Martini, & Guffey, 2010, p. 6). In addition, traditional allies of the US have started to reflect on diversifying their security partnerships towards other major or emerging powers such as Russia or China (ibid., p. 6). If China takes this opportunity and aims at changing the current power equilibrium of states, the PRC will most probably seek to distinguish its approach from the US' example. The hypothesis here is that Chinese conflict interventions will only take place with the consent of the international community. In this case, however, China might want to take on leading roles in the missions and create both an environment of (military) cooperation with states in the MENA region and Africa and foster the establishment of a world military force.

3. THEORETICAL FRAMEWORK

2. China uses UN peacekeeping missions to promote the country's soft image and proclaim the foreign policy narrative of a "peaceful rise".

Since 2011, the Syrian civil war has threatened not only regional security and stability but also illustrated how major powers instrumentalise their actions to pursue geopolitical aspirations in the wake of a humanitarian crisis (Guimarães & Nasser de Carvalho, 2017, p. 66). The Syrian crisis is just one of the most recent cases in which the role of the United Nations and the Security Council in particular has been paralysed by the decision of major powers to use their veto to block resolutions (ibid., p. 66). On the one hand, the absence of a resolution prevents visible action and may contribute to the popular image of the UN as a toothless tiger. On the other, without a clear mandate by the Security Council, any action by states, most importantly the use of force, is not legitimised under international law (Nye, 2007). The UN may not hinder nation states from intervening militarily in other countries as the US did when invading Iraq in 2003 (ibid.). However, without a UN mandate, the costs of intervention are a lot higher for the intervening parties, and even traditional allies of the US usually refrain from offering their support (ibid.). While the UN's own hard power remains limited, soft power can thus affect and leverage governments' hard power decisions (ibid.). One important tool to prevent conflicts from escalating are UN peacekeeping missions (Erendor, 2017, p. 61). While they were originally not foreseen in the UN Charter, they have become an essential element of the Security Council's efforts to maintain international peace and security (ibid., p. 63). In December 2020, the UN counted 81,832 UN troops and police contributions by member states, yet peacekeeping missions are often under-funded and lack adequate resources and equipment (Sarjoon & Yusoff, 2019, p. 207; UN Peacekeeping, 2020). Whilst the USA has progressively decreased its contributions to the UN since 2016, the Chinese government under Hu Jintao has begun to promote a cooperative soft power approach with regard to foreign security relations (Lanteigne, 2014, p. 114). With peaks in 2020 and 2015, China's contributions to UN peacekeeping operations have increased significantly in terms of both personnel and financial support (UN Peacekeeping, 2020). By increasingly contributing to legitimised peacekeeping missions, China thus has the opportunity to create a soft image of its military forces as being devoted to international peace and security and at the same time to influence the UN's soft power. In addition, China may use these opportunities for international attention to represent its ideology and culture and shape international conflict resolu-

3.5. Formulation of Hypotheses

tion. China's traditional non-intervention policy adequately corresponds to the need for a host country's consent before the start of a peacekeeping mission. Thus, the second hypothesis of this thesis is that China's attempts to become an indispensable promoter of UN peacekeeping are motivated by the PRC's goal to extend its soft power image. Hence, Chinese military contributions to international peace and stability are intended to reflect China's "peaceful rise" as a world power.

3. China puts a regional focus on the MENA region and Africa to emerge as a regional hegemonic power and guarantor of regional security and stability while, at the same time, establishing strategic state relations.

In the past, Chinese imperial dynasties established relations with Persian kingdoms and the Ottoman Turkish empire, in particular along the mainland ancient Silk Road (Rózsa, 2020, p. 2). Yet, traditionally, the Middle East and North Africa have been regions of peripheral interest to China. Chinese–Arab relations have only recently intensified with the development of the revived Silk Route trade route (ibid., p. 2). China has attracted a number of Arab countries[32] to join the BRI while, at the same time, Beijing has refrained from positioning itself in the numerous regional conflicts among them (ibid., p. 2). In addition, China's official 2016 Arab Policy Paper outlines the comprehensive approach the PRC now pursues towards Arab states. In the paper, not only are economic relations such as investments and trade outlined. The focus also lies on political, social and cultural partnerships as well as collaborations on peace and security (Ministry of Foreign Affairs of the PRC, 2016).

However, intra-regional economic and political cooperation in the MENA region has remained among the lowest worldwide (Ekanayake & Ledgerwood, 2009, p. 19f). Mostly, the lack of intra-regional integration can be attributed to the large spectrum of political violence the region has experienced in the past (Hiltermann, 2017, p. 3). Civil wars, revolutions and terrorism have caused a conflict trap in many states in the region, which has hindered economic and political development (Alaaldin & Mezran, 2018, p. 23ff). In his analysis of conflict lineages, Hiltermann (2017) suggests at least five sources of conflict for the region: the dysfunctional post-world war state system in the Ottoman Empire, the Arab–

---

32 Bahrain, Egypt, Iran, Iraq, Israel, Jordan, Kuwait, Lebanon, Oman, The Palestinian Territories, Qatar, Saudi Arabia, Syria, Turkey, the UAE and Yemen.

3. THEORETICAL FRAMEWORK

Israeli conflict starting with the creation of the state of Israel in 1948, the rise of Iran and the emergence of the Sunni-Shiite debate triggered by the 1979 Islamic Revolution, radicalisation movements among Sunnis resulting from their defeats in 1967[33] and 1979[34], and finally the uprisings during the Arab Spring in 2011, with several states experiencing collapse and civil war (Hiltermann, 2017, p. 3).

Yet, despite the notorious instability of several countries in the region, MENA is an immediate neighbour to Europe and of strategical importance in terms of trade in goods, not only with regard to inter-regional trade but also transit routes to Africa and Asia (Giovannetti & Enrico, 2019, p. 270f). A decisive moment in the relations between Europe and countries in the MENA region was the beginning of European Imperialism in the 19th century (Maerk, 2012, p. 56). During that time, many Arab countries were under the control of major colonial powers, among them France, Great Britain and Italy: France was mostly present in the West (Maghreb) and Great Britain in the East and was later followed by the United States (ibid., p. 56f).

With the retreat of Italy, France and Great Britain, particularly during the Cold War, the two major powers, the Soviet Union and the United States, started competing for the Middle East. The role of the Soviet Union is comprehensively summarised by Gaub & Popescu (2018). The Soviet Union's influence in the Middle East and North Africa began when the monarchy was overthrown in Egypt and President Gamal Abdel Nasser came to power in 1954 (Gaub & Popescu, 2018, p. 14). Nasser needed weapons, which the Soviet Union provided to implement Nasser's Arab socialism and get access to the Suez channel (ibid., p. 14). Moscow opened up support bases in Egypt and Syria, signed agreements with Damascus, Cairo and Baghdad and provided assistance to Algeria and Libya (ibid., p. 14). During the Cold War, however, both the Soviet Union and the USA refrained from getting involved in direct military confrontations (ibid., p. 18). On the whole, the Soviet Union never managed to fully implement

---

33 Arab–Israeli War/Third Arab–Israeli War, fought between 5 and 10 June 1967 by Israel and the neighbouring states of Jordan, Syria and Egypt.
34 The Grand Mosque seizure occurred in November and December 1979 when armed civilians called for the overthrow of the House of Saud and temporarily took over Masjid al-Haram in Mecca, Saudi Arabia. After the attack, stricter enforcement of Sharia (Islamic law) was applied by Saudi King Khalid, which gave the Ulama and religious conservatives more power over the next decade, and the religious police became more assertive. The occupation is considered a key event in the emergence and development of Islamist terrorism.

its political system of socialism in the region and did not succeed in binding Middle Eastern states as satellites or vassal states (ibid., p. 20). Gaub & Popescu name several reasons why Arab countries refused to accept socialism, such as distrust in the idea of ending nation states, the focus on working classes (which were not numerous in Maghreb due to a large agricultural sector), the minor importance of religion in socialism and, finally, the Soviet Union's reluctance to openly fight Israel (ibid., p. 18f). While the Soviet Union's efforts to gain influence in the region were strongly motivated by the quest to promote socialist ideas but also to get access to the Mediterranean Sea, the USA was focused on commercial interests in relation to oil extraction instead (Campbell, 1972, p. 127). In this regard, the USA viewed the Middle East as "part of the free world", whose people as well as their natural resources, which were considered essential to Western peace, deserved protection against an aggressive Soviet Union (ibid., p. 127). As opposed to the Soviet Union, the US' objective was thus not to achieve long-term territorial control over sovereign states but rather to ensure that the principles of a liberal worldwide economic order were followed, so that a focus could lie on the market (Bromley, 1998, p. 19). US hegemony in the Middle East was, however, also characterised by the American readiness to launch violent interventions and its capacity to destroy enemies (Yom, 2020, p. 75). One of the most prominent of those invasions is the above-mentioned American invasion of Iraq in 2003, which was announced as a "war on terrorism" to protect American and Western citizens as well as political and economic interests (Danju, Maasoglu, & Maasoglu, 2013, p. 682). As Collins outlines, this war not only caused many thousands of people dead or wounded and cost billions of dollars to US taxpayers, but it has also caused the US to lose its reputation as a "moral leader" among its international allies and Muslim nations in the Middle East (Collins, 2008, p. 1). While the objective of the operations in Iraq were announced as aiming to safeguard US national security, Collins (2008) concludes that they, at least in part, aggravated the local terrorist threat, while, at the same time, enabling Iran to increase its influence and become a more important actor in the Middle East (ibid., p. 1). On the whole, American hegemony in the MENA region has been manifested by the US' capacity and ability to intervene in local and geopolitically important crises (Yom, 2020, p. 76). Thus, the US would intervene in local balances of power regardless of local and regional states and societies (ibid., p. 76). With regard to the US' presence in the capitals of the MENA countries, US embassies, notably, are always the second tallest building in the capitals, which can be considered a subtle statement to express

3. THEORETICAL FRAMEWORK

their superpower domination (ibid., p. 76). Yet, Yom (2020) finds that in recent years, especially during President Trump's term in office, the US has increasingly refrained from intervening in further Middle Eastern conflicts (Yom, 2020, p. 76). One reason might be that, unlike the oil crisis, recent threats such as the emergence of the so-called Islamic State as well as Iran's quest to become a nuclear power are rather regional crises that have very limited direct effects on the American population (ibid., p. 76).

By contrast, Russia has started a remarkable comeback to several volatile places in the Middle East (Trenin, 2018, p. 21). Most prominently, the launching of the Astana process has decisively shaped the outcome of the Syrian crisis so far (ibid., p. 22). In this regard, Russia understood that the national interests of its allies Turkey and Iran had to be respected to make this situational alliance work. This implied both Russian acceptance of Turkish intervention in northern Syria in 2018 as well as Iran's connection to the Lebanese Hezbollah, which Russia does not consider a terrorist group but distrusts because of their threats towards Israel (Trenin, 2018, p. 23). While the US is reducing its presence in major conflicts in the Middle East, interventionist opportunities are emerging for both Russia and new global actors such as China, who may aspire to influence local governance (Yom, 2020, p. 76). If China aims at shaping affairs and changing the current power equilibrium in the MENA region, the current shift in the presence of former major powers represents a favourable momentum.

While the attention of the US' military presence during the last few decades has certainly been on the Middle East, one must not neglect Africa's strategic position between the USA and Asia (Ahmad, 2015, p. 57). While the US influence on Africa has largely been developed with regard to education and technology, the first US military involvement in Africa can be traced back to the beginning of the 19th century (ibid., p. 57). While the US was involved in the Second World War as well as the Persian Gulf crisis during the Cold War, US air and naval military bases were opened in Africa to safeguard supplies and evacuate US nationals if needed (ibid., p. 57). An overview of US military bases has been provided by Lutfalah Mangi (1987). In the aftermath of the 9/11 attacks, the US changed its foreign military approach to Africa and established US Africa Commands known as US AFRICOM in 2007 (Ahmad, 2015, p. 57). The objective of this US initiative is reflected in the US Strategy Towards Sub-Saharan Africa of 2012, in which the introductory remarks of the former president Barack Obama outline the goals for Africa as

> "strengthening democratic institutions and boosting broad-based economic growth, including through trade and investment [as well as

strong,] accountable, and democratic institutions, sustained by a deep commitment to the rule of law, generate greater prosperity and stability [met] with greater success in mitigating conflict and ensuring security" (The White House, 2012).

The US' approach to Africa can thus be seen as highly motivated by the political goal of spreading Western values, particularly democracy. A doctrinal approach was also the objective of the Soviet Union's efforts during the Cold War, which aimed at supporting African countries in bypassing capitalism and directly introducing socialism (Giles, 2013, p. 3). Yet, just as in Afghanistan, the Soviet Union had not considered African regional and local circumstances such as political instability and rivalry, which finally led to the overthrow of pro-Soviet leaders in Algeria (1965), Ghana (1966) and Mali (1968) (ibid., p. 3). These incidents introduced a period of Russian disinterest in Africa that seems to have changed only recently. Russia has started reclaiming its lost influence, in particular with regard to energy resources, as well as developing new economic markets, as stated in Russia's energy strategy for the year 2030 (Giles, 2013, p. vii; 23; Ministry of Energy, Russian Federation, 2009). In addition, Russia's concerns about a spread of terrorist activities towards the Russian sphere of influence can be seen as its motivation to consider cooperating with US AFRICOM (Giles, 2013, p. 36). During the 2000s, Russia thus restarted to increase its presence in African countries and avoided leaving the field to emerging powers such as India, Brazil and especially China, while the latter has already increased its footprint in Africa during the last few decades (Giles, 2013, p. 8).

Therefore, the third hypothesis of this study is that by increasing China's military contributions to both the MENA region and Africa, the PRC seeks to become a hegemonic regional power and guarantor of regional security and stability. China may attempt to gain conflict-affected states' loyalty and confidence and evolve as a new powerful actor in conflict resolution.

4. China intervenes in conflicts if they are relevant for the realisation of the Belt and Road Initiative and if the countries involved host a large number of Chinese citizens.

In view of the BRI, a number of new imperatives result from it with regard to China's security concerns. The different levels and layers relate to both the securing of trade routes and resource supply chains but also the safety

3. THEORETICAL FRAMEWORK

of more and more Chinese migrants in conflicting foreign environments. If China aims at using its participation in UN peacekeeping missions to meet domestic demands to secure its resource supplies, it should focus on conflict-affected countries with a high relevance in terms of resource supply to China. The PRC aims to extract the necessary resources which contribute to increasing its latent power, which again will foster its military power. By doing so, China will secure its internal energy and resource requirements and accelerate its economic growth. Furthermore, resources are needed to realise China's giant infrastructure projects under the umbrella of the BRI.

China is seeking to revive its ancient network of trade routes along the traditional silk road via both terrestrial and maritime routes. Through China's efforts to become a global economic and political power, the sphere of countries China approaches is further widening. On the whole, the BRI covers five areas of cooperation. First, a policy coordination area which will lead to jointly formulated development plans with other states to resolve problems through consultations (Wolff, 2016, p. 4). The second area concerns the facilitation of connectivity and covers the construction of infrastructure such as ports and land and water passages to connect Asia, Europe and Africa (ibid. p. 5). The third relates to unimpeded trade by reducing investment and trade barriers. Fourth, financial integration is promoted by managing financial risks along the route and by increasing the scope of local currency exchanges (ibid. p. 4). Finally, the fifth area covers people-to-people bonds to enhance exchanges and dialogues between cultures (ibid. p. 4). Remarkably, the five areas that the BRI comprises do not cover any aspect of security. Yet, a large number of countries relevant for the realisation of the project are affected by conflict, in particular the MENA region and Africa, which calls for an increased focus on safety-related issues by Beijing.

In addition, China's increased economic activities abroad have been accompanied by growing Chinese communities in conflict-affected countries. The development of increasing Chinese migrants worldwide has been comprehensively analysed by Daniel Goodkind (2019), who used data by the UN Department of Economic and Social Affairs on International Migration and outlined the development during the years 1990, 1995, 2000, 2005, 2010, 2015 and 2017. Goodkind concludes that, over time, Chinese migrants have become increasingly wealthy and high-skilled (Goodkind, 2019, p. 15).

David Dollar provides an analysis of Chinese human resources as part of China's engagement with the African continent. The author finds that concrete numbers of Chinese workers per African country are difficult to determine due to a lack of data (Dollar, 2016, p. 95). Given the current migration regulations of many African countries, the author suspects, however, that not all Chinese workers have entered legally. While China itself used to have relatively strict controls on how many workers international investors were allowed to invite for their projects in China, the PRC focuses on employing its own workers in Africa (Dollar, 2016, p. 95). A recent report by Alessandro Arduino outlines that public and private Chinese companies are facing a broad threat spectrum including the risk of both criminal and political violence (Arduino, 2020, p. 3). Therefore, security concerns have become increasingly important, in particular for Chinese companies in hostile regions. Arduino states that, compared to American or Russian private security companies, Chinese ones have only recently joined and do not provide any military services or equipment (2020, p. 3). According to the author, Chinese private security companies used to act in relatively safe environments in mainland China and were only about to adapt their activities to high-risk areas (ibid., p. 3). In October 2009, the *Regulation on the Administration of Security and Guarding Services* was published by China's State Council to set up a regulatory framework for private security companies, but it still mainly focused on their domestic activities (PRC State Council, 2009). With the official start of the BRI in 2013, this development had to accelerate to meet the new foreign security demands, such as protection from terrorism, riots, the execution of anti-piracy missions or mass emergency evacuations (Arduino, 2020, p. 3). As Arduino (2020) notes, China's domestic laws are based on a socialist market economic structure, which—from a Western perspective— may complicate clear differentiation between private companies and state-owned organisations (ibid., p. 5).

Until 2016, about twenty Chinese private security companies evolved employing about 3,200 security professionals abroad, as mentioned in the Chinese media (Zhong, 2016). Compared to their well-known Western counterparts with mostly five-digit numbers of staff and up to 620,000 employees, the size of current Chinese companies remains miniscule (Security Degree Hub, 2020). With regard to current trends in the development of Chinese private security companies, Sergey Sukhankin provides a valuable overview. The author predicts that China's model will most probably be different from both the Western and Russian approach (Sukhankin, 2020). While the Western model focuses on transparency, independence from the state and a greater role for private ownership, Russia's approach stresses zero accountability (ibid., p. 24). Both models pose risks for China since

3. THEORETICAL FRAMEWORK

the PRC's political system might hesitate to allow a larger role for private ownership but will not risk damage to its international reputation (ibid., p. 24). Moreover, both models are based on the availability of large numbers of trained and experienced personnel, which China, unlike Russia and many Western countries, does not have (ibid., p. 24). In addition, the use of private security actors is always a risky endeavour for their country of origin since their activities may be difficult to control (Legarda & Nouwens, 2018, p. 4). Even if, in the case of China, these companies are frequently staffed with former PLA officers and have at least indirect connections to Chinese officials, they may have an unpredictable impact on Chinese interests in the country of operation (ibid., p. 4). Legarda & Nouwens (2018) thus outline that Chinese private security companies cannot be fully regulated by domestic or international legal frameworks since the final responsibility for their activities may be denied on both sides (Legarda & Nouwens, 2018, p. 4). If Chinese private security companies, however, attract attention through misconduct, this poses a risk to China's reputation on the international stage (ibid., p. 4). The killing of 14 Iraqi civilians by security contractors from the US private security company Blackwater in Baghdad in 2007 was an alarming example of this (Gafarov, 2019, p. 42).

While China is thus still developing the use of private security companies, the PRC's referral to international security efforts represents an alternative Chinese approach to dealing with hostile environments. Fostering international missions to stabilise conflict-affected regions, however, needs efforts on international platforms such as the UN Security Council. Hence, the fourth hypothesis is that China's increased military engagement in African and Middle Eastern conflicts is motivated by both its increased economic activities and the growing Chinese communities as part of the BRI. The choice of China's participation in conflict resolution and UN peacekeeping missions in particular may thus be influenced by the economic importance of the conflict-affected country as well as the number of Chinese citizens residing there.

The assumptions can be summarised in different categories: political development, economic factors, social and historical factors, and the centrality of the military to regional and international security. These categories are tested empirically in the QCA study of this thesis. This study thus investigates the structural components of Chinese foreign policy behaviour in conflict resolution. This theoretical relationship between conflict management and power determines a probable shift in the international power equilibrium.

3.6. Summary of the Theoretical Framework

The aim of chapter 3 was to situate the study within existing strands of theory. Overall, the investigation aims to contribute to the development of three different theoretical streams.

First, analytical concepts in the field of Chinese foreign policy analysis will be considered. Second, a concentration on conflict studies allows us to focus on the field of military diplomacy as a relevant analytical model in foreign policy analysis. While existing research literature also provides some examples of Chinese contributions to mediation activities, Beijing's efforts in international conflict resolution remain focused on multilateral military diplomacy. Third, the study considers the role of power and power relations to understand China's behaviour in foreign policy. A close consideration of different aspects of power is necessary to identify which elements of power are relevant for Chinese foreign policy decisions.

The theoretical categorisation and positioning of this study forms a basis for establishing hypotheses to be tested in the operationalisation that follows. Finally, chapter 3.5. formulated four hypotheses on the drivers of Chinese (non-) intervention practices:

1. China aims at changing the international power equilibrium of states by taking on leading roles in conflict resolution within the UN framework.
2. China uses UN peacekeeping missions to promote the country's soft image and proclaim the foreign policy narrative of a "peaceful rise".
3. China puts a regional focus on the MENA region and Africa to emerge as a regional hegemonic power and guarantor of regional security and stability, while, at the same time, establishing strategic state relations.
4. China intervenes in conflicts if they are relevant for the realisation of the Belt and Road Initiative and if the countries involved host a large number of Chinese citizens.

The hypotheses provide guidance for the following chapters and outline possible directions of a Chinese road map for conflict resolution. In the following chapter, the methodology used to test these hypotheses will be presented.

4. METHODOLOGY

The previous chapters covered an introduction to the topic and provided a general overview of the context and discourse relevant to international military interventions. Furthermore, the theoretical framework was presented, and hypotheses were derived. In the following, the methodology used in the analysis of specific cases of intervention in the MENA region and Africa will be outlined.

4.1. Introduction of the Research Design: Qualitative Comparative Analysis

Most previous studies on China's contributions to conflict resolution cover case studies, with a majority of studies focusing on Mali and Sudan (Benabdallah & Large, 2020; Lanteigne, 2019; Seesaghur & Ansong, 2014). Such case studies provide valuable insights into specific constellations of conflicts and China's bilateral connections to the country. In addition, Bennett (2015) presents a study on *Causes of Third Party Military Intervention in Intrastate Conflicts*. The knowledge gained in such studies is useful in understanding historical circumstances as well as recent developments in a specific country. Yet, a comprehensive comparison of particular Chinese interventions in conflict cases in the MENA region and Africa is not found in previous literature. Both in its analysis of bilateral relations between China and another country and its analysis of Chinese relations with entire regions, such as Africa or the Middle East, scholarly work focuses predominantly on individual research areas, such as trade or resources (Butts & Bankus, 2009; Sun, 2018). However, to make comparative and generally valid statements, a critical mass of cases must be considered along the same criteria. This study fills this methodological gap with regard to research on China and the PRC's involvement in conflict resolution.

The dissertation consists of a medium N analysis for which the method of a qualitative comparative analysis (QCA) is used. The method was originally established by sociologist Charles C. Ragin (1987) to combine configurative and case-oriented approaches with set theoretical thinking (Buche & Siewert, 2015). QCA has become a commonly used tool in analysing political and social phenomena with a limited set of cases (ibid.

4.1. Introduction of the Research Design

p. 386). In this regard, cases can be compared by combining qualitative and quantitative approaches, which makes detailed knowledge about each case necessary (Lambach, Johais, & Bayer, 2016, p. 41). The aim is to discover underlying complex causal chains of social phenomena. QCA was first developed by Ragin (1987) and can be considered very useful in systemic comparisons of cases since both qualitative and quantitative elements are combined.

In general, QCA can either be operationalised as classical crisp-set QCA (csQCA), as fuzzy-set (fsQCA) or multi-value QCA (mvQCA). The classical approach of crisp-set QCA allows binary coding for both conditions and outcomes (Rihoux & De Meur, 2009, p. 36). Accordingly, all data is allocated a "0" or a "1". If, for example one condition was "gross domestic product" (GDP), a threshold value has to be defined. The latter could be a sum of USD 3 trillion. Every country with a GDP of less than USD 3 trillion would be coded "0", all those equal or above with a "1". The results of all countries considered would be collected in a truth table. Binary categorisation, however, may cause a loss of information, which can result in misleading conclusions. In the example just mentioned, France with a GDP of about USD 2.7 trillion[35] would be in the same category as Ghana with a GDP of USD 67.2 billion[36]. Both might be considered countries with a "low" GDP since the two of them are in the category of "under USD 3 trillion". To avoid a loss of information, Ragin's method of QCA has constantly been extended over the years. One approach which allows more than two categories is the "fuzzy-set" method (Regan, 2000). The latter allows multiple variables for both conditions and outcomes. While the related "multi-value" approach of QCA also allows more than two variables for conditions, outcomes stay binary in this version (Cronqvist & Berg-Schlosser, 2009).

When one is comparing drivers for state interventions, existing literature helps to identify criteria. The conditions are defined and split up into measurable factors. Where three variables are needed, the conditions are reworded since binary codes are preferred. One example could be a country's "oil wealth". Binary codes would be 1 for "yes" and 0 for "no", whereby 1 means that a country possesses natural oil reserves and 0 means that a country does not. Theoretical thoughts and considerations for each factor were summarised in a table. Additionally, indicators of each factor and data sources are listed. In the aforementioned example, a theoretical

---

35 World Bank figures for 2019.
36 World Bank figures for 2019.

4. METHODOLOGY

thought could be that China has an interest in stability within a country in order to exploit oil. China might, therefore, intervene in a country that possesses a significant amount of this natural resource. The size of what "oil wealth" means could be defined by data from OPEC.

The rationale behind QCA is that social phenomena may have complex causal structures and more than one cause. Sometimes, different causal structures may lead to the same outcome (Lambach, Johais, & Bayer, 2016, pp. 41-44). To identify various combinations of qualifications, QCA uses Boolean Algebra (ibid. pp. 41–44). When QCA is applied, it is possible that outcomes result in *contradictions*. For example, Switzerland and Germany are both democracies in Europe, but only Germany is part of the European Union. One way to avoid this contradiction is to add another variable in which the two countries are different. Another challenge when working with QCA can be *logical remainders*. They emerge if a combination of causes exists theoretically but has not been observed empirically. Both *contradictions* and *logical remainders* can indicate that more research needs to be done or that variables need to be redefined (Herrmann & Cronqvist, 2006, p. 6).

The investigation conducted for this study covers nine main cases of Chinese military intervention in the Middle East and Africa where China was present in the year 2013, when OBOR was first announced. Additionally, four synchronic and seven diachronic comparative cases were taken into consideration. The main cases were successively compared to these control groups. The first control group consisted of states which were relatively similar to the main case and experienced a similar conflict situation in the same period of time. Yet, these states differed in the observation that no Chinese intervention took place. The choice of cases for the synchronic comparison was made by the logic of "most similar, different outcome" (Rihoux, 2006, p. 685). In order to maintain the constancy of the variables, synchronic cases were at best chosen in the same region of the main case (Lambach, Johais, & Bayer, 2016, p. 39).

The second control group consisted of diachronic cases. Conflicts within the same countries were looked at which differed in the time period of their occurrence. During this diachronic comparison, other periods of instability in the country were observed which did not lead to Chinese intervention. While the synchronic comparison is supposed to outline structural differences between the cases, the diachronic comparison is meant to help understand differences in temporal circumstances.

To examine the research questions guiding this inquiry, the use of a qualitative comparative analysis helps to understand if a conditionality chain of Chinese military interventions in extraterritorial conflicts can be discovered and what drivers lead to an outcome of intervention. Just as the causes of conflicts can be very diverse, a decision for third-party intervention depends on various criteria. Since the questions of this thesis asks about variables that drive China's intervention in a given conflict, QCA provides a valuable method of searching for drivers. The study at hand was conducted using crisp-set QCA.

While the main component of the study is a QCA, it became apparent during the course of the investigation that the findings needed to be supplemented with other research methods to obtain comprehensive results. The following two chapters outline how this was achieved.

4.2. The Added Value of Process Tracing

The objective of this study is to find causal links for Chinese interventions in conflict regions in the Middle East and Africa. The QCA considers a range of possible relevant factors. The use of the term "causality", however, cannot be automatically assumed due to the simultaneous occurrence of two events (Lambach, Johais, & Bayer, 2016, p. 45). For example, China was present militarily in Mali in 2013 and Mali is participating in the Rail Infrastructure plan of the African Union. The method of QCA does not provide information about causality between the appearance of a particular condition and an outcome. A causal statement is, however, a necessary element for theory development.

To close this gap in the application of QCA, process tracing is performed. Process tracing aims at discovering causal mechanisms instead of purely causal factors (Beach & Pedersen, 2013, p. 2f). The use of process tracing has increased in qualitative research and is often applied as a supplement to QCA (Lambach, Johais, & Bayer, 2016, p. 44). Accordingly, it is possible to enrich a study with the implications of possible causal mechanisms. In their work on process tracing methods, Beach & Pedersen (2003) propose differentiating between three different types of causal mechanisms: theory-testing, theory-building and explaining-outcome research approaches (Beach & Pedersen, 2013, pp. 53-67). As a result, the relation between condition X and outcome Y can be identified in more detail and the historical outcome can be explained (explaining-outcome) in a case-centric investigation (Beach & Pedersen, 2013, p. 11; 21). In this regard, the process tracing method is intended to both support a theory-

4. METHODOLOGY

centric and case-centric approach to theory building (Beach & Pedersen, 2013, p. 21).

Table 3: Purpose of Process Tracing

Question	Purpose	Basis
What is the causal relationship between X and Y?	Theory-building	Theory
Does the causal mechanism function as expected?	Theory-testing	Theory
Which mechanism can attest to the outcome?	Explaining the Outcome	Single Case

Source: Based on Figure 2.1 in Beach and Pedersen (2013, p. 12)

In general, process tracing requires a profound knowledge of the cases under investigation. While such information is not necessarily relevant for regression analysis, QCAs require detailed in-depth knowledge about individual cases (Lambach, Johais, & Bayer, 2016, p. 44). In the study at hand, the use of process tracing in addition to the QCA proved to be a valuable supplement to the study. This is due to the fact that the results of the QCA did not reveal a clear picture about a theoretical model on China's motivation for intervention. Unfortunately, clear types of intervention paths were not obvious. Nevertheless, both adequately causal and coincidentally causal factors could be found (see chapter 8.2). The presence of various different solution terms did not lead to a coherent model which could have been tested with further case studies in the framework of a nested analysis. Process tracing thus provided a valuable possible way to develop a theory model.

During the implementation of the process tracing, information collected for the QCA provided useful preparatory work. Some conditions had already been eliminated due to missing data. To arrange and classify the remaining conditions, process tracing was used to find out which conditions and combinations of conditions could be considered real reasons for China's intervention and which of them might rather be side factors which were not crucial for the outcome observed. In this regard, the questions of *how* the conditions had an impact on the outcome and *how* they were related to other conditions were addressed. In this way, it was possible to establish a causal model for China's intervention practices (see chapter 9.1). The use and application of the process tracing method was based on the work of Beach & Pedersens (2013) as well as on the example of Lambach, Johais & Bayer (2016). Beach and Pedersen propose a

4.2. The Added Value of Process Tracing

"theory-centric variant, [where] mechanisms are understood as midrange theories of mechanisms that transmit causal forces from X to Y and are expected to be present in a population of cases, assuming that the context that allows them to operate is present" (Beach & Pedersen, 2013, p. 34).

Consequently, the aim is to develop and understand the mechanism that connects the two observations. Figure 1 illustrates this logic.

During the implementation of the process tracing method, findings from the QCA were able to be used. Therefore, not only single factors, but also the combination of conditions of a path were examined. In this regard, each case consisted of three solution terms resulting from the main case, a synchronic comparison and a diachronic comparison. In the following, the conditions found which appeared at least once in one of the three terms were further examined in the process tracing. This method had been used by Lambach, Johais & Bayer (2016) in their study on state collapse and seemed likewise applicable for the study at hand.

Figure 1: Opening the Black Box with Empirical Narratives

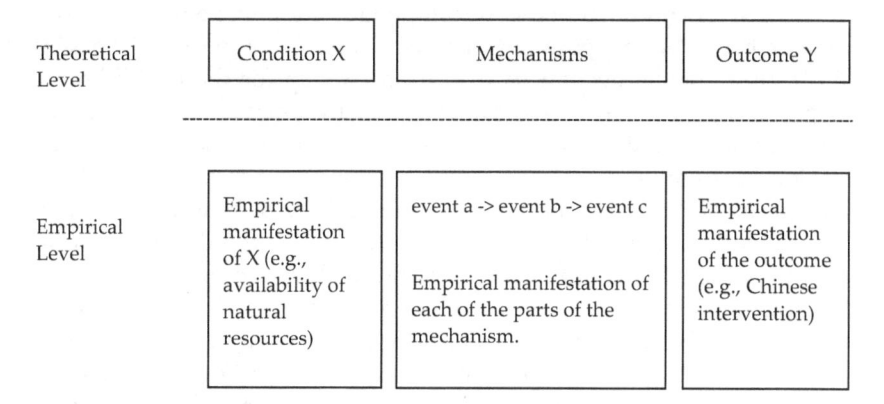

Theoretical Level	Condition X	Mechanisms	Outcome Y
Empirical Level	Empirical manifestation of X (e.g., availability of natural resources)	event a -> event b -> event c Empirical manifestation of each of the parts of the mechanism.	Empirical manifestation of the outcome (e.g., Chinese intervention)

Source: The author based on Beach & Pedersen (2013, p. 35)

In doing so, the aim was to better understand the particular cases and search for possible cumulative effects in the different cases. At best, a theory model should be established to explain the necessary conditions for the outcome. For the analysis of possible causal mechanisms, the categorisation proposed by Patrick Thaddeus Jackson was referred to (Jackson, 2011). By using Jackson's categorisation, the conditions applied in the QCA were further investigated (see chapter 8). Consequently, an assess-

4. METHODOLOGY

ment of their causal influence on the outcome was able to be established. The analysis was conducted by using additional sources such as studies on intervention theories, professional literature as well as newspaper articles. Additionally, studies and reports on the specific conditional factors were collected. In this regard, the availability of information varied among the factors, especially concerning data for particular years. If data was available from one year before or after the event, this was taken as orientation. The results of the process tracing are presented in chapter 8.

4.3. The knowledge gained from a keyword analysis

The QCA conducted as part of this study helped me to gain knowledge about drivers that increase the likelihood of China's intervention in conflicts in the MENA region and Africa. Yet, this empirical evidence was not sufficient to make comprehensive statements about China's influence on international conflict resolution and a possible change in the global balance of power. Thus, another analytical step was necessary to complement the study. The assumption was that China's increased power in the field of conflict resolution and peacekeeping might not only be deduced from the number of leading positions in peacekeeping but also from the design and content of the documents that are drawn up for the establishment of peacekeeping missions, namely UN Security Council resolutions. For this reason, the study also covers an analysis of 300 UN Security Council resolutions from 2001 to 2020, which dealt with conflicts in the MENA region, sub-Saharan Africa or general issues related to conflict resolution. The resolutions were searched for using specific keywords derived from the causal model of Chinese interventions. With regard to China's model for peace outlined above, the assumption was that if China has already changed the global balance of power in Beijing's favour, the occurrence of certain keywords such as "non-interference", "stability" or "economic development" should have increased over time. At the same time, the stagnation of or a decrease in "human rights", "governance" or "institutions" was expected. The results of the keyword analysis finally provided evidence of the fact that Chinese priorities in conflict resolution have already become visible on the global stage.

4.4. Summary of the Methodology

Chapter 4 has outlined the methodology of this study. The investigation covers a QCA and comparatively analyses cases of conflict-affected countries in the Middle East and Africa with and without Chinese intervention. Nine cases of conflict are tested in relation to chosen factors. The methodology of QCA was chosen since it requires detailed knowledge about each case and allows their comparison in relation to chosen qualitative and quantitative factors. In this way, complex causal chains as well as specific patterns of Chinese intervention practices can be identified. The idea was to find out if the prevalence of certain factors or a combination of factors—drivers—determine China's decision to intervene in a conflict. The method of QCA was thus used to test the hypotheses laid out in chapter 3 and to find out if China's potential road to conflict resolution is characterised by specific drivers.

In addition to the QCA research design, which forms the core of this study, chapter 4 outlined that the method of process tracing was added, with the result that major factors identified in the QCA were tested with regard to possible causalities. Moreover, a keyword analysis provided evidence of how China's priorities are already reflected within United Nations peacekeeping. The combination of QCA, process tracing and an additional keyword analysis represent a novel approach with regard to research on China's new role in international conflict resolution. Unlike previous case studies on individual conflicts, the chosen research design allows political scientists to make general statements on China's orientation in the field of conflict resolution.

Finally, tendencies in Chinese foreign policy can be identified and China's approach to military diplomacy can be recognised. Consequently, the design of a Chinese "road map for peace" can be outlined.

After the presentation of the methodology used for this research, the following chapter covers outlines the operationalisation of the study.

5. OPERATIONALISATION

As stated in the introduction to this thesis, the aim of this study is to provide insights into China's foreign policy behaviour in conflict resolution and its intervention policy in particular. The previous chapters provided the context of this research field and outlined the theoretical framework and methodology of this study. The subsequent chapter outlines the operationalisation of the study, covering the presentation of the main and control cases, which form the central components of this research project.

5.1. Concept Development

This chapter provides an overview of the concept development used for the operationalisation of the thesis. At first, relevant cases of Chinese military interventions had to be identified. To this end, data provided by the UCDP in its version 20.1 was used. The database covers data on a collection of military conflicts since 1946, with at least one party being the government of a state, and is managed by the University of Uppsala in cooperation with the Peace Research Institute Oslo (PRIO).

As part of this study, relevant cases were determined. Conflicts in Africa and the Middle East were identified in two time periods that were of interest for this study: before and after 2013[37]. This timely differentiation allowed me to find out if the introduction of the BRI in 2013 had an effect on China's attitude and behaviour with regard to conflicts and the PRC's intervention practices. In a second step, the dates of Chinese intervention were looked at during both periods. This was done by using UCDP&PRIO data as well as UN data on multilateral UN missions with Chinese participation (UN Peacekeeping, 2021). Accordingly, conflicts with Chinese involvement were identified in the two regions and during the time periods under consideration. As a result, nine conflicts with Chinese military involvement in 2013 were identified in Morocco, DR Congo, Liberia, Ivory Coast, Lebanon, Sudan, South Sudan, Mali and Israel/Palestine. An overview of the cases identified is provided in the

---

37 The period "after 2013" includes the year 2013.

following sub-chapters. China's bilateral relations to the specific countries are additionally outlined.

To find out what drivers led the PRC to intervene in these particular conflicts, control cases had to be identified. In quantitative QCA research, scientists often use so-called random sampling, which results in a coincidental allocation of control cases (Lambach, Johais, & Bayer, 2016; King, Keohane, & Verba, 1994). Yet, this method was neglected for this study since it might have produced very general results. Instead, the choice of control cases was conducted deliberately to allow a comparison of both the states that are affected by the conflict while the PRC intervenes in only one of them. At first sight, all states affected by conflict without Chinese intervention could have served as possible comparative control cases. It was thus necessary to draw up a shortlist with specified criteria. As regards synchronic cases, the aim was to identify structural differences that occurred between conflict-affected countries after 2013. Diachronic cases were considered to explore dynamic factors that may cause Chinese military intervention at a later point in time.

In the choice of relevant control cases, the possibility principle presented by Mahoney and Goertz (2004) was applied. The authors recommend that "[i]n particular, nonpositive cases that closely resemble positive cases, including [on] key hypothesized causal factors, are seen as highly useful" (ibid., p. 654). In addition, Ragin (2000) recommended the choice of cases that share the most similarities with the positive cases (Ragin, 2000, p. 59ff). When choosing control cases, scholars thus refer to the logic of Most Similar, Different Outcome (Caramani, 2009; Lambach, Johais, & Bayer, 2016; Rihoux & Ragin, 2008).

5.2. Selection of Cases with and without Chinese Intervention

Many countries worldwide suffer from violent conflicts or even state collapse. Yet, China's military interventions have been concentrated on MENA and African countries. Therefore, several sub-questions shall be dealt with here. Does the PRC, for instance, follow international political considerations or is its engagement motivated by domestic political strategies? To what extent does China's interest in these conflict situations reflect Chinese perceptions of world order? Which implications can be outlined regarding China's quest to redefine the current balance of powers? How might bilateral Chinese support for conflicting parties help Chinese leaders in implementing the BRI? A mix of both internal and

5. OPERATIONALISATION

external drivers might also be possible. The subsequent analysis of cases will provide answers to these questions..

For many years, relations between China and countries in the MENA region have been rather constant, although some relations were more intense than others (Cantori, 2016). Arabic Gulf countries, for example, have been of interest to the PRC for a long time due to China's need for fossil fuels. Apart from that, the Chinese leader Mao Zedong widened relations with MENA countries to promote the image of China as a partner of developing countries. By using this image for China's external relations, Mao positioned China in opposition to the capitalist United States of America (USA) (Olimat, 2013). China's introduction of the BRI, however, started a new period of bilateral relations with several Arab countries (ibid.). While some of the Gulf states are partly connected to both land and sea routes, the Arab countries of North Africa are not connected to either land or sea routes, except for Egypt[38]. These countries have, nevertheless, also experienced an increase in investments and closer ties with China in recent years (Hammond, 2017; Rakhmat, 2015).

At the same time, Chinese relations to the African continent have greatly expanded during the last few years (Li & Rønning, 2013, p. 1f). In particular, China has been investing in African oil and mining sectors as well as other natural resources (ibid. p. 9). Not only are Chinese investors interested in the manufacturing sector, but also in infrastructural projects as well as telecommunications and the agricultural sector (ibid. 9f). Moreover, Chinese political and military involvement is also apparent. While only the eastern country of Tanzania is directly connected to the maritime road of China's BRI in the early maps of the project, China's economic and military activities are widespread over the MENA region and Africa. Moreover, recent maps of the BRI cover extensions to east Africa and along the Maghreb, suggesting that the transcontinental initiative might be oriented at but not limited to the ancient routes of the historic Silk Road (Sprangers, van der Putten, & Forough, 2021).

After having provided an overview of the regional focus of this study, the following table summarizes cases of conflicts which were considered in this research project:

---

38 This refers to the majority of maps available from the BRI. Some of the more recent maps also show an extension of the original land and sea routes, which occasionally also pass through the Mediterranean Sea along the northern coast of the African continent. Thus, various scholars are considering an expansion of the routes into a worldwide network and numerous trade centres.

5.2. Selection of Cases with and without Chinese Intervention

Table 4: Overview of Cases of Conflict

Case	Period of Conflict	Geographical Region	Characteristics of Conflict
Morocco	1991 – today	North Africa	Independence movement
DR Congo	1993 – today	sub-Saharan Africa	Civil war, tribal conflicts
Liberia	2003 – today	sub-Saharan Africa	Civil war, rebel groups
Ivory Coast	2003 – 2017	sub-Saharan Africa	Civil war
Lebanon	2006 – today	Middle East	Inner-state conflict, Israeli–Palestinian conflict
Sudan	2003 – today	sub-Saharan Africa	Darfur Conflict
South Sudan	2011 – today	sub-Saharan Africa	Civil war, Secessionist war
Israel/Palestine	1948 – today	Middle East	Inner-state conflict, Israeli–Palestinian conflict
Mali	2012 – today	sub-Saharan Africa	Islamist Terrorism

The above conflicts with Chinese military intervention form the main research objects of this study. To find out if these cases can be distinguished from other conflicts without Chinese intervention using certain characteristics, comparative cases need to be identified. In this regard, a comparative synchronic case refers to an incident or period of conflict that occurs in another country at about the same time as the main case. A synchronic comparison was sought for each case and chosen under consideration of the following criteria:
1. The period of conflict must be the same with a scope of five to ten years[39]
2. The geographical region has to be as similar as possible
3. The cause of conflict has to be as similar as possible

Both conflicts and countries should have similar characteristics to ensure their comparability. When the selection criteria were applied, the allocation presented in table 5 was the result.

---

39 Due to the limited empirical selection of similar cases and because of the commonalities of the circumstances in Morocco and Iraq, an exception was made here.

5. OPERATIONALISATION

Table 5: Overview of Synchronic Comparative Cases

Case Synchronic Control Case	Period of Conflict	Geographical Region	Characteristics of Conflict
Morocco	1991 – today	North Africa	Independence movement
Iraq	2017	Middle East	Demands for autonomy
DR Congo	1993 – today	sub-Saharan Africa	Civil war, tribal conflicts
Central African Republic	2012 – 14	sub-Saharan Africa	Civil war, rebel groups
Liberia	2003 – today	sub-Saharan Africa	Civil war, rebel groups
Republic of Congo	2016 – 2017	sub-Saharan Africa	Rebel groups
Ivory Coast	2003 – 2017	sub-Saharan Africa	Civil war
No control case			
Lebanon	2006 – today	Middle East	Inner-state conflict, Israeli–Palestinian conflict
No control case			
Sudan	2003 – today	sub-Saharan Africa	Darfur Conflict
No control case			
South Sudan	2011 – today	sub-Saharan Africa	Civil war, Secessionist war
No control case			
Israel/Palestine	1948 – today	Middle East	Inner-state conflict, Israeli–Palestinian conflict
No control case			
Mali	2012 – today	sub-Saharan Africa	Islamist Terrorism
Nigeria	2009 – today	sub-Saharan Africa	Islamist Terrorism

The selection process of appropriate and comparable synchronic cases proved to be difficult when applying all three criteria. All in all, four synchronic control cases were found. In the cases of Ivory Coast, Lebanon, Sudan, South Sudan and Palestine, no similar crisis or conflict could be found in a Mena or sub-Saharan African country during the period concerned. However, to ensure the comparability of the cases, I decided not to increase the flexibility of the criteria.

In addition to a synchronic comparison, this study considers diachronic control cases. The latter relate to conflicts or crisis in the same countries that have been identified as main cases. However, these diachronic cases took place prior to the investigation period, that is, before 2013. During the selection progress, crisis were chosen that were concluded before the beginning of the conflict under investigation in the main cases. To select the cases, data by PRIO as well as secondary sources on the specific countries and historic conflicts were considered.

5.2. Selection of Cases with and without Chinese Intervention

The aim of adding diachronic control cases was to find out if circumstances had changed over time that made Chinese intervention in the same country likelier after 2013 than before. Such changes might have taken place in the country under consideration or in the PRC and its role in conflict resolution.

Table 6 provides an overview of the diachronic control cases identified. Overall, seven control cases were found, although the same diachronic case was applied to the main cases Sudan and South Sudan since both countries were united and belonged to one state in the past. In the following sub-chapters, each diachronic case will be presented. The length of the summaries depends, among other things, on the availability of secondary sources.

Table 6: Overview of Diachronic Comparative Cases

Case / Dyachronic Control Case	Period of Conflict	Geographical Region	Characteristics of Conflict
Morocco	1991 – today	North Africa	Independence movement
West Saharan Conflict	1975	North Africa	Independence movement
DR Congo	1993 – today	sub-Saharan Africa	Civil war, tribal conflicts
Second Congo War	1998 – 2003	sub-Saharan Africa	Tribal conflict
Liberia	2003 – today	sub-Saharan Africa	Civil war, rebel groups
First Liberian Civil War	1989 – 1997	sub-Saharan Africa	Civil war
Ivory Coast	2003 – 2017	sub-Saharan Africa	Civil war
First Ivorian Civil War	2002 – 2007	sub-Saharan Africa	Civil war
Lebanon	2006 – today	Middle East	Inner-state conflict, Israeli–Palestinian conflict
Lebanese Civil War	1975 – 1990	Middle East	Civil war
Sudan	2003 – today	sub-Saharan Africa	Darfur Conflict
Second Sudanese Civil War	1983 – 2005	sub-Saharan Africa	Civil war
South Sudan	2011 – today	sub-Saharan Africa	Civil war
Second Sudanese Civil War	1983 – 2005	sub-Saharan Africa	Independence movement, civil war
Israel/Palestine	1948 – today	Middle East	Inner-state conflict, Israeli–Palestinian conflict
No Control Case			
Mali	2012 – today	sub-Saharan Africa	Islamist Terrorism
Agacher Strip War between Mali and Burkina Faso	1974 – 1985	sub-Saharan Africa	Territorial conflict

5. OPERATIONALISATION

5.2.1. Further Regional Conflicts since 2013

In addition to the cases of conflict under investigation in this research project, two further major conflict phenomena were characteristic of the post-2013 period and shall be addressed briefly here. The first relates to the emergence of Islamist terrorist cells, especially the so-called Islamic State of Iraq and Syria (ISIS), which constitutes a threat to the stability and security of the whole Middle East and beyond (Chaziza, 2016, p. 25)[40]. Since the end of the Cold War, China's Middle Eastern focus has been concentrated on trade and energy security, while establishing and maintaining peaceful relations with regional countries (ibid., p. 25). Stressing its non-interference policy, China refrained from interfering in conflicts in the region, as opposed to great powers such as the US, which intervened in Iraq in 2003 and only justified its intervention in retrospect (Chase, 2017). As regards the increasing impact of ISIS activities in 2014 as well as the destabilising effects of terrorist activities of other militias, which also resulted in attacks in Xinjiang Province, speculation about possible increased Chinese involvement in the fight against ISIS grew (Chaziza, 2016, p. 25f). In particular, this was reasoned by the former ISIS leader Abu Bakr Al-Baghdadi's attempts to recruit Chinese Uighur Muslims as well as his proclaimed plans to expand ISIS's territorial influence towards Xinjiang Province (Gambhir, 2016, p. 24). In this regard, China defined separatism, terrorism and religious extremism as "three evil forces", although without a clear distinction between these phenomena (Wacker, 2018, p. 50)

Until now, however, China has refrained from joining the Global Coalition to defeat the Islamic State of Iraq and Syria, which was announced by the United States in 2014 (U.S. Department of State, 2014). The 82 members of the Coalition aim at eliminating ISIS networks and at countering ISIS' activities, including the cells' financing, economic infrastructure and the recruitment of fighters (Global Coalition, 2014). While being criticised for refraining from the Coalition, Beijing stressed the need to respect the United Nations Charter and thus the sovereignty of the countries concerned (Bree, 2014; Reuters, 2015).

With regard to Chinese nationals who have joined ISIS, China's massive surveillance activities and restriction of movement, particularly in Xinjiang, are likely to have a deterrent effect on Uighur fighters who consider

---

40 The abbreviation ISIS is sometimes also translated as Islamic State of Iraq and Al-Sham. Further names are Islamic State of Iraq and the Levant (ISIL) or the Arabic acronym Daesh.

5.2. Selection of Cases with and without Chinese Intervention

returning to China (Wacker, 2018, p. 56). Xinjiang plays a major role in the land route corridor of China's BRI, which is why the Chinese government is particularly engaged in securing stability in the region (ibid., p. 56). In 2015, China passed a new anti-terrorism law which allowed Chinese security forces to be deployed abroad (Zhou, 2015). Moreover, China has remained committed to building up anti-terrorism ties with Arab states, including information sharing, joint military exercises or the extradition of Chinese citizens (Wacker, 2018, p. 56). In addition, China voted in favour of UN Resolution 2170 of August 15, 2014, and Resolution 2178 of September 24, 2014, which both acknowledge the threat to international peace and security posed by terrorist groups such as ISIS, al-Nusra-Front and other associates of Al-Qaeda. Both Resolutions call for measures against financing terrorism as well as the flow of fighters (UNSC Resolution 2170, 2014; UNSC Resolution 2178, 2014). Resolution 2178 (2014) particularly extended states' obligations regarding the treatment of foreign fighters. China, furthermore, voted in favour of UN resolution 2199 of February 12, 2015, which targeted illegal oil exports and the illicit export of cultural heritage that were both used as financial sources by ISIS (UNSC Resolution 2199, 2015). Chinese military participation as defined in the present study, however, has not taken place with regard to the Global Coalition to defeat ISIS. Therefore, the subject has not been further considered here.

A second prominent conflict case relates to the security situation at the Horn of Africa. The civil war in Somalia with attacks by terrorists from Al-Shabaab, the threat of piracy in the waters off the Somali coast as well as conflicts in Yemen, Ethiopia, Sudan and South Sudan make the region particularly fragile. (Ursu & van den Berg, 2018, p. 1). Between 2000 and 2011, piracy off the coast of Somalia threatened important international shipping routes and hindered the delivery of humanitarian assistance to millions of Somalis (Aftab Khan, 2007). Ongoing crises, a civil war and instability created a legal vacuum in Somalia that was soon used by militias to extend their business with weapons and threaten the waters off the coast of Somalia (Baniela & Ríos, 2012, p. 693ff; Bruton, 2010, p. 12). However, since 2001, international military deployments have arrived in the region to address the problem of piracy and secure maritime trade routes along the Horn of Africa (Melvin, 2019, p. 1). Naval forces of

5. OPERATIONALISATION

16 principal contributors[41] have started patrolling along the coast and land-based facilities have been opened (ibid., p. 1; 30). Additionally, since 2002, a total of six international military missions have been operating, of which the first was the US-led 33-state coalition of combined maritime forces for the Red Sea, the Gulfs of Aden and Oman and the Indian Ocean, which was extended to the Gulf in 2004 and to the Somali Coast in 2009[42] (Melvin, 2019, p. 30). Since 2008, the EU Operation Atalanta has started to operate in the Gulf of Aden, the Red Sea and the Somalian Coast. In 2010, an EU training component for Somalian security forces was added (ibid., p. 30). Between 2009 and 2019, piracy attacks were subsequently reduced from 163 to one (Operation ATALANTA, 2020). As a result, military bases were built in the region and caused militarisation by external forces. One prominent actor is the Chinese People's Liberation Army Navy that joined international anti-piracy operations in 2008 (Kaufman, 2009, p. 1). Until 2018, China had deployed a total of 26,000 personnel and escorted almost 6,600 ships (Zhuo, 2018).

The particular importance of this regional logistical hub became obvious in 2011 when China managed to evacuate about 35,000 Chinese nationals from conflict-affected Libya as well as during the evacuation of 800 Chinese from Yemen in 2015 (Melvin, 2019, p. 3). In 2017, China opened its first overseas naval base in Djibouti, which is used for logistical support of China's regional anti-piracy mission. Moreover, it serves as the PRC's contribution to several peacekeeping operations in the region such as UNMISS in South Sudan, MONUSCO in the DR Congo as well as MINUSMA in Mali and UNMIL in Liberia (ibid., p. 3). China's 2015 anti-terrorism law paved the way for foreign deployment of security forces and enabled China to engage in counterterrorism activities outside the country's borders (Zhou, 2015). In addition, the Chinese naval base in Djibouti plays an important role in the realisation of China's economic interests, particularly in view of the BRI's maritime route (Melvin, 2019, p. 4). Moreover, China has developed intense financial and commercial relations with Djibouti and Ethiopia and invested in infrastructural projects

---

41 The principal naval forces at the Horn of Africa are China, Egypt, France, Germany, India, Iran, Italy, Japan, South Korea, Russia, Saudi Arabia, Spain, Turkey, United Arab Emirates, the United Kingdom and the United States.

42 The Gulf covers waters known historically and internationally as the Persian Gulf. However, with the emergence of pan-Arabism and Arab nationalism in the 1960s, the term Persian Gulf became contested. As a result, the acronyms Arabian Gulf and the Gulf are widely used in Arab countries today and can be found in official documents on the mission.

such as a railway connecting both countries, a water pipeline and most of all the Doraleh Port for both military and commercial purposes (Wang, 2018). The announcement and opening of the Chinese naval base raised international speculation about China's strategic ambitions in the region and China's growing role as a sea power in the region. China's military engagement in the Horn of Africa illustrates China's ambitions and readiness for a stronger role in questions of security in the region. The Chinese deployment of a significant number of military personnel in the Horn of Africa has facilitated support for additional Chinese military activities in Africa such as UN peacekeeping missions. However, this is not direct military intervention in a conflict within a country such as Somalia. Instead, Chinese personnel have been stationed in Djibouti, a relatively stable location compared to some neighbouring countries. Moreover, the mission is used as a superordinate supply station, which can also be used to evacuate Chinese citizens in an emergency. Chinese naval efforts at the Horn of Africa thus illustrate the PRC's regional approach as a contribution to stability and security. Yet, the case does not represent military intervention in the sense of the cases investigated in this study.

5.3. Summary of the Operationalisation

Chapter 5 has covered the identification of conflict-affected states in the MENA region and sub-Saharan Africa between 1946 and 2012 as well as between 2013 and 2019. Cases were also categorised into main cases with Chinese military participation. Two other categories consisted of synchronic and diachronic control cases without the official involvement of the Chinese military. The categorisation of cases was relevant to obtain an overview of the existing baseline data for this study. The year 2013 was considered with a special focus as it marked the beginning of the BRI.

Chinese troop contributions were found in nine cases after 2013, three in the MENA region and six in sub-Saharan Africa. These cases represent the main ones to be investigated in this study and were presented individually in chapter 5.2. In addition, both synchronic and diachronic comparative cases were identified from the population of conflict cases in the UCDP&PRIO data set, which were also briefly presented in chapters 5.3. and 5.4.

The presentation of cases has added value to the study since it provided a first overview of the variety of conflicts and countries with Chinese (non-) intervention. To find out whether the cases with Chinese intervention

5. OPERATIONALISATION

were characterised by certain attributes, it was necessary to compare the cases on the basis of specific factors. The purpose of conducting a QCA was to clarify whether the main cases differed from the comparative cases in these factors. If yes, these differences could explain China's foreign policy decision-making in the field of conflict resolution and provide evidence of a Chinese "road map for peace". With the help of research literature and previous research, relevant factors were identified and are presented in the following chapter.

6. IDENTIFYING DRIVERS FOR INTERVENTION

The chapter above outlined that the method of a QCA will be applied in this study and that the results will be enriched and verified by process tracing. To conduct the QCA, testing factors have to be selected carefully in order to achieve meaningful results about possible determinants for China's military interventions. Chapter 6 covers the identification of factors relevant in foreign policy, conflict studies and power relations and outlines the selection process of twenty-six conditions to be analysed with regard to China.

Previous research literature has provided a range of analyses on worldwide military interventions considering their historical contexts as well as legal and normative circumstances. Most studies refer to particular cases and highlight how intervention practices have changed over time. As early as in 1921, international law professor Ellery C. Stowell wrote a legal analysis of occasions on which the use of force or the threat of force by one state towards another would be justified (Stowell, 1921). Stowell argued that the rule of conduct in international law would not allow states' egoistic decisions to enable them to act independently and violate the independence of their neighbours. The investigation was one of the first to suggest that states would unreasonably pursue their interests, thereby denying the rights and interests of a second state. If efforts to find a compromise were refused, this would be a violation of international law, which would consequently allow for an appeal for intervention (ibid., p. 23). Almost one hundred years later, political scientists Martha Finnemore and Gary J. Bass traced the changes in norms and the application of interventions over time (Bass, 2008; Finnemore, 2003). Finnemore claimed that the normative value of the use of force has increasingly weakened until today (Finnemore, 2003). While single states refrain from intervening, multilateral interventions have become more common. Interventions on the international level have become legalised, which contrasts with the Weberian idea of the state as a rational and legal authority (ibid. p. 52ff). In particular, Finnemore considered three types of interventions where she observed a systemic change over time. In her chapters on sovereign default, humanitarian military intervention and interventions to uphold international order, the author traces normative changes in the importance of humanity with regard to intervention practices. Political scientist Gary

6. IDENTIFYING DRIVERS FOR INTERVENTION

Bass (2008) focused on the perception of humanitarian interventions. Bass stated that interventions based on humanitarian emergencies were able to be observed in the 19th century and were thus not a novelty (Bass, 2008). Bass, however, also illustrated how the revival of this type of intervention led to the removal of interventions being a topic of foreign policy which were the exclusive preserve of governments (ibid.). At the same time, Bass expressed concerns about whether the public would fulfil their responsibility to seek information about international events or if the sudden public attention on humanitarian interventions would merely result in showmanship (ibid.).

The focus on a normative debate about interventions in the post-Cold War period was furthermore captured by Davis et al (2004). The authors differentiated between humanitarian interventions within the framework of the UN and those under the so-called war on terrorism which emerged after the 9/11 attacks (Davis, Dietrich, Scholdan, & Sepp, 2004, p. 3). David et al. stress the necessity of a debate about the normative basis of both types of intervention and elaborate on the establishment of international courts for justice (Davis, Dietrich, Scholdan, & Sepp, 2004, p. 74). As early as in 1994, US diplomat Richard N. Haass, who worked for the former US president George W. Bush, elaborated on the meaning of the changes in military intervention norms after the end of the Cold War with regard to US foreign policy (Haass, 1994). Haass criticised the loss of surprise when referring to humanitarian interventions as well as the element of nation building (ibid.).

In 2000, the political scientist and peace researcher Patrick M. Regan added a contribution on conditions he found to be most likely to result in intervention in civil wars (Regan, 2002). By examining empirical cases, the author also analysed those conditions that proved to be most successful. For instance, Regan found that interventions on the governmental side were more than twice as likely to be successful as supporting an opposition party (Regan, 2002, p. 30). Finally, in 2003, geopolitical scientist Pascal Boniface illustrated a European perspective on interventions with a "regime change" character (Boniface, 2003). In this regard, the author represented complex political challenges concerning the decision to embark on military interventions. Boniface sees only two justifications for military interventions, which are self-defence or a decision by the UN Security council (Boniface, 2003, p. 61). Even if international actors insist on respecting the principles of national sovereignty and non-interference in international theory and law, empirical cases such as the interventions in Somalia (1992), Rwanda (1994) and Kosovo (1999) have shown that

6.1. Political Factors and their Influence on Conflict Intervention

they have never been fully respected in practice since the end of the Cold War (Silverstone, 2016). Furthermore, the US-led invasions of Afghanistan (2001) and Iraq (2003) have reopened the discussion on military interventions as well as associated questions on political and social challenges (ibid.).

The previous literature review has shown that military interventions and, in particular, the type of humanitarian military interventions have been subject to political scientists' discussion. This chapter gives an overview and summarises four sections of causal fields that are related to literature-based findings, namely political, economic, sociocultural, historical, international and regional factors. Each paragraph has further sub-themes which concretise these fields. In this way, a set of causal conditions can be extracted. In total, twenty-six causal factors are identified, which will be used for the following comparative analysis.

6.1. Political Factors and their Influence on Conflict Intervention

Beijing's role in international politics has been changing rapidly since the PRC's political strategy of "opening up" started in the 1980s. Subsequent reforms which allowed the country to lift millions of people out of poverty further accelerated this trend. Furthermore, Beijing has become a relevant actor in the international community and joined international institutions or meetings such as the G20 or Davos summits (Noesselt, 2014, p. 10). China's internal development also affects its foreign policy. It is, therefore, necessary to include political factors in an analysis of the causes of Chinese interventions abroad.

6.1.1. Special Relationship

Strong and special bilateral ties between two countries may result in particular support between governments in times of crisis. Often, ideologically similar parties especially support each other[43]. This can currently be observed in the Syrian crisis where Russia and Iran are supporting President

---

43 The term "The Special Relationship" is often used to describe the historical relations between the United Kingdom and the United States of America as well as the intense political, economic, military and cultural collaboration of both states' leaders until today. However, this study uses the term "special relationship" as

6. IDENTIFYING DRIVERS FOR INTERVENTION

Bashar al Assad's regime (Bishara, 2015). Special bilateral ties can have various forms such as Memorandums of Understandings, treaties or other documents. As early as in ancient times, kingdoms used to have bilateral relations with allies to establish trade relations or increase their methods of defence against enemies (Rana, 2015, p. 2). In ancient Greece, Egypt and China, bilateral diplomatic practices developed over time (ibid., p. 2). However, modern bilateral diplomacy can be considered a "Western product" that emerged as a result of the European Renaissance and was only adopted by Asian states in the late 19th century (ibid., p. 3). Rana (2015) classifies three types of priorities for bilateral relations, namely "core" countries that might be neighbouring states, "priority" countries with political, economic or cultural commonalities and finally "peripheral" countries which consist of the rest (ibid., p. 4). In a recent study about China's partnerships with other countries between 1990 and 2014, Georg Strüver found that bilateral relations helped China to achieve economic and diplomatic gains (Strüver, 2016, p. 24). The scholar Nantulya concentrates on China's military bilateral relations with African states and outlines that these are mostly based on strong party ties and ideological content and can also be traced back to support for anti-colonial movements (Nantulya, 2019). In return, China is expected to support Chinese positions at the United Nations and other bodies in order to strengthen China's voice at the global level (ibid.).

Lanteigne (2018) emphasises that supporting PKOs with military personnel has traditionally been the responsibility of smaller or poorer countries within the UN (Lanteigne, 2018, p. 1). However, China's involvement in PKOs has helped the People's Republic to expand its diplomacy in many developing countries, thus distinguishing it from other major powers (ibid. p. 1). China is now in a position to actively push ahead with mission reforms and to determine more parameters through its increased financial contribution to the UN (ibid. p. 2). Since 2017, China has thus been calling for a holistic approach that addresses country-specific problems and, at the same time, respects the national sovereignty of the countries in question (ibid., p. 3). As part of this study, the type and intensity of bilateral relations between China and conflict-affected countries is included as a factor that might determine Chinese military interventions.

---

one of several factors to be tested in cases of Chinese intervention in conflict-affected countries.

6.1.2. Regime Type

Recent research suggests that the regime type of a country influences both the initiation, the duration and the results of wars (Filson & Werner, 2004; Reiter & Stam, 2002). For example, Reiter & Stam (2002) found advantages of democratic regimes in the chances of winning wars. Earlier studies even suggested that wars fought by democratic regimes would be shorter and more cost-efficient (Bennett & Stam, 1998; Siverson, 1995). The advantages diminish, however, the longer a war continues, and democracies are more likely to accept an undecided outcome and stop fighting (Bennett & Stam, 1998; Reiter & Stam, 2002). At the same time, several authors found that democratic regimes are more likely to be attacked than other regime types (Gelpi & Grieco, 2001; Leeds & Davis, 1999). Democratic regimes are also characterised by a higher cost-sensitivity towards war expenses, which results in a more considered choice of fights (Filson & Werner, 2004). Filson and Werner conclude that

> „Because [democratic regimes] are more willing to make concessions, democracies are more likely to be targeted and less likely to be able to threaten to use force with credibility. Because they are often targeted under the least advantageous circumstances, but attack only under the most advantageous, democracies tend to win when they do fight" (Filson & Werner, 2004, p. 311).

In addition, Gelpi & Grieco point out that democratic leaders are usually in office for limited and rather short periods of time and might be less experienced compared to autocratic leaders (Gelpi & Grieco, 2001, p. 794). The longer a leader is in office, the lower domestic resistance towards costly decisions in favour of violent attacks might be (ibid., p.915). In addition, Koga finds that autocratic regimes mostly conditioned interventions with the chance of extracting resources from the country in question, while democracies were rather concerned about conflicts where they share ethnic ties (Koga, 2011). Bennett (2015), however, disagrees with Koga by pointing out that democratic intervening parties were highly interested in resources such as oil, especially during the Cold War era (Bennett, 2015, p. 25f). With regard to China's socialist identity, Noesselt outlines a rather limited role of a state's ideological preferences and states that it was no longer a decisive element of Beijing's foreign policy in bilateral relations (Noesselt, 2014, p. 20).

Overall, scientific evidence suggests a close connection between regime type and the initiation, configuration and outcome of wars. Hence, external intervention in a conflict with at least one democratic party might promise greater prospects of achieving early satisfaction compared to conflicts between autocratic regimes. If the intervening party strives for reputational gain in conflict resolution, considering the regime type can be a decisive factor. To assess if the regime type of a host country plays a role in China's decision to intervene in a conflict, the criteria of regime type has been included in the QCA. The inclusion of the criteria "regime type" in the QCA of this study furthermore aims to help to identify if and to what extent this factor influences China's behaviour in conflict resolution towards countries in the MENA region and Africa.

6.1.3. Civil War

The reasons for the outbreak of civil wars have been examined by numerous scholars. Collier and Hoffler as well as De Soysa, for example, investigated greed and grievances (Collier & Hoffler, 2004; De Soysa, 2002). Heraclides furthermore provided a study on the relevance of secessionist minorities in civil wars (Heraclides, 1990), while the involvement of third parties in civil wars since the end of the Cold War has been examined by Mitchell (1970).

In general, civil wars present an opportunity for intervening states to demonstrate their own power status and significantly determine the future political orientation of the country (Bennett, 2015, p. 15). Yet, the factor of civil war is closely connected to other potential reasons for unilateral or bilateral state intervention such as a country's location or its ethnic composition and the extent to which the intervening country is connected. The aspect of humanitarian interventions, however, is a relevant feature which is connected to civil wars. Decisions by governments to militarily intervene in a foreign civil war have caused intense discussions both on the political level but also among ordinary citizens (Woo, 2017, p. 2f). While the US intervention in Vietnam in 1965 was among the first and, until today, probably most prominent cases of third-party military intervention, it has not remained the sole one. In 2001, for instance, the United States intervened in Afghanistan, in 2015 Saudi Arabia intervened in the conflict in Yemen, and Russia entered the Syrian Civil War in 2015. Interventions in civil wars may either be explained by third parties' self-interest or by humanitarian concerns. While self-interest is of high importance in unilateral or bilateral interventions, humanitarian justifications are highly relevant

6.1. Political Factors and their Influence on Conflict Intervention

in relation to multilateral action within the framework of the United Nations, for instance (Kim, 2012).

As Woo (2017) illustrates, military interventions are not without risks for the intervening party and there is no guarantee of a positive outcome. For example, Turkey's intervention in Cyprus in 1974 has had long-term effects on Turkey's relations with the EU and has even affected the country's pending EU accession process (Woo, 2017, p. 3). Furthermore, third-party interventions can result in negative effects for the host country and even intensify conflicts (Carment & James, 2004, p. 11). An example of where the intervening parties even contributed to the casualties in a civil war are the two civil wars in the Democratic Republic of Congo in 1996 and 1998. Up to eight external third parties supported different conflict parties during the conflict, thus exacerbating the internal conflict (Woo, 2017, p. 3). Another example is the ongoing war in Syria, where the US is providing military support for opposition parties and Kurdish fighters, whereas Russia is backing the government regime (Eksi, 2017). In 2005, Krain furthermore examined the effects of military interventions in order to prevent further killings in ongoing genocides (Krain, 2005). In this regard, Pickering investigated the war weariness of the parties involved (Pickering, 2002). Finally, Regan provided a comprehensive study on the circumstances which may be favourable for third-party interventions in civil wars (Regan, 2002).

On the whole, previous research gives reason to suspect that the existence of a civil war may be a significant factor in third-party intervention. It is thus included in the QCA investigation carried out in this study.

6.1.4. Self-Defence

Self-defence is probably the most uncontested justification for military (re-)action on the global political stage. It is of such importance to global actors that the member states of the United Nations have included a right to self-defence in the UN Charter. Article 51 states:

> "Nothing in the present Charter shall impair the inherent right of individual or collective self-defence if an armed attack occurs against a Member of the United Nations, until the Security Council has taken measures necessary to maintain international peace and security. Measures taken by Members in the exercise of this right of self-defence shall be immediately reported to the Security Council and shall not in any way affect the authority and responsibility of the Security Council

under the present Charter to take at any time such action as it deems necessary in order to maintain or restore international peace and security."

Article 51 can be considered an exception to the general prohibition of the "threat or use of force against the territorial integrity or political independence of any state, or in any other manner inconsistent with the Purpose of the United Nations", as stipulated in Article 2(4) (UN Charter, 1945) . The exception of self-defence has been universally accepted and its scope largely discussed in academic analyses. In many interpretations, the term "armed attack" in Article 51, however, limits the scope of the article's applicability. It indicates, for instance, that the use of self-defence is not allowed to justify pre-emptive or anticipatory attacks (Richter, 2003, p. 57).

This limitation contrasts with the understanding of self-defence in international customary law that has been developed since the 19th century. States have been allowed to use preventive measures under the umbrella of self-defence in cases when they were anticipating an armed attack (Dinstein, 2017; Richter, 2003). As regards a state's right to self-defence, this fundamental difference between the UN Charter and international customary law has led to disagreements on the concept. The question arises of whether the United Nations Charter is the only legal source of international law or if it includes only some of several conditions that may justify attacks under the concept of self-defence.

The interpretation of self-defence in international customary law relates to an incident which became known as the "Caroline case" in the 19th century. At that time, Canada was under British rule. Yet rebels, supported by the United States of America, fought for the country's independence. In 1837, British soldiers destroyed the American boat Caroline by lighting a fire and referring to self-defence because they claimed that the boat would have shipped equipment to Canadian rebels (Arend, 2003, p. 90). Subsequently, American Secretary of State Daniel Webster condemned the British actions but recognised the right of a preventive attack under certain circumstances. In doing so, he set up elements that have to be present to justify such an attack as self-defence. Webster noted:

> "It will be for that Government to show a necessity of self-defence, instant, overwhelming, leaving no choice of means, and no moment for deliberation. It will be for it to show, also, that the local authorities of Canada,—even supposing the necessity of the moment authorized them to enter the territories of the United States at all,—did nothing unreasonable or excessive; since the act justified by the necessity of

6.1. Political Factors and their Influence on Conflict Intervention

self-defence, must be limited by that necessity, and kept clearly within it. It must be strewn that admonition or remonstrance to the persons on board the "Caroline" was impracticable, or would have been unavailing; it must be strewn that daylight could not be waited for; that there could be no attempt at discrimination, between the innocent and the guilty; that it would not have been enough to seize and detain the vessel; but that there was a necessity, present and inevitable, for attacking her, in the darkness of the night, while moored to the shore, and while unarmed men were asleep on board, killing some, and wounding others, and then drawing her into the current, above the cataract, setting her on fire, and, careless to know whether there might not be in her the innocent with the guilty, or the living with the dead, committing her to a fate, which fills the imagination with horror." (Webster, 1837).

Following the explanation by Webster, the right to self-defence could be applied to pre-emptive attacks if the elements stated were fulfilled. However, in 1986, the International Court of Justice referred to Article 51 of the UN Charter and found that the USA had violated international law by supporting rebels and mining Nicaraguan ports (ICJ Reports, 1986, p. 93). The Court stated that the USA had to pay compensation to Nicaragua and that "the exercise of [the right of self-defence] is subject to the State concerned having been the victim of an armed attack" (ICJ Reports, 1986, p. 93)[44]. As a result, any use of force before being attacked was declared unlawful.

After the tragic attacks of September 11, 2011, US President George W. Bush introduced a new national strategy for security (The White House, 2002). This strategy included the concept of preventive attacks in anticipation of a use of military force by the enemy. In the introduction to the document, Bush explained this new approach with the need to adapt to modern adversaries.

> "Defending our Nation against its enemies is the first and fundamental commitment of the Federal Government. Today, that task has changed dramatically. Enemies in the past needed great armies and great industrial capabilities to endanger America. Now, shadowy networks of

---

44 For further information concerning the case Nicaragua vs. United States of America, see
https://www.icj-cij.org/public/files/case-related/70/070-19841126-JUD-01-00-EN.pdf.

6. IDENTIFYING DRIVERS FOR INTERVENTION

individuals can bring great chaos and suffering to our shores for less than it costs to purchase a single tank." (The White House, 2002).

The concept of pre-emptive military attacks is still referred to in the 21st century and used under the justification of self-defence. The latter is thus a relevant factor in military interventions and therefore considered in this study.

6.2. Economic Factors and their Influence on Conflict Intervention

China's increasing international investments are often made in unstable environments such as fragile states or conflicting regions. With diplomatic costs rising, the disadvantages of China's noninterventionist approach become visible (Sofer, 2012). The importance China dedicates to economic relationships with countries is often not coherent with the PRC's efforts for these countries' populations. The following four economic factors might thus be relevant in China's decision-making on whether or not to intervene in foreign countries' conflicts.

6.2.1. Resource Wealth of the Conflict-Affected Country

Haroz (2011) points out what is undisputed today: China needs far more resources than the country itself has available for its economic rise. Many of the loans China issues to African countries are secured by resources. At the same time, many of these states are affected by conflicts, which puts China's resources at risk (Haroz, 2011). Third parties' national interests such as access to resources in conflict-affected states can influence their decision to intervene (Bennett, 2015, p. 20). In particular, non-renewable resources such as natural gas, diamonds or oil are of concern. Yet, their relevance depends on the number of worldwide suppliers and the possibility of alternative trade routes (ibid. p. 20).

China's imports of natural resources for energy consumption have been on the rise since Deng Xiaoping's economic reforms in 1978 (World Bank, 2018). By turning away from the Maoist planning system and opening markets up to competition, the Chinese leadership succeeded in raising the country's gross domestic product from slightly over USD 149 billion in 1978 to more than USD 14 trillion in 2019 (World Bank, 2019). While China remained an energy-exporting nation until 2001, the country has meanwhile become one of today's major importers of natural resources

6.2. Economic Factors and their Influence on Conflict Intervention

such as coal, iron, oil or gas (Sofer, 2012, p. 4; U.S. Commercial Service, 2017). This resulted in business deals with states rich in resources such as North Korea or Iran but also with Venezuela or African states such as Sudan (Sofer, 2012, p. 4). On the one hand, China did not face large competition from Western companies in these states. The opposite was the case. Many new trade partners were internationally known as pariahs and conflict-driven countries (ibid. p. 4). Chinese companies started businesses with rather unstable states to profit from the absence of other international stakeholders that had already established close ties in energy trade with more stable producers (ibid. p. 4).

In general, there is no universal definition of resource wealth. One possibility is to consider a country's share of natural resource exports divided by its gross domestic product. Within the World Bank Group, the "Fragile, Conflict and Violence Group – Investment Climate" team considers countries rich in resources if the natural resource rents as a percentage of GDP have surpassed ten per cent of the GDP for the past three years (The World Bank Group, 2018). From a global perspective, on average, the number of total natural resources rents as a percentage of GDP is at about 1.89 per cent (ibid.). In this thesis, resource abundance in the countries under investigation is able to provide evidence about the drivers of Chinese military intervention.

6.2.2. Trade Balance between China and the Conflict-Affected Country

Recent research suggests that an increase in trade among states diminishes the threat of conflict and war[45] (Polachek, 1980, p. 55). Put differently, conflict hinders business and instability and destruction make investors retreat. Hence, from the perspective of external parties, Nantulya states that conflict intervention might be an option in securing economic and business relations (Nantulya, 2019). Theoretically, intervention should be likelier the larger trade relations are between a third party and a conflict-affected country.

In 2017, China was rated the world's largest exporter by value with goods worth about USD 2.27 trillion (Workman, 2018). This constituted more than one eighth of global exports estimated in 2016 (ibid.). As regards the destinations of Chinese goods, almost 50 per cent were delivered

---

45 Polachek found that a doubling of trade decreases belligerence by about 20 per cent (Polachek, 1980, p. 55).

to other Asian countries. More than one fifth was sent to North America, while almost one fifth was exported to Europe. In addition, Latin American as well as African countries imported about four per cent of Chinese exports (ibid.). While no developing state is listed among the Chinese top ten export destinations, Angola is ranked eighth in the list of countries with which China has the largest trade deficits (Workman, 2018). Countries rich in resources like South Korea, Brazil and Saudi Arabia are also listed at the very top, while China's deficit with Saudi Arabia rose fastest between 2016 and 2017 by 170 percentage points (ibid.).

Bilateral trade relations between China and African countries resulted in a volume of USD 192 billion in 2019, with most exports to China originating from Angola, South Africa and DR Congo (Comtrade, 2021; Johns Hopkins China-Africa Research Initiative, 2021). Most goods from China were delivered to Nigeria, South Africa and Egypt (ibid.). Chinese trade relations with Middle Eastern countries were less extensive compared to those with African countries in 2019 (Comtrade, 2021). Whilst Chinese imports mostly originated from Saudi Arabia and Oman, China exported most goods to the United Arab Emirates and Saudi Arabia (ibid.). When excluding Gulf countries from the rankings, most Chinese imports originated from Egypt, Mauritania and Morocco (ibid.). The majority of Chinese exports were delivered to Egypt, Algeria and Morocco, although the volume was a lot smaller compared to trade relations with Gulf countries (ibid.).

The intensification of trade between China and the MENA region and Africa suggests that China has also become more sensitive and vulnerable with regard to conflicts that might break out in these regions and disrupt trade relations. Once a conflict breaks out and the longer it continues, a settlement to the hostilities might become more difficult. In his study, researcher Hannes Mueller assessed the economic risks and costs of conflicts and made recommendations about military or diplomatic third-party interventions (Mueller, 2013, p. 13ff). Cho suggests that countries which are important export markets for Chinese products play a significant role in China's decision to participate in UN missions (Cho, 2019, p. 482). The author further considers a country's importance as an export market as even greater than a country's exports of natural resources to China (Ibid., p. 483).

This study includes "trade balance" between China and conflict-affected countries as a possible factor in Chinese conflict intervention in the QCA. By taking a closer look at this factor, it provides evidence on the question of if China is more likely to intervene in conflict-affected states if they are of high economic interest for the PRC. China's trade balances with conflict-affected states are analysed with World Bank data (World Integrated Trade Solution, 2018). In addition, import and export figures for the countries under investigation are compared for the year 2013 by using data from the UN Comtrade Database (UN Comtrade Database, 2020).

6.2.3. Financial Relations between China and the Conflict-Affected Country

China's economic activities in the MENA region and Africa are largely characterised by a "golden triangle that exists between Chinese companies, the state and quasi-commercial lending institutions" (IDE-JETRO, 2009, p. 77). Loans provided by China's state-backed financial institutions have been decisive in the success of numerous projects, in particular in the resource and infrastructural sector (ibid., p. 77)[46]. Supported by state-backed subsidised interest rates, Chinese development banks have been able to offer discounted loans, thus providing Chinese companies an advantage over Western ventures (ibid., p. 77f). China's ExIm[47] bank is one of the world's largest export credit agencies and has additionally introduced a new business model which has become known as the "Angola Model" and allows repayment of loans with natural resources (ibid., p. 78). Chinese financial institutions have furthermore started to buy into international banks with large portfolios in African countries (ibid., p. 78). During the last two decades, China's financial relations to foreign countries have seen a significant increase. By January 2018, Chinese outward investments by more than 740 registered enterprises had grown to a contract value of more than USD 12,000 billion (Ministry of Commerce of the PRC, 2018). Chinese investors have concentrated mostly on non-financial direct investments in 99 countries and regions worldwide (ibid.).

In 2006, an additional China–Africa Development Fund (CADF) was established to facilitate Chinese investments in Africa by offering both fund investments, management and consulting services, particularly for projects in the sectors of agriculture, infrastructure, industries or resource development (China Development Bank, 2015).

---

46 Examples of Chinese banking institutions are the China Development Bank (CDB), the Industrial and Commercial Bank of China (ICBC), the China Export-Import Bank and the China Export and Credit Insurance Corporation (CECIC).
47 Export-Import Bank.

6. IDENTIFYING DRIVERS FOR INTERVENTION

The increase in China's efforts deepen financial relations mostly with African countries increases Chinese bank's vulnerability to conflicts in host countries. China may thus have an increased interest in assisting conflict-affected countries militarily if intensified financial relations exist. It therefore seems interesting to consider Chinese financial flows and investments in conflict-affected countries in the MENA region and Africa. However, a huge variety of actors are involved on both sides, including not only financial and trade institutions but also state-actors such as ministries. When data was collected to include this factor in the study, it became evident that financial relations are often opaque when it comes to China's activities in Africa and the MENA region. Instead, various political actors such as ministries and banks seem to be involved in rather "hidden" local competitions (Corkin, 2013). It became apparent that influential provincial governments as well as Chinese companies acting below the central government in Beijing are important factors in power competition and might influence China's role at the UN. Yet, a lack of sufficient available data inhibited a profound consideration of the relevant financial relations between the PRC and countries under consideration in the QCA of this study. The indicator could thus not be included in the inquiry. However, considering financial aspects in future studies which may have the chance to refer to more comprehensive financial data sets is worthwhile.

6.2.4. Infrastructural Projects with Chinese Participation in Conflict-Affected Countries

During the last few years, China has been among a number of non-OECD countries that have started to play a bigger role in financing infrastructural projects in the Middle East and Africa[48]. In this regard, Chinese financiers mostly focus on large-scale projects and about 35 African countries such as Angola and Sudan have already agreed on corresponding deals (Foster, Butterfield, Chen, & Pushak, 2008, p. 2). Often, Chinese infrastructure finance is combined with the development of natural resources (see chapter 6.2.1) (ibid. p. 2). Most African leaders have welcomed Chinese investments in recent years, in particular because Beijing's approach differs from traditional Western cooperation in that it does not connect agreements to conditions regarding good governance or democratisation efforts. Such an alternative model of development was attractive for African statesmen

---

48 Other non-OECD financiers include India and the Gulf states.

6.3. Sociocultural and Historical Factors

since China considers human rights or environmental standards less than Western partners (Foster, Butterfield, Chen, & Pushak, 2008, p. 8). By 2012, China had become the largest single government to support the closing of Africa's infrastructural deficit (ICA Annual Report, 2012, p. 31). In 2015, Chinese investments in Africa amounted to USD 20.9 billion (Infrastructure Consortium for Africa Secretariat, 2017, p. 56). This sum marked a peak in the period between 2011 and 2016 with average investments of about USD 12 billion (ibid.). Financing is managed by the China ExIm Bank. In 2016, China, for example, contributed more than USD 7 billion to a railway that would connect Burundi, Rwanda and Tanzania. Furthermore, coal plants (USD 3 billion) or energy projects were supported with USD 4.6 billion in 2016.

Breuer (2017) argues that the OBOR initiative, often referred to as the Eurasian Infrastructure Network, extends beyond infrastructure development. While a maritime route through the Suez Canal is planned, tracks are to be laid all the way to East Africa. Such tracks will connect Nairobi with Southern Sudan, Uganda, Rwanda and Burundi as well as ports in Togo and Nigeria with the hinterland. In light thereof, Breuer considers a "Second Belt" across Africa, which will link the continent and open up markets to become part of the new Silk Road (Breuer, 2017, p. 4). Nantulya furthermore, explains how China is building rail links in landlocked Mali to connect the country with ports in Dakar (Senegal) and Conakry (Guinea) (Nantulya, 2019). Some of the tracks run through areas that are partly controlled by violent extremists in northern Mali and endanger Chinese workers. Nantulya (2019) sees this as one of the main reasons for China's participation in the United Nations' Multidimensional Integrated Stabilization Mission in Mali (MINUSMA) to stabilise the West African country. The large number of investments in transportation projects and other infrastructural sectors such as energy explain China's interest in a stable environment. The more support a country has experienced, the likelier it is that China will become active in a conflict. Infrastructural projects might thus be a driver of Chinese military interventions and are thus included in the QCA in the study at hand.

6.3. Sociocultural and Historical Factors and their Influence on Conflict Intervention

Sociocultural and historical factors as motives for military intervention have not been discussed largely in research literature. In the case of China,

6. IDENTIFYING DRIVERS FOR INTERVENTION

however, the two following aspects might be relevant for the PRC's decisions to intervene in foreign conflicts.

6.3.1. Number of Chinese Citizens Abroad

Counting the number of Chinese migrants abroad strongly depends on the criteria used. In some calculations, only the so-called first generation of Chinese migrants is counted, which relates to Chinese people who were born in China and settled in another country but excludes their foreign-born children (Goodkind, 2019, p. 2). By contrast, other countries would include all Chinese descendants regardless of their birthplace and would sometimes also include people from Singapore and Taiwan (ibid. p. 2). For example, the Academy for Cultural Diplomacy stated that the number of ethnic Chinese citizens living outside China, Hong Kong, Taiwan and Macau in 2007 was 46 million people, which would make Chinese expatriates the largest migrant group worldwide (Academy for Cultural Diplomacy, 2018). For 2020, however, recent UN figures estimate a total of 10.7 million Chinese migrants worldwide (IOM, 2020, p. 3). A comprehensive UN data set furthermore shows that the number of Chinese citizens living in worldwide diasporas more than doubled between 1990 and 2017. While in 1990, about 4.2 million Chinese people resided abroad, this figure increased to almost 10 million in 2017. David Goodkind (2019) identifies the following composition of these Chinese migrants:
1. First generation international migrants from China (10 million)
   - 1.0 labourers
   - 1.0 million current students
   - 2.0–3.0 million former international students
   - 0.5 million investors, entrepreneurs or highly skilled migrants
   - 0.5 million traders, mercantilists or family-run businesses
   - 4.0–5.0 million family-related migrants (formal reunification of immediate relatives, family preference, international intermarriage, etc.)
2. Second or later-generation descendants of those born in China (35 million)

Source: (Goodkind, 2019, p. 15)

The UN Department of Economic and Social Affairs provides valuable data on the number of international migrants and their origin and destinations between 1990 and 2017. While the total rise in Chinese migrants worldwide from 4.2 million in 1990 to 10 million in 2017 was largely due to migration towards more developed regions (from 1.5 million to 5.5 million), the numbers of Chinese citizens migrating to less developed regions also increased (from 2.8 million to 4.4 million) (UN Department of Economic and Social Affairs, 2017). Taking a closer look at less developed countries shows that the number of Chinese migrants arriving there remained constant for least developed countries (from about 246,000 to 247,000)[49]. In comparison, the number of Chinese migrants to less developed regions increased from 2.5 million to 4.2 million in the same period (ibid.)

On the whole, several typologies of Chinese migrants can be identified. One categorisation has been made by Wang (1991), who was later cited by Poston, Mao and Yu (1994, p. 631) and also Goodkind (2019, p. 2). While the Chinese word *hua* refers to Chinese heritage, the different migrant groups can be classified as

- *Huashang* (mercantilists who have travelled to Southeast Asia for hundreds of years and still consider themselves Chinese),
- *Huahong* (Chinese labour migrants who worked in America's railroad industry during the 19th century),
- *Huaqiao* (well-educated and highly-skilled professionals who went abroad in the 19th century but often came back to China after a certain time) and
- *Huayi* (similar to *Huashang* but travelling to other destinations abroad) (Wang, 1991, p. 5).

In his report, Goodkind (2019) outlines that *Huagong* workers have become very widespread until today, in particular with China opening up (Goodkind, 2019, p. 3). At the same time, Goodkind observes that the migration of *Huagong* has become more and more temporary and better monitored, while the number of educated migrants has increased steadily (ibid., p. 3). Many Chinese have left their home country to work in Chinese investment projects overseas, strongly supported by the government's going out strategy (Sofer, 2012, p. 7). Goodkind (2019) adds two more categories of contemporary Chinese migrants: family members who join their relatives abroad and Chinese who travel abroad with a mandate to foster and strengthen China's image and interests abroad such as diplomats and

---

49 For the categorisation of least developed countries, low-income countries, lower-middle-income countries, middle-income countries, upper-middle-income countries and high-income countries, see UN Department of Economic and Social Affairs, Population Division.

6. IDENTIFYING DRIVERS FOR INTERVENTION

other businesspeople but also students equipped with governmental sponsorship (Goodkind, 2019, p. 3).

Chinese traders in less developed countries are often prone to conflicts which interrupt trade routes and lead to economic losses, for example when goods are stolen or destroyed, or workers injured. With conflicts continuing in their destination countries, Chinese residents abroad increasingly demand action by the Chinese government. In 2011, for instance, China evacuated 35,860 Chinese nationals from Libya when violent uprisings began after the downfall of former leader Muammar Al-Gaddafi's regime (Zerba, 2014, p. 1093). In 2013, another 400 Chinese workers were evacuated from South Sudan, where fighting broke out between the government and rival groups (Vasselier, 2016).

Apart from civil wars, violent outbreaks of fighting or general political instability, many regions in which Chinese nationals have settled are affected by piracy and kidnapping (Sofer, 2012, p. 8). In 2012, more than twenty Chinese road workers were seized by a Sudanese rebel group while working in an oil-rich region that had become a battlefield in the conflict between Sudan and South Sudan (Bradsher & Gettleman, 2012). Another incident happened in Egypt in the same year when 25 Chinese workers were kidnapped by a Bedouin tribesman but freed the next day (Wee, 2012).

These examples make clear that China is not exempt from international security risks in its global engagement. China's abilities to protect Chinese migrants abroad have been rather limited. On top of that, former protection by actors such as the United States can no longer be relied on since the US military is reducing its presence, for example in Middle Eastern countries such as Iraq and Afghanistan (Erickson & Collins, 2012). Where companies' security is not ensured by the Chinese government, some enterprises might hire private security contractors to protect their workers (Erickson & Collins, 2012). In the case of the Chinese nationals kidnapped in Sudan, private forces are reported to have supported Sudanese troops in their rescue efforts (ibid.).

Paul Nantulya (2019) points out that China's activities in the field of security have increased in parallel with the establishment of the Belt and Road Initiative (Nantulya, 2019). In 2015, China passed a law allowing the People's Liberation Army to operate abroad. In 2017, China's first Maritime Military Base was opened in Djibouti (ibid.). Nantulya argues that China is particularly interested in military training for African states in the areas of anti-terrorism and infrastructure protection. This measure would make it clear that China is expanding its security presence to expand the

BRI into the Sahel and further into West Africa. Lanteigne, furthermore, underlines China's need for security and stability along the BRI and sees PKOs that also accompany the transition from war to peace as a way to achieve this (Lanteigne, 2018). Chinese companies thus increasingly rely on their own government for security. Until now, Chinese investors have continued to develop mines and support infrastructural projects, which has kept the numbers of Chinese residents abroad at a high level. This development puts pressure on the Chinese government to take a stronger approach in the protection of their citizens and might be a reason for a change in China's noninterventionist policy (Sofer, 2012).

The number of Chinese citizens abroad thus seems relevant for Chinese bilateral relations and the decision of whether or not to intervene in foreign conflicts. Due to a lack of data, the number of Chinese citizens abroad can only be included for a limited number of cases in the QCA.

6.3.2. The Question of Taiwan

The question about the status of Taiwan was one of the most challenging topics in international relations during the last decades of the 20th century. In essence, the question of "two Chinas" has urged the international community to decide which "China" will be recognised internationally and thus accepted as a member state in the United Nations (Hsieh, 2009).

In 1971, the UN General Assembly voted on a resolution determining that the People's Republic of China is the only government of China and has the legitimacy to rule over its territory and people. As such, Resolution 2758 (XXVI) was a decision to replace the Republic of China (Taiwan) as a permanent member of the UN Security Council (Dumbaugh, 2009; UN Security Council, 1971). In total, the resolution was adopted with 76 members voting in favour, 35 voting against and 17 abstentions (UN Security Council, 1971). With the adoption of Resolution 2758 (XXVI) Beijing's one-China principle was officially recognised by the international community, whilst Taiwan had to give up its permanent seat at the United Nations (Hsieh, 2009, p. 59). In order to maintain diplomatic relations with Taiwan, countries started to develop unconventional legal concepts (ibid. p. 59). The country's strategically important geographical location in the South China Sea certainly played a role in nations' interest in remaining on good terms with the Republic of China even after it lost international recognition as a representative of China. Even today, China and Taiwan continue their efforts to persuade countries to adopt either position. This especially relates to a number of developing countries in Central America, Africa and the Pacific. Often, generous aid packages were used as incentives (Rich & Banerje, 2014, p. 149). China regards Taiwan as a province without the right to sustain diplomatic state ties. By contrast, Taiwan has attempted to convince other actors of its right to be recognised as a sovereign state (ibid. p. 150f). Money diplomacy by both states resulted in numerous countries switching between the recognition of China and then Taiwan and vice versa (Scharping, 2002, p. 3). For example, in the 1990s, six countries changed their support from Beijing to Taipei and five other countries switched it from Taipei to Beijing. In total, seven countries made several changes depending, for example, on which country offered larger aid packages (ibid. p. 3). Currently, the majority of states, however, follow the PRC's argumentation. In 2017, even Taiwan's long-term ally Panama changed sides in favour of China (Hsieh, 2009; Mendez & Alden, 2019, p. 2). While in 2018, a total of nineteen UN members still recognised Taiwan as a sovereign state, this number fell to fourteen in 2020 (Gilbert, 2018; World Population Review, 2020). Several other states maintain unofficial diplomatic relations with Taiwan (Rich & Banerje, 2014, p. 145). In the United Nations, however, Taiwan remains represented by the People's Republic of China, which considers the island part of its country (Dumbaugh, 2009).

For the purpose of this thesis, the question of Taiwan is considered since Chinese bilateral relations to other countries were often non-existent if the latter did not recognise the one-China principle. It might thus be possible that decisions for military intervention are influenced by a country's choice of recognition for China.

6.4. Regional and International Factors and their Influence on Conflict Intervention

This chapter considers geopolitical aspects that may influence China's decision to intervene in conflicts. The relationship between geographic proximity, the international system and a state's own interests are of particular relevance. The assumption is that the rate of intervention increases, the closer a country is located to the conflict (Khosla, 1999, p. 1143). External actors might, furthermore, be more willing to interfere in a conflict if other third parties are already involved (Shirkey, 2016). In such cases, military intervention could be used to uphold regional and international order by a country taking sides with one of the conflicting parties (Finnemore, 2003).

6.4. Regional and International Factors

Moreover, the relevance of a country as a recipient country of aid might be relevant. The following categories provide an overview of which factors are considered in this study.

6.4.1. Country Location

A country's geographical location can be critical to a third party's decision on whether or not to intervene in a conflict or civil war. The location criterion becomes even more relevant when national interests such as trade routes or access to resources are affected (Bennett, 2015, p. 52). If trade routes are blocked or not safe because of internal violent fighting, trading goods must be transported along alternative routes that might be costlier and take more time. Costs might also increase due to the risk of losing commodities after confiscation or destruction. If a conflict-affected country exports natural resources such as oil or gas, several third parties and destination countries may have an interest in securing trade routes for these products (ibid. p. 83). Yet, third parties might not directly intervene militarily in such conflicts. Diplomatic talks or economic sanctions are usually attempted first to settle the conflict. In addition, if the supplying country can easily be substituted by other providers, interest in military involvement may also decline. In the case of China, the geographic location of conflict-affected countries could also be relevant even though Middle Eastern and African countries, which are considered in this study, are not neighbouring countries of the PRC. However, some of them are located along China's Belt and Road Initiative. The Silk Road Economic Belt connects Central Asia with Europe by crossing through Iran, Iraq, Syria and Turkey in particular. The 21st Century Maritime Silk Road, furthermore, passes through African countries such as Tanzania, Kenya, Djibouti and Egypt. Geographical extension has thus moved the boundaries of Chinese interests far beyond national borders and China's immediate neighbouring states (Rolland, 2019, p. 2).

By using the BRI as a means of economic integration along the routes, China is trying to establish a production chain with the PRC as the origin of innovation and standards (Cai, 2017, p. 5). Conflicts and civil wars along these routes might endanger China's plans to realise this production chain. In addition, neighbouring countries can affect security along the routes. In the case of Afghanistan, for instance, China urged the North Atlantic Treaty Organization (NATO) not to leave the country too early since attacks by the Taliban might spread violence and instability in the region

(Weitz, 2015). Other surrounding countries, while not directly located along the routes, might still be strategic partners in supplying resources for the construction of ports, roads, bridges, airports or other infrastructural projects along the BRI. If conflicts arise in these countries, their location may be one criterion for China to consider military intervention.

6.4.2. Situation in Neighbouring Countries

One reason to interfere militarily in countries could be the situation of neighbouring states. In secondary literature, the role of regional circumstances is stressed when considering third-party intervention in civil wars (Kathman, 2010; Khosla, 1999). The authors Gleditsch, Salehyan and Schultz found that neighbouring states are more likely to intervene as a third party in a civil war than other external states, which increases the likelihood of regionalisation of the conflict (Gleditsch, Salehyan, & Schultz, 2008, p. 13). The danger of conflict spillovers into neighbouring countries is also central as far as the security of trade routes as well as resource extraction and supply are concerned. Hence, the situation of bordering states plays a role in third parties' decisions to intervene in conflicts and "a third party's interests in a neighbouring conflict must be substantial enough to produce a willingness to intervene" (Kathman, 2010, p. 991). Lambach, Johais & Bayer (2016) also consider bad neighbourhoods a risk factor for instability. In addition, civil wars limit economic ties and trade relations and often lead to displacement and military infringements (Schneckener, 2006). Moreover, internationalisation of the conflict through transnational ethnic ties or military unification could endanger regional and international stability (Joyce & Braithwaite, 2013, p. 598). Possible spillovers of conflicts into neighbouring countries increase the potential of regional conflagration, which might also threaten international investors in a region.

In view of the PRC's BRI, however, infrastructural projects and investments are not concentrated on single nation states. Instead, Beijing has introduced the presentation of six so-called "economic corridors" which cover some of the world regions that are most rich in resources (OECD, 2018, p. 10f). The corridors are spread all over Asia and Europe and are connected to the land routes of the BRI covering
(1) a New Eurasia Land Bridge,
(2) a China, Mongolia, Russia Economic Corridor,
(3) a China, Central Asia, West Asia Economic Corridor,

(4) a China Indochina Peninsula Economic Corridor,
(5) a China, Pakistan Economic Corridor and finally
(6) a China, Bangladesh, India, Myanmar Economic Corridor (ibid., p.11). Whilst African countries are not part of these corridors, the third corridor passes through Iran and Turkey and covers Middle Eastern countries such as Lebanon, Iraq, Syria, Jordan and the Palestinian Authority (ibid., p. 12). Beijing's approach of summarising countries into corridors and seeking regional development instead of solely bilateral projects will most likely expand to other world regions. China's support of an African railway network which aims at stronger connectivity among African states is one example which supports Beijing's regional approach outside Asia (Githaiga, Burimaso, Bing, & Mohammed Ahmed, 2019). Against this background, Beijing may not only pay attention to conflicts within partner countries but also in neighbouring countries that are part of the same region.

This thesis focuses on conflicts in the MENA region and Africa to identify characteristics that drive conflict interventions by China. Many countries in both regions have borders with states or sub-regions that are affected by violent conflicts or civil war. If China has an interest in keeping whole regions—or corridors—stable and secure, the situation in neighbouring states may be a relevant factor in China's contribution to conflict resolution. Conflicts in neighbouring states are thus included as a criterion for military intervention within the QCA of this study.

6.4.3. Conflict Involvement by Other States or Parties

Recent research literature suggests that the chances of settling a conflict become more complicated the more parties are involved (Shirkey, 2012, p. 321). If a third party decides to intervene, it is reacting to information revealed about both the power status of the conflicting parties as well as possible outcome scenarios (Shirkey, 2016, p. 417). The more parties intervene, however, the more issues and interests are added to the list of topics which need to be solved in order to end the conflict (Shirkey, 2012, p. 321). In 1980, the authors Yamamoto & Bremer provided one of the earliest studies on the effects of third-party intervention by great powers (Yamamoto & Bremer, 1980). The authors found that a major power's decision to intervene in a conflict depends on political circumstances and especially on the decision of other great powers (ibid.). Yamamoto & Bremer (1980) added that the number of intervening parties also increases if a great power takes part in an intervention. In such circumstances, the chances of successfully resolving the conflict might appear greater to other smaller third parties. The method used by Yamamoto & Bremer (1980) was later also applied by Corbetta & Dixon (2005), who used new data and confirmed previous results (Corbetta & Dixon, 2005, p. 59).

While intervening parties mostly take the side of one of the conflicting parties, the party supported does not always have to be the ruling power of a country. One example of disagreement between intervening powers is the ongoing civil war in Syria. Russia has supported the Syrian regime under President Bashar Al Assad, while the United States and other Western powers have, at least for some time, assisted oppositional groups (Laub, 2017). The decision to intervene or not remains a trade-off between the possible gains and losses of intervening or the maintenance of the status quo (Bennett, 2015, p. 68). The more powerful an allied power that has already intervened, the likelier the chances are of a third party intervening as well and benefiting from a successful outcome. Corbetta & Dixon add that "the most effective way for a third party to manage a conflict is to bring that conflict to an end by helping one side in that conflict achieve a decisive victory" (Corbetta & Dixon, 2005, p. 40). When deciding to support one party in a conflict, the intervening party may influence the process of the conflict, which might either prolong and complicate the outcome or facilitate a settlement. In an analysis of conflicts between 1900 and 1976, Cusack & Eberwein found that the involvement of major powers in disputes led to them escalating into war in one fifth of the cases (Cusack & Eberwein, 1982). Petersen, Vasquez & Wang added that war was more probable in multiparty disputes, especially if the topic of the conflict related to territorial questions (Petersen, Vasquez, & Wang, 2004, p. 89f). The topic of this thesis is based on the observation that China has increasingly become active and involved in global crisis policies. It is therefore of interest to investigate whether the PRC's decisions to intervene in conflicts are related to other actors' involvement in these conflicts.

6.4.4. Multilateral or International Conflict Intervention

After the failures of the UN Security Council to prevent ethnic cleansing in Rwanda (1994) and in Kosovo (1999), the 2001 report by the International Commission on Intervention and State Sovereignty (ICISS) presented a new principle which introduced the responsibility for the international community to protect people at risk of mass killing, ethnic cleansing or other crimes against humanity (ICISS, 2001). The Responsibility to Protect gave member states of the United Nations new justification in international intervention and has been used as a reference in numerous resolutions (Global Center for the Responsibility to Protect, 2018).Yet, Weiss (2014) observed that members often only seem to call upon the principle when international action is in their interest. Current examples are the wars in Syria and Yemen, where numerous resolutions have been vetoed in the Security Council.

In the case of China, US annual reports to Congress about the military and security developments of the PRC indicate that the country is expanding its international contributions. One area China seems particularly interested in is peacekeeping missions. After Chinese troops had followed the US-led command during a UN mission to support South Korea[50] during the Korean War between 1950 and 1953, China remained sceptical towards further involvement in UN activities (Gill & Huang, 2009). While China rejected any involvement during the 1970s, this political position changed throughout the 1990s and resulted in its increased participation in international missions from the beginning of this millennium (Butler & Wheeler, 2012, p. 9). In 1981, China participated in a UN mission for the first time and sent 20 troop members to Namibia to support peaceful elections[51] (Gill & Huang, 2009, p. 2). Hence, Africa was China's first destination within a multilateral UN mission, followed by its participation in the UN Truce Supervision Organization (UNTSO) in the Middle East, where China has remained active until today (ibid. p. 2). Peacekeeping missions are established on the basis of resolutions by the UN Security Council (United Nations Peacekeeping, 2020). The UNSC defines how many military personnel are needed for the mission and consults member states for their provisioning (ibid.). This procedure often takes considerable time and delays the beginning of missions (ibid.). Around the year 2000, China deployed only about 100 peacekeepers. By August 2020, China had become the 9th largest troop contributor to UN missions with 2,441 men and women involved (UN Peacekeeping, 2020). For the purpose of this thesis, the presence of a UN peacekeeping mission is thus a relevant indicator of Chinese international conflict involvement.

---

50 The mission is known as United Nations Command (UNC).
51 UN Transition Assistance Group (UNTAG).

6. IDENTIFYING DRIVERS FOR INTERVENTION

6.4.5. Chinese Official Development Aid

After the end of the Cold War, the number of civil wars increased, particularly in the MENA region and Africa. As a consequence, the international community and Western actors especially increased their efforts to support democratic changes in former colonies (Uvin, 1999, p. 2). In 1997, *Guidelines on Conflict, Peace and Development Cooperation* were published within the OECD-DAC and formed a new framework for aid among the donor community (ibid., p. 2). Over the past few decades, the amount of international official development assistance given by the OECD-DAC countries has become the most stable external source of funding for developing countries (Ahmad, Bosch, Carey, & Mc Donnell, 2020, p. 6). In parallel, many former recipients of Official Development Assistance (ODA) from OECD countries have become "new donors" themselves (Altenburg & Weikert, 2007). For example, India, Brazil, South Africa and China have developed their own aid programmes. China, however, does not publish a transparent overview of its official financial support or project data. A research lab at the William & Mary's Global Research Institute in Williamsburg tracks underreported financial flows and has published Chinese aid data online (Aiddata, 2021). Since the beginning of the new millennium, Chinese total official development aid has largely been increased with peaks in 2009 and 2011 (Aiddata, 2021). After 2011, a slight but constant decrease can be observed until 2014 (ibid.). Whilst official figures on China's development aid are not publicly available, estimations of Chinese ODA amount to USD 5.4 billion for the year 2020 (Kitano & Miyabayashi, 2020, p. 2). In comparison, Germany's Official Development Assistance (ODA) amounted to almost USD 33 billion compared to USD 24 billion from EU institutions and almost USD 36 billion from the USA (OECD, 2021). When adding "Other Official Flows" and "Vague Official Finance" to China's record, the total sum of development aid also amounts to USD 38 billion (Aiddata, 2021). If China has provided a large amount of development aid to countries in the MENA region and Africa, the PRC might be interested in keeping those countries stable since conflicts and destruction undermine the positive effects of aid. In a comparison of four case studies in 1999, research professor Peter Uvin outlined the role of aid in the case of conflicts in destination countries and drew four main lessons from his investigation (Uvin, 1999, p. 4):

Aid creates both incentives and disincentives for conflict, which need to be managed.

Aid is political and can be used for political purposes, whilst both the volume of aid and the recipients are crucial decisions to ensure stability and peace.

Aid is just one factor among many that influence the dynamics of conflicts.

The impact of aid is determined by the broader relations between the recipient country and the international community.

Whilst the discussion about aid effectiveness has been covered by many scholars[52], this study considers aid as a potential factor in conflict intervention. The amount of development aid paid by China to the countries under consideration is therefore included as a causal factor to be tested in the QCA of this study.

6.5. Summary of the drivers for intervention

Chapter 6 has covered a major preparatory step in the implementation of the QCA. The identification of causal factors for the realisation of a QCA was conducted using the theoretical strands of foreign policy, conflict studies and power relations. The relevance of each factor for China's decision to intervene was deduced. By testing conflict cases using the factors identified, we can find concrete determinants of a possible Chinese "road map for peace". The analysis of research literature focusing on state interventions resulted in a total of fifteen topics in four categories that led to twenty-six causal factors to be tested in this study. Table 7 provides an overview of the factors by category.

---

52 See, for example, (Easterly, 2001) or (Banerjee & Duflo, 2019).

6. IDENTIFYING DRIVERS FOR INTERVENTION

Table 7: Overview of Causal Factors to be tested in the QCA

Political Factors	Economic Factors	Sociocultural and Historical Factors	Regional and International Factors
Special Relationship	Resource Wealth	Number of Citizens abroad	Country Location
Regime Type	Trade Balance	Question of Taiwan	Situation in Neighbouring Countries
Civil War	Financial Relations		Conflict Involvement by other States or Parties
Self-defence	Infrastructural Projects		Multilateral or International Conflict Intervention
			Chinese Official Development Aid

With the study having outlined both the cases of conflict and the factors to be tested, the following chapter presents the results of the QCA.

7. IMPLEMENTATION OF THE QCA

Chapter 7 summarises the results of the QCA on conflicts in the MENA region and in Africa. In chapter 6, four categories of risk factors were presented. They resulted from hypotheses derived from secondary literature and theoretical concepts (see chapter 3). During the QCA these factors were tested empirically on a case-by-case basis. Hence, coding guidelines were established and used to conduct studies of the cases chosen. The following table provides an exemplary illustration of two factors that were included in the QCA. All factors were assigned a code name and two expressions, one and zero. The table furthermore includes the theoretical implications behind the factors as well as data sources..

Table 8: Coding Examples

Condition risk factors QCA-Short name	Coding	Theoretical Consideration	Indicator	Sources of Data
Country Location IR1a LOC_OBOR_LAND	0 = not located along OBOR land route 1 = located along OBOR land route	If a country is located along China's New Silk Road, the PRC might have a strong interest in a peaceful environment and thus be more likely to intervene in conflicts.	Map of One Belt One Road land and maritime routes	Secondary Sources
Resources E1 RE-COURCES	0 = total natural resource rents make up less than 10 per cent of the country's GDP 1 = total natural resource rents make up 10 per cent or more of the country's GDP	To realise the country's investment plans and respond to the nation's demand for energy resources, China needs large amounts of natural resources such as oil and gas but also other minerals. To trade with countries rich in resources, China is interested in a stable political situation in these countries. China would, therefore, rather intervene in such countries than in those with lesser resource wealth.	Total natural resources rents (% of GDP) are higher or lower than the world average in the country in the year of the intervention/non-intervention.	World Bank Data

157

7. IMPLEMENTATION OF THE QCA

7.1. Results of the QCA

The implementation of a Qualitative Comparative Analysis reveals a diversified picture. The aim was to identify a structure of characteristics to cluster China's conflict interventions. Within the QCA, nine conflicts in Africa and the Middle East were considered which began or were ongoing in 2013. The analysis was conducted on the basis of data from the Uppsala Conflict Data Program. Furthermore, twenty-six conditions in fifteen categories were derived from existing research literature (see chapter 6). The conditions were categorised as political, economic, sociocultural, historical, regional and international factors. It was expected that a structure of drivers would be found which characterises conflicts in which China has intervened and thus distinguishes them from other conflicts without Chinese intervention in the regions under consideration.

The QCA, however, did not reveal a coherent picture of Chinese preferences. Political features were very diversified in the countries under consideration. When considering the official Chinese list of countries with which China has signed trade and economic cooperation agreements, investment protection agreements and double taxation relief agreements, the analysis shows that at least one agreement was in place in 2013 in all the cases except South Sudan. This deviation might be explained by the fact that South Sudan only gained independence in 2011.

The regime type of countries was not decisive for China's interventions. Both autocracies (Sudan), democracies (Lebanon, Liberia, Israel) and hybrid regimes (DR Congo, Ivory Coast, Mali, Morocco, South Sudan) were identified by using systemic peace data. The criterion of a civil war within the country of intervention also led to different results. The Chinese need for self-defence did not apply in any of the conflicts since China was not attacked by any of the states under consideration here.

Out of the nine cases, five countries were identified as suffering from civil wars in 2013 (DR Congo, Israel/Palestine, Lebanon, South Sudan, Sudan). Political instability within the cases was also prevalent. World Bank data for governance indicators showed that six countries (DR Congo, Lebanon, Mali, Sudan, South Sudan) were considered politically unstable in 2013. Finally, data from the Global Terrorism Index showed that Lebanon was categorised as a country with high security risks.

As far as economic factors are concerned, China's infrastructural investments in almost all cases were distinctive. China's infrastructural investments cover a range of projects including highways (Morocco, Mali, Ivory Coast, Sudan), hospitals and clinic equipment (Morocco, DR Congo, Mali,

South Sudan, Sudan), the (re-)construction and renovation of ministries (Liberia, Mali, Ivory Coast, Palestine), investments in water supply projects (DR Congo, Ivory Coast), airport construction support (South Sudan), schools (Liberia), bridges (Mali) and investments in the energy sector (Sudan) (Aiddata, 2018).

In addition to infrastructural investments, trade relations were considered in the section on economic factors. Positive Terms of Trade[53] (ToT) for China were found with Israel, Ivory Coast, Lebanon, Liberia, Mali and Morocco, while they were negative with DR Congo, South Sudan and Sudan in 2013. Finally, natural resource rents were considered in the nine cases. The results of the QCA show that four cases had higher natural resource rents as a percentage of GDP than the world average in 2013, namely DR Congo, Liberia, Mali and Sudan.

During the planning of the QCA at hand, additional financial drivers such as the number of Chinese banks operating in conflict-affected countries as well as the possibility of payments with Renminbi were considered. Yet, due to a lack of data, these factors could not be integrated into the operational part of this study during the time frame of this research project and thus remain subject to future research.

In the category of sociocultural and historical aspects, all the countries agreed to resolution 2758 (XXVI) of 1976 and thus accepted the PRC as one representative in the United Nations. The number of Chinese citizens in conflict-affected countries could, unfortunately, not be considered in relation to many cases due to a lack of official data.

Finally, international and regional indicators showed that the geographical locations of conflicts involving Chinese intervention in Africa and the Middle East cannot be found along previous maps of the BRI. The main conflict cases are neither located along the land route, nor the maritime route of China's new Silk Road. A majority of six cases are, however, located along African railways that have been built as flagship projects by the African Union and are intended to form an African Integrated High-Speed Railway Network by 2063 (African Union, 2019).

With reference to regional drivers, the situation in neighbouring countries was looked at. In five cases (DR Congo, Israel/Palestine, Lebanon, South Sudan, Sudan), civil wars were ongoing in bordering countries. Ad-

---

53 Terms of Trade (ToT) consider the relative prices or index of prices of exports and imports to calculate a ratio. If the export prices are higher than the import prices, an economy has a positive ToT and can purchase more imports per unit of export goods.

7. IMPLEMENTATION OF THE QCA

ditionally, conflict involvement by external parties was found in all nine cases, with US bilateral military interference in five conflicts. Multilateral missions by NATO or the EU were found in two cases and related to the EU National Indicative Programme for Mali as well as the EU and NATO assistance for the African Union's mission in Darfur. In all nine cases, China's military involvement was part of a United Nations Peacekeeping Mission. Finally, aid flows from China to the countries under consideration were looked at and found in all countries with the exception of Israel (Aiddata, 2021).

7.1.1. Evidence from the Synchronic Comparison

During the synchronic comparison of the QCA, conflicts in 2013 without Chinese intervention were analysed by applying the same criteria as to the main cases. Soon, it became clear that the synchronic cases displayed very similar distributions among the criteria. As regards political factors, both autocratic, democratic and hybrid regimes were found. All countries had good overall relations with China during their year of conflict. Two countries were affected by civil war, but China did not intervene.

Economically, resource rents were higher than the world average in four of the five cases. ToT were positive for China in one case (Nigeria 2009-today), with data lacking for Iraq (2017). Infrastructural investment projects were found in all cases similar to the main conflicts. With respect to sociocultural and historical factors, all countries in the synchronic comparison agreed to the policy of One China.

Regional and international factors similarly revealed a broad mix of political instability, Chinese aid flows, multilateral conflict involvement and security risks. One country (Iraq) is located along the land route of China's New Silk Road. All three African countries in the synchronic comparison (Central African Republic, Republic of Congo, Nigeria) are considered in the African Union's plan for an extended railroad network.

Yet, the results of one factor reveal a major difference in comparison to the main cases. The presence of a United Nations Peacekeeping Mission could only be found in one of the four synchronic cases. Here, China's troop contributions started shortly after the finalisation of this study. The factor of "UN Mission" was thus identified as a necessary criterion for Chinese military conflict intervention.

7.1.2. Evidence from the Dyachronic Comparison

Seven diachronic cases were analysed additionally. Data constraints affected the criteria on countries' "special relationship" with China, "ToT" as well as political instability, security risks and aid data. In general, less data was found for diachronic cases the longer ago these conflicts occurred.

The diachronic cases did not encompass democracies but four autocracies (DR Congo, Liberia, Mali and Morocco) and three hybrid regime systems (Ivory Coast, Lebanon[54] and Sudan). Chinese self-defence was not the case. Six out of the seven conflicts were classified as civil wars (Lebanon, Morocco, DR Congo, Liberia, Sudan, Ivory Coast).

As far as economic drivers are concerned, three countries had rents from natural resources that were higher than the world average in the year of conflict (Liberia, Mali, Sudan). China invested in infrastructural projects in two countries (Sudan, Ivory Coast). Historically, all countries had agreed to the One-China principle.

With regard to regional and international factors, the distribution was similar to the that found among the synchronic cases. Strikingly, UN missions were initiated in all conflicts of the countries considered in the diachronic comparison. China's contribution to most cases[55], however, only started in 2003 (Ivory Coast). Ever since, China has continuously increased its contributions both in terms of the number of missions as well as the number of troops sent to each mission.

7.1.3. Overall Findings of the QCA

Both the synchronic and the diachronic comparisons showed that conflicts and cases with and without Chinese intervention had very similar patterns. Hard economic factors such as resource wealth or geographical location along China's New Silk Road could not be identified as major drivers for Chinese military intervention. Neither did political and sociocultural factors highlight major differences between conflicts with and without Chinese intervention.

One international factor, however, seemed to be especially relevant for China's decision to engage in military intervention. As shown both in the

---

54 Whilst Lebanon was categorised as a hybrid (anocracy) state until 2006 in the Polity IV Index, this status changed to democratic afterwards.
55 Except for Morocco, where China has been contributing troops since 1991.

7. IMPLEMENTATION OF THE QCA

synchronic and diachronic comparisons, China's interventions before and after 2013 were always conducted within the framework of United Nations peacekeeping missions. Moreover, if we compare the number of troops contributed, a strong increase can be observed over time and throughout the missions (UN Peacekeeping, 2021). In this regard, the need for security for the BRI may be one decisive factor in this development. China's military activities in conflict regions thus seem to be connected to multilateral conflict management within the UN. The diachronic comparison showed that China did not participate in the majority of UN missions that took place in the same countries before 2003. This observation indicates that China's reluctance to embark on conflict intervention was not be determined by a lack of missions but a different attitude towards this international instrument of conflict resolution. With the beginning of the new millennium and China's increasing contributions, this seemed to change. Unexpectedly, China's involvement in international conflict resolution thus seemed to have already increased before the official announcement of the BRI in 2013.

The observation from the operational part of the QCA can thus be concluded as follows: A direct correlation between Chinese military intervention and solely political, economic or sociocultural factors cannot be verified in Africa and the Middle East for the cases under consideration. Rather, the presence of an international peacekeeping mission by the United Nations is identified as the major driver of Chinese participation in conflicts after 2013. UN peacekeeping missions therefore represent a tool of Chinese foreign policy in Africa and the Middle East and enable Chinese military involvement in conflicts.

7.2. Summary of the QCA

In chapter 7, the results of the QCA were presented. Overall, the results showed a large number of solution terms for the different cases. Thus, after the QCA had been conducted, the clear identification of general drivers of Chinese interventions was not yet possible. Evidence from the year 2013 was not enough to gain significant results with regard to a clear Chinese "road map for peace". Hence, the study had to be extended using the method of process tracing, which will be presented in chapter 8. This expansion of the research allowed the consideration of circumstances in the first year of Chinese intervention before 2013. The aim was to find out which factors could be identified at the beginning of the intervention and to identify whether they could lead to general statements about Chinese drivers in addition to the results gained from the QCA. The combination of both methods provides an innovative approach and leads to a better understanding of China's foreign policy in the field of conflict resolution.

8. PROCESS TRACING

Building on the results obtained from the QCA, this chapter presents an overview of the implementation of the process tracing component. In the previous chapter, the QCA provided evidence about whether or not certain factors were met or rejected in conflicts with Chinese intervention. The underlying concept of causality is, however, limited to the simultaneous appearance of a condition and the outcome of a case (Lambach, Johais, & Bayer, 2016, p. 45). The method of process tracing thus helped to discover causally relevant conditions and to distinguish these factors from merely accompanying manifestations. In this regard, each case was evaluated again with a special focus on the first year of China's intervention. The realisation of the method was oriented on the logic of process tracing introduced by Beach and Pedersen (2013). The authors assume that a causal factor and the result are known, while the challenge is to understand the mechanism that leads from condition to outcome (ibid. p. 33ff). Since the exercise of process tracing was based on the QCA already conducted, each case study provided not only a single factor but a solution term consisting of several factors. Whilst Beach and Pederson define the objective of process tracing as a quest for causal mechanisms in a single case, this study combines several single cases in an attempt to establish a superior theory on Chinese interventions (Beach & Pedersen, 2013, p. 75). For this purpose, a multitude of sources was considered for each case such as traditional research literature and contemporary studies from the time of intervention. The number of sources varied between the cases. Whereas rather extensive literature was, for example, available for Sudan and South Sudan, less information was found about the historical circumstances of the conflict in Ivory Coast. By analysing each case in increased depth and in addition to the QCA previously conducted, this study succeeded in establishing a causal model for Chinese military interventions, which will be presented in chapter 10.1. The combination of the QCA and process tracing represents a novel approach to research on China's foreign policy in the field of conflict resolution.

8.1. Analysis of Cases during Process Tracing

8.1. Analysis of Cases during Process Tracing

In the following, each main case of the QCA was analysed in the year of China's intervention. This helped to identify and compare the prevalence of specific factors in the cases. With regard to economic factors, the analysis of the trade volume of imports and exports was extended to a comparison of figures in the respective year of intervention for each case. Only the case of Morocco could not be considered due to a lack of data for 1991. A ranking helped to identify China's most important trading partners in imports and exports in the first year of the PRC's intervention in each respective conflict (2003, 2004, 2006, 2007 and 2013). Two groups of countries were defined based on the classification of the United Nations (UN Department for General Assembly, 2020). One group included all sub-Saharan African states. The second group comprised the countries of North Africa (including Mauritania) and the countries of the Middle East, which were also considered in the QCA. This group, however, differed from the official UN classification, which also covers Asian-Pacific countries. Given the focus on Africa and the Middle East of this study, the group was amended. In this way, the economic importance of each state for China within a region was determined.

8.1.1. Morocco 1991

The conflict in Morocco relates to territorial disputes between the Moroccan government and the people of Western Sahara, who claim that they are not just a southern province of the country but a state in its own right. This conflict has its origins in 1975, when Spain abandoned its colonies in the northwest of Africa (Pabst, 1999, p. 71). With support from Algeria, a liberation movement was established in Western Sahara in 1976. The movement was called *Fente Popular para la Libération de Saguia el Hamra y de Río de Oro* (short: Frente POLISARIO) and proclaimed the Democratic Arab Republic Sahara (SADR) (ibid., p. 71). Subsequently, however, Mauritania and Morocco agreed to divide the land among themselves. When Mauritania gave up its share in 1979, Morocco incrementally occupied the whole territory (Zoubir, 1996, p. 177). Until 1991, a bloody guerrilla war was fought between the POLISARIO Front and Morocco (ibid. p. 177). While about 85 per cent of the Western Sahara territory was taken under the control of the Moroccan government, the remaining 15 per cent remained under the sovereignty of POLISARIO (Boukhars, 2013). In 1991,

8. PROCESS TRACING

after a ceasefire agreement between the two parties, the Security Council voted in favour of resolution 690 and thus adopted the United Nations Mission for the Referendum in Western Sahara (MINURSO) (MINURSO Fact Sheet, 2020). The purpose of MINURSO was to enable a prompt referendum for the people in the territory concerned (MINURSO Fact Sheet, 2020). Yet, due to controversies about the voting lists between Morocco and POLISARIO, the referendum was constantly postponed and has not taken place until today[56] (Theofilopoulou, 2006, p. 2). Until such a referendum takes place, the Resolution ensures Morocco de facto territorial control over two thirds of Western Sahara. The SADR only exists in the outback of the desert at the Mauritanian and Algerian border as well as in Algerian refugee camps near Tindouf (Zoubir, 1996, p. 178). To date, the official border status has not been clarified. Since the beginning of MINURSO, China has contributed personnel in the form of observers and experts. In 2007, Major General Zhao Jingmin was appointed Force Commander (FC) to the Western Sahara, which was the first time China had assumed the lead in a UN mission (OCHA, 2007). From 2016 until 2019, another Chinese, Major General Xiaojun Wang of China was force commander for the mission (MINURSO Fact Sheet, 2020). Yet, Chinese personnel contributions for MINURSO have diminished in numbers since the beginning of China's participation in the mission.

Table 9: Overview of Chinese Contributions to MINURSO

Year	1991	1992	1993	1994	1995	1996	1997	1998	1999
Personnel	20	20	20	20	20	16	16	16	16

2000	2001	2002	2003	2004	2005	2006	2007	2008	2009
16	16	16	19	19	18	14	13	12	10

2010	2011	2012	2013	2014	2015	2016	2017	2018	2019	2020
11	7	7	10	10	10	11	12	13	10	15

Source: (UN Peacekeeping, 2021)

Relations between China and the Sahrawi Arab Democratic Republic (SADR) in Western Sahara began in the 1950s in the context of China's support for national liberation movements in colonised countries (Olimat, 2014, p. 123f). The PRC provided military equipment and political support for the North African states of Algeria, Libya, Tunisia, Morocco and

---

56 July 2021.

Mauretania (ibid. p. 123f). Especially after China's admission to the United Nations in 1971 and until 1978, China's main concern for many African states was to support decolonising movements (Olimat, 2014, p. 123f). By the end of the 1970s, however, China's economic reform period had begun, and Beijing changed the PRC's external focus towards internal economic development questions and growth (Olimat, 2014, p. 124).

Whilst all northern African states had gained their independence at that time, SADR declared its independence only in 1976 (Polisario, 2020). At that time, China was no longer focused on independence movements but interested in establishing an active role for itself within the UN and in international affairs instead (Olimat, 2014, p. 124). Whereas the USA continued to support Morocco, China and also the Soviet Union no longer backed SADR even though POLISARIO had joined the Socialist International (Olimat, 2014, p. 124). China ceased its policy of independence support for SADR and instead committed itself publicly to the UN resolution (Olimat, 2014, p. 125). Moreover, China emphasised its bilateral ties with Morocco, focusing on trade ties and fisheries, natural resources such as oil and gas and minerals which also covered the Sahara region. The urgency of resolving SADR's claims was thus neglected (Olimat, 2014, p. 125f). Apart from China's economic ambitions being in competition with other prospective customers in Morocco such as India or Australia, another aspect appears relevant for China's reluctance to accept POLISARIO's demands. The PRC's open support for a referendum could have had the potential to be understood as motivation for several Chinese provinces and their independence efforts, such those as in Tibet Xinjiang or Tibet (Olimat, 2014, p. 126). China therefore stuck to its principle of territorial integrity while deepening trade negotiations with Morocco and Mauritania. Yet, China had to appease its long-term ally Algeria, where a large community of Sahrawis had settled (ibid. p. 126). In addition, China's interest in the exploitation of natural resources met with less resistance concerning judicial and environmental questions from the Moroccan government than from Algeria or SADR (ibid. p. 126). The SADR government furthermore strongly promoted values such as human rights, democracy and pluralism which have never been priorities for Beijing (SADR, 1999, p. 2). The uncertainty about POLISARIO's future political policies and the leader's orientation towards Europe offers another explanation for China's lacking support (Olimat, 2014, p. 126). Moreover, in light of China's admission to the UN, reputational threats and opportunities at the beginning of the PRC's membership also played a role in China's participation in MINURSO.

8. PROCESS TRACING

With regard to research and literature on Sino-Moroccan relations, a range of journal articles can be found. In 2015, the African Research Bulletin included an overview of trade agreements between Morocco and China (Africa Research Bulletin, 2015, p. 20624C). Strikingly, in November 2014, over 30 such agreements and memorandums of understanding had been signed, particularly in sectors such as energy, tourism and finance (ibid., p. 20624C). In 2016, the Fondation pour la Recherche Stratégique published a note on *The economic presence of China in the Maghreb: Ambitions and limits* focusing on investment and business relations (Lafarge, 2016). In 2019, the ChinaMed Report was published by Enrico Fardella and Andrea Ghiselli to answer the question of what effects China's growing role is having on the Mediterranean region (Fardella & Ghiselli, 2019, p. I). In the same year, the Brookings Doha Centre published a policy briefing on *China's Growing Footprint in North Africa*, outlining China's engagement in the Maghreb region as a cross section between Africa and the Mediterranean (Ghafar & Jacobs, 2019). Finally, a 2020 Chatham House report covers expanding Sino–Maghreb relations with a focus on Morocco and Tunisia (Zoubir, 2020). The authors observe that China's interest in the Maghreb region has risen since the launch of the BRI and particularly focuses on the widening of construction and infrastructure projects (ibid., p. 2). In addition, they argue that by opening Confucius Institutes, China is trying to promote its culture and language in a region with otherwise rather scant knowledge about China (ibid., p. 24).

8.1.2. DR Congo 2003

In DR Congo two eastern provinces called North Kivu and South Kivu have been affected by several conflicts in the past (Stearns, 2012, p. 27). Approximately 1.2 million Hutu fled to neighbouring DR Congo in response to the 1994 genocide in Rwanda (MONUC Peacekeeping, 2010). Many of them had taken part in the genocide and now arrived in the eastern parts of DR Congo, formerly known as Zaïre, where mostly Tutsis lived (ibid.). Some of the new arrivals soon began to attack DR Congo's Tutsi population. Ethnic tensions escalated and led to the mass displacement of both Hutu and Tutsi people. While the Tutsi mostly fled to Rwanda, Hutus also arrived in Uganda (Lange, 2010, p. 48). During a rebellion in 1996, the Tutsi leader Laurent Désiré Kabila was supported by Rwandan and Ugandan forces and conquered the capital city of Kinshasa to become President (MONUC Peacekeeping, 2010). Yet, in 1998 Hutu militia started an uprising against Kabila in the eastern parts of the country, where they received support for their so-called Congolese Rally for Democracy from Rwanda and Uganda (ibid.). Kabila, however, was militarily supported by Angola, Chad, Namibia and Zimbabwe (ibid.).

Since the outbreak of the First Congo War in 1996, about 70 different rebel groups have been established (ibid., p. 27). Ongoing rivalry between several rebel groups provoked the Second Congo War, which has become known as one of the deadliest wars in modern African history and lasted from 1998 to 2003 (Stearns, 2012, p. 32). Rebels tried to overthrow the government in Kinshasa, which had only been in power since 1997, when the First Congo War ended (ibid., p. 32). During the Second Congo War, various fighting groups recruited their fighters along ethnic lines and were supported by local chiefs (ibid., p. 34). The Second Congo War ended when an agreement was reached during an Inter-Congolese Dialogue that marked the beginning of national unification. Moreover, external military forces from Rwanda and Uganda left the country (ibid., p. 35). However, the accord enabled a rebel group called *Mouvement du 23 Mars* (M23) to keep its command structure intact (Stearns, 2012, p. 36). Although an armistice agreement has been in place since 2003, most rebel groups in these two regions have remained active (UN MONUC, 2010). While different parties in the conflict put forward ethic reasons for their interference, their involvement was largely considered a proxy war, with the real interest being the exploitation of DR Congo's large natural resources (Jacquemot, 2010, p. 6). The discovery of minerals such as coltan, which can be used in the electronic industry, and gold was another reason why different militias and armies fought for power over mining sites (ibid., p. 6). Both national and international actors have remained in competition to gain control over mining facilities. Local groups especially often employ violence in their fights and aim to control territories that are rich in resources (Lyall, 2017). Paul Collier was the first researcher to draw a link between the outbreak of civil wars and a country's reliance on primary resources, of which DR Congo served as an example (Collier, 2011).

Throughout the past conflicts in DR Congo, the UN introduced missions to support the country's peace processes. As early as in 1999, the UN Security Council adopted Resolution 1279 and initiated a mission in the Democratic Republic of the Congo (MONUC) (UN MONUC, 2010). The mission's objective encompassed an observation plan on a ceasefire agreement (ibid.). In 2010, the United Nations Security Council adopted resolution 1925 and established the United Nations Organization Stabilization Mission in the Democratic Republic of the Congo MONUSCO,

8. PROCESS TRACING

which replaced MONUC (MONUSCO Fact Sheet, 2010)[57]. The new mission aimed at the protection of civilians and humanitarian personnel and at defending human rights. In addition, the government of the Democratic Republic of Congo was to be supported in its efforts to stabilise the country and promote peace and security (ibid.). Compared to other missions, China has contributed large numbers of personnel to both MONUC and MONUSCO over the years (see tables 10 and 11).

Table 10: Chinese Contributions to MONUC

Year	2003	2004	2005	2006	2007	2008	2009
Personnel	230	230	230	230	234	234	234

Table 11: Chinese Contributions to MONUSCO

Year	2010	2011	2012	2013	2014	2015	2016	2017	2018	2019	2020
Personnel	234	234	233	234	231	232	230	229	231	226	230

Source: (UN Peacekeeping, 2021)

The Second Congo War is often referred to as Africa's World War and was subject to an investigation report by the UN Security Council in 2002 which concentrated on the topic of illegal resource exploitation in DR Congo (UN Security Council Report, 2002). The investigation identified transit points for the illegally exploited resources in eleven African countries (ibid.). Moreover, a list of 85 international companies was published, which were accused of violating OECD principles for multilateral corporations. Most of the companies cited were part of the mining sector and originated predominantly from Belgium, Great Britain, the USA, South Africa, Canada, Germany, Zimbabwe, Switzerland, Finland and France (Putzel, et al., 2011, p. 4). With regard to Asian companies, China, Hong Kong, Malaysia and Thailand were listed (ibid. p. 4).

While formal industrial mining used to be dominated by the state-owned *Générale des Carrières et Mines* (Gécamines) commodity trading and mining company, the sector has been liberalised since 2002. Although Gécamines still holds most of the concession titles, the Mining Regulations of 2003 reformed the mining sector by both allowing new private actors to enter the market and introducing guidelines for granting land and taking into account social and environmental impacts (Constituent

---

[57] The French acronym for Mission de l'Organisation des Nations Unies pour la Stabilisation en République Démocratique du Congo.

and Legislative Assembly DR Congo, 2002; Government of the DR Congo, 2003).

Since 2003, China has officially supported the so-called Kimberley Process[58] to prevent illegal trading in rough diamonds in mostly African conflicts (UN Security Council Report, 2002, p. 27). However, a study by the UK-based organisation Rights and Accountability in Development (RAID) in the Congolese province of Katanga unveiled activities by Chinese companies both in the formal and informal mining sectors (Goethals, Okenda, & Mbaya, 2009, p. 20). During the war and in the transition time that followed until 2006, informal middlemen would buy minerals directly from artisanal miners and transfer them to Zambia for further manufacturing (ibid. p. 20). While Western countries dominated the import of coltan from DR Congo during the 1990s, they had been replaced in direct imports by China and other Asian countries by 2000 (Bleischwitz, Dittrich, & Pierdicca, 2012, p. 13). This development was accompanied by an overall increase in trade between China and African countries mostly rich in resources (UNCTAD, 2010). Between 2000 and 2009, the value of China's total imports of African ores and minerals rose from USD 350 million to USD 7 billion per year (Putzel, et al., 2011, p. 14). In this regard, the biggest quantities were exported from Congo Basin countries (ibid. p. 14). By 2009, China had become the number one importer of coltan from DR Congo (Global Witness, 2010, p. 15). As regards the resources of tantalum and niobium, China's direct imports from DR Congo rose from 435 tons in 2000 to 3,154 tons in 2009 (Bleischwitz, Dittrich, & Pierdicca, 2012, p. 13). Direct imports from Rwanda were, however, even greater, which may be explained by extended smuggling routes from DR Congo to Rwanda (Global Witness, 2010, p. 12). While coltan prices increased in DR Congo, they remained constantly low in Rwanda, which may have served as an incentive for transfers from DR Congo before the coltan was shipped to its destination countries (Molintas, 2013, p. 10f).

The year 2003 was decisive in two ways. First, the Security Council approved Resolution 1457, which renewed a mandate for a panel of experts to investigate the issue of illegal exploitation of natural resources and other forms of wealth in the DR Congo (UN Security Council Resolution 1457, 2003). The panel published its report in October that same year, highlighting the extent of illegal exploitation in the context of the conflict, particularly the trade in small and light weapons (UN Security Council

---

58 The Kimberley Process is a complex system designed to prevent trade in so-called blood diamonds through government certificates of origin.

Report 1027, 2003). Second, the year 2003 saw an upswing in the bilateral relations between DR Congo and Uganda when the two countries started to discuss the implementation of the so-called Luanda Accord, which they had signed in 2002 to normalise their bilateral relations and implement a ceasefire (Alusala, 2004, p. 94).

While the role of resources had played a major role in previous conflicts in DR Congo, the control over their main extraction sites has continued to cause hostilities between different rebel groups, which provoked calls for an extension of the MONUC mandate (Alusala, 2004, p. 94). As a result, MONUC was updated to a Chapter VII mandate of the UN Charter, which allowed peacekeepers to use force when necessary. At the same time, the mission's strength was increased from 8,126 blue helmets in August to 10,649 blue helmets in December 2003 (Alusala, 2004; UN Peacekeeping, 2020). China had started its personnel support for MUNOC in January 2003 with 10 observers and troops and extended its contribution to 230 by the end of that year (UN Peacekeeping, 2020). In light of the Kimberley Process, the factor of reputational threats can be considered a major driver of China's contributions to the UN mission in DR Congo.

In previous literature on relations between China and the DR Congo, several studies already focus on China's quest for resources in the African country. A report by Global Witness in 2011 addresses the so-called "deal of the century", which was signed between the two countries in 2007 with a value that exceeded DR Congo's state budget (Global Witness, 2011, p. 4). In exchange for access to copper and cobalt mines, China promised to finance the construction of projects relating to transportation infrastructure, hospitals, schools and dams (ibid., p. 9). While the deal was promoted as a win-win agreement, Global Witness claims that its conditions were opaque and the actual benefit for the Congolese state unclear (ibid., p. 21). An overview of this win-win relationship between China and the DR Congo is also provided by Claude Karemba (2016). Karemba argues that the established commercial relations are beneficial to both parties, yet lacking state structures risk this fragile African country collapsing again (Karemba, 2016, p. 83). A stable state is thus necessary to preserve the large infrastructural investments and allow them to become a win-win result (ibid., p. 78f). While China promotes its engagement as being non-political and keeping out of internal political affairs, state-building shortcomings may risk the infrastructural developments achieved (ibid., p.83).

8.1.3. Liberia 2003

After the electoral success of Charles Taylor in 1997, the US supported the new Liberian President, who won 75 per cent of the seats in parliament and was thus able to rule with an uncontested majority (Kamara, 2003, p. 1). The election was, however, marked by a discussion about human rights violations and previous war crimes (ibid. p. 1). Moreover, the situation of about 700,000 refugees as well as 1.4 million internally displaced people resulting from the war remained a challenge for the newly elected leader (ibid. p. 1). Taylor had been supported by Libya's president Muammar Al-Gaddafi, who trained and armed Taylor's movement to oust the former Liberian president Samuel Doe, whom he considered a "Western puppet" (International Crisis Group (ICG), 2002, p. 1). Taylor instrumentalised the election process to justify further abuses. With his majority, he excluded any possibility of state institutions with checks and balances, which would have been necessary to restore a judicial system after years of war. However, Taylor's new power marked the beginning of a recurring pattern in the international assessment of events in Liberia (Kamara, 2003, p. 1). The international community's support for Taylor's election campaign was inter alia motivated by the effort to enable a rapid restart for the country (ibid., p. 1). The United Nations as well as the African Union therefore silently observed Taylor's rise (Anderson, 1998). The haste in finding and promoting a face-saving end to years of bloody wars in many African states also characterised Liberia's situation in 2003 (Kamara, 2003, p. 1f). Taylor, in turn, contributed troops to peacekeeping missions to ensure regional stability (ibid. p. 1). Yet, he upheld his network of rebels in neighbouring Sierra Leone to ensure his personal security and survival (ibid., p. 1). In doing so, Taylor upheld the breeding ground for a return to war, while preventing the creation of an environment of reconciliation and peace-building (ibid., p. 2). At the same time, this behaviour was an expression of the mistrust he had for the different groups within the Liberian population (ibid., p. 1). Indeed, violence soon returned after Taylor's election. The killing of an opposition politician and his family marked the start of the government's attack on villages of the ethnic group of the Krahns (Kamara, 2003, p. 2). Many fled to neighbouring countries such as Ivory Coast (ibid. p. 2). Additionally, the ethnic group of the Mandingos, who traditionally had their roots in Guinea, were attacked and deprived of their homes (ibid. p. 2). While Taylor blamed the US and Great Britain for the conflict outbreaks, Guinea prepared for vengeance against Liberia, which resulted in killings and fighting (ibid. p. 2).

8. PROCESS TRACING

In the year 2000, after the kidnapping of 500 UN soldiers of UNOMIL, which had been in place since 1993 to observe a former Cotonou peace agreement, the Security Council imposed a travel ban on Taylor and implemented an arms embargo (Kamara, 2003, p. 5; United Nations UNMIL, 2018). In this regard, the Security Council also considered the smuggling of weapons and diamonds with links to terrorist groups such as Al-Qaeda (Kamara, 2003, p. 4).

In 2003, Moses Blah became President of Liberia, and a comprehensive Peace Agreement was signed with the rebels (Gerdes, 2013, p. 172). The very same year, the United Nations Security Council voted in favour of resolution 1509 to support the ceasefire agreement and accompany a peace process that had been established by the conflicting parties. With progress being made, the Security Council adopted Resolution 2239 in September 2015, stating that security responsibilities had been handed over to the Liberian government. UNMIL was deployed in March 2018 (United Nations, UNMIL Factsheet, 2018).

Table 12: Chinese Contributions to UNMIL

Year	2003	2004	2005	2006	2007	2008	2009	2010	2011
Personnel	77	597	595	593	581	569	582	584	583

2012	2013	2014	2015	2016	2017	2018
587	729	721	667	271	142	Mission Completed

Source: (UN Peacekeeping, 2021)

The Liberian civil war as well as its aftermath were marked by many factioned rebel movements and governmental cross-border support for various ethnic groups (Kamara, 2003, p. 8). Finally, in 2003, combined pressure from the international community and the Economic Community of West African States (ECOWAS) forced Taylor to resign (Moumouni, 2014, p. 5). Subsequently, a two-year transitional period paved the way for elections in 2005 (ibid. p. 5). With the new president Ellen Johnson-Sirelaf, a period of stability began, including the first approaches towards national rejuvenation (ibid. p. 5). The new political leadership in Liberia had significant meaning for Beijing and gave China a relevant role in Liberia's post-war reconstruction. Until 2005, Liberia's ties with the PRC were characterised by it switching between recognition of China and Taiwan (Moumouni, 2014, p. 6). China's diplomatic relations with any state were

8.1. Analysis of Cases during Process Tracing

conditional upon the state's non-recognition of Taiwan. In the case of Liberia, this has changed several times in the country's past, starting with a twenty-year relationship with Taipei (ibid. p. 6). In 1977, however, Liberia approached the PRC, only to abandon Beijing again in 1989 (ibid. p. 6). Diplomatic relations were restored with Beijing, but when Taylor tried to revive relations with Taipei simultaneously, Beijing inflicted the respective consequences (ibid. p. 6). In 2003, however, the Joint Declaration and Memorandum of Understanding was signed in Liberia's capital Monrovia, which included the recognition of China (ibid. p. 6). This decision was reinforced by Resolution 001, which was passed by the Liberian Senate and House of Representatives in 2005 (ibid. p. 6). China's membership as one of the P5 in the UN Security Council was a decisive factor in Liberia's decision in favour of Beijing (Moumouni, 2014, p. 6). After the recognition of the One-China principle, Liberia had gained an ally in voting for the UN resolutions it needed to restore peace and security in Liberia (ibid.). Additionally, China's ambitions for economic investments and increasing development aid presented attractive opportunities to Monrovia (ibid. p. 6).

From Beijing's perspective, China's socio-economic development offered additional resources in the form of human and financial capital as well as materials that could be used for peacekeeping missions at the beginning of the 2000s (Moumouni, 2014, p. 7). In 2001, the terrorist attack on New York's World Trade Centre may additionally have illustrated the need for a common strategy against terrorism within the international community (ibid. p. 7). In September 2003, China thus voted in favour of the UNSC Resolution 1509 on the situation in Liberia (UNSCR, 2020). Beijing already deployed its first troops in November 2003 (Moumouni, 2014, p. 8). China's UNMIL presence was, however, not only limited to its military contribution to the mission. Examples were the construction of hospitals and roads which were provided for both the population but also for wounded UN soldiers and illustrate China's holistic approach to the mission (Kaure, 2006, p. 34f).

With regard to research literature, a 2008 report by Benner & Blume summarises the legacies of Liberia's eleven years of civil war. While outlining the country's "poisoned legacy" of political culture and security challenges, Liberia's natural richness is seen as an opportunity for economic reconstruction and as an appeal to external actors such as China (Benner & Blume, 2008, p. 40).

Additionally, a comprehensive summary of China's engagement in Liberia since 2003 is provided by Guillaume Moumouni (2014). The author makes Liberia's "win" dependent on China's support within UNMIL as well as China's diplomatic efforts to lift sanctions on diamond mining and timber trade (Moumouni, 2014, p. 19). In addition, China's technical assistance and contribution to infrastructure investments are mentioned. Moreover, China's "win" resulted from Liberia's approval of the One-China principle in 2005 as well as the advantages of trade and the development of an export market (ibid., p.11; 19).

8.1.4. Ivory Coast 2004

Since gaining independence from France in the 1960s, Ivory Coast has developed as one of Africa's leading economic powers. Especially in the production of cocoa and coffee, the country has attracted international companies and foreign investment (World Peace Foundation, 2017). Due to its economic strength, the country has also attracted many migrants, which led to political movements against foreigners during a period of political instability in 1993 (ibid., p. 1f). In 2002, a coup d'état resulted in another political crisis, the displacement of up to one million people and violence against civilians (ibid. p. 1). Due to its colonial history, Ivory Coast has retained close relations with France, which assumed a leading role in establishing a peacekeeping mission within the United Nations (World Peace Foundation, 2017).

The complex causes of the conflict's outbreak in Ivory Coast date back to colonial times and historical migration in the region (Werthmann, 2005, p. 221). The conflict led to a geographical division of the country into the North and South. The North was controlled by rebels and a Muslim majority, while the South remained government-controlled and predominantly Christian (Werthmann, 2005, p. 228). Since the introduction of a national ideology of Ivoirité in 1995, members of the Northern ethnic group called Dioula faced discrimination and exclusion. Due to their origins from Mali, Burkina Faso and Guinea, they were accused of not being true Ivorians (Crook, 1997, p. 222; Ogwang, 2011, p. 4). Shortly after the outbreak of the conflict, Ivory Coast's politicians turned to France for logistical support (Global Security, 2002). Additionally, ECOWAS sent a delegation to Abijan in an attempt to negotiate a cease-fire (ibid.). After a peace agreement had been signed in 2003, a UN mission was established in 2004 to facilitate its implementation (UNOCI Fact Sheet, 2004).

China joined the UN mission in 2004, thus extending its security-related activities in the country only shortly after the PRC had begun a consider-

8.1. Analysis of Cases during Process Tracing

able increase in economic exchanges with several African states, among them Ivory Coast (Sahui, 2018, p. 924). Since 2000, Chinese projects and the number of Chinese companies within Ivory Coast have constantly increased (ibid., p. 925). In this regard, the year 2003 stands out since it marked the beginning of a constant increase in imports from China until 2013, when a peak was reached (ibid. p. 925). While imports from China accelerated in terms of mass and volume, exports from Ivory Coast to China stayed roughly the same in this time period (ibid. p. 925). Throughout 2002 and 2010, a time of major crisis in the country's history, the volume of trade between China and Ivory coast constantly increased (Auregan, 2011). China, furthermore, began to explore oil sources in Ivory Coast and signed its first deals in 2004 (Hurst, 2006, p. 6).

In February 2004, the UN Security Council voted in favour of Resolution 1528 and established the UN Operation in Côte d'Ivoire (UNOCI) (UNOCI Fact Sheet, 2004). The aim of the mission was to support the implementation of a peace agreement signed between different parties from Ivory Coast in 2003 (ibid.). In 2010, however, a political crisis followed the presidential election, and UNOCI was used to protect civilians and facilitate the government's efforts to disarm, demobilise and reintegrate (DDR) former combatants (ibid.). After a decision of the Security Council in 2016, UNOCI was ended the subsequent year. Until the completion of the UN mission in 2017, however, Chinese personnel contributions remained below ten staff members per year. As one of the smallest Chinese staff contributions compared to other UN missions, UNOCI was also one of the less dangerous ones, aiming at the disarmament, demobilisation and reintegration of armed groups. As such, UNOCI provided an opportunity for China to display and increase its reputation as a "guardian of peace" in the face of relatively lower security threats than in other missions.

Table 13: Chinese Contributions to UNOCI

Year	2004	2005	2006	2007	2008	2009	2010	2011
Personnel	3	7	7	7	7	7	6	6

2012	2013	2014	2015	2016	2017
6	6	6	6	3	Mission Completed

Source: (UN Peacekeeping, 2021)

In previous literature on the relationship between Ivory Coast and China, the historical development of their bilateral relations is covered with a recent focus on the BRI. In 2017, Gamassa and Chen investigated the impact of OBOR on the development of Abijan Port. The authors found out that the port has become an important entry point for Chinese goods, not only for Ivory Coast but also for neighbouring countries in the hinterland (Gamassa & Chen, 2017, p. 147). In 2018, Magby Henri Joel Regis Sahui furthermore provided an analysis of bilateral trade during the 20-year period between 1995 and 2015 (Sahui, 2018). The author identified a large trade deficit on the part of Ivory Coast due to much larger exports from China to the African country than vice versa (Sahui, 2018, p. 936). In 2019, Kadidiatou and Baolong contributed a report on the impact of China's investments as part of the OBOR Initiative on the agricultural sector in Ivory Coast (Kadidiatou & Baolong, 2019). The authors found that agricultural investments had a positive effect and predicted an increase in people engaged in the agricultural sector (Kadidiatou & Baolong, 2019, p. 31).

8.1.5. Lebanon 2006

Tensions between Lebanon and neighbouring Israel escalated in 2006 when a 34-day conflict erupted and transformed the local conflict between Palestinians in the Gaza Strip and Israel into a regional crisis (Fontana, 2010, p. 3). In this regard, Hezbollah played a significant role. After the kidnapping of two Israeli soldiers by Hezbollah, for which Israel made the whole Lebanese government responsible, Israel responded with artillery fire on Lebanon, which destroyed and damaged many roads and other infrastructure such as Beirut airport.

The hostilities between Lebanon and Israel began on July 12, 2006 and ended on August 14, 2006 in light of a ceasefire agreed upon in UNSC Resolution 1701 (UNEP, 2007, p. 10). Despite the relatively short duration of the conflict, severe damage was reported. Almost 1,200 people were killed and over 4,400 injured. Additionally, more than 900,000 people became displaced due to widespread destruction of about 30,000 houses, roads and other infrastructure (ibid. p. 10).

On August 11, 2006, the UN Security Council, therefore, extended UNIFIL to Lebanon. This was remarkable since the mission was originally initiated as an observer mission to confirm the retreat of Israeli troops from Lebanese territory after the Israeli invasion in spring 1978 (UNIFIL, 2019). In contrast to the resolution of 1978, the 2006 extension was now based on Chapter VII of the UN Charter. The mission, therefore, became an armed blue helmet mission, which meant that UN troops became entitled to implement their mandate with force under Article 42 of the

8.1. Analysis of Cases during Process Tracing

Charter (UN Resolution 1701, 2006). The mission's size was furthermore extended to a maximum of 15,000 troops.

One year after the start of UNIFIL, another internal conflict emerged and 2007 marked a year of conflict in Lebanon. In May 2007, the Lebanese Armed Forces (LAF) and a hitherto unknown Islamist fundamentalist group called Fatah al-Islam clashed inside the UN-led refugee camp Nahr al-Bared in northern Lebanon (International Crisis Group , 2012). The camp was founded in 1949 to host Palestinian refugees in an area of about 200,000m² (Halkort, 2013). The area was rented by the United Nations Relief and Works Agency for Palestine Refugees in the Near East (UNRWA) and soon became too small to host subsequent generations of refugees (ibid.). Never really welcome in Lebanon, Palestinians also never had a legitimate body to represent their interests and were categorised as foreigners in Lebanon (International Crisis Group , 2012).

Despite long-existing tensions, the event that triggered the hostilities occurred unexpectedly on May 19, 2017. A group of armed Fatah al-Islam members robbed a bank, whereupon Lebanon's prime minister sent Lebanon's internal security forces to defeat the group (Refugee Review Tribunal, 2009). Prime Minister Siniora, however, did not inform the Lebanese army of his actions, which resulted in Lebanese soldiers being exposed to brutal revenge by Fatah al-Islam members outside Nahr al-Bared camp (ibid. p. 2). Pictures of fatally wounded soldiers led to broad backing for a governmental reaction against the camp among the public. Subsequently, Lebanese forces stormed the camp, which the government had stayed out of since 1969. During the hostilities in 2007, however, much of the camp was destroyed or damaged and many of the 40,000 refugees were forced to flee their homes (ibid. p. 2). Rising Islamist movements such as Fateh al-Islam in the Nahr al-Bared camp and continuing violence remained a challenge to the Lebanese army (Abdel-Latif, 2008, p. 1). Due to increasing unemployment and a lack of basic services and prospects, particularly for young men in the northern areas, several militant groups, which pose an increasing security challenge to the country and the whole region, have emerged (Abdel-Latif, 2008, p. 21). Moreover, to defend their existence, Islamist movements refer to regional and international developments and rise up against what they frame as "aggression" against Muslims (ibid., p. 21).

Aside from the triangular rivalries between actors in the Gaza Strip, Israel and South Lebanon, the situation had long become internationally relevant. The USA and Great Britain interfered by supporting Israel and Syria, while Iran kept bolstering Hezbollah (Fontana, 2010, p. 3). In this

8. PROCESS TRACING

context, the mandate of UNIFIL covered several tasks such as support for Lebanese forces in securing their borders and demilitarising militant groups in the South (UNIFIL, 2019). Furthermore, Israel was asked to withdraw from Lebanon and humanitarian access was to be ensured (ibid.). In 2006, the mission was supported by 11,563 troops from twenty-six countries (UN Peacekeeping, 2020). From April 2006 onwards, China participated in the United Nations Interim Force in Lebanon (Ibid.). In 2018, the PRC was among the top ten contributors to the mission. The underlying aim of the mission was to restore peace and security in the region after Israel's withdrawal from the South Lebanon conflict, also known as Operation Litani (UNIFIL, United Nations Peacekeeping, 2018). The incident had its roots in the long-running conflict between Israel and Palestine. After 1968, the Popular Front of the Liberation of Palestine (PLO) united with other Palestinian groups to create a quasi-state in the south of Lebanon. After the Jordanian Civil War of 1970 and 1971, a large number of PLO fighters came to southern Lebanon, where they were attacked by Israel (Gurses, 2014).

In 1978, the UN Security Council installed UNIFIL to support the Lebanese government in regaining effective control over the state's territory. In 2006, fighting between the Lebanese party Hezbollah and Israel resulted in the Lebanon War, which lasted one month (Tür, 2006, p. 109). Subsequently, UNIFIL had to be adapted and has since then been in place to monitor the cessation of violent fighting and hostilities. Additionally, Lebanese armed forces have been supported, and internally displaced people have been accompanied in returning to their homes (UNIFIL, 2018).

As of December 2020, China's contribution to the mission consisted of 419 peacekeepers and was the 9th largest compared to all contributing members. The overview of China's troop contributions since 2006 shows an overall rise in numbers for the mission—especially in 2015.

Table 14: Chinese Contributions to UNIFIL

Year	2006	2007	2008	2009	2010	2011	2012
Troops	190	343	343	344	342	344	343

2013	2014	2015	2016	2017	2018	2019	2020
343	218	418	418	418	418	410	419

Source: (UN Peacekeeping, 2021)

China's attitude and behaviour towards the Lebanese–Israeli conflict followed a pattern that displays typical patterns in Beijing's behaviour. If asso-

8.1. Analysis of Cases during Process Tracing

ciates of the PRC were involved in the dispute, China preferred to distance itself from the conflict area (Shichor, 2006). Instead, Beijing advised fast and peaceful internal settlement of the conflict by the parties to avoid implications for Beijing's economic interests (ibid.). In the early 2000s, China was even reluctant to support external interventions by the United Nations since it would probably have provoked international calls for Chinese participation and therefore a need for Beijing to position itself (Shichor, 2006). In his analysis of the Chinese–Lebanese relationship in 2006, political scientist Yitzhak Shichor presents two levels of China's approach to the conflict: A local–particularistic micro-level and a global–universalistic macro-level (ibid.).

On the micro-level, China continued a balancing act between the parties involved. While condemning the Hezbollah kidnapping of Israeli soldiers, it also criticised the Israeli violation of Lebanon's sovereignty (Shichor, 2006). Yet, the hostilities did not spare UN facilities in Lebanon. Missiles launched by both Hezbollah and Israel hit buildings and shelters of UN personnel, killing four UN troops including one Chinese observer serving in the United Nations Truce Supervision Organization (United Nations Press Release, 2007). Moreover, Chinese UNIFIL and other soldiers were wounded and the Chinese contingent headquarters damaged (ibid.). China, however, had to provide an explanation when some of the missiles used in the conflict were identified as having been produced in China. Hezbollah, for example, used Chinese-made C-802 or Yingji-8 (82) (Shichor, 2006; U.S.-China Economic and Security Review Commission, 2006, p. 92). While China had not provided Hezbollah with arms, Iran was a major buyer of Chinese weapons (Gill, 1998, p. 355). To what extent China knew about the Iranian–Hezbollah cooperation is questionable. Intended Chinese support for the group was rather unlikely since the group was internationally classified as a terrorist organisation. Moreover, since 1997 China had been confronted with domestic terror by a group called the Eastern Turkistan Islamic Movement (ETIM). The ETIM, also known as East Turkistan Islamic Hezbollah, spread in the Chinese region of Xinjiang and was connected to the Lebanese branch of the organisation (Shichor, 2006; TRAC, 2020). Nevertheless, it is unlikely that China was completely unconscious of the Iranian–Hezbollah relationship since Chinese arms provisions were not sold to the Iranian Army but to the Islamic Revolutionary Guard, which traditionally had close ties with Hezbollah (Shichor, 2006). Additionally, China's ambassador to Iran from 2003–2007, who is considered to be one of China's specialists on the Middle East, had been China's ambassador to Lebanon from 1999 to 2002 (Shichor, 2011, p. 109).

8. PROCESS TRACING

It can thus be assumed that at least some intelligence was provided to the Chinese government.

Apart from local circumstances, China also regarded the broader context of the conflict by considering interests on a macro-level as a quest for hegemony in the region between Iran, Syria and Israel supported by the USA (Shichor, 2006). On July 24, 2006, a comment on the online news page of People's Daily stated:

> "Israel wants precisely to thwart with its heavy strikes the intention of Hezbollah to coordinate Hamas and come to the aid of Syria and Iran by coordinated actions, and its consideration has won the support of the United States, which also likes Israel to deal effective blows at Hezbollah" (People's Daily, 2006).

China thus recognised the interests of the different players in the region. However, after the loss of one Chinese troop member, opposing views on the conflict became obvious between China and the USA. While the US government tried to prevent a UN Security Council Resolution that would condemn Israeli attacks on UN entities, China's UN Ambassador Wang Guangya was quoted on July 28, 2006 as saying that a strong signal by the UN was necessary to assure seriousness concerning "the protection of our peacekeepers" (China Daily, 2006). In the view of political scientist Shichor, the Lebanon case illustrated that neither China nor the USA, despite being superpowers, were able to handle and end the conflict. In 2006, the PRC seemed not (yet) ready to appear and perform as a responsible stakeholder in the Middle East (Shichor, 2006).

Yet, apart from China's involvement in the Lebanese conflict in summer 2006, China's ambitions to raise its voice within the international community had been underlined in May 2006 when the PRC was elected a member of the newly found UN Human Rights Council (Kinzelbach, 2013, p. 59). With 146 votes in favour, the PRC thus became a founding member of the Council (ibid. p. 59).

In previous literature covering the relationship between China and Lebanon, a dialogue by Jiemian, Gemayel and Suleiman provides an analysis of a new era of Chinese–Arab and in particular Chinese–Lebanese relations since President Xi Jinping's visit in 2016 (Jiemian, Gemayel, & Suleiman, 2016, p. 421). China's Arab Policy Paper of 2016, furthermore, paved the way for new bilateral relationships between China and Arab countries such as Lebanon (Ministry of Foreign Affairs of the PRC, 2016). David Perez-Des Rosiers (2019) provided a comparative analysis of China's relations with Syria and Lebanon and found that the instability of both countries poses a major challenge to China in particular with regard to their geostrategic position for the infrastructural needs of the BRI (Perez-Des Rosiers, 2019). The European Council on Foreign Relations (2019) concluded, however, that China's military campaigns in sectarian conflicts between Sunni, Shi'ites and Maronites in Lebanon remained minimal and could be considered "[...] merely a gesture of goodwill" (Lons, Fulton, Sun, & Al-Tamimi, 2019, p. 20).

8.1.6. Sudan 2007

The crisis in Darfur, the western part of Sudan began in 2003 when the non-Arab African majority attacked the minority of Arab Africans in the region (Brosché, 2008) (Dagne, 2004, pp. 1-4). Their claim was that the government discriminated against African and Arab ethnic groups in the region (ibid. pp. 1-4). In addition, the conflict relates to control over resources in the region since Arab nomadic groups often enter territories of farmers in Darfur to graze and water their cattle (ibid. pp. 1-4). Violence had also spilled over to the neighbouring countries Chad, Libya and the Central African Republic (ibid.). While the Sudanese government tried to calm the riots, the uprising periodically escalated. In essence, many of both the Arab and non-Arab participants in the conflict were Muslims, which indicates that the causes of the conflict are more ethnic than religious (ibid. Pp. 1-4).

Numerous actors were and are still involved in the conflict. Since the beginning, the Sudanese government supported the so-called Janjaweed militia, which consists of local Arab tribes (Mullins & Rothe, 2017, p. 143). On the opposite side, the Justice and Equality Movement and the Sudanese Liberation Movement have become the most prominent rebel groups. They are closely connected to other tribes such as the non-Arab African Fur, the Zaghawa or the Masalit, who have dominated and lived in the Darfur region for a long time (Brosché, 2008, p. 109).

While violence occurred on all sides of the conflict, Janjaweed militias became popular due to their particularly cruel actions against the civil population. While former President Omar al-Bashir denied any involvement, he was still accused of supporting Janjaweed killings, which were categorised as genocide by the United States in 2004 (Brosché, 2008, p. 91). Additionally, the National Islamic Front is said to govern in favour of Arab ethnic groups while marginalising African and non-Arabs (ibid. p. 91).

8. PROCESS TRACING

In 2006, the UN Department of Peacekeeping Operations (DPKO) and the already existing African Union Mission in Sudan (AMIS) prepared a joint AU/UN peacekeeping operation for the region of Darfur, which was implemented in 2007 (UNAMID, 2019). It was approved by UN Security Council Resolution 1769 and aims at ensuring stability in Darfur and accompanying peace talks between the parties (UNAMID Fact Sheet, 2007). Until today, UNAMID has been renewed every year with the mandate to ensure both the protection of civilians and the provision of humanitarian assistance (ibid.). In addition, mediation between the conflicting parties was to be enabled on the basis of the Doha Document for Peace in Darfur (DDPD) (ibid.).

In July 2007, the Security Council unanimously adopted Resolution 1769, which authorised the deployment of joint United Nations–African Union forces to be sent to Sudan's Western region Darfur (SC/9089, 2007). Since 2003, government supported militias had been fighting against various rebel groups in the Western Sudanese province of Darfur about influence and power over resources in the region (Danielová, 2014, p. 42f). The conflict was characterised by a particularly high level of violence against the civil population, causing refugees to flee to neighbouring countries such as Chad, which has been a traditional destination for Sudanese refugees (ibid., p. 44) (Hastrup, 2013, p. 91). In 2007, Human Rights Watch reported "massive civilian deaths and […] the displacement of some 2.4 million people since 2003" (Human Rights Watch, 2007). The number of direct victims in the conflict varied between 10,000 and up to 400,000 depending on the source (Danielová, 2014, p. 45).

The UN peace mission involved 26,000 troops and was deployed to reduce the violence and fighting between guerrilla groups and pro-government militias (SC/9089, 2007). UN personnel met with 7,000 troops provided by the previously established African Union Mission in Sudan (ibid.). This hybrid mission called African Union/United Nations Hybrid Operation in Darfur was the first of its kind and approved under Chapter VII of the UN Charter, which allowed UN troops to make use of armed force in emergency situations even without the consent of the host country Sudan (ibid.). This part of the resolution had long been refused by veto power China, which finally gave in to pressure from the international community (bpb, 2007). In return, China negotiated that troops were not allowed to confiscate weapons or prosecute war criminals, with the aim of transferring them to Den Haag (ibid.). Furthermore, initial sanctions against the government of Khartoum were taken from the resolution (ibid.). This compromise had been discussed between China and Sudan during a meeting in early April 2007 (Human Security Baseline Assessment, 2007, p. 1). Sudanese President Omar al-Bashir had long rejected a UN mission but was persuaded by Chinese foreign minister Zhai Jun (ibid. p. 1). China's direct attempt to persuade a conflict-affected country to agree to a UN mission was a novum during China's UN membership and was followed by China's announcement to deploy 3,000 troops to the mission in Darfur (ibid. p. 1). In December 2020, 6,226 UN personnel were present in UNAMID, which makes the mission the sixth largest out of 23 UN missions currently in operation (UN Peacekeeping, 2020).

Table 15: Chinese Contributions to UNAMID

Year	2007	2008	2009	2010	2011	2012	2013
Personnel	3	321	324	325	323	323	234

2014	2015	2016	2017	2018	2019	2020
230	235	231	375	374	371	364

Source: (UN Peacekeeping, 2021)

Beijing's efforts in favour of the UN mission expressed China's strengthened role as a veto power. At the same time, it was contested by international accusations of an "arms and oil" deal with Khartoum (ibid.). China did not declare its arms sales to Sudan or any other country to the UN Register of Conventional Arms Transfers, and data on small arms and light weapons have remained incomplete. However, it has been found that China was a major exporter of arms to Khartoum between 1992 and 2005 (Human Security Baseline Assessment, 2007, p. 5). Additionally, Beijing was a major importer of Sudanese oil, which indicates that China's lobbying for a UN mission might not necessarily have been a confession to the international community, but rather motivated by Chinese national economic and political interests (Human Security Baseline Assessment, 2007, p. 1).

China's bilateral relations to Sudan commenced in 1959 when Sudan officially recognised the PRC (ibid. p. 1). China's support for Sudan's suppression of a communist coup d'état in 1971 marked the beginning of a close relationship between the two countries (ibid. p. 1). Sudan profited from Chinese military equipment, including aircrafts as well as economic grants, loans and technical assistance (ibid. p. 1). The relationship was characterised by China's non-interference policy, which continued throughout Sudan's first post-independence civil war until 1972 and the civil wars in Southern Sudan after 1983 (Large, 2008, p. 94f). While China was displeased with the strengthening of the National Islamic Front (NIF) in Sudan in 1989, it upheld its relations with and arms transfers to Sudan in the context of its own international isolation following the incidents in Tiananmen Square that same year (Human Security Baseline Assessment, 2007, p. 1).

From 1994, the government of Sudan closely cooperated with China in the development of its oil sector (ibid. p. 1). China profited from Khartoum's international isolation and was thus able to enter the mostly Western-dominated oil market by using previously unexploited areas as a testing ground for technical development (Human Security Baseline Assessment, 2007, p. 2). By 2002, Sudan supplied about 40 per cent of China's African oil imports (ibid. p. 2).

China's diplomacy towards Sudan has historically been characterised by its support for the sovereignty of Sudan (Human Security Baseline Assessment, 2007, p. 7). Although threatening to use its veto in votes on several UN resolutions on sanctions against Khartoum over the Darfur conflict, China's voting behaviour has been limited to abstentions (Ibid.). At the same time, China supported regional initiatives such as the 2005 African Union Mission in Sudan (AMIS) (ibid. p. 7).

Yet, China's policy of non-interference changed from 2006 onwards when international criticism of the conflict was rising. This shift can be connected to Chad turning away from Taiwan and the country's recognition of the PRC in August 2006 (Large, 2008, p. 100). From this moment, Beijing took into account Chad's stability and security interests in western Sudan (ibid. p. 100). Recognising the political risks of the conflict for the whole region as well as its international reputation, China started to play an active role in negotiations on the so-called "Annan plan", which included an extended role of the UN in Darfur and paved the way for UNAMID in 2007 (ibid. p. 100). Beijing subsequently stressed its proactive engagement on al-Bashir's consent to the mission (ibid. p. 100).

Within Sudan, China's role in the Darfur conflict is highly politicised. Pro-governmental parties accuse Beijing of not having defended it enough on the international level, while armed rebel groups would have expected more leverage on the government and criticise China's involvement in Sudan's oil economy (Large, 2008, p. 101). With repeated ultimatums for withdrawals and attacks on Chinese oil fields, China remains most exposed to enmity in Sudan (ibid. p. 100). On the global stage, China has not yet been able to convince the international community of its role as a responsible stakeholder in Sudan. Its close ties to the Sudanese government have been expressed rhetorically in the UN Security Council

8.1. Analysis of Cases during Process Tracing

as well as militarily (Large, 2008, p. 101f). According to Large, however, China's balancing act between seeking to maintain the principle of non-intervention, its obvious support for the Sudanese government and its performance within the international community have not yet led to the country's expected recognition as a peacekeeper (ibid. 101f).

In previous literature, a 2012 summary of China–Sudan–South Sudan relations has been provided by Moro. The author found that the relationship between China and the "old" Sudan has always been dominated by oil companies (Moro, 2012). Since the development of oil fields has always been a highly politicised issue in Sudan, China's principle of non-interference has been challenged (ibid., p. 24). Moreover, since the separation of North and South Sudan, China has been performing a balancing act between the leaders of both sides to allow oil companies to continue their business (ibid., p. 25). In addition, Daniel Large (2007) provided a comprehensive overview of the relations between China and Sudan. In particular, Large argued that China's influence in the region has become visible in the oil sector (Large, 2007, p. 57). Large also mentioned the historical development of bilateral ties between Sudan and China and the importance of China's non-intervention principle in this regard (ibid., p.57). In one of Large's studies, the author particularly concentrated on China's role in the conflict between North and South Sudan that ultimately led to Sudan's separation into two independent countries (Large, 2009).

8.1.7. South Sudan 2013

Since the time of the Anglo-Egyptian condominium (1899–1956), Sudan had been composed of an Arab and Muslim-dominated North and a predominantly African South (Ottaway & El-Sadany, 2012, p. 4). While available resources had been exploited from the North early on, the Southern regions had remained remote (ibid. p. 4). An official border between the two regions was, however, not defined, which caused long-lasting future conflicts, especially after Sudan's independence in 1956 and the subsequent disadvantaged position of the South (ibid. p. 4). While the North struggled politically between left and Islamist governmental shifts, the South remained divided along tribal lines but united in its resentment towards the dominant North (Ottaway & El-Sadany, 2012, p. 5).

Open fighting between the North and the South mainly took place in central Sudan along the contested border which turned out to be rich in oil resources (ibid. p. 5). The rise to power of Sudan's new President

8. PROCESS TRACING

Jafaar Nimeiri in 1969 and the subsequent introduction of Islamic Sharia Law caused grievances and anxiety among Sudanese Christians. It was the beginning of a war-torn period which brought Islamist extremist military groups to power and peaked in a coup d'état that brought President Omar al-Bashir to power in 1993 (Ottaway & El-Sadany, 2012, p. 6). The war in central Sudan continued with tribal clashes from the South and was further complicated when international actors became interested in Sudan's oil wealth (Ottaway & El-Sadany, 2012, p. 6). While Western companies withdrew from Sudan due to its political standpoints, Asian investors did not hesitate to cooperate with the regime in Khartoum (ibid. p. 6).

The conflict continued between North and South over oil and territories although a comprehensive peace agreement was signed in 2005. One of the key principles of the agreement was a referendum for the people of South Sudan, in which they had to choose between full unity with the North or independence (Kumsa, 2007, p. 521). In its outcome, a large majority voted for South Sudan's secession from Sudan (Ottaway & El-Sadany, 2012, p. 10). Several conflicting topics relating to the South's independence were, however, not covered in the decision. These included clear border tracts, the status of the border city Abyei as well as South Kordofan and the Blue Nile State (ibid. p. 10). Complex disputes over water resources and tribal use of grazing lands in the border regions remained unresolved, too (ibid. p. 10). Hence, violent clashes continued in 2012, with the governmental Sudanese Armed Forces becoming an official actor in the conflict and attacking the town of Heglig located in the north of the border region (ibid. p. 10). South Sudan's government in Juba had difficulty providing a functioning administration while being undermined by prevailing tribal structures and armed militias (Ottaway & El-Sadany, 2012, pp. 6-8). Whilst the North had already developed administrative and infrastructural capacities in the past, it has still been confronted with civilian and military internal conflicts such as in Darfur (Large, 2008).

International actors such as the African Union, Ethiopia and China have long tried to mediate in the conflict, especially concerning the status of Abyei and the withdrawal of troops from the border (ibid. p. 10). Economic interests in the conflict have continued since Sudan's oil wealth is located in the South, while the pipelines in the North are needed to export the oil (Attree, 2012, p. 3).

In 2011, a six-year peace process in Sudan resulted in the separation of South Sudan as the world's youngest recognised independent state (UNMISS Fact Sheet, 2011). Since the United Nations Security Council considered that the situation in the region remained a threat to international peace and security, Resolution 1996 was adopted (ibid.). The United Nations Mission in the Republic of South Sudan (UNMISS) was established, which China has supported with troop contributions since 2012. The mission was deployed after violent incidents broke out in 2013 and was aimed both at the protection of the civil population and at supporting the Cessation of Hostilities Agreement, which was agreed to by the various South Sudanese parties (ibid.).

Table 16: *Chinese Contributions to UNMISS*

Year	2012	2013	2014	2015	2016	2017	2018	2019	2020
Personnel	347	359	359	1,051	1,055	1,061	1,068	1,058	1,061

Source: (UN Peacekeeping, Troop and Police Contributions, 2021)

What began as a political conflict between South Sudanese President Salva Kiir and his Vice President Riek Machar in 2013, turned into an ongoing civil war, although Machar fled into exile in 2016 (Human Rights Watch, 2017). The British writer and expert Alex de Waal claimed that the South Sudanese crisis arose due to severe political errors made by the elites shortly after the country's independence (de Waal, 2016). This included the sudden stopping of the country's oil production, which made up almost 100 per cent of the government's revenue (ibid.). Political elites explained the decision with a dispute with Sudan. At the same time, financial resources leaked away among elites or were spent on military investment, while the population remained in poverty (ibid.). Finally, President Kiir accused Machar of preparing a coup d'état and violent conflict broke out (ibid.). The latter included war crimes such as torture, rape and crimes against humanity, from which the populations continue to suffer (de Waal, 2016; Johnson, 2014, p. 306). Meanwhile, about four million people have either been internally displaced or have fled to neighbouring countries and six UN bases (Johnson, 2014, p. 307; de Waal, 2016).

China first deployed troops to the mission in 2012, including combat personnel (UN Peacekeeping, 2020). Due to repeated violent outbreaks, however, the mission was extended and was still ongoing in 2021[59]. While trade and resources have certainly played a major role in China's interest in the settlement of the conflict, UNMISS also provided a reputational opportunity for Beijing to act as a regional "guardian of peace".

---

59 See UN data on peacekeeping missions. In May 2021, China's contribution to UNMISS was 1,064 troops and other staff (experts, police, officers).

8. PROCESS TRACING

In previous literature, research often focuses on the relationship between China and South Sudan in the energy and oil sectors. One very prominent author is Daniel Large (2016), who provided an analysis of China's role in the South Sudanese civil war between 2013 and 2015. Large describes the case of South Sudan as a point of departure for more comprehensive Chinese engagement in political and security affairs on the African continent (Large, 2016, p. 36). Moawia adds a study on the South Sudanese grievances and mistrust on the community level towards China's longstanding support of the government in Khartoum (Moawia, 2018). Finally, Yan provides a discussion on the asymmetric relationship between China and South Sudan as an underlying structural factor between the two countries (Yan, 2019, p. 149).

8.1.8. Mali 2013

In 2012, several Malian insurgent groups began to fight against their government with the aim of gaining independence for a territory called Azawad in northern Mali (Chauzal & van Damme, 2015, p. 8f). In particular, the Islamist National Movement for the Liberation of Azawad (MNLA) strived to turn these lands into an independent country for the people of a larger Berber ethnic confederation, called the Tuareg (ibid. p. 8). In March of the same year, President Amadou Toumani Touré lost his presidential position in a coup d'état which was followed by political instability in the country (Chauzal & van Damme, 2015, p. 10). Rebellious groups profited from the inability of the government to act and took over control in the large northern cities (Timbuktu, Gao and Kidal). On April 5th, 2012, the MNLA proclaimed the independence of Azawad (Chauzal & van Damme, 2015, p. 11). Thousands of combatants remained armed, which increased criminality, violent incidents and exploitation of the civil population, particularly in the north of the country. In addition, insecurity impeded the delivery of medical care, education and humanitarian services in several parts of the country. The Tuareg rebels caused a political and territorial crisis in Mali and devastated the security situation, not only within the country but in the whole region (Cold-Ravnkilde, 2013, p. 9). Many members of the Tuareg had previously been involved in fighting in support of Muammar Al-Gaddafi in Libya and were now returning to Mali's North where they joined paramilitary Tuareg groups (ibid. p. 9). While Mali had been considered a relatively stable country with prospects of evolving democracy in Africa, the overthrow of President Touré in 2012, the declaration of independence of the Tuareg in Mali's North as well as the uprising instigated by Islamist movements were regretted by the international community (Besenjö, 2013, p. 247). The coup against Touré and its aftermath led to a political crisis in Mali, which uncovered the weakness of Mali's state institutions, high levels of corruption and the systematic abuse of power, which had been ignored until then (Cold-Ravnkilde, 2013, p. 9). For their part, government forces continued counterterrorism activities including execution and torture (Chauzal & van Damme, 2015, p. 30; 50). At the same time, the rule of law has remained weak and Islamist groups have stepped in as providers of security and the daily needs of the population such as medical aid, food or financial donations for marriages and fuel (ibid.).

On a regional level, ECOWAS first responded to the violent outbreaks in Mali by pressuring the coup leaders to install a transitional government under the newly appointed president Diaconda Traoré (Cold-Ravnkilde, 2013, p. 14). While the transitional government lacked legitimacy among the population and although the political unrest continued in Bamako, the chances of pushing back insurgents in Mali's north diminished (Cold-Ravnkilde, 2013, p. 14f). After several months of kidnapping and violence, the Islamists started to move to Mali's southwestern regions. With the Islamists gaining territory, Bamako called for help from Mali's former colonial power France, which intervened with "Operation Server" in January 2013 (Besenjö, 2013). The French initiative was backed by UN Secretary General Ban Ki Moon (Besenjö, 2013, p. 257). UN Security Council Resolution 2100 established the United Nations Multidimensional Integrated Stabilization Mission in Mali (MINUSMA) on April 25th, 2013 (MINUSMA Factsheet, 2013). The aim of the mission is both security-related and covers the support of political progress by Mali's transitional politicians (ibid.). In 2014, the Security Council extended the mission's tasks to the protection of civilians, the insurance of human rights and reconciliation support (MINUSMA Factsheet, 2013). Since 2013 China has contributed an increasing number of troops to the mission.

Table 17: *Chinese Contributions to MINUSMA*

Year	2013	2014	2015	2016	2017	2018	2019	2020
Personnel	157	402	402	401	395	395	426	422

Source: (UN Peacekeeping, 2021)

Apart from the discussion on Chinese migrants in Mali and the resulting implications for small and medium local entrepreneurs, the topic of China's engagement in peacekeeping in Mali is very prominent in research literature. MINUSMA was the first UN mission in which Chinese combat personnel was sent to. Hence, in his works, the author Marc Lanteigne considered China's participation in the UN mission in Mali in contrast to the unilateral approach by France (Lanteigne, 2014, p. 10). Lanteigne concluded that the Malian case was a turning point for Chinese peacekeeping efforts due to Mali's role as source of China's trade with Africa, in particular fuel and minerals (ibid., p. 15).

In April 2013, the UN Security Council passed Resolution 2100, which covered a UN peacekeeping mission to Mali consisting of 12,600 peacekeeping forces (Security Council 10987, 2013). The UN mission was initiated to continue the French-led operation and has been supported by China since late 2013 (van der Putten, 2015). China's involvement comprised the protection of UN personnel, which led to the deployment of a Chinese infantry unit to Mali (ibid., p. 8). In the history of Chinese peacekeeping, this was only the second time a Chinese infantry company was involved after 2012, when China sent a unit to South Sudan to protect Chinese engineers and medical staff (Hartnett, 2012, p. 3). The deployment of Chinese infantry with the task of protecting international UN staff of MINUSMA was a novum. The Chinese military were confronted with frequent attacks on UN personnel in a generally dangerous security environment (van der Putten, 2015, p. 10). Although China has contributed to a multilateral initiative, language barriers have hindered Chinese troop members in their communication with locals. The general Chinese approach of avoiding or at least restricting the interactions of Chinese troops with the local environment hindered the full integration of China's contribution to the mission (ibid., p. 11). At the operational level, Chinese troops, furthermore, connected more easily to troops from developing countries than from Western countries. This may be explained by the different positions within UN peacekeeping. In response, China's contributions to UN peacekeeping missions have seen diversification of troops (ibid., p. 12). Criticism of China may also be explained by expectations that were not fulfilled. Van der Putten presents the example of a Chinese-built hospital that did not meet the standards expected by European members of the mission (ibid., p. 11). Whilst European troops are mostly used to multilateral cooperation from their joint work within the North Atlantic Treaty Organization (NATO), cooperation with China has still remained unusual, especially considering the geopolitical differences between China and the USA (ibid., p. 12).

On the whole, China's involvement in and contribution to MINUSMA exemplarily portrays China's developing desire to play an active role in global conflict zones (Lanteigne, 2015). This development furthermore reflects China's acknowledgement of the regional and international effects of local conflicts, especially in Africa, where China's economic and trade interests have long crossed national borders (ibid.). The sole bilateral economic links between China and Mali remain rather modest, which supports the presumption about China's focus on whole regions. MINUSMA can thus be seen as an example which shows that Chinese engagement in Africa has moved beyond solely bilateral economic scope (ibid.).

In previous literature on the relations between China and Mali, both China's engagement in business and peacekeeping as well as social aspects such as Chinese nationals settling in Mali are covered. In 2010, Antoine Kernen provided a comparative analysis on medium-sized businesses in Mali and Senegal. Kernen outlined that while Chinese entrepreneurs are often perceived negatively by locals and accused of unfair competition or violation of human rights, they also have difficulty approaching locals due to language barriers (Kernen, 2010, p. 253). In contrast to the findings by Kernen, Laurence Marfaing (2010) stated that small Malian entrepreneurs are capable of coping with the Chinese competition (Marfaing, 2010, p. 1). Yet, Marfaing is not consistent in his argumentation since he also pointed to the inferiority of Malian products compared to Chinese ones at a later point (ibid., p. 1). Nevertheless, Marfaing additionally argued that Malian workers are able to find employment opportunities in Chinese companies (ibid., p. 1).

8.1.9. Israel/Palestine 1990

The conflict between Palestine and Israel dates back to 1948 when the state of Israel was found. Towards the end of the 1947, the United Nations General Assembly proposed a plan for the partition of Palestine into an Arab and a Jewish State, while the capital Jerusalem was to be assigned an international status (UNTSO, 2020). From the beginning, this state foundation was accompanied by violent disputes between Israelis and Palestinians, which were essentially about a dispute over the settlement of the territory (Bayeh, 2014, p. 206).

When the United Kingdom officially gave up its mandate over the territory of Palestine in 1948 and the State of Israel was proclaimed, hostilities began between Palestinian Arabs supported by other Arab States and Israel (ibid). On May 29, 1948, the Security Council adopted Resolution 50 (1948), which called for a "cessation of hostilities in Palestine without prejudice to the rights, claims and position of either Arabs or Jews" (UN Security Council, 1948). The resolution further called for the truce between both parties to be mediated by installing the first group of UN military observers, which became known as UNTSO (ibid). After 1949 UNTSO was intended to supervise an armistice agreement between Israel and its neighbouring states, thus extending activities to Egypt, Jordan, Lebanon and the Syrian Arab Republic (UNTSO, 2020).

The situation changed with Israeli occupations of Palestinian territories during the Six-Day War in 1967 (Lintl, 2018, p. 7). The conflict has since remained unresolved and violence between the conflicting parties has become a characteristic of the dispute (ibid, p. 7). A breakthrough seemed possible in the 1990s, when the idea of a two-state solution became evident. In 1993, negotiations in Oslo seemed promising. Both parties had agreed on peaceful coexistence and mutual recognition, including Israel's right to exist (Declaration of Principles, Oslo I, 1993). The aim of the agreement covered an autonomous Palestinian administration in Gaza and the West Bank and required Israel to withdraw from both regions (ibid). In 1995, a second agreement, Oslo II, followed in which both the West Bank and the Gaza Strip were categorised into three types of areas, A, B and C, with increasing security control of Israel (Declaration of Principles, Oslo II, 1995). Additionally, the agreement included steps towards a democratically elected Palestinian Council (ibid). Yet, several developments hindered the realisation of both agreements, such as the failure of further talks and the Second Intifada[60] in the 2000s (Lintl, 2018, p. 7). In addition, confrontations with Hamas increased in subsequent years (ibid., p. 7). After the three wars of 1956, 1967 and 1973, the conflict reached another climax during the Gaza War in 2014, also called Operation Protective Edge[61] (Bayeh, 2014, p. 207). This Israeli military operation in the Hamaz-ruled part of Gaza was initiated in response to the kidnapping and killing of three Israeli teenagers (ibid. p. 207). During the conflict, Hamaz fired rockets into Israel, which were responded to with airstrikes. People in the Gaza Strip suffered most, as evidenced by high death tolls (ibid., p. 207f). While Israel's aim was to stop Hamaz from firing rockets, Hamaz wanted to bring international attention to Israel's blockade and

---

60 Also known as Al-Aqsa Intifada. This Intifada refers to a Palestinian uprising after the failure to reach a final agreement on the Israeli–Palestinian peace process during a summit at Camp David in the year 2000.
61 Israel's name for the incident.

prevent global players from lifting their pressure on Israel[62] (ibid. p. 207f). Since 1989, the conflict has caused over 8,000 deaths (UCDP, 2020). Data from the UN Office for the Coordination of Humanitarian Affairs (UN OCHA) shows that between 2008 and May 2020, 5,580 Palestinian and Israelis were killed or injured in the context of the conflict, with a peak of 2,327 casualties in 2014 alone (UN OCHA, 2020). Civilian victims make up a large proportion of the total casualties, and concerns have been raised about both the neglect of international law and a lack of accountability in the conflict (ibid.). International political sanctions have remained a theoretical concept until today and the possibility of international arbitration began to shrink after the pro-Israel US president Trump came to power (Lintl, 2018, p. 5).

As early as 1948, the UN Security council adopted Resolution 50 and the established United Nations Truce Supervision Organization (UNTSO) to monitor agreed ceasefires and prevent incidents from escalating (UNTSO, 2020). In addition, UNTSO has supported other UN peacekeeping missions in the region (ibid.). While China's contribution to the UN mission dates back to 1990, its personnel numbers have remained limited until today.

Table 18: *Chinese Contributions to UNTSO*

Year	1990	1991	1992	1993	1994	1995	1996	1997	1998	1999
personnel	5	5	5	5	5	5	5	5	5	4

2000	2001	2002	2003	2004	2005	2006	2007	2008	2009
5	4	5	4	5	4	4	5	2	2

2010	2011	2012	2013	2014	2015	2016	2017	2018	2019	2020
5	4	4	4	4	4	4	4	3	4	2

Source: (UN Peacekeeping, 2021)

China's position on the Israeli–Palestinian conflict and the PRC's contribution to UNTSO must be seen in the broader context of China's attitude towards the Middle East. Only after the death of Mao Zedong in 1976 and the rise to power of pragmatic Chinese leaders, did China's behaviour in

---

62 Additionally, in May 2021, the most recent military escalations occurred between the ruling party of Gaza, Hamaz and Israel before a ceasefire was reached after ten days of mutual missile fire. This incident happened after the finalisation of this study and is thus mentioned here.

the UN and particularly the Security Council begin to change (Shichor, 1991, p. 261). This became particularly evident during the 1980s and China's voting in several UN resolutions on the Middle East (ibid., p. 261). The number of Chinese votes in favour increased simultaneously with China's approval of UN peacekeeping missions (ibid., p. 261). Moreover, China began to identify ways to join a UN peacekeeping mission in the Middle East in 1985 (ibid., p. 265). Yet, only after China's official admission to the UN Special Committee on Peacekeeping Operations in 1988, did China begin to concretise its personnel contributions to UNTSO (ibid., p. 265). Finally, in 1990, five officers were stationed with the Observation Group Golan in neighbouring Syria (ibid., p. 266).

China's membership of the Committee on Peacekeeping Operations resulted in further votes in favour of three new UN missions: United Nations Iraq–Iran Military Observer Group (UNIIMOG), which lasted from 1988 to 1991, United Nations Good Offices Mission in Afghanistan and Pakistan (UNGOMAP), which extended from 1988 to 1990, and the United Nations Observer Group in Central America (ONUCA) from 1989 to 1992 (ibid., p. 266).

To conclude, China's contribution to UNTSO can be seen as part of its rising role within the United Nations after the Mao era. Compared to the missions in the conflicts between Iraq and Iran as well as between Afghanistan and Pakistan, a position in Syria to monitor the Golan Heights may have been perceived as less risky. Nevertheless, China's contribution to UNTSO can be seen as the PRC's entry point to a proactive role in conflict resolution in the Middle East.

In previous research literature, Israel–China relations were analysed by Orion and Lavi in 2019. The authors stressed that Israel does not have a long historical relationship with China comparable to that of Israel and Europe or the USA (Lavi & Orion, 2019, p. 9). Rather, political, economic and cultural connections have been established in parallel with the rapid rise of the PRC (ibid., p. 9). Therefore, Israel and China were still in a phase of getting to know each other (ibid., p. 9).

Moreover, Yoram Evron (2016) wrote about Israel's dilemma of being dependent on the US. The author stated that Israel's position has been tailored to Washington's demands, even accepting conflicts with Beijing (Evron, 2016, p. 392). This problematic triangle between China, Israel and the US is also part of a contribution by Kumaraswamy (2013). The author suggested that China's increasing influence in the Middle East at a time when America is retreating in the region may lead to a change in Israel's no-arms policy, which it was pressured into by the US, towards China (Kumaraswamy, 2013).

In addition, Roie Yellinek provided a paper on China and the Palestinian question and considered the possibility of Chinese intervention in the conflict. While China may use its presence in the conflict to gain "credit points" at the United Nations, the author concluded that China was generally not interested in becoming involved in conflict resolution processes without a clear chance of success, which is clearly the case in Israel/Palestine (Yellinek, 2017).

8.2. Identifying Causal Factors

The results of the process tracing analysis illustrate a selection of causal factors that seem particularly important for China's decision on whether to intervene in a conflict. The application of the method allowed the role of different causal factors to be assorted. This exercise was important to distinguish between factors that were particularly relevant in a special case and others that proved important across several cases. The sorting of different options demanded a particular knowledge of each case. Guidelines for sorting the relevance of factors are given by Patrick Thaddeus Jackson (2011), who presents three categories on how to order the conditions, which are of varying relevance. The categories read as follows.
1) Adequately causal (part of an ideal and typically specified causal configuration without which we cannot imagine the outcome having occurred)
2) Coincidentally causal (we cannot imagine the outcome having occurred without it, but it is not part of a systematic ideal type)
3) Not causal, or incidental (we can imagine the outcome having occurred regardless of whether the factor was involved) (Jackson, 2011, p. 150)

By applying Jackson's (2011) leading questions, the specific cases were organized. . In this regard, the aim was to find case-specific arguments to obtain an insight into the given situation (Jackson, 2011, p. 150). Hence, there were no fixed rules about the decision of how to categorise each factor (ibid. p. 150). Instead, the decision depended on empirical plausibility given by the context (ibid. p. 150). Furthermore, a decision for an ideal-type factor may have created room for other factors to be explanatory (Chernoff, 2005, p. 100ff). An example of such an observation can be found in Kenneth Waltz's theory of International Politics (1979), in which he describes that even in the case that a state acts in a way its structural ide-

8. PROCESS TRACING

al type would anticipate, the explanation of the state's actions would cover more aspects than just systemic pressure (Waltz, 1979, p. 70ff). Waltz thus allows causes to be introduced that may be special to particular cases (ibid. p. 70ff). Consequently, this opens the possibility of suggesting interaction between an ideal-type systemic condition and further elements and factors that prove to be relevant for specific outcomes (Jackson, 2011, p. 150).

In this study, different causal factors proved to be relevant in the different cases, and regional trends for one or more factors were identified. In the case of Morocco in 1991, global political events played a crucial role. With the disappearance of the Cold War and the accompanying bipolarity between the USA and the Soviet Union, the number of reciprocal vetoes on resolutions in the Security Council declined to a minimum (Ayenagbo, Njobvu, Sossou, & Tozoun, 2012, p. 23). The early 1990s were thus characterised by cooperation between the former enemies in favour of a peacekeeping doctrine which was intended to be built upon negotiated peace agreements between the conflict parties, which provided, at least theoretically, a peaceful environment for the work of UN missions (ibid. p. 23). Members of the Security Council would not have to take sides anymore but could focus on the very mission itself, with both the US and the Soviet Union stressing their efforts to revalue the United Nations (ibid. p. 23). These significant developments and changes within the framework of the UN also urged China to adjust the PRC's role within the international community. Chinese leaders changed their behaviour from reluctance to a more proactive role, which particularly affected the Chinese attitude towards and involvement in UN peacekeeping missions (ibid., p. 23). The Moroccan case concerning the status of Western Sahara illustrates an example of these time-related circumstances. While POLISARIO still relied on China's support as a socialist ally, the PRC did not support their claims any longer but became in favour of the UNSC proposal to establish a transitional phase. In doing so, China took the chance to integrate itself into this new international community without pressuring socialist values. Instead, China's foreign policy focused on cooperation and stability (Ayenagbo, Njobvu, Sossou, & Tozoun, 2012, p. 24). While Beijing had been very sceptical of the UN's peacekeeping activities during the previous forty years, China supported the UN mission in Morocco both with its vote and troop contributions. The factors in China's involvement in MINURSO in 1991 were strongly linked to international political circumstances. China's conduct, however, displayed an interest in intensified new cooperation within the UN and was also a chance for China to reposition itself as a member state of the international community. China's efforts in favour

8.2. Identifying Causal Factors

of MINURSO at the expense of neglecting the call for support from a socialist partner marked the beginning of a new Chinese position towards UN peacekeeping. The opportunity for new profiling on the international level was crucial for China's decision and marks a coincidentally causal condition for China's intervention within the mission.

China's increasing interest in contributing to UN peacekeeping became a key element in Beijing's communication of the PRC's interests abroad (Institute for Security and Development Policy, 2018, p. 2). With Beijing's engagement and expansion of non-violent interventions, the image of a brutal regime, which had been created after the Tiananmen incidents, was mitigated (ibid. p. 2). In addition, China had started to promote the narrative of a "peaceful rise" in the 1980s and 1990s, which was to be intensified by the creation of a collaborative perception of Beijing (ibid. p. 2). The years 2003 and 2004 thus saw a rapid increase in Chinese troop contributions to UN missions, which occurred in parallel with both China's rapid economic rise and the globally contested US invasion of Iraq (ibid. p. 2). Temporal circumstances thus allowed China to position itself internationally, a chance which Beijing inter alia used by extending its contributions to UN peacekeeping and thus emphasised the opposite of the military behaviour of the US. Peacekeeping provided a relatively low-cost opportunity for China to display its support for not only international security and stability but also international institutions (Institute for Security and Development Policy, 2018, p. 3). China's attempt at profiling furthermore played a role in Lebanon, the second Middle Eastern case under investigation. By maintaining relations with all parties involved, China tried to appear as a valuable intermediary in the conflict. After the PRC's efforts to find a settlement on the micro-level remained unsuccessful, China agreed to a UN mission. In this regard, China's personnel contributions to the mission were on a high level from its inception on. UNIFIL was supported with a large number of personnel and troops (He, 2007, p. 63f). In the case of Lebanon, China's participation stressed Beijing's political will, and also equipment and troop capabilities, to support UN missions (ibid. p. 63f).

A regional focus of China's efforts, however, was clearly established in West Africa, where Beijing became involved in three missions between 2003 and 2004. China's previous history with the countries concerned had been characterised by economic relations, in particular in the mining sector. After the end of the Cold War, Beijing's motivator for a post-Cold War order can be seen in economic interests, which were predominantly fulfilled in Africa (Institute for Security and Development Policy, 2018,

p. 3). The quest for stability has thus been a necessary requirement for China's expanding trade and access to resources. While economic interests in West Africa consisted to a large extent of trade in resources, another reputational element needs to be considered. From 2003 onwards, the Kimberley Process put the issue of blood diamonds on the international agenda and was followed by a general discussion on mining methods in African countries. After the discovery of Chinese weapons and missiles having been used by the conflicting parties in DR Congo, Sudan and Lebanon, a coincidentally causal element can be added to China's decision since Beijing was confronted with reputational risks.

Apart from mining, the exploitation of oil has played a major role in the cases of Sudan and South Sudan, where trade routes were at risk due to the conflicts. The extended regionalisation of the conflicts in DR Congo, Liberia and Ivory Coast furthermore illustrated the cross-border implications of conflicts in these countries, which were inter alia justified by a population structure that has been characterised by many tribal formations and ethnic groups. China's involvement in all three missions hints at a regional Chinese perspective and an understanding of common efforts against terrorism to ensure regional stability. The factor of regional threats in the form of terrorism has increasingly become important and can also be considered a decisive element in China's decision to join the 2013 UN mission to Mali.

Nevertheless, the case of Libera unveiled another crucial element in China's positioning towards a UN mission within the Security Council. Only after Liberia's recognition of the One-China policy, did Beijing favour a peacekeeping mission. This political conditionality was understood as an indispensable request for China's support at the UN and can be counted as an adequately causal factor in China's involvement in peacekeeping missions here. Remarkably, in the case of Sudan, the recognition of the One-China principle by Sudan's neighbouring country Chad played a crucial role in China's decision to participate in a respective mission. Additionally, the PRC's election to the Human Rights Council in spring 2006 was another push for China's recognition within the UN and may have inspired greater participation in UN peacekeeping.

The analysis of economic factors in this study produced diversified results. Within the classification group of African states, all cases but Mali ranked in the upper half of the most important countries which China's imports originated from. Yet, two cases from the synchronic comparison also ranked very high in the year they experienced a conflict without China's intervention. Among the Middle Eastern countries, however, Lebanon

8.2. Identifying Causal Factors

was ranked last of all the 16 cases. Hence, the importance of a country as China's source of imports can only be classified as coincidentally causal.

Table 19 shows an overview of the ranking. The reference groups are oriented towards the United Nations' regional groups of member states.. In addition, the figures on Chinese exports were analysed and ranked for comparison (see table 20). While the majority of countries in the main cases are ranked in the upper half within their classification group, synchronic cases without Chinese intervention show a similar importance as export markets for China.

Table 19: Ranking of China's Import Trading Partners

Main Case and Date of Chinese Intervention	Ranking of Importance (for Chinese Imports within Reference Group)	Control Case	Ranking of Importance (for Chinese Imports within Reference Group)
DR Congo (2003)	20/48	Central African Republic (2003)	33/48
Liberia (2003)	12/48	Republic of Congo (2003)	4/48
Ivory Coast (2004)	14/48	No control case	-
Lebanon (2006)	16/16	Palestine (2006)	No data available
Sudan (2007)	3/48	No control case	-
South Sudan (2013)	7/48	No control case	-
Mali (2013)	25/48	Nigeria (2013)	9/48
Israel/Palestine[63] (1990)	-	No control case	-

Table 20 provides an overview of the ranking of China's export destinations among the same reference groups. It can be seen that even if Sudan ranked fourth in 2007 when China intervened, Nigeria was China's second largest export market in 2013. Yet, China did not intervene in Nigeria's conflict. Instead, Beijing participated in the UN mission to Mali, a country which was only China's 30th most important export market. At best, a country's status as an important export market can thus be classified as coincidentally causal in terms of Chinese intervention and needs to be considered on a case-by-case basis.

---

63 According to the UN categorisation, Israel is listed as a special case in the group of "Western European and Others". For the purpose of this study, however, Israel has been compared within the group of Middle Eastern countries for the year 2013.

8. PROCESS TRACING

Table 20: Ranking of China's Export Trading Partners

Main Case and Date of Chinese Intervention	Ranking of Importance (of the Case as an Export Market for China within the Reference Group)	Control Case	Ranking of Importance (of the Case as an Export Market for China within the Reference Group)
DR Congo (2003)	27/48	Central African Republic (2003)	43/48
Liberia (2003)	26/48	Republic of Congo (2003)	19/48
Ivory Coast (2004)	15/48	No control case	-
Lebanon (2006)	10/16	Palestine (2006)	No data available
Sudan (2007)	4/48	No control case	-
South Sudan (2013)	40/48	No control case	-
Mali (2013)	30/48	Nigeria (2013)	2/48
Israel/Palestine (1990)	-	No control case	-

A study by Cho (2019) suggests that the importance of a country as an export market for China was a decisive factor in the choice of UN missions China participated in. Yet, the process tracing conducted as part of this study did not provide evidence of Cho's (2019) assumption. Instead, the results have shown that China did not intervene in conflicts in Congo and Nigeria even though their ranking as trading partners in both imports and exports was similar to that of the main cases. Instead, China intervened in countries with lower rankings than those of cases covered by the synchronic comparison. The results rather suggest that China did not intervene in conflicts without a UN mission. This even holds true for conflicts that took place in countries which are important trading partners for China.

In addition, the comparison of Chinese major import and export markets illustrated another important factor, namely that of the geographical location and proximity of a source of conflict to other important economic markets. On the international level, an often-stated reason for intervention is the level of danger and threat to stability both regionally and globally as well as the proximity of the conflict and the potential or actual number of refugees (Dowty & Gil, 1996; Elia & Bove, 2011, p. 8). The overview of cases with Chinese involvement suggests that this might also be valid for the concentration of Chinese trading partners in a particular region. From the tables in this chapter, it can be seen that the main cases in West Africa have very similar rankings in terms of import and export trade with China. In terms of imports to China, both Sudan and South Sudan are ranked among the top ten trading partners. The difference in the export ranking might be caused by South Sudan's previous secession. Two regional hubs can therefore be identified, while West Africa clearly dominates with four interventions by China.

8.3. Summary of the Process Tracing

Chapter 8 presented the results of the process tracing method in addition to the QCA conducted earlier. The chapter provided an in-depth analysis of the main conflict cases in the year in which China's involvement began. In addition to the local circumstances of the conflict, it also included a consideration of the relations between the respective country and the People's Republic of China. Furthermore, geopolitical circumstances were taken into account. This detailed analysis of the cases at the beginning of Chinese intervention in them was important since it allowed the identification of particular determinants and priorities for China's "road map for peace". As a result, both adequately causal and coincidentally causal factors were found. Adequately causal factors covered the recognition of the One-China principle, the consent of the host state and the existence of a UN mission. Coincidentally causal factors were intense trade relations particularly in resources, the threat of the regionalisation of the conflict and reputational risks for China. Every case showed its particularities with different combinations of drivers. Most importantly, however, evidence was gained about the crucial role of the existence of a UN mission for China's efforts in military conflict resolution. After the realisation of both the QCA and the process tracing method, drivers of Chinese participation in conflict interventions were derived. The results consisted of a combination of factors related to the national, regional and international levels, which are summarised in table 21.

Table 21: Summary of Causal Factors

National level	Regional Level	International Level
Significant trade in resources; Intense general trade relations; Recognition of One-China principle; Consent of the host state	Threat of regionalisation	Reputational threat/opportunity UN Mission
Outcome: Chinese intervention in the conflict		

Following the empirical evidence gained in this study, the next chapter covers a keyword analysis that shows how Chinese priorities in conflict resolution have already become visible on the international level. This becomes evident when considering changes in the occurrence of pertinent keywords over time.

9. KEYWORD ANALYSIS

9.1. Analysis of UN Security Council Resolutions

The realisation of the QCA and subsequent process tracing provided evidence about drivers that increased the likelihood of China's intervention in conflicts in the MENA region and Africa. A respective model for Chinese interventions will be presented in chapter 10.1. Yet, this research project aimed at taking another step and complementing the previous results with insights into the extent to which Chinese priorities in conflict resolution have reached the international level. To this end, UN Security Council Resolutions were considered a valuable source. Thus, a keyword analysis was added to the inquiry. To find evidence about changes to and developments of the design of resolutions over the twenty-year period, resolutions were clustered into four sub-periods from 2001–2005, 2006–2010, 2011–2015 and 2016–2020[64]. Throughout the whole period under investigation, the total number of resolutions adopted by the UNSC fluctuated slightly with an average of 62 resolutions per year.

Table 22: Number of Resolutions adopted by UNSC per year

2001	2002	2003	2004	2005	2006	2007	2008	2009	2010
52	68	59	59	71	87	56	65	48	59

2011	2012	2013	2014	2015	2016	2017	2018	2019	2020
66	53	47	63	65	78	61	54	52	76

In each five-year period, 75 resolutions were randomly selected and examined for key words. The results were listed in tabular form with the occurrence of a term coded with a "1" and the absence of a term coded with a "0" . The table below provides an overview of the occurrence of each keyword per five-year period.

---

64 Duration of the period until 12th November 2020.

9. KEYWORD ANALYSIS

The following table covers the list of keywords and their position in the resolutions that were considered:

Table 23: Selection of Keywords

Keywords	Position
Human Rights	Preambulatory Clauses
Human Rights	Operative Clauses
Infrastructure	Operative Clauses
Governance	Operative Clauses
Institutions	Operative Clauses
Economy, economic	Operative Clauses
Development	Operative Clauses
Stability, stabilise, stabilisation	Operative Clauses
Region, regional	Operative Clauses
Neighbour, neighbouring	Operative Clauses
Sovereignty, sovereign	Operative Clauses
Non-interference	Operative Clauses

For the term human rights, a differentiation was made depending on the location of the term in resolutions. While the preambulatory clauses contain introductory remarks, the operative clauses imply implementation and require direct action.

Overall, the comparison of 300 UNSC resolutions showed that the appearance of all the keywords chosen increased over the last twenty years, albeit with differences in the level of that increase. The term "human rights" was found in the preambulatory clauses of 137 out of 300 resolutions. In addition, 54 resolutions included human rights in the operative clauses. While the term's occurrence has more than doubled in the preambulatory clauses since 2001, the number remained rather stable in the operative clauses with a peak between 2011 and 2015. This shows that whilst an increasing number of resolutions cover human rights as part of their introductory remarks, this has not yet translated into an increase in operative calls for action to defend human rights in peacekeeping operations.

9.1. Analysis of UN Security Council Resolutions

Table 24: Keyword Analysis of UNSC Resolutions 2001–2020

Keyword	2001 – 2005	2006 – 2010	2011 – 2015	2016 – 2020	Total
Human rights (in preamble)	20	23	48	46	137
Human rights (in operative clauses)	13	11	19	11	54
Infrastructure	1	2	7	5	15
Governance	2	5	21	13	41
Institution(s)	10	17	23	28	78
Economy, economic	21	16	32	27	96
Development[65]	26	25	44	36	131
Stability, stabilisation, stabilise	30	34	52	51	167
Region, regional	53	60	64	68	245
Neighbour, neighbouring	27	28	39	35	129
Sovereignty, sovereign	31	40	43	39	153
Non-interference	15	16	23	25	79

The occurrence of the term "infrastructure" has multiplied since the beginning of the period under investigation, albeit on a very small basis. Even in the period between 2016 and 2020, "infrastructure" occurred in fewer than ten resolutions out of 75 and thus remains considered to a very limited extent in peacekeeping resolutions. Similarly, the occurrence of the term "governance" increased on a small scale with an outstanding peak in the period between 2011 and 2015. Moreover, institutions seem to increasingly play a large role.

For terms related to "economy", the figures were rather stable throughout all four periods, although they underwent a slight overall increase. The same could be observed for the term "development", although its level of increase over the four five-year periods was more obvious. At the same time, a very prominent increase was seen for the appearance of the term "stability", which occurred in over 50 resolutions out of 75 in the last two five-year periods. The number of terms related to "regions"

---

65 Development is understood as the process of economic or institutional progress within a country. Resolutions that included development in the sense of recent events or as a verb were not counted.

9. KEYWORD ANALYSIS

or "neighbouring states" remained stable in all 300 resolutions over the entire twenty-year period, as did the term "sovereignty". Remarkably, the keyword "non-intervention" experienced a larger increase.

While the consideration of changes over all five-year sub-periods showed an increase in all terms, peaks were found in the period between 2011 and 2015, which flattened in the period afterwards. To obtain a clearer picture of the level of increase, the four five-year periods were combined into two ten-year periods from 2011 to 2010 and 2011 to 2020. This step facilitated the calculation of increases and allowed statements on the occurrence of keywords to be concretised. The following table provides a comparison of the two periods including the percentage rise. To put the percentage increases into perspective, the following overview also includes the absolute increase in the number of keywords used.

The direct comparison of the two ten-year periods showed that the largest proportional development occurred with the terms "infrastructure" and "governance" both with over a 70 per cent increase. Yet, as outlined above, both terms remained on small absolute occurrence levels over all resolutions. In both percentual and absolute terms, however, the increase in references to "human rights" in preambulatory clauses was remarkable, while the total change in operative clauses is very limited. Outstanding increases in absolute numbers of keywords were furthermore observed for the terms "development" and "stability", both highly relevant elements with regard to China's peacekeeping model. By contrast, Chinese priorities in relation to economic development and infrastructure as well as its focus on states' sovereignty seem less reflected in the percentual increase in keywords over the twenty-year period. Assuming that the global balance of power is reflected in the content of resolutions adopted by the UN Security Council, the following conclusions can thus be made.

Table 25: Comparison of Keywords in Two Ten-Year Periods

Keyword	2001 – 2010	2011 – 2020	Total Increase	Increase in percentage points (pp)
Human rights (in preamble)	43	94	51	+54 pp
Human rights (in operative clauses)	24	30	6	+20 pp
Infrastructure	3	12	9	+75 pp
Governance	7	34	27	+79 pp
Institution(s)	27	51	24	+47 pp
Economy, economic	37	59	22	+37 pp

9.2. Analysis of Security Council Meeting Records

Keyword	2001 – 2010	2011 – 2020	Total Increase	Increase in percentage points (pp)
Development	51	80	29	+36 pp
Stability, stabilise	64	103	39	+38 pp
Region, regional	113	132	19	+14 pp
Neighbour, neighbouring	55	74	19	+26 pp
Sovereignty, sovereign	71	82	11	+13 pp
Non-interference	31	48	17	+35 pp

Chinese priorities became increasingly included in UNSC resolutions, albeit with different levels of occurrence. This particularly relates to terms related to "stability" and "development". To a lesser degree, the numbers for the keywords "infrastructure", "economics" and "non-intervention" rose. At the same time, however, "Western" priorities resulting from a liberal peace model also rose in their occurrence in UNSC Resolutions. This relates to increased citation of "human rights", especially in preambulatory clauses. Since this increase is not equally reflected in operative clauses, the observation appears like a temporary compromise between Western and non-Western actors. Whilst the mentioning of human rights might appease human rights defenders, it does not result in direct action, which might make it acceptable to sceptical actors and prevent their veto. Moreover, the occurrence of "governance" and "institutions" rose over the twenty-year period under consideration. While neither were identified as a Chinese priority in conflict resolution and peacekeeping, the PRC seems to accept their entry into UNSC Resolutions without vetoing them.

9.2. Analysis of Security Council Meeting Records

Meeting records of speeches delivered during the passing of resolutions in the Security Council support the findings made above. The texts of four randomly selected meeting records illustrate this exemplarily and are presented in the following.

9. KEYWORD ANALYSIS

Table 26: Security Council Meeting Records

Topic	Date	Meeting Number	Related to Resolution
International Peace and Security	October 9, 2015	7531	2240 (2015)
UN Peacekeeping	June 20, 2019	8556	2475 (2019)
UNMISS	March 15, 2019	8484	2459 (2019)
UNIFIL	August 29, 2019	8610	2485 (2019)

In the meeting records of Resolution 2240 (2019), China stressed that "[China hopes] that Member States will implement the resolution in a comprehensive and accurate manner by scrupulously respecting the independence, sovereignty and territorial integrity of countries concerned and [...] in strict compliance with the relevant rules of international law" (UN Security Council, Meeting No. 7531, 2015, p. 6). The Chinese representative, Mr. Liu Jieyi, continued that "the will of the countries concerned must be respected. Communication and coordination with regional and subregional organizations are essential" (ibid., p. 6). By contrast, the representative of the United States, Ms Power, stressed that "[w]e strongly believe that States have the responsibility to protect the human rights of everyone in their territories, including migrants and refugees" (ibid., p. 8). Moreover, Power directly criticised the governments of Syria, Eritrea and Sudan for repressing their own people and thus increasing waves of refugees (ibid., p. 8).

In the meeting records of Resolution 2475 (2019), which covers the topics of Peacekeeping and the Protection of Persons with Disabilities in Conflict, the United States stressed that "the rights of persons with disabilities across the United Nations [are] an area of the United Nations where we have not done enough on the topic" (UN Security Council, Meeting No. 8556, 2019, p. 3). The representative of the Russian Federation, Mr. Kuzmin, criticised the focus on people with disabilities as a separate category in need of special protection. The Chinese representative, Mr. Yao Shaojun, agreed with these concerns and stressed that "[t]he key to tackling the issue lies in stamping out the root causes of armed conflict" (ibid., p. 4). Yao Shaojun continued that "[t]he Governments of countries in situations of armed conflict should play a primary role and take on the primary responsibility in tackling matters related to persons with disabilities" (ibid., p. 4). While the USA promoted a rather active role, China considered respective governments as mainly responsible for the topic. Remarkably, the representative of the United Kingdom, Mr.

9.2. Analysis of Security Council Meeting Records

Allen, thanked Russia and China for voting in favour of the resolution "despite the doubts they expressed today" (ibid., p. 5).

In the meeting records of Resolution 2459 (2019) concerning the UN mission in South Sudan, the PRC representative Mr. Wu Haitao stressed the important role of the mission for "maintaining peace and stability in South Sudan" (UN Security Council, Meeting No. 8484, 2019, p. 2). Remarkably, China further outlined that, in particular, countries contributing troops should be involved in the further design process of the mission (ibid., p. 3). The representative of South Sudan highlighted and thanked all such countries for their efforts (ibid., p. 4). Finally, Mr. Wu Haitao underlined that "China is ready to continue to play a constructive role in achieving peace, stability and development in South Sudan" (ibid., p. 3). In contrast, the United States' representative, Mr. Cohen, considered the core of the mission to be "to protect civilians, support the delivery of humanitarian assistance, monitor and investigate human rights and support the peace process" (ibid., p. 3). The Russian Federation abstained from voting, which was explained by the Russian representative, Mr. Polyanskiy, who stated that "[w]e are concerned about the fact that a document that is supposed to outline the peacekeeping mandate clearly and succinctly is overloaded with text on gender issues and human rights" (ibid., p. 3). This statement suggests that Russia is critical of the consideration of human rights in UN resolutions and that Russia's role must not be neglected when discussing the design of UN Security Council resolutions. While the investigation of keywords presented here focuses on China, it does not exclude the possibility of other actors' influence on the design of UN resolutions. P5 member states especially may try to introduce their own agenda in the Security Council. A particular analysis of Russia's influence would be interesting but is beyond the scope of this study.

Finally, the meeting records for Resolution 2485 (2019), which considers the United Nations Interim Force in Lebanon, includes another statement by the PRC highlighting "the great dedication of the troop-contributing countries and all peacekeeping personnel [...]" (UN Security Council, Meeting No. 8610, 2019, p. 5). In addition, the Chinese representative, Mr. Zhang Dianbin, outlined that the mission "is conducive to maintaining stability in southern Lebanon" and due to the PRC's position "[a]ll parties should effectively respect Lebanon's sovereignty, independence and territorial integrity" (ibid., p. 4f). Remarkably, the US representative also outlined that "[t]he United States remains steadfast in its commitment to UNIFIL and to Lebanon's security, stability and sovereignty" (ibid., p. 3). On the whole, seven out of eight speakers men-

9. KEYWORD ANALYSIS

tioned the importance of stability for the region and Lebanon in particular and stressed the important contributions of UNIFIL.

The next chapter presents the overall results of this study and implications for China's role in conflict resolution practices. To this end, the drivers identified are arranged in a causal model. Thereafter, evidence about Chinese (non-) intervention will be summarised by responding to the hypotheses formulated/identified in chapter 3. Moreover, theoretical implications cover both China's place in international relations and China's (soft) power status on the global level.

10. RESULTS AND IMPLICATIONS

10.1. Development of a Causal Model

The objective of this study was to identify specific factors which drive Chinese military intervention in conflict-affected countries. Moreover, this study considered the question of the existence of a Chinese "road map for peace" with particularly "Chinese characteristics".

After the completion of the QCA with both synchronic and diachronic comparisons, however, a systematic model for Chinese intervention could not yet be found. This was due to the wide variety of causal factors and the heterogeneity of the cases. In their study about state collapses, Lambach, Johais & Bayer (2016) added process tracing to their QCA to establish hypotheses on typical causal relations between their cases (Lambach, Johais, & Bayer, 2016, p. 135). Building on the example of Lambach, Johais & Bayer (2016), the process tracing here built upon results gained from the QCA. A special focus lay on causal factors which had proven relevant in the solution terms of the QCA. While some factors had been coded with 1 in the QCA, they had a rather low importance in the subsequent process tracing of the cases and vice versa. By adding the process tracing procedure, conditions and combinations of factors were examined which played a decisive role in China's intervention. These factors were now able to be distinguished from merely accompanying phenomena (Lambach, Johais, & Bayer, 2016, p. 46).

Through process tracing, greater knowledge was attained in understanding Chinese interventions. At the same time, causal effects were discovered for four of the twenty-six factors that were included in the QCA. These were resources (RESOURCES), trade (TRADE_BA), the recognition of the One-China principle (ONE_CHINA) and the prevalence of a UN peacekeeping mission (UN_MISSION). The close investigation into the cases led to an improved understanding of the causality between these conditions and the outcome. Moreover, four additional factors were discovered that can be assumed to have had effects on China's decision-making process. These were the relevance of the host state's consent to the intervention, the threat of regionalisation of the conflict, reputational threats to China if it did not intervene, and Beijing's quest to establish a more prominent role within the UN. The results of the process tracing method allowed for

10. RESULTS AND IMPLICATIONS

the establishment of a causal model on Chinese conflict interventions. The model displays how matching different configurations of factors resulted in China's conflict intervention. In this regard, the factors are categorised into three levels: the national level of the conflict state, the regional level and the international level.

Both the QCA and the subsequent process tracing of cases, however, illustrated differences in the significance of the causal factors for the outcome. Some of these causal factors proved to be particularly important and even indispensable in specific cases but were of minor or no relevance in others. These factors were thus categorised as coincidentally causal. Three causal factors proved to be part of an ideally typical specified causal configuration and essential for the outcome. First, this related to the recognition of the One-China principle of the host state and, in the case of Sudan, even the neighbouring state. Secondly, the existence of a UN peacekeeping mission was indispensable in China's conflict intervention. China's favouring of such missions in the UN Security Council in turn was dependent on the host country's consent.

Throughout all the cases, no bilateral Chinese involvement was determined. The causal model for Chinese conflict interventions thus consists of three adequately causal and four coincidentally causal conditions. All other factors which were part of the QCA were found to be neither causal nor incidental since it was possible to imagine the outcome having occurred regardless of whether the factor was involved. Figure 2 presents the causal mechanisms of drivers that led to Chinese intervention in conflicts in the MENA region and Africa.

10.1. Development of a Causal Model

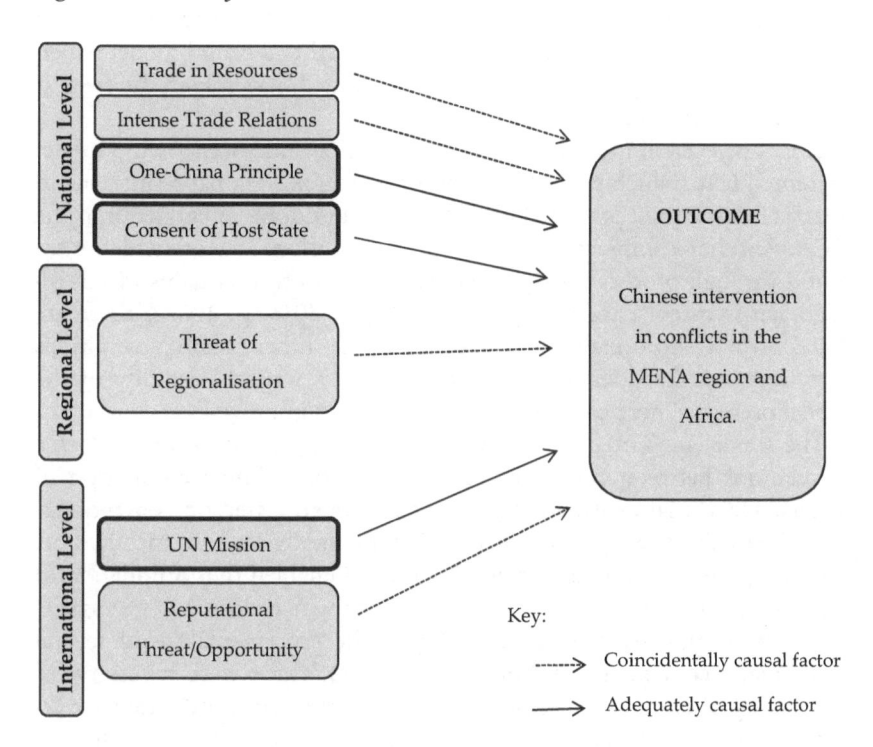

Figure 2: Drivers of Chinese Intervention

National Level
- Trade in Resources
- Intense Trade Relations
- One-China Principle
- Consent of Host State

Regional Level
- Threat of Regionalisation

International Level
- UN Mission
- Reputational Threat/Opportunity

OUTCOME: Chinese intervention in conflicts in the MENA region and Africa.

Key:
- ----> Coincidentally causal factor
- ⟶ Adequately causal factor

Source: The author

In general, it can be said that the more factors that can be observed in a case, the likelier Chinese participation in a UN peacekeeping mission is. The visualisation in the model does not display a temporal sequence of the occurrence of factors. Rather, the arrows in the model describe the causal relation between the different factors. Adequately causal conditions are highlighted using a thicker frame and arrows with a solid line. Dashed arrow lines visualise coincidental causal factors that can additionally appear and may be decisive in some cases.

The causal model displays how different causal factors interact and finally lead to the outcome observed. The combination of factors is the result of the comparison of nine conflict cases with Chinese intervention and different cases of synchronic and diachronic comparison of the previous QCA investigation. In addition, detailed qualitative research into each case allowed for a comprehensive understanding of the cases and the relation

10. RESULTS AND IMPLICATIONS

between causal factors. This study is thus based on a broad empirical foundation. The derivation of its concept and research design were presented transparently and the methods chosen finally led to a causal model which adds knowledge to political science research on China's role in the context of (international) conflicts.

It is, however, important to be aware of the limitations of the model presented here, which should be understood as a provisional result. Due to a lack of data, some proposed conditions could not be integrated into the QCA. Another comparative analysis of the additional factors which were found through process tracing would also lead to further gains in knowledge across cases (Lambach, Johais, & Bayer, 2016, p. 138; Lieberman, 2005). It may additionally be interesting to add other possible conditions that were not considered in this study. In this way, the validity of the model presented here could be further tested and improved.

The model presented as a result of this study represents an ideal type of relations between conditions and goes beyond simple covariation of factors. The causal explanations presented here are based on concrete cases and explain how specific causal relations finally lead to an outcome. The comparison of a range of empirical cases enabled the formulation of evidence about a reasoned general statement which does not necessarily have empirical, universal validity. During the process analysis of several cases, many contextual conditions were found which were necessary for the totality of circumstances of the particular case. The model thus covers both adequately causal conditions and coincidentally causal conditions, which were increasingly observed. The explanation of the outcome thus consists of a combination of systematic causal factors as well as case-specific elements.

10.2. Evidence about Chinese (non-) interventions

The development of a causal model for Chinese interventions in conflicts in chapter 10.1. enabled the answering of hypotheses two, three and four, which were presented in chapter 3.

2. China uses UN Peacekeeping missions to promote the country's soft image and proclaim the foreign policy narrative of a "peaceful rise".

Beijing's reasons for choosing the UN as a significant tool for conflict resolution appear numerous. While China's presence in peacekeeping missions in countries with large Chinese investments is often explained by economic reasons, another factor might appear more subtle. China's quest for good publicity both on the domestic and the international level has been illustrated by the Chinese media as well as Chinese officials in multiple speeches (see chapter 2.3.1). While China's presence in conflict regions poses a threat to the soldiers on duty, it also leads to greater visibility of the Chinese military among the local population and on the global level. The country's personnel contributions have already been honoured and awarded with peace medals in the case of China's engagement in Lebanon (see chapter 8.1.5). Although the number of troops per mission still seems relatively moderate, the communication by the Chinese leadership is already changing the perception of China as an actor in conflict management. Moreover, the deployment of Chinese peacekeepers is portrayed as proof of China's support for multilateralism and multilateral conflict resolution. The Chinese government fully understands the need to present its participation in UN peacekeeping missions as contributions to global stability. In his speech to the UN in 2017, Chinese Foreign Minister Wang Yi underlined that:

> "Peace is hard to make and even harder to keep. As a permanent member of the Security Council and the largest developing country, China knows full well the value of peace. We will continue to work shoulder to shoulder with other peace-loving nations to give concrete support to UN peacekeeping operations and in particular to African countries. Together, we will make our planet a place of durable peace" (Wang, 2017).

By increasing military troop contributions to UN missions, China might thus aim at achieving what other major powers have not succeeded in doing in bilateral conflict interventions. While the 2015 Chinese announcement to provide an 8,000-strong standby force was renewed in 2017, the numbers of troops actually provided in fact decreased from 3,045 in 2015 to 2,531 in August 2020 (Wang, 2017; UN Peacekeeping, 2021). Moreover, in 2020, Chinese contributions were just enough for China to remain

10. RESULTS AND IMPLICATIONS

among the top ten providers of troops and police forces[66]. While the figures reveal a discrepancy between China's official statements and the actual deployment of troops, the latter is still by far higher than those of the other P5 members[67]. It remains to be seen if a turning point in China's orientation towards UN peacekeeping has already been reached. Nevertheless, contrary to other P5 members, China has become a visible actor for the local population and among the international community. The image of Chinese troops as guardians of peace is underlaid with concrete assignments of personnel. Hence, the PRC is pursuing maximum differentiation from other world powers such as the USA, which have traditionally provided only limited numbers of personnel to the UN and have recently also started to reduce their financial contributions.

China's distinction from other P5 members also becomes clear with regard to its overall conflict intervention practices: While Russia, France, the United Kingdom and the USA would not refrain from intervening in conflict-affected countries without a resolution by the Security Council, China's interventions have been limited to UN-authorised missions only. Just as Janka Oertel concluded in his analysis on China and the United Nations under Hu Jintao, this study confirms that China uses UN policies and tools to legitimise and stabilise its own power (Oertel, 2014, p. 239). Remarkably, China uses hard power tools to improve its soft image as well as its strategy of increased soft power. With regard to power seeking in international relations, a theoretical extension of Joseph Nye's soft power approach makes a theoretical understanding of China's involvement in military interventions possible (see chapter 10.4.2). Accordingly, China's increased activities in military conflict resolution as part of the PRC's foreign policy strategy are placed in the larger framework of international relations.

Therefore, China's support for peacekeeping missions increases the PRC's bargaining power within the UN system towards stronger consideration of Chinese priorities. Beijing's rising contributions to the United Nations have, inter alia, been reflected in China's taking over of leadership roles. For example, China temporarily led MINURSO in Morocco. Chinese military efforts within the UN furthermore meet previous demands and expectations of a rising power. China thus sets an example of a

---

66 In 2020, the top ten troop and police contributors were Ethiopia, Bangladesh, Rwanda, Nepal, India, Pakistan, Egypt, Indonesia, Ghana and China.
67 Troop contributions by the P5 in December 2020: China: 2,520, France: 717, United Kingdom: 540, Russia: 68 and USA: 30.

10.2. Evidence about Chinese (non-) interventions

redefined definition of the role of a P5 member in the UN by allowing for a more flexible interpretation of its five principles of peaceful coexistence. The rhetorical efforts in keeping up the traditional non-intervention strategy represents a balancing act which the Chinese government is currently performing. While the aim of Western interventions has been the introduction of liberal peace, Chinese efforts today do not seek to introduce socialist communism in conflict-affected countries. Instead, Beijing's focus lies on the establishment of bilateral governmental relations, identifying new markets for Chinese (construction) companies and finally presenting Chinese values to the world (Kuo, 2015, p. 172). By employing Chinese workers in the field, Beijing's approach once more differs from the West's handling via offices in the capital (ibid., p. 172). The example of Liberia has shown that Chinese contributions to UN peacekeeping missions are focused on these characteristics (International Monetary Fund, 2008). With increased Chinese contributions to UN peacekeeping and a possible lack of personnel and funding for further components such as good governance, it is quite likely that Chinese characteristics will further influence the design and content of peacekeeping to achieve maximum visibility. The study at hand furthermore provides evidence about the specific missions which China has been involved in so far.

3. China puts a regional focus on the MENA region and Africa to emerge as a regional hegemonic power and guarantor of regional security and stability while, at the same time, establishing strategic state relations.

This study has shown a general increase in China's participation in UN peacekeeping operations. If China's military activities aim at strengthening this UN instrument as a whole and without a regional focus, one would expect that the number of Chinese troops sent to each mission should be roughly the same and distributed over all UN peacekeeping missions. Yet, an analysis of the missions with Chinese participation has shown that over the last 21 years (2000–2020), an average of 50 per cent of the missions were located in Africa. In addition, an average of 31 per cent were in the Middle East and North Africa. Therefore, more than 80 per cent of China's participation in UN peacekeeping missions was focused on these two regions. In the MENA region, China constantly contributed to the United Nations Mission for the Referendum in Western Sahara (MINURSO) as well as the United Nations Interim Force in Lebanon (UNIFIL) and the United Nations Truce Supervision Organization in Palestine/Israel

10. RESULTS AND IMPLICATIONS

(UNTSO). In 2001 and 2002, China additionally contributed to the United Nations Iraq–Kuwait Observation Mission (UNIKOM) with eleven and twelve personnel. In 2004 and 2017, China additionally sent one individual police officer to the United Nations Assistance Mission in Afghanistan (UNAMA) which is, however not considered part of the MENA region in this study. A more nuanced picture emerges considering peacekeeping missions in Africa, although constants in Chinese contributions exist. In particular, China has perpetually supported the United Nations Mission in Liberia (UNMIL) since 2003 and has been present in both in the United Nations Organization Mission in the Democratic Republic of the Congo (MONUC) and its follow-up mission United Nations Organization Stabilization Mission in the Democratic Republic of the Congo (MONUSCO). Additional constant support is the Chinese participation in the UN missions in Mali (MINUSMA) and Ivory Coast (UNOCI) as well as three missions in Sudan and Southern Sudan (UNMIS, UNAMID and UNMISS). Between 2013 and 2016, even 90 per cent of all Chinese peacekeeping contributions were located in Africa and the MENA region, while in the same period only about 72 per cent of all UN peacekeeping missions were located in both regions. It can thus be concluded that the increased Chinese support is not a general, equally distributed supply of personnel to all UN peacekeeping missions but rather characterised by a regional focus. In 2020 (August), 89 per cent[68] of missions with China's contributions were found in Africa and the MENA region, while the percentage is 73 per cent[69] for all UN peacekeeping missions (UN Peacekeeping, 2020).

With the exceptions of UNTSO (Palestine/Israel) and MINURSO (Western Sahara), where China has contributed since 1990 and 1991, the regional focus on UN missions in Africa and the MENA region has become particularly evident since the increase in Chinese support at the beginning of the 21st century. While conflicts in both regions prevailed throughout the 20th century and several UN peacekeeping missions were initiated after World War II, China's involvement began only recently. In the case of DR Congo, for instance, the Security Council authorised the deployment of UN military personnel in 1999 (UN Resolution 1258). China, however, only started contributing to the Mission in 2003 (230 personnel staff). Similarly, contributions to the UN mission in Ivory Coast began in 2007 (seven personnel staff), while the missions had been in place since 2004.

---

68 Eight out of nine missions.
69 16 out of 22 missions.

10.2. Evidence about Chinese (non-) interventions

A similar picture arises in relation to the number of personnel per mission, albeit with an even stronger focus on missions in Africa. By August 2020, about 17 per cent[70] of Chinese troops were deployed in the MENA region, while about 83 per cent[71] were involved in the five ongoing peacekeeping missions in Africa. China's largest contribution was to UNMISS in South Sudan with a deployment of 1,072 troops in 2020 (August). Another 1,019 troops are spread among the UN missions in Mali (MINUSMA, 426 troops), DR Congo (MONUSCO, 226 troops) and the Darfur conflict in Sudan (UNAMID, 367 troops), resulting in China's presence all over the continent. Outside Africa, a significant number of troops were deployed to Lebanon (UNIFIL, 419 troops) (UN Peacekeeping, 2020).

The QCA conducted in this study observed that the increase in Chinese participation in UN missions has been accompanied by an increase in trade relations between China and the conflict-affected states, particularly in Africa. Most prominently, this relates to trade in resources, with Chinese imports encompassing oil, gas and minerals (see chapters 8.1 and 8.2). China's quest for resources certainly plays a major role in China's support for international conflict management and stabilising activities. In DR Congo and Sudan, coincidentally causality was observed for the factor of natural resources. Yet, the mere existence of resources could not be identified as a general adequately causal factor since several African countries affected by conflict but without Chinese intervention also possess a great wealth of resources.

Chinese missions to the Middle East have been limited to Morocco, Lebanon and Palestine. In Africa, a geographically wider distribution of China's presence can be observed in both East (Sudan, South Sudan), West (Liberia, Mali, Sierra Leone, Ivory Coast) and Central (DR Congo) Africa. While the Chinese Middle Eastern approach thus seems focused on particular conflicts with historically long-standing Chinese peacekeeping support, China's support for African missions seems to have a more wholistic approach in order to stabilise the continent as a whole.

Overall, the clear dominance of Chinese participation in UN peacekeeping missions in the MENA region and Africa can be observed over all existing missions. The hypothesis tested here can, however, only partially be confirmed. China's efforts to ensure regional stability focus on a multilateral approach which is justified by a Security Council mandate. Instead of hegemonial tendencies, China's increased support for interna-

---

70 432 of 2,531 troops.
71 2,093 of 2,531 troops.

10. RESULTS AND IMPLICATIONS

tional peacekeeping suggests that Beijing is interested in promoting the instrument as such. Yet, the number of Chinese troop contributions varies significantly between missions, which indicates that China regards the conflicts as having different levels of relevance.

4. China intervenes in conflicts if they are relevant for the realisation of the Belt and Road Initiative and if the countries involved host a large number of Chinese citizens.

The years 2002 and 2015 marked significant increases in the numbers of Chinese military troops sent to UN peacekeeping missions. The results of this study thus suggest at least an indirect connection to the BRI. Most notably, this is due to China's sine qua non need for stability for both the extraction of resources abroad and the securing of trade routes. Since 2001, the keyword "stability" has occurred increasingly often in UNSC resolutions dealing with conflicts in the MENA region and Africa as well as peacekeeping in general (see chapter 10.3). In addition, the parallel developments in both China's engagement in conflict resolution through military involvement and the PRC's economic initiative, Belt and Road, can at least be considered interconnected. China's approach to conflict zones seems not only focused on a conflict-affected country but takes into consideration whole regions, which was observed in the case of West Africa. Without China appeasing some of the most volatile regions in Africa and the Middle East, both resource extraction, trade routes and export markets would be endangered.

Although security and stability are not included in the five areas of co-operation in the BRI, they display major if not the most important preconditions for the expansion of the initiative. The success and sustainability of the new routes highly depend on the security and stability of the countries they cross or pass in Asia, Europe and Africa. Moreover, the safety situation of countries that supply China with resources also has an effect on the advancement of the BRI. At the same time, the BRI supports the mitigation of security threats by establishing economic interconnections and thus aims at a more predictable and stable environment (Ghiasy, 2017). Even if the cases under consideration are not located along the official land and maritime routes of the Belt and Road Initiative, they are both important suppliers of resources and sales markets for products that are shipped or carried by train along the BRI routes. Additionally, they may be relevant for future extension of the routes. A peaceful environment in African

10.2. Evidence about Chinese (non-) interventions

and Middle Eastern countries or regions thus corresponds to China's core interests. Both the Belt and Road Initiative and China's increased military engagement can be considered parts of China's goal to become a global power in terms of infrastructure, politics and the military by 2049. China's efforts can be seen as parallel developments, and the dependency of the BRI on stability and interdependencies between China's economic and security efforts can be recorded. While the realisation of the BRI depends on peaceful and stable partner countries, these countries also benefit from economic trade interactions that accompany the BRI's expansion. This may even mitigate conflicts which are based on economic disputes. With regard to the number of Chinese citizens abroad, available sources did not cover sufficient data to provide sophisticated evidence about the weight of this factor in affected countries. The relevance of Chinese citizens abroad to Beijing's efforts at conflict resolution is thus left open for further research.

Overall, the cases examined do not provide sufficient evidence that China's main motivation for military intervention in conflicts lies in the economic advantages of ending the conflicts. This conclusion arises in particular from the fact that the economic significance of conflicts in states with Chinese intervention does not clearly differ from that of other states that are also affected by conflicts but in which China does not intervene. For example, if its main motivation was to secure the economic viability of the BRI, China should also be interested in intervening in the conflicts in Egypt or Yemen since these countries are directly located on the Maritime Silk Road. Whereas in Egypt a UN mission is still lacking, the United Nations Mission to Support the Hudaydah Agreement (UNMHA) was established in relation to Yemen on January 16, 2019. It remains to be seen if China will join the mission in the coming years . On the whole, China's choice of which missions to participate in is not necessarily dependent on whether a country's location is along the main routes of the BRI or even on the degree of economic importance of that country for the realisation of the project. Yet, the BRI can be considered one of several drivers that have made China become more committed to international conflict resolution. On the one hand, the BRI increases the necessity for Beijing to become involved in international conflict resolution. On the other, China presents the BRI as key to harmony and peace. A mutual dependency therefore has to be recognised and must be seen as a central influencing factor in a Chinese "road map for peace".

10. RESULTS AND IMPLICATIONS

10.3. Findings about China's Quest for Power

This dissertation does not only add knowledge to a better understanding of criteria that characterise China's intervention in conflicts, but it also provides findings about the PRC's changing role on the international stage through Beijing's participation in multilateral military diplomacy, particularly UN peacekeeping missions. This study sheds light on particular Chinese priorities and the formulation of a Chinese "road map to peace" in conflict-affected countries. Four hypotheses were presented in chapter 3.5 and assessed throughout the course of this study. Hypotheses two, three and four were answered in chapter 10.2. In the following, the findings obtained with regard to the question of China's changing power status on the international level (see chapter 3.5, hypotheses) will be outlined to find answers to the first hypothesis.

1. China aims at changing the international power equilibrium of states by taking on leading roles in conflict resolution within the UN framework.

The QCA conducted in this dissertation has shown that the unifying element in all cases of intervention with Chinese participation is the existence of a United Nations peacekeeping mission. China thus understands its role as a responsible power as a commitment to the international community and the UN institution of peacekeeping missions in particular. A Security Council vote and thus a UN mandate is required for Chinese interventions. By referring to UN Security Council mandates, China thus bases its military conflict engagement on the only global institution with the power to authorise military action. Within this framework, China's military actions in conflict regions differ from those of other world powers such as unilateral involvements or coalitions of the willing by the USA (Iraq 2003), France (Mali 2014) or Russia (Syria 2015). By contributing not only financially but also with personnel to UN peacekeeping missions, China differs from the other P5 members in its understanding of a powerful actor in conflict regions. China's contributions to UN peacekeeping missions as a global instrument of conflict resolution can be interpreted as a clear sign of strengthening international military cooperation. In this regard, however, China's model of peacekeeping seems different from Western ideas. Whilst the latter have always focused on the introduction of liberal peace based on democracy and free-market economic policies, China's approach is based on China's traditional political philosophy as well as its development over the past 40 years (Kuo, 2020).

After World War II and the introduction of UN peacekeeping, the missions had a neutral character and were mostly implemented to supervise ceasefires and observe armistices, as was the case with UNTSO in Israel in 1948 (Usden & Juergenliemk, 2014, p. 1). During the Cold War, however, the number of UN peacekeeping operations remained limited due to the frequent use of vetoes by the P5 (ibid., p. 1). While missions had to be strictly based on the three premises of impartiality, consent and limited force, the size and scope of missions was extended towards comprehensive reconstruction and peacebuilding during the 1990s (ibid., p. 1). With the end of the Cold War and the shift in Peace and Conflict studies from international conflicts to topics such as democratisation and development, authors discussed the neo-liberal ideology underpinning peacekeeping projects. Roland Paris (2004) argued that "transforming war-shattered states into stable democracies is basically sound, but [...] can have damaging and destabilizing effects" (Paris, 2004, p. ix). Paris even predicts that if turned over in a hurry, the process of liberalisation can produce social tensions and thus jeopardise the peace in conflict-affected and typically rather unstable contexts (ibid., p. ix). Paris (2004) suggests that instead of focusing solely on fast elections, international peacebuilding efforts should first support local institutions that will be able to mitigate the possibly negative effects of a systemic change towards democracy and political and economic liberalisation (ibid., p. ix). Critics such as Richmond and Franks (2007), however, consider the implementation of a neo-liberal ideology a liberal hybrid between intellectual theory and practice that has not been as successful as expected, at least in their case study of Cambodia, where deep-rooted legacies of top-down institutions, semi-feudalism and corruption still hinder the resolution of the Cambodian situation for large parts of the population, even after almost two decades of liberal peacebuilding (Richmond & Franks, 2007, p. 45f). Western debates on how to merge international peace operations with local traditions and indigenous practices thus continue (Mac Ginty, 2010, p. 392).

By contrast, China puts economic development and societal stability at the forefront of its peace model and hereby considers the animation of infrastructure to be key to economic growth (Kuo, 2015, p. 166). Beijing aims at distinguishing Chinese peacebuilding efforts from previous Western approaches and thus at establishing recognisable Chinese characteristics (ibid., p. 166). The principle of non-interference is still upheld in official documents such as *China's Second Africa Policy Paper* of 2015

10. RESULTS AND IMPLICATIONS

(Government of the PRC, 2015). The roots of this principle are China's own experience with Western and Japanese invasions during the 19th and 20th centuries, which are remembered today as part of the Century of Humiliation which lasted from 1939 until 1949 and still shapes China's contemporary interaction with other nations (Kaufman, 2010, p. 1) (also see chapter 2.1). In addition, Beijing remains sensitive to any outside intervention in its own internal affairs, notably concerning the Chinese provinces such as Tibet and Xinjiang, where the topic of minorities such as the Uyghurs has become of international interest (Clarke, 2010, p. 213f). Beijing's emphasis on non-interference is thus motivated by its own interest in avoiding external interference in domestic affairs, which has, however, not prevented Western actors from addressing issues such as Taiwan, Tibet, Xinjiang and the topics of human rights or freedom of the press so far (Pang, 2009, p. 245).

Additionally, China's model for peace is focused on political stability and national interest, which override individual interests, and is reflected in China's own development and the PRC's activities in developing countries, especially in Africa (Jiang, 2009, p. 585). Beijing's focus on political stability as a precondition for development can be traced back to Deng Xiaoping's initiative of opening-up (Kuo, 2015, p. 169). After the end of the Cold War and against the backdrop of the Tiananmen Square massacre, Deng understood China's biggest need to be stability (Yahuda, 1991, p. 564). Today, this premise is still valid and shapes not only Beijing's domestic policy but also China's international presence. In conflict-affected countries such as in Africa, where Chinese investments are expanding, China's success highly depends on political stability (Hinga, Jun, & Yiguan, 2013, p. 30). While the traditional Western model for peacebuilding relies on a basic liberal position and assumes liberal democracy encompassing good governance as the key to human rights and security, China follows a different approach (Benabdallah, 2016, p. 21). In particular, Beijing's priority is on stability and (economic) development to reduce conflicts and crises (ibid., p. 21). Moreover, Beijing even considers forced democratisation as a cause of instability (Kuo, 2012, p. 31ff). The Chinese presumption states that political stability and sovereignty without Western interference are essential for the development of a country (Shen, 2001). In a speech to the United Nations Security Council in 2001, Chinese Ambassador Shen Guofang said:

"In our view, preventive measures such as pre-conflict mediation and good offices are essential and sometimes can play an important role. However, to uproot the causes of conflicts, we must help developing countries, especially the least-developed countries, to seek economic development, eradicate poverty, curb diseases, improve the environment and fight against social injustices" (ibid.).

China stresses the importance of political stability and a basic supply of human services as more relevant than holding elections, since in contrast to democratic politics, development is considered a necessary ingredient for peace (Alden & Large, 2013, p. 23).

Finally, the third component of China's model for peace can be found in infrastructural economic development. In this regard, China copied its own economic path of the 1980s and 1990s to its foreign aid approach, which was mainly applied to Africa (Brautigam, 2009, p. 2; Kuo, 2015, p. 171). As Brautigam (2009) writes, "China's aid and economic cooperation differ, both in their content and in the norms of aid practice [from traditional donors]" (Brautigam, 2009, p. 11). Chinese support has been characterised by simplicity and continuity and has been based on the request of the recipients (ibid., p. 11). In particular, China has extended its offer of loans for infrastructural programmes and university scholarships (ibid., p. 11). China's recognition as a donor in the Global South can be connected to its own previous status as a developing country. China's own development success in both economics and in poverty reduction aroused the confidence of many African states (ibid., p.11). As outlined in Ian Taylor's book *International Relations of Sub-Sahara Africa*, Beijing leaves African governments the choice of infrastructure priorities and refrains from "dictating" conditions, which is traditionally associated with Western donors (Taylor, 2010). China's official abstention from political decisions by African leaders with regard to their development focus was pronounced by China as being part of its principle of non-interference (Kuo, 2015, p. 171; Taylor, 2010). Yet, a common condition of receiving Chinese loans has been links to contracts with Chinese firms, for which the process of bidding often remained non-transparent (Brautigam, 2009, p. 11). China's focus on construction projects has also been reflected in its contributions to UN peacekeeping missions. One prominent example is the mission to Liberia between 2003 and 2018, which was based on Liberia's Poverty Reduction Strategy. The strategy's four pillars were focused on security, economic revitalisation, governance and rule of law, and infrastructure and basic services (International Monetary Fund, 2008). Remarkably, Chinese aid contributed to all the pillars but governance and rule of law (Blankson-Ocansey, 2009, p. 19). In UNMIL, China provided support in engineering, medical aspects and transportation, which reflects China's simple but very concrete aid practice (Blankson-Ocansey, 2009, p. 20; Kuo, 2015, p. 172).

10. RESULTS AND IMPLICATIONS

One major disagreement between Western donors and China has emerged on the question of human rights. While traditional donors have accused China of disregarding human rights, China stresses the higher relevance of improving welfare over the civil liberties of minorities (Osondu-Oti, 2016, p. 52). Western actors have traditionally emphasised that early elections in conflict-affected states are a sign of progress. Yet, China stresses the danger of violent unrest and riots as well as the political instability that often follows electoral processes (Kuo, 2020).

Overall, China's approach has given new impetus to the international donor community and has already left its mark on the international institution of peacekeeping. China stresses the peaceful intentions of its troops and presents its intervention in conflict regions as a commitment to global peace. This new impetus, however, has also put pressure on China and has raised expectations about how successful Beijing's efforts may be.

This study has provided evidence that China's contributions to peacekeeping missions reflect China's readiness to engage in conflicts in Africa and the Middle East. One important driver for China's efforts can thus be seen as a quest to develop Beijing's status within the international community. In addition, the examination of China's recent contributions to the United Nations shows that Beijing is using opportunities within established institutions, such as peacekeeping, to support the PRC's economic and political objectives. By claiming the status of a rising power, China can hold on to the international system and key institutions. Until now, several experts have already dealt with the American retreat from international institutions and the decline of US power (Ikenberry, 2003; Nye, 2004). Moreover, multiple authors have begun to examine the growing influence of new actors on the world stage. Etzioni (2013), for example, expects that instead of another global power, several regional powers will emerge (Etzioni, 2013, p. 13). Chan et. al. focus on the PRC's involvement in global governance (Chan, Lee, & Chan, 2012). Moreover, Beeson and Li claim that China is trying to develop a new international order with new institutions like the Asian Infrastructure Investment Bank (AIIB) (Beeson & Li, 2016). In addition to previous research, this inquiry provides evidence that China's rise has not been reflected in a change of governance structures so far. In the field of peace efforts, the established institution of peacekeeping has instead remained an essential platform. As an emerging power, China is thus strengthening its position through the United Nations. To answer how these efforts influence global governance, their connection to the international balancing of power has to be outlined. In this regard, Abbot and Snidal state that "states are able to achieve goals that they cannot accomplish on a decentralized basis" (Abbott & Snidal, 1998, p. 29). Šabič and Pejič (2019) add that emerging actors "need to challenge institutional power" and will consequently cause a rebalancing of powers that "affects international organisations whose members may need to recognise the changes occurring on the "map" of world powers and respond accordingly" (Šabič & Pejič, 2019, p. 375). While Beijing has challenged the World Bank by establishing the AIIB and has refused to join the International Criminal Court (ICC) so far, Beijing has neither tried to establish a competitor nor withdrawn from UN institutions.

In international conflict resolution, however, China is engaged in achieving a more prominent status in international peacekeeping. As Šabič and Pejič outline, this option allows newcomers to introduce their norms and values to the international organisation and challenge the organisation's constitution from within (Šabič & Pejič, 2019, p. 375). As the comparison of different conflicts in the MENA region and Africa has shown, China supports the functioning of UN peacekeeping missions. By increasing its contributions, China is promoting a new role for itself within the institution. With regard to peacekeeping operations, China might, for example seek more frequent representation in leadership positions such as Force Commander (FC), who is responsible for both military strategy and the use of force in missions, or becoming Special Representative of the Secretary General (SRSG) for a mission. While the choice is made by the UN Secretariat, three criteria are focused on: "satisfying powerful member states by appointing their nationals; recognizing member states' contribution to the work of the organization; and ensuring that leaders have the necessary skill set" (Oksamytna, Bove, & Lundgren, 2020, p. 1). While a Chinese national became FC in MINURSO in 2007, no Chinese has taken the post of a SRSG so far[72]. By contrast, a comprehensive study by Bove, Ruffa and Ruggeri shows that the United States, Great Britain and Germany were the top three nationalities among the SRSGs in Asia and Africa between 1991 and 2017 (Bove, Ruffa, & Ruggeri, 2020, p. 107). As regards China's massive increase in troops and also financial contributions, Beijing's quest for leadership positions does not only relate to missions, but was also expressed with regard to the post of the Under-Secretary-General for Peacekeeping missions in 2016 (Lynch, 2016; Oksamytna, Bove,

---

[72] In 2019, Secretary General António Guterres appointed Huang Xia (Chinese diplomat) as his special envoy for Africa's Great Lakes region. It was the first time a nominee from China had been selected for such a high-level position. However, Huang Xia is not in charge of troops or police forces.

10. RESULTS AND IMPLICATIONS

& Lundgren, 2020, p. 2). Beijing pointed out China's growing number of troop contributions, which largely exceeded the contributions of personnel by all other P5 members combined, which is why Beijing aimed at ending the 20-year leadership of France in this position. While France has kept its position, Beijing's claims will most probably not fall silent. In this regard, China's reluctance towards international human rights protection in UN peacekeeping remains challenging among Western representatives and scholars (Lagon & Lou, 2018, p. 243). In view of the PRC's troop and financial contributions, Beijing remains underrepresented in leading peacekeeping positions. As Oksamythna et al. point out, "the nationality of key [International Organizations (IOs)] officials is linked to states' quest for influence in IOs and has a significant effect on organizations' work" (Oksamytna, Bove, & Lundgren, 2020, p. 2). For the moment, the rest of the P5 have successfully kept China out of leadership positions. Yet, the results provided in this study suggest that China will make further attempts to obtain appropriate recognition in the form of leadership positions in return for its contributions. China has recognised the relevance of international organisations in changing the current balance of powers. At the same time, a shift in power relations will also affect the structure of IOs.

The USA has reduced its budget to the UN since the 1980s and President Trump announced he would limit financial contributions to UN peacekeeping to 25 per cent of the country's total budget in 2019 (Morello, 2019). Moreover, Trump also withdrew the USA from the UN Human Rights Council in 2018, while the US had already withdrawn from UNESCO in the 1980s (Galbraith, 2018; Šabič & Pejič, 2019, p. 286). Whilst the US is thus apparently retreating from the "road map of peace" at the UN, China has discovered this international platform and particularly the institution of peacekeeping as an opportunity to not only control the set-up of UN missions using its veto power but also introduce the PRC's input to the organisation (Šabič & Pejič, 2019, p. 285). Whilst the implementation of UN peacekeeping is not dependent on US troop contributions, a strong dependence on US financing still exists, as China provided—albeit ranked second behind the US—only half the share of the US in 2019 and 2020[73].

---

[73] In 2019 and 2020, China's share was about 15 per cent while the US contributed around 27 per cent of the total peacekeeping budget. See https://undocs.org/A/73/350/Add.1.

10.3. Findings about China's Quest for Power

This study has shown that China is combining national economic and political goals with a stronger presence at the UN. The PRC's outstanding contributions to conflict resolution within UN peacekeeping has resulted in requests for it to have stronger representation in leading positions. The latter have, however, not been appointed to China so far. If China continues both its financial and troop contributions and refrains from establishing a parallel competing organisation related to peace and security (such as the AIIB as a new development bank), traditionally powerful member states will have difficulty denying Beijing's nominations for leadership positions permanently, despite their reservations with respect to human rights.

In addition to its quest for leadership positions, China's increasing influence on the structure and design of international conflict resolution becomes evident with regard to UN Security Council resolutions. The results obtained from the keyword analysis in chapter 9 showed that Chinese priorities—or "characteristics"—are on the rise in resolutions dealing with the MENA region and Africa as well as general resolutions on peacekeeping. The observation of this development in combination with the results obtained from the QCA conducted at the beginning of this study allows the following conclusion to be drawn. China's increased contributions to conflict resolution within UN peacekeeping have resulted in a change of the global balance of power, which is reflected in the formulation of UNSC resolutions and thus the design of peacekeeping missions. The number of certain keywords has changed remarkably during the last two decades. Like other fields of research that include a search for specifically Chinese "characteristics", the terms themselves are not necessarily derived from an exclusively Chinese tradition (Romano, 2020, p. 5). Rather, they are also known from previous approaches to peace missions and thus from other, for example, Western cultures. The type of wording has remained the same, but the occurrence of keywords and thus also the qualitative weighting of elements has changed. What is promoted as exclusively Chinese "characteristics" in peacekeeping and a new "road map for peace" can thus rather be seen as the new organisation of elements referring to Chinese priorities. In particular, "stability" has become an increased focus, an element that is especially important for China's BRI. However, the interpretation of terms remains open, which might facilitate agreement on the wording on the international level. Yet, a peacekeeping concept is emerging that is more in line with Chinese priorities today than it was ten or even twenty years ago. At the same time, Western liberal characteristics have neither disappeared nor diminished in UNSC Resolutions.

10. RESULTS AND IMPLICATIONS

On the contrary, many of them have equally been on the rise, such as human rights, governance and institutions. It can therefore be concluded that these elements have not been replaced but rather supplemented by an increasing number of Chinese priorities. The critical question is how much funding and personnel will be available to implement the respective elements on the ground.

As part of this study, the occurrence of certain terms and keywords in UN resolutions was examined and a number of conclusions have already been drawn from the findings. Additional studies could focus on the meaning of these keywords in Chinese and Western use of language. It is possible that the Chinese understanding of "stability", for example, primarily encompasses economic and security-related aspects, while Western actors may well also include good governance or human rights issues. Different interpretations of terms leave room for the configuration and realisation of missions on the ground, where Chinese troops have become increasingly present.

China's military activities have resulted in a greater share of Chinese influence on decision-making and power. Hence, the field of conflict resolution is a valid example of the PRC's approach to the global stage. Instead of abandoning established institutions, Beijing is aiming to achieve an indispensable role within these structures to be considered a great power. This study shows that this has already led to changes in the global balance of power.

10.4. Theoretical Implications

In chapter 3 of this study, different theoretical approaches were presented and possible causal conditions for Chinese interventions in conflicts were derived from these theories. The study at hand will help to classify China's role in conflict resolution against the backdrop of power seeking. After my empirical research covering a QCA enriched by process tracing of the cases under investigation, it can be said that clear evidence has been found about China's increased involvement and participation in multilateral military diplomacy. China seems to be realising its proclaimed support for the world community with regard to military action to ensure security and stability, as stated in Article 66 of the PRC's Law on National Defence (see chapter 3.3.). By focusing on multilateral military diplomacy, China is engaging in non-traditional security cooperation and has assumed a more prominent role on the international stage. The cases under investigation made clear that China's efforts in terms of sending military personnel to conflict regions is focused on contributions within UN peacekeeping operations. China thus accepts the United Nations and the Security Council as international forums which allow for interventions in international conflict resolution efforts. China's close attachment to established international structures may counter fears about China's rise as a threat to the present global order. However, several coincidentally causal factors that were identified during the QCA of this study also point to Chinese domestic motivations, such as the existence of and trade with natural resources or the recognition of the One-China policy. To explain China's quest to increase its power status through efforts in international conflict resolution, attempts at explanation using established theoretical approaches reach their limits. Rather, previous theoretical concepts must be revised to understand China's power relations in international affairs. This exercise is important to gain knowledge about the intentions and key priorities of a possible Chinese "road map for peace". The results gained in this study will thus be presented in the following.

10.4.1. China's Placement in International Relations

The empirical results of this study have shown multiple drivers that have made China contribute to UN peacekeeping missions in Africa and the MENA region. Pragmatic Chinese needs and interests such as resources and trade have played a significant role in this respect.

This analysis has shown that national interests have been important in Beijing's decision to foster the country's activities in international conflict resolution. In the case of China, recognition of the One-China principle has been a major concern for the PRC. Moreover, at the beginning of this study, a connection between China's security concerns and the BRI was assumed. Even if a direct link could not be verified in this investigation, the factor of trade remains an important driver for China's multilateral relations framework. Whilst the MENA region is not yet among Beijing's key partners, some of the main suppliers of oil and gas are located here (Sidło, 2020, p. 7). Additionally, countries in the MENA region have become important export markets for Chinese goods and are thus relevant for the PRC's security interests abroad (ibid., p. 7). The more China's economic activities grow in the region, the more difficult it will be for China to keep economic and geopolitical interests apart and present itself as a neutral partner (Andersen, Lons, Peragovics, Rózsa, & Sidło, 2020,

p. 24). Selim (2019) states that China's increased efforts in joint military exercises, counterterrorism activities and a stronger naval presence have resulted in a military image that "undermines the integrity of China's traditional principle of non-interventionism, in favour of an assertive and, if necessary, interventionist policy to safeguard what China's leaders see as the state's strategic interests" (Selim, 2019, p. 260). Yet, whilst China's arms trade with MENA countries might have positive short- and medium-term effects on its trade balance, unconditional possession of weapons might also backfire if they are not used to ensure a secure environment but to enhance greed and grievances (Rózsa & Peragovics, 2020, p. 70).

Immediate national interests have thus played a role in China's policy on multilateral military diplomacy. A realism-oriented policy analysis would conclude that China was attempting to increase its material wealth through multilateral military interventions. This demonstration of military strength would thereby foster China's total power and increase trade relations. While the prevalence of natural resources has been identified as a coincidentally causal factor, such as in the case of South Sudan, it cannot explain the full picture of China's efforts at peacekeeping. For instance, natural resources only played a minor role in Liberia and Lebanon, where Beijing has also sent troops to. Instead, China's quest to be seen as a responsive power and a guardian of common peace and security within the UN has become very prominent. China's opening-up strategy during the 1980s and 1990s has certainly contributed to a change in the PRC's attitude towards UN peacekeeping since stable international environments were considered favourable for the domestic economy (He, 2019, p. 255). Yet, at least since the beginning of the new millennium, China's increased activity with regard to both financial and personnel support for UN peacekeeping cannot be fully explained with pragmatic interests. Rather, this study provides evidence that at least two further motivations have played a role in China's increased military activities: the quest to become a responsible and reliable power and a guarantor of peace and stability as well as the attempt to upgrade and strengthen the United Nations as a forum for international conflict resolution.

To understand this shift in China's attitude, it is valuable to look at a state's understanding of its identity, which defines its interests and thus also shapes its resulting actions. With regard to the case of China, the change of the PRC's participation in conflict resolution within UN peacekeeping missions would therefore have been caused by a changed understanding of China's role on the international level. The author He outlines this change and identifies two major historical turning points (He, 2019, p.

256). China's transformation from a withdrawn state without involvement at the international level during the 1970s to a full member of the international community from the 1980s and onwards (ibid., p. 256). Moreover, since the beginning of the new millennium, China's understanding of its role has developed to that of a rising great power, which is inter alia reflected in its increased participation in conflict resolution activities within the UN (ibid., p. 256). The diachronic comparison conducted in this study confirms this shift over the decades. In the 21st century, China's identity towards the international community seems increasingly shaped by the PRC's efforts to establish its position within international institutions in line with its growing comprehensive national power (Johnston, 2008, p. 34; 42). In 2014, Janka Oertel examined how the Chinese leadership under Hu Jintao increased Chinese contributions to the United Nations and used its UN policy strategically to foster domestic positions (Oertel, 2014).

The observation of this development leads to the question of to what extent China will reflect its identity on the international level and how Beijing's increased activities will change the field of conflict resolution. The study at hand identified drivers that promote China's participation in UN peacekeeping missions. These drivers can be seen as "Chinese characteristics" that are positioned as decisive factors in China's contributions. In this regard, the results of this study allow features that do not necessarily contradict the Western liberal peace model to be identified. However, drivers may be weighted differently. The Chinese features identified can be categorised under the thematic priorities presented in Table 27.

With regard to economic development, China's emphasis on infrastructural reconstruction in host countries has been recognised as Beijing's priority (Zhao, 2010, p. 419). This developmental preference by China precedes the Western focus on democratisation and is—based on China's own experience—presented as a fast-track form of growth "without visible social and political disorder that often comes as a by-product of democratization", as stated by Zhao (ibid., p. 432).

Table 27: Chinese Drivers of and Priorities in Peacekeeping

Driver	Priorities of a Chinese Peacekeeping Model
Significant trade in resources / Intense trade relations	Economic development and infrastructure
Recognition of One-China principle / Consent of the host state	State-centred sovereignty
Threat of regionalisation	Stability
Reputational threat/opportunity	(Soft) image building

10. RESULTS AND IMPLICATIONS

Even though or maybe exactly because China remains authoritarian, the enormous economic success of the PRC has raised attention among developing countries and has made this so-called "Beijing Consensus"[74] more attractive than the hitherto tried "Washington Consensus", which demands democratic governmental structures to make market economics work (Nye, 2005). As a result, China offers infrastructure-led development instead of focusing on liberal democracy. The most prominent example of this prioritisation is the BRI with its extensive demand for natural resources. The attractiveness of China's promotion is thus also rooted in the example China is setting itself.

China's concept of state-centred sovereignty is vital and has resulted in a rather traditional approach towards the design of UN peacekeeping missions. Beijing's vision of peacekeeping remains focused on non-intervention in the internal affairs of the host state by holding to the principle of neutrality and impartiality (Fravel, 1996, p. 1106f). Due to China's own experience of being subjected to colonialisation, China has attached great importance to sovereignty and mostly refrained from supporting UN missions under Chapter VII, which deals with procedures for economic and military measures of constraint against states in the event of a threat to or breach of peace and acts of aggression (Fravel, 1996, p. 1107; Zhu, 2010, p.18). China's concerns about Western humanitarian interventions are rooted in the PRC's concern about external involvement in the question of Taiwan (Gill & Reilly, 2000, p. 46). In 1993, however, Beijing overcame this attitude for the first time and voted in favour of a UN mission to Bosnia, where peacekeepers were to be allowed to use military means for self-defence (Stähle, 2008, p. 644). Yet, in the majority of cases and by using its permanent seat in the UN Security Council, China has promoted an international order that retains sovereignty as a central element. The 2008 case of Darfur is a very prominent example since China insisted on

---

74 The Beijing Consensus is also referred to as the China Model or China Economic Model and describes the political and economic policies of the PRC after Mao Zedong's death in 1976. The policies were introduced by Deng Xiaoping and led to an "economic miracle" with fast and large growth rates of China's GNP by the beginning of the new millennium. The term represents an alternative model to the Washington Consensus, which is based on liberal policies and has been the basis of the work of international institutions such as the International Monetary Fund (IMF) or the World Bank. Whilst scholars such as Joshua Cooper Ramo (2004) understand the Beijing Consensus as a means to achieve peaceful and high-quality growth, a universal definition of the term does not exist (Ramo, 2004).

the approval of the Sudanese government before agreeing to a UN–AU hybrid mission. Pressure on China was high since Europe and the USA even called for a boycott of the 2008 Olympic Games unless the UN mission could take place (Holslag, 2008, p. 80). However, the greater the role China has assumed within the international community, the fewer Beijing's concerns have become about external interventions in domestic subjects (Kuo, 2015, p. 169). The example of Darfur illustrates the double-edged sword China faces when choosing a norm to follow. On the one hand, insisting on non-intervention has many supporters, in particular among developing countries. In addition, China may not yet have enough capacity to meet international expectations when it officially abandons its non-intervention policy (Zhu, 2010, p. 46). On the other, international humanitarian crises may not be mitigated without humanitarian intervention by the international community. By making use of its veto power in cases of severe humanitarian catastrophes, however, the PRC risks its desired reputation as a provider of peace (ibid., p. 46). This study has shown that since the beginning of the new millennium, China has increasingly supported interventions in conflict regions on the condition of a UN mandate and mission. By focusing on UN missions, China has tried to maintain its official doctrine of non-intervention on the political level. Within a multilateral framework, Beijing has thus endeavoured to prevent or halt war crimes and crimes against humanity. Yet, recent cases of China's veto on UN missions to Syria in the years 2012, 2014, 2016, 2017 and 2019 prevent a general conclusion on a changing Chinese attitude towards RtoP. Rather, China must be convinced that intervention would not implicitly aim at reforming the internal political structures of the host country (Fung, 2016). Another focus of the Chinese motivation to intervene concerns the quest for stability. With China's own political experiences, stability is considered a central pillar of development and instability and a main factor of conflict in Africa and the MENA region (Kuo, 2012, pp. 24–43). Moreover, by focusing on stability as a condition for development, China often dismisses democratisation processes as obstructive potential causes of turmoil (ibid., p. 31f). China does not only consider the stability of single states but focuses on regional stability instead, which was seen in the distribution of Chinese peacekeepers throughout Africa and the MENA. China's priorities in the choice of peacekeeping missions thus significantly differ from Western ones. Additionally, the PRC's participation in peacekeeping missions in Africa and the MENA region are central elements of Beijing's projection of it being a responsible power while, at the same time, keeping up its national identity. This provides Beijing with

10. RESULTS AND IMPLICATIONS

a valuable platform to promote Chinese practices and thus shape international order (ibid., p. 169). The following chapter outlines the theoretical implications of Beijing's soft attempts to increase its power status.

10.4.2. China's Quest for a Military (Soft) Power Status

The previous chapter outlined Beijing's push for revitalisation of the instrument of peacekeeping and how the future design of individual missions may be shaped and influenced more strongly by the Chinese priorities of regional and international stability. China's quest for establishing a peaceful image of its military is of particular relevance. The exercise of political power and influence in international relations on the basis of increased attractiveness is a central feature of the theoretical concept of soft power by the political scientist Joseph Nye. In his works, Nye (1990, 2004, 2013) illustrated the importance of a country's image (see chapter 3.4.2).

China has increasingly used this knowledge and invested in its ability to make the country attractive to other countries and develop preferences consistent with Beijing's interests. The awarding of the 2008 Olympic Games to Beijing, the influx of Confucius Institutes but also the often-neglected soft influence of the film industry are some examples. While Joseph Nye mentioned the popularity of American films in the 1990s, Chinese productions are on the rise. While the share of top global 50 films shot in China was two per cent in 2010, this proportion rose to 12 per cent in 2017 (Woetzel & et al., 2019, p. 43). Two popular examples of China's attempts to convey political messages through entertainment are the movies Operation Red Sea (2018) and Wolf Warrior 2 (2017). Analyses of the so-called "visualistic turn" highlight the effects of the media and entertainment on political narration and public opinion (Sachs-Hombach & Rehkämper, 2013). Recently, the image of Chinese military forces as heroic units in securing peace was furthermore addressed in the Chinese movie production *Chinese Peacekeeping Forces* (2018) (Walter, 2020). China's efforts to increase its global soft power are evident and manifold. In this regard, China breaks up Nye's classification of power in the international order. Nye (2013) clearly distinguishes between hard power, consisting of military or economic power, and soft power, which is composed of ideological and cultural resources and agenda setting.

The QCA conducted in this study has shown that China's military involvement in conflict regions in Africa and the Middle East implies a soft power component. The fact that China solely intervenes within the parameters of UN peacekeeping missions enables the country to both express its support for international institutions and allows it to take official and international reward and credit for its military efforts, a tribute that no single intervening state has ever achieved from the international community. In doing so, China invests far fewer financial and personnel resources than the United States has invested in international conflicts to acquire the image of the world's police. Clearly, the era of Chinese international participation has only begun and cannot yet be fully compared to the long history of US conflict involvement worldwide. Nevertheless, China's way of only intervening in conflicts on a multilateral basis expresses a new approach to claiming power.

In the case of China, Nye's theory of 1990 would thus need to be adapted as follows: Instead of clearly defining behaviour and policies for both hard and soft power, a pool of tools exists. Elements of this pool are used by states to exercise either hard or soft power. The question is not which tool is used but in which way it is used and how each particular use is communicated. In concrete terms, this implies that an investment can both result in hard and soft power outcomes. For instance, the investment of a country in the water supply of another country might result in people's sympathy for the investing country, especially in places where the central government is incapable of ensuring such an infrastructure. At the same time, the population becomes dependent on the investor's willingness to supply and, in the long term, is obliged to do what the investing state wants to avoid the suspension of its water supplies. Similarly, even military activities may result in hard and soft power outcomes depending on the recipient's point of view. Those attacked will certainly consider the intervention an act of hard power. Contrarily, a government that is supported in its fight against rebels may develop sympathy for an intervening power and be willing to do what it wants without being forced to do so. Whether power elements are perceived as normatively good or bad strongly depends on the recipient's perspective. In this regard, multinational coalitions and in particular UN peacekeeping missions play a special role. Before a mission takes place, the UN Security Council has to approve of the mission. This international approval of the initiation of military action provides legitimacy and acceptance of the use of traditionally considered hard power elements. In particular, the awarding of UN medals for outstanding contributions to international peace makes the soft power element evident.

This dissertation provides insights into the way in which China uses specific military tools in order to increase its soft image and implicitly its

10. RESULTS AND IMPLICATIONS

soft power status. Chinese soldiers within UN troops are not sent to conflict countries as warriors but to influence China's image abroad positively. Nye's theory about hard and soft power thus needs to be amended in such a way that tools, behaviour or government policies are not a priori defined as belonging to a specific type of power. Traditionally, the use of military force has been an expression of coercion, deterrence or protection that resulted in threat, war or alliances and expressed the military power of an actor. The same applies to economic power, which has traditionally been expressed through investments and could result in coercion, economic support or public diplomacy. Both military and economic power have traditionally been defined as hard power and have been contrasted to soft power tools such as policies and institutions that aim at building an agenda to result in bilateral and multilateral diplomacy. Yet, the results of this study imply that the strict distinction between both hard and soft power is not applicable to the case of China. Instead, both forms of power are merged and need to be regarded as an integrated concept to understand China's approach. The example of China illustrates that both traditional hard and soft power tools can be instrumentalised for either hard or soft power depending on the configuration of their use. For instance, Chinese military troops are presented as guardians of peace to counter any assumption about China's aggressive appearance on the international stage and instead promote the image of peaceful guarantors of stability and security.

The theoretical addition to Joseph Nye's approach of 1990 does not contradict the concept of smart power, which he developed in 2013. Nye argues that effective strategies result from combining hard and soft power resources (Nye, 2013). A combination of both types of power will lead to a smart power status (ibid.). However, this study starts at an earlier point and explains how military means which were originally regarded as an undoubted instrument of hard power are now used as a tool of soft power. The case of China illustrates that the use of the military, which was a clear example of hard power in Nye's theory, can be used as a soft power instrument. This investigation thus clarifies that China's actions cannot be classified by simply applying traditional theoretical categories. Neither does the combined concept of smart power provide a solution. Instead, China's increased activities on the international stage suggest a comprehensive "Chinese" understanding and interpretation of power as a wholistic concept that combines both hard and soft power elements. This observation is illustrated by China's changed military activities and the willingness of the People's Republic to increase its military contributions to international UN peacekeeping missions. The adaptation of Joseph

Nye's approach helps us to better understand China's role and behaviour on the global stage and the cases in Africa and the Middle East presented here in particular.

10.5. Summary of Results and Implications

Two research questions were raised at the beginning of this study (see chapter 3). To answer the first research question—*What variables drive China's interventions in the MENA region and in Africa?*—the results of the QCA and process tracing methods were presented and summarised. When nine cases of conflict in the MENA region and sub-Saharan Africa were compared, seven factors on the national, regional and international levels proved to be important for China's intervention. By categorising three adequately causal and four coincidentally causal factors, I developed a model for Chinese interventions in conflicts in the MENA region and sub-Saharan Africa (see chapter 10.1). Three factors proved to be essential for the outcome of intervention: the recognition of the One-China principle, the existence of a UN mission and the consent of the host state. The more these factors were fulfilled in a case, the likelier China was to participate in intervention. Most notably, China's interventions remain limited to UN-authorised missions only. Unlike other great powers that have not refrained from bilateral interventions in conflicts in the past, Beijing benefits from the generally peaceful image of UN peacekeeping and presents its troops as international guardians of peace. This attempt to create a positive reputation for the PRC's military supports China's rhetoric narrative of a "peaceful rise" in foreign policy (see chapter 10.2, second hypothesis). Remarkably, Chinese troop support for UN peacekeeping has largely been concentrated on the MENA region and Africa. Whilst many conflict-affected countries possess crude resources and have increased trade relations with China in recent years, the establishment of strategic relations with particular countries was not found to be decisive in China's military efforts at conflict resolution. Rather, this study finds that China focuses on both the MENA region and Africa as a whole and strives for regional stability, which supports the implementation of the BRI (see chapter 10.2., third and fourth hypotheses).

The second research question—*How do China's contributions to conflict resolution affect the PRC's power status?*—was answered with an analysis of UN peacekeeping designs.

10. RESULTS AND IMPLICATIONS

The combination of factors identified in the QCA and process tracing methods and the results of an additional keyword analysis in UN resolutions allowed the establishment of a Chinese peacekeeping model. The elements of this model consist of four drivers that make up the core of China's "road map for peace": Economic development and infrastructure, state-centred sovereignty, stability and (soft) image building. When the ingredients of this Chinese "road" were compared, they appeared similar to the ones used by previous actors in international conflict zones. Hence, one major finding here is that the composition of elements of a Chinese peace model remains the same as in previous decades. What is promoted as "Chinese characteristics", however, apparently encompasses a new weighting of factors. By promoting and imposing new priorities in international conflict resolution, China underlines its claim to leadership and is thus changing the international power equilibrium of states (see chapter 10.3., first hypothesis).

The results of this study provide scientific knowledge on the question of the decisive elements of Chinese (non-) interventions in areas of conflict and outline the priorities of a possible Chinese "road map for peace" as part of Beijing's increased contributions to international conflict resolution. A conclusion on all the findings arrived at in this study is provided in the next chapter.

11. CONCLUSION

This study undertook a critical analysis of China's recent interventions in conflict-affected countries in the MENA region and Africa. In the preparation of the study, it was assumed that cases of conflict-affected countries in which China intervenes militarily were characterised by certain factors. Furthermore, it was assumed that the combination of factors in the different solution terms would lead to conclusions about the PRC's foreign policy strategy in the area of conflict resolution. Hence, the objectives of the study were (1) to obtain a better understanding of the factors that determine China's interventions in conflicts and (2) to gain knowledge about how these drivers shape China's role in international conflict resolution and beyond. The cases under investigation covered all official Chinese military interventions in the MENA region and Africa that were recorded by UCDP&PRIO (2020) before and after the announcement of China's OBOR/BRI in 2013. The analysis of the cases should thus help to achieve a more detailed understanding of China's behaviour in conflict resolution. The realisation of the comparison indeed allowed for the conclusion of general statements. Hence, the results provide evidence about characteristics of a Chinese "road map for peace".

The results add to knowledge about China's evolving role on the international stage in multiple ways. Empirical findings about drivers that make China intervene in conflict regions in the MENA region and Africa were identified and contribute to a better understanding of Chinese foreign policy decisions. The definition of "intervention" provided in chapter 2.2. covered the official deployment of military forces in countries affected by conflict in both the regions under investigation. This inquiry covered all Chinese interventions that corresponded to this definition, which facilitates the presentation of profound conclusions. The study acknowledges that in addition, other informal Chinese military interventions may take place, such as in the form of arms deliveries. However, this investigation aimed at contributing to a better understanding of the PRC's official foreign policy decisions and the role China is about to take on within the international community. Therefore, a focus on official military missions was chosen. Most importantly, the cases showed that Beijing concentrates on a multilateral approach in conflict resolution, which differentiates China from other great powers, especially the US. However, the cases also clar-

11. CONCLUSION

ified how national interests influence China's decisions to participate in international peacekeeping missions. This relates to China's both economic and political ambitions to achieve its overall goal of becoming a great power by 2049. Furthermore, the study filled gaps in previous methodological approaches by applying a unique combination of methodologies. An analytical approach to identifying important factors in China's behaviour in conflict resolution was established. Finally, the inquiry contributed to the development of theoretical concepts about power and has revealed the complexity of power relations in China's foreign policy decisions. Given that the research framework of the study aimed at a detailed understanding of Chinese foreign policy decisions, the explanatory power of the study is limited with regard to the extent to which other global actors, such as Russia, influence the design of international peace operations.

At this point, it is important to mention that this study was finalised in June 2021, when the 2020 worldwide outbreak of the coronavirus (COVID-19) had already had noticeable effects on several countries in countries in the MENA region and Africa. Whilst the first reports of the new disease originated in Wuhan (China), the virus spread quickly, which caused a worldwide pandemic that was not yet over at the time this study was finalised. It is still too early to know how the spread of the virus and its consequences might affect China's role on the international level as well as Beijing's image abroad. However, like every research project, this study needs to adhere to its allocated schedule. If not, the thesis would never be completed but remain in a spiral of constant updates. Therefore, the pandemic situation as well as its partially severe consequences with regard to economics, livelihoods and also conflict resolution were not taken into consideration. This was also due to the fact that the operationalisation of the methods used in the study had already been accomplished in spring 2020. In any case, possible follow-up studies need to address and evaluate the effects of the pandemic.

11.1. Empirical Findings: Introducing China's Road Map to Peace

While China seems to have departed from its traditional principle of non-intervention, and Chinese military troops have become present in an increasing number of conflict-affected countries in the MENA region and Africa, political science has lacked knowledge about the factors that have motivated Beijing's behavioural change towards international conflict resolution. This study provided evidence of China's drivers and their implica-

11.1. Empirical Findings: Introducing China's Road Map to Peace

tions on the international balance of power by analysing and comparing different cases of conflict. The results obtained in chapter 9.2 showed that China has not only increasingly participated in international peacekeeping missions but also has introduced Beijing's priorities into the designs of missions in UN Security Council resolutions.

Chapter 8.2 showed that cases of conflict with Chinese participation are characterised by certain factors. In the analysis, it became apparent that with regard to conflict resolution, China focuses on the economic development and state-centred sovereignty of the host state. Ensuring stability plays a major role, as does the opportunity for China to enhance Beijing's soft image. For one thing, these drivers are the prerequisite for Beijing's support for missions. For another, these drivers are precisely those elements that China advocates when designing missions. This illustrates the establishment of what Beijing may label "Chinese characteristics" for conflict resolution at the international level. In the MENA region and sub-Saharan Africa, China's focus lies on a multilateral approach within the framework of UN peacekeeping. China has largely increased its troop contributions, which thus distinguishes the PRC from other major powers such as the P5. Moreover, China uses these conflict interventions to illustrate Beijing's visions of security and the safety of nations in the "new era". The PRC has actively introduced these drivers in the creation of peacekeeping designs in the United Nations and linked its support for the implementation of missions to their consideration. This became evident with regard to the increased occurrence of specific keywords in UNSC resolutions that correspond to China's priorities in conflict resolution activities. China's focus on stability has become increasingly reflected in UNSC resolutions over the past twenty years, although a definition of stability (economic, political or social) as well as sub-categories such as the absence of violence or institutional stability are still lacking.

The combination of the QCA and the analysis of keywords in UNSC resolutions led to the finding that the PRC is strategically making use of UN peacekeeping to increase its influence and power in international conflict resolution. In this way, China demands participation at the international level and expresses its claim to be an emerging world power. The previous concept of UN peacekeeping missions is not questioned as such. Rather, China is building on existing structures and defining new priorities within these frameworks. Rhetorically, China stresses the new weighting of "Chinese characteristics" to offer an alternative "road map for peace" to the road of traditional major powers. The discourse analyses provided in chapter 2.3 showed that China promotes these priorities in speeches and

11. CONCLUSION

via public media to export this road map internationally. By doing so, Beijing is working on a future design of international conflict resolution to eventually become a globally leading peacekeeping model. These findings are thus relevant for the academic discussion about alternatives to the liberal peace model (Debiel & Rinck, 2016). The conclusion is furthermore related to contemporary research about the question of whether China additionally is attempting to export its model of governance as a guarantee of regime stability in the MENA region and Africa (Boone & Doshi, 2009; Murphy, 2009; Seesaghur, 2015). The connection of China's BRI to the momentum for changes in global governance and the world order is also discussed in scholarly research and connected to the results of this study (Carrai, Defraigne, & Wouters, 2020; Godement, Rudolf, Julienne, Schwoob, & Isenring-Szabó, 2018; Noesselt, 2010; Noesselt, 2018; Zhang, 2017). Several authors consider China's outreach and discuss the question of authoritarianism and the effects on host countries (Bader, 2015; Davidsson, 2020; Melnykovska, Plamper, & Schweickert, 2012). This is relevant since autocratic regimes prevail in many countries in the MENA region and Africa, and their leaders are trying to create increasingly authoritarian regimes to enhance the socio-economic development of their countries (Onyalo, 2020; Vollmann, Bohn, Sturm, & Demmelhuber, 2020).

For the sustainable and long-term implementation of alternative peace and governance models, China will inevitably have to defend its approaches against other models (Hartmann, 2020, p. 94f). A return to a policy of non-intervention is therefore unlikely in the foreseeable future. The inclusion of Chinese drivers in recent designs of UN peacekeeping missions illustrates that Beijing's propositions are being heard on the international level and have the potential to find majorities in the Security Council. A reorientation and development of the international approach can thus be found. This observation challenges traditional leading powers and their attempts at international conflict resolution. With regard to the US, the former president Donald Trump downplayed the role of the UN and its institutions, calling the UN "a club of people to get together, talk and have a good time", and highlighted his opinion about "the utter weakness and incompetence of the United Nations"[75]. Whilst the Trump administration has not left many good marks on the UN and UN peacekeeping in particular, this study has shown the great importance Beijing attributes

---

75 President Donald Trump via Twitter on December 26, and March 21, 2016. For a collection of Donald Trump's Twitter postings on the United Nations, see (Reuters, 2017).

11.1. Empirical Findings: Introducing China's Road Map to Peace

to this international instrument. This has not only been illustrated by China's increased financial and personnel contributions to UN peacekeeping missions and troops but also by Beijing's increased influence on the development of peacekeeping designs and the institution as a whole. Moreover, this study recognises China's ambitions in conflict resolution as part of the PRC's goal of becoming a great power by 2049, considering economic, military and soft power elements. Beijing's aspirations are reflected in the choice of conflicts it has contributed the Chinese military to. Moreover, the PRC's efforts to reprioritise elements of international peacekeeping missions shows that Beijing wants to play a leading role in international peace and security.

China is thus ready to take on a leading role wherever the US lets go of its claim to leadership. During his presidential campaign, President Joe Biden has already recognised China as a powerful competitive power that challenges America's economic, political and military position in the world (Council on Foreign Relations, 2020). Yet, while focusing on US–China competition in the fields of trade, space and cyberspace, the topic of conflict resolution has not been addressed by the new US administration so far. Instead, the US is "coming back" from international conflict zones and President Biden has started the withdrawal of soldiers from Iraq and Afghanistan to "end forever wars" (Biden, 2019). Whether this retreat will actually end the wars or just US involvement in these conflicts remains to be seen. With regard to the increasing number of conflicts worldwide, the need for international conflict resolution seems at another historical peak. In an interview for the New York Times, Biden stated that

> "We do have a moral duty, as well as a security interest, to respond to genocide or chemical weapons use. Such cases require action by the community of nations, not just the United States. But the United States has a special ability and responsibility to mobilize others to such collective action" (Beswetherick, Astor, & Sanger, 2020).

Whilst Biden mentioned the need for collaboration with other nations, he did not specify how and where this should take place. Compared to Donald Trump's statements, the rhetorical shift by the new US leader suggests that Joe Biden might introduce a new Western position in the field of conflict resolution. This corresponds to one of the suggestions in this study. If values such as democracy and human rights are to play a role in future peacekeeping, they will need prominent defenders. As outlined in the study, Beijing has chosen the United Nations as a platform on which to discuss conflict resolution and peacekeeping. This might be a chance for

11. CONCLUSION

Western actors since the rules of the instrument are well known. In contrast to other major powers such as Western representatives among the P5, Beijing has increased both its financial and personnel contributions and is eager to take on a leading role in the design of peacekeeping missions.

While this study recognises China's own economic and political interests in its selection of interventions in the MENA region and Africa, there is an overriding recognition of China's desire to be recognised as an influential actor in the field of peacekeeping. By strengthening international institutions, China is increasingly dictating where decisions on conflict resolution are made. As an emerging great power, China is offering the global community an alternative "road map for peace", which is also reorienting itself in terms of content. Beijing is thus putting conflict resolution on the agenda in the international competition for power and is challenging the positioning of major actors. Whilst public attention and also scholarly work is mostly focused on Sino-US competition in the fields of economics and trade, this study has shown that China is also challenging the US and other mostly Western actors in the field of conflict resolution.

If traditional leaders of multilateral military diplomacy have an interest in continuing their role in conflict resolution, they need to acknowledge China's increased activities in the prevention, management and resolution of conflicts and refocus their attention on the very institution they once established to navigate countries from conflict to peace. President Biden's first speeches on the topic are a first indication of such a change of direction. If other powers return their focus to UN peacekeeping as well and strengthen the Security Council as a globally recognised body for decision-making on conflict resolution, this will also relieve many African states of the concerns of being caught between the fronts of two rival great powers, as was the case during the Cold War. The results of this study outline that as an emerging world power, China is moving the topic of conflict resolution back to the United Nations, where Beijing is actively introducing the PRC's vision of a new "road to peace". In a joint press conference in 2015, the former US president Barack Obama reminded President Xi Jinping of their common responsibility towards world peace as the two biggest world economies (Obama, 2015). In 2021, this study suggests that it may now be China's turn to recall this joint responsibility.

11.2. Filling Methodological Gaps: Identifying China's Drivers

Previous studies on China's relations with the MENA region and Africa and Chinese interests in intervening in conflicts in these regions mostly focused on specific fields such as trade, economics or the role of natural resources (Butts & Bankus, 2009; Grieger, 2019; Marafa, 2009; Sun, 2018). So far, the concentration on specific aspects of Sino-African or Sino-Middle Eastern relations has resulted in conclusions such as:

"The major reason for China's renewed involvement in Africa is the need for access to Africa's natural resources, primarily energy and minerals" (Butts & Bankus, 2009, p. 3).

> "Building on its experience in Sudan, China has continued to play an active role in conflict resolution processes aimed at political stability in those African countries where it has major economic interests" (Grieger, 2019, p. 8).
>
> "China's military presence is designed to protect such commercial interests in the Middle East" (Sun, 2018, p. 8f).
>
> "China is forging deep economic relationships with most African countries with the aim of securing access to their vast natural resources" (Marafa, 2009, p. 19).

Whilst the concentration on particular elements of China's bilateral or regional relations adds detailed knowledge to these research fields, they do not allow for a generalisation of drivers behind China's approach. Natural resource extraction and trade may be important elements of China's bilateral relations with other countries. However, reducing academic work to these elements poses the risk of oversimplification and ignoring recognition of other influencing factors as well as their interplay. Moreover, simplified conclusions have been promoted by official statements and declarations by high-ranking political actors in the Trump administration. In 2018, Secretary of Commerce Wilbur Ross and Senator Chris Coons commented in an article published on CNBC that

"China is pursuing a neo-mercantilist vision that uses investment in infrastructure to secure an economic foothold, from which it is attempting to secure political, diplomatic, and in some cases military access" (Ross & Coons, 2018).

Additionally, former National Security Advisor Ambassador, John R. Bolton stated that

"We are already seeing the disturbing effects of China's quest to obtain more political, economic, and military power"

11. CONCLUSION

and he continued

"In short, the predatory practices pursued by China and Russia stunt economic growth in Africa; threaten the financial independence of African nations; inhibit opportunities for U.S. investment; interfere with U.S. military operations; and pose a significant threat to U.S. national security interests" (Bolton, 2018).

However, many of the statements on China's engagement and motivations remained without scientific validation. Particularly with regard to the USA's pronounced understanding of competition with China, the statements must be classified against the background of the respective ideological adherence of the speakers. John Bolton[76], for example, is known as a neo-conservative politician who promoted a policy style of rigid nationalism, which suited Trump's America First policy.

With the aim of scientifically investigating the drivers and background of China's engagement in the field of conflict resolution and the intention to pronounce well-founded statements that go beyond the consideration of individual factors, this study offers a comprehensive analysis. Its results show that the combination of drivers that make China intervene in conflict regions in the MENA region and Africa are not conditioned by natural resources or trade relations only. Rather, China considers the United Nations a responsible and authorised international institution, in which conflict resolution should be prepared. Consequently, China only intervenes in conflicts within the parameters of UN peacekeeping missions. Moreover, the recognition of the One-China principle plays a significant role.

The findings arrived at in this thesis were achieved by applying a distinctive combination of methodological approaches (see chapter 4). The combined use of a QCA, process tracing and keyword analysis allowed general conclusions about China's role in international conflict resolution to be drawn. In addition, the analysis of speeches and interviews were taken into account to gain knowledge about the academic and public discourse on this topic.

After the development of a catalogue of criteria in chapter 6, the implementation and results of the QCA was presented in chapter 7 and combined with the method of process tracing (chapter 8). This procedure enabled the identification of generally relevant factors in China's decisions to intervene in conflicts abroad. Twenty-six causal factors from four cat-

---

76 In January 2021, Beijing imposed sanctions on Bolton and 27 other US citizens, including many former confidants of Donald Trump.

11.3. Theoretical Contributions: Understanding Chinese Soft Power

egories were tested, with the result that a limited number of factors were identified as adequately causal[77] and others as coincidentally causal[78]. With this method, specific drivers of Chinese military intervention as well as priorities of a supposedly Chinese "road map for peace" were identified. In this way, previous methodological concepts used to understand China's behaviour in multilateral military diplomacy were enriched by a comparative approach that allowed the formulation of general statements about China's (non-) intervention practices. As a result, this study adds a model for Chinese military contributions to international conflict resolution that both helps to understand China's current choice of conflict interventions and can be used to predict possible future contributions. Moreover, this study also provides evidence about how China's contributions to UN peacekeeping affect its quest to become a great power. The analysis of 300 UN resolutions provided valuable findings about how Chinese priorities have increasingly been reflected in the design of UN peacekeeping missions. The innovative combination of different research methods applied in the study represents a wholistic approach to both identifying general drivers of China's military activities in conflict-affected countries and to gaining insights into the establishment of these priorities at the international level.

11.3. Theoretical Contributions: Understanding Chinese Soft Power

The field of China's foreign policy analysis consists of a variety of different concepts that can be used to understand the state's decision-making processes (see chapter 3.1). Most approaches relate to the analysis of internal and external influencing factors during particular time periods or under specific domestic or international circumstances (Fairbank, 1969; Kim, 1984). Theoretical concepts that can be used to understand Chinese foreign policy decisions have, however, not been concretised on drivers that influence the outcome of military interventions in conflict regions. This study offers a comprehensive framework to test the relevance of specific internal and external factors in China's involvement in conflict resolution practices. Hence, the results contribute to the development of theoretical

---

77 Factors were part of an ideal-typically specified causal configuration, without which we cannot imagine the outcome having occurred.
78 We cannot imagine the outcome having occurred without it, but it is not part of a systematic ideal type.

11. CONCLUSION

concepts with a wide scope of applicability on the analysis of future cases of conflict. Furthermore, the results of this study have shown the relation between China's conflict intervention practices and the countries quest for a greater power status on the international level.

In this regard, the study contributes to the theoretical development of Joseph Nye's soft power approach. Whilst scholarly debate has concentrated on China's upgrading in hard power sectors such as economics or the military, China's efforts in making use of the country's soft power to gain influence in the world through attraction instead of coercion or payments have not been sufficiently reflected in previous academic debate. Only a few studies cover the implications of China's increased soft power and how Beijing is using this power strategically to implement the country's policy goals (d'Hooghe, 2010; Glaser & Murphy, 2009). This study finds that soft power plays an important role in China's quest to become an internationally recognised actor in conflict resolution. Strikingly, China presents its use of hard power tools in the framework of a peace-loving narrative which aims at creating a soft image of Chinese troops as guardians of peace and stability. This indicates a novelty with regard to the concept of soft power, which originally provides a clear distinction between hard power tools such as military assets or weapons and soft power tools such as the number of Nobel prizes, students abroad or the number of music and movie sales (Nye, 2004, p. 76f). This study therefore contributes knowledge on whether China's soft power corresponds to the common Western understanding of soft power and how China is making use of its own soft power tools such as Chinese culture, which is considered a core element of Beijing's power (Glaser & Murphy, 2009, p. 10; Zheng & Zhang, 2021).

China has noticed the potential of using soft power to introduce a new peace model and is using this framework to increase its hard power presence with military troops abroad. China has responded to rising demands for it to play a more prominent role in international crises by using and strengthening existing structures. China's contributions to international missions such as peacekeeping provide Beijing with a platform on which to present its efforts and become an indispensable actor in conflict resolution within the established forum of the United Nations. Hence, China is making use of existing structures of international conflict resolution to promote a soft image of the PRC's military diplomacy. While the military has traditionally been a tool of hard power throughout all theoretical approaches, it is now used as an ingredient of soft power for the first time.

A major change in conflict resolution methods that would neglect the use of military means and provide an actual alternative to previous efforts

11.3. Theoretical Contributions: Understanding Chinese Soft Power

by great powers cannot be observed. Based on the findings of this study, future research could focus on how China's military efforts within the framework of UN peacekeeping are perceived in the host countries. Does the presence of Chinese peacekeepers enhance China's local reputation over time? And can such an effect also be observed among the Chinese population or in other countries that contribute troops? Interviews and polls in the respective countries would be necessary to gain such knowledge, which was beyond the scope of this research.

However, the findings gained add knowledge to the understanding of power and power sources to Joseph Nye's illustration of hard and soft power. While Nye (2004) considered both elements to be two opposing forms of power, this does not hold true for the study presented here. Instead, China's appearance on the international stage is characterised by a merging of both types of power into a new form of power that can possibly be measured by China's own method of Comprehensive National Power. Beijing has noticed the importance of soft power elements in increasing CNP[79] by referring to Chinese cultural values.

To comprehend China's efforts at becoming a guardian of peace and thus increasing Beijing's power status, traditional theoretical concepts of power have to be adapted. Compared to previous great powers such as Russia or the USA, China's choice of tools when acting in international conflict resolutions remains with the military and is thus no different to those of other powers. This is remarkable, since Beijing's rhetoric of "harmony", "love and humanity" and "happiness" raise expectations about a possible increase in China's contributions to other methods of conflict resolution such as mediation. While Beijing instead opts for deployment of its military forces, the way it uses and presents Chinese troops has turned out to be different than known from other major P5 powers. Whilst Beijing tries to disassociate the Chinese approach from former great powers, the application of tools remains very similar. The PRC refrains from intervening in conflicts bilaterally; the use of the military, however, remains its instrument of choice for conflict resolution. Beijing's chances of winning the hearts and minds of countries thus lies in the credible realisation of China's soft power strategy, which the US has never achieved in the MENA region (ibid., p. 263f). This analysis has shown that China's involvement in conflicts is strongly focused on multilateral diplomacy and

---

79 While the CNP allows for the calculation and ranking of powers, the concept does not provide theoretical evidence about the implications of changes in the rankings.

11. CONCLUSION

relies on the original use of hard power assets under a soft power umbrella of peacekeeping.

11.4. Outlook

While China's presence in the MENA region and Africa is growing, Beijing's contributions to conflict resolution differ from the approach of the United States, which has been characterised by the strong presence of US military forces and the tough enforcement of hard power since the 1990s (Selim, 2019, p. 263). Based on the results of this study and in addition to the conclusions provided so far, the following five points are relevant to consider for the observation and analysis of the further development of China's role in international conflict resolution.

First, China still lacks a geopolitical strategy. According to some authors, the "developmental peace" introduced by Beijing as opposed to a Western-dominated "democratic peace" still lacks a geostrategic overview (Lons, Fulton, Sun, & Al-Tamimi, 2019, p. 3; 10). So far, the PRC has been concentrating on the elements laid out in China's 2015 Paper on the *Vision and Actions on Jointly Building [the] Silk Road Economic Belt and 21st Century Maritime Silk Road* as well as the 2016 *Arab Policy Paper*, which focus on local infrastructure, trade and investments. While the importance of common security is mentioned, the papers lack concretisation of China's role in this field. As Sun writes, China has been able to balance security and economic interests along the BRI so far (Sun, 2019, p. 55). However, Beijing might need to diversify its "whole-of-region" approach and adapt its foreign policy to the different sub-regions in the MENA region[80] (ibid., p. 64). Sun furthermore concludes that "in the long run, China needs to build up its capacity on overall planning, strategic design and agenda setting, especially in the fields of security and political cooperation where principles of pragmatism and utilitarianism are dominant for the time being" (Sun, 2019, p. 58).

Second, differentiation between regional issues and general questions of global order is necessary. As long as oil remains the most consumed energy source transported via the maritime route through the Middle East, conflicts in the region will have economic consequences for China (Sayin

---

[80] Sun (2019) lists at least four sub-regions in the MENA region, namely the Gulf region, the Red Sea region, the Eastern Mediterranean region and the Maghreb region in North Africa.

& Kilic, 2020, p. 48). So far, China has reacted by diversifying its energy imports to reduce Beijing's dependence on Saudi Arabia in favour of greater imports from Russia or Brazil (ChinaMED, 2021)[81]. The interest in a stable MENA region to maintain energy flows and secure shipping lanes is shared by China, most Gulf countries and the US (Fulton, Propper, & Fahmy, 2021). While China and the Gulf Cooperation Council (GCC)[82] benefit from the current status quo of US security protection, however, a growing sense of Washington's unreliability emerged after the US reneged on the Iran nuclear deal of 2015 (ibid.). Countries in the MENA region might also appreciate a certain rivalry between two powers as an opportunity for strategic bargaining. At the same time, China's increased investments in digital data protection in the MENA region have alarmed US security concerns (ibid.). However, as Fulton, Propper & Fahmy (2021) state, China and the US should differentiate between solving regional issues and general questions of global order to avoid turning the MENA "into a great power contest" (ibid.). Politically, this remains a challenge between China and the US since many countries in the MENA region are still in transition in terms of their governmental systems and economic development models after the 2011 Arab Spring (Alijla & Aghdam, 2017; Mabey, Schulz, Dimsdale, Bergamaschi, & Amin, 2013). Moreover, the Israeli–Palestinian conflict or the question of the Western Sahara, which have been part of this study, illustrate the complexity of national sensitivities in the MENA region.

Third, China's relations with Iran might affect security-related questions in the Middle East. Arab Gulf countries have recently envisaged a stronger alignment with China to find an alternative provider of security in view of US retrenchments in the use of force (Lons, Fulton, Sun, & Al-Tamimi, 2019, p. 6). However, China has remained reluctant to take on a more active role on the question of Iran's nuclear energy programme (Yilmaz, 2015, p. 54). Instead, Beijing's emphasis on Iran's right to develop nuclear technology for civilian purposes illustrated China's reserved and cautious positioning in long-lasting disputes in the region, which contrasts with the US' position of tough enforcement (Yilmaz, 2015, p. 58f). The revitali-

---

81 The ChinaMED INDEX is a quantification of China's interest in economic, military and diplomatic cooperation resulting from various data sources. The ChinaMED Project is a research platform promoted by the Torino World Affairs Institute.
82 The GCC was established in 1981 and is a union of six bordering Arab Gulf states. The members are Bahrain, Kuwait, Oman, Qatar, Saudi Arabia and the United Arab Emirates.

11. CONCLUSION

sation of negotiations about the 2015 nuclear deal by President Joe Biden would give Beijing the opportunity to introduce China's model for international conflict resolution into multilateral negotiations. Yet, it remains questionable how much Beijing is actually waiting for an opportunity provided by the US to raise its profile. In March 2021, China took matters into its own hands and signed a 25-year cooperation agreement with Iran (Al-Sharif, 2021). The agreement provides for Chinese investments of USD 400 billion, in return for which Iran guarantees a constant supply of cheap oil (ibid.). In addition, the stationing of 5,000 Chinese soldiers in Iran was agreed (ibid.). When Beijing first offered Iran an alliance in 2016, Iran remained hesitant to avoid jeopardising its nuclear deal with the USA (Vatanka, 2021). As a result of President Donald Trump's "maximum pressure" on Iran, which included the US cancelling the deal, Iran's scope for a decision in favour of Beijing's offer widened (ibid.). Thus, the signing of the agreement between China and Iran has left President Joe Biden with a more difficult scope for negotiation to revive the 2015 nuclear deal. The intensification of Beijing's relations with Teheran has also been strengthened by their shared sentiments about world order, such as their objection to US hegemony and emphasis on sovereignty (Vatanka, 2021).

Fourth, China's "road map for peace" could refocus UN missions geographically. The results of this study have shown that in terms of conflict resolution, China's focus lies on a multilateral approach via the United Nations. This raises the expectation that China and the US will engage in diplomatic disputes to reorient international conflict resolution, rather than in bellicose confrontation, as happened between the US and Russia in Syria. Beijing's increased contributions to UN peacekeeping missions are, however, underpinned by China's own political interests in conflict regions. This may lead to new unofficial criteria for the implementation of UN peacekeeping missions in conflict-affected countries unless Western powers reorient their efforts in conflict resolution to the UN as well. Otherwise, war-torn countries with a less important trade relevance for China may be neglected in favour of UN support. A possibly new Chinese "road map for peace" could shift the geographical focus of future UN missions, particularly in view of overall scarce financial and troop funding. In addition, scholarly debate has been discussing what influence China's authoritarian practices will have with the country's rising power. Bader concludes from a study between 1993 and 2008 that bilateral engagement between China and both authoritarian and democratic states may increase the likelihood of autocratic systems' survival (Bader, 2015). A study by Broich, however, states that "Chinese development finance does not sys-

11.4. Outlook

tematically target more authoritarian countries" (Broich, 2017, p. 34). Nevertheless, prominent empirical examples such as the sentence on Nobel Peace Prize winner Liu Xiaobo in 2010 or Beijing's 2019 rule for Hong Kong to extradite its citizens to the mainland have renewed the debate about authoritarian tendencies, not only within China but also abroad (Lee, Yuen, Tang, & Chen, 2019, p. 1; Minzer, 2011, p. 1). Yet, the results of this study do not suggest a particular contribution to the survival of authoritarian regimes in the MENA region and Africa through China's increased military interventions in conflict regions.

Fifth and finally, China's military activities may be an incentive and a challenge for other major powers to reflect on their input to conflict resolution if they want to continue their role in international peacebuilding. Beijing's new flexibility in the interpretation of the principle of non-intervention can be considered part of a wholistic approach to reshaping global power balances. Both China's contributions to multilateral conflict resolution and Beijing's efforts to establish cross-continental economic belts can be seen as parts of the PRC's ambitions to act and be perceived as a major global power. China's attention to the question of security and stability relates to an understanding of peace as a common global good. The PRC's increased support for UN peacekeeping brings new momentum to this multilateral instrument and may be a chance for reforms and further development. Western actors are thereby challenged to defend and promote their priorities. The increased occurrence of keywords related to Chinese priority areas in conflict resolution hints at Beijing's increased influence on the design of UN peacekeeping resolutions. The ability to include specific clauses in UNSC resolutions illustrates both increased participation by and influence from China on the international stage. By promoting peacekeeping resolutions with Chinese "characteristics" and supporting missions both financially and with troops, Beijing has the power to redefine and shape future conflict resolution and peacekeeping and urges other powers to return to the UN Security Council as an international arena for peacekeeping.

While Chinese priorities for a new orientation of peacekeeping missions are increasingly reflected in the wording of UN resolutions, the question of the costs of the implementation of these elements follows. China has been keen on funding infrastructure but has lobbied to cut budgets on human rights and democratisation. If particularly Western actors, who have traditionally been in favour of these elements, cut their funding, future UN missions may indeed be reshaped and will embark on a new road. China's increased activities may thus be an incentive and a challenge

11. CONCLUSION

for other major powers to reflect on their input to conflict resolution if they want to continue their role in international peacebuilding. Whilst President Joe Biden, elected in 2020, had already co-chaired a peacekeeping summit as Vice President of the United States in 2014 and agreed with over 30 countries on strengthening UN peacekeeping, it remains to be seen if Biden will use his presidency to revive this path (The White House, 2014). Several announcements by Biden during the first six months of his presidency at least point to a narrative shift in the US' position compared to Donald Trump's approach and seem to introduce the revitalisation of Western concepts for conflict resolution. During his presidential campaign, for example, President Joe Biden announced that the US would "revitalize [their] national commitment to advancing human rights and democracy around the world" (Biden, 2019). It remains to be seen if and how the new US administration will implement this goal throughout Biden's presidency and if an increase in human-rights related efforts and budget will counter China's design for peacekeeping missions.

So far, developments since the turn of the millennium have pointed to the steady expansion of the Chinese position within the multilateral framework of the United Nations. Outside the UN, however, China has remained reluctant to adopt a clear position towards major conflicts, especially in the MENA region. Time will show how China's position and influence on UN peacekeeping and international conflict resolution will develop. In this regard, the development of China's representation on UN committees will be relevant to assess which possibilities Chinese experts use to incorporate Chinese priorities into the design of peacekeeping missions. It remains to be seen whether and to what extent Chinese involvement in peacekeeping will actually lead to a change in the image of the PRC's military and the realisation of a Chinese-shaped new road to peace on the international level. After decades of increasing numbers of conflict-affected countries, the Chinese approach may be worth considering. This study provides another step towards a better understanding of China and its role in conflict resolution activities in particular. Yet, if nations have doubts about China's propositions, the time to respond has come. And those coming back on the road might consider a return to the international stage of peacekeeping.

12. ANNEXES

Annex 1: Background Information on Synchronic Control Cases

Iraq 2017
In 2017, the President of the Kurdish region in Iraq held a referendum on Kurdistan's independence (Pichon, 2017, p. 1). Iraq's prime minister strongly opposed the referendum and demanded its cancellation (ibid. p. 4). Yet, the referendum was held, with a majority voting in favour of an independent state (ibid. p. 1). The situation escalated into a diplomatic and violent crisis, during which Iraq moved its military to Kurdish territories around Kirkuk and occupied important lands with large oilfields (International Crisis Group, 2020, p. 9; 19). The case is comparable to Morocco since minorities are fighting for independence and their own land within an existing state.

Research literature on Chinese–Iraqi relations is, however, very limited. In Jeremy Garlick and Radka Havlova's paper on China balancing diplomacy between Saudi Arabia and Iran in their battle for supremacy in the Persian Gulf, the authors also consider the role of Iraq (Garlick & Havlova, 2000). Historically, China supported both Iran and Iraq in their bilateral war during the 1980s by providing weapons to both sides (ibid., p.12). When the war ended, China promoted post-war construction in both countries (ibid., p.12). In general, however, the authors consider Iran and Saudi Arabia important regional powers with whom China has to boost its relations to implement the PRC's trade and infrastructure goals for the BRI in the Persian Gulf (ibid., p. 18). Yet, Blanchard and Fuji (2012) consider an indirect role of Iraq with regard to China's soft power status in the region. Since China's scope of soft power also depends on other actors' actions, China was able to gain ground when the US' soft power started to weaken after George W. Bush's intervention in Iraq in 2003 (Blanchard & Lu, 2012, p. 579f).

Central African Republic 2012–14
Between 2012 and 2014, a civil war took place between the government of the CAR and rebels from an alliance of mostly Muslim rebel militia groups called Séléka (Dukhan, 2016, pp. 2-10). Séléka accused CAR's president of violating a peace agreement that had been negotiated in 2007

(ibid. pp. 2–10). The militia stormed the Republic's capital city and forced the President to flee. Shortly after Séléka's rebel leader took over the country's presidency, another militia group, the Christian Anti-balaka started to contest him, and violent fighting continued (ibid. pp. 2–10). Séléka's power, however, had diminished due to a loss of unity (ibid. pp. 2–10). The war mostly revolved around religious identity and ethnic differences between the various groups (Bax, 2017). Anti-balaka attacks mostly affected the country's Muslim populations and forced many to flee (ibid.). In 2014, former Séléka fighters and the Anti-balaka signed a peace agreement to conclude the civil war. Yet, conflicts have continued between various clans and smaller military factions (Dukhan, 2016, pp. 2-10). The civil war in the Central African Republic thus serves as a control case for the conflict in DR Congo.

In research literature on bilateral relations between China and the Central African Republic, Abdurrahim Siradağ (2016) describes how first economic and political exchanges were established in the 1960s opposed to the former colonial power France's interests (Siradağ, 2016, p. 94). The new partnership with China also influenced the CAR's relationship to neighbouring Chad (ibid., p. 100). A report by the International Peace Information Service (2014) further outlines that China's economic relations with the CAR have been dominated by the oil industry, where a number of licences have been provided to the China National Petroleum Corporation (Weyns, Hoex, Hilgert, & Spittaels, 2014, p. 38). In view of the 2012–2014 conflict in the CAR, a report by Conflict Armament Research states that Sudan and China were the main suppliers of weapons and ammunition used on all sides (Conflict Armament Research, 2015, p. 6). The UN mission MINUSCA was established in 2014. Yet, China did not participate in it until 2020[83] (UN Peacekeeping, 2020).

Republic of Congo 2016–2017
Between 2016 and 2017, the government of the Republic of Congo was involved in violent fighting with members of the Ninjas' militia in the region of the Pool department (Acaps, 2017, p. 1; Humanitarian Response Plan Update, 2018, p. 8). During the first six months of 2017, nine provinces were affected by the conflict and about 1.4 million people were

---

83 The Chinese contribution to MINUSCA started after the operationalisation of this study had been finalised. The case of the CAR was thus kept as a synchronic control case. It remains up to future research to conduct a case study on the changed behaviour of China in this particular case.

Annex 1: Background Information on Synchronic Control Cases

forced to flee their homes (Humanitarian Response Plan Update, 2018, p. 8). On 23rd December 2017 both sides signed a peace accord, due to which the Ninjas had to hand over their arms (Reuters, 2017). Due to the similarities in both conflicts, the case of the Republic of Congo serves as a synchronic comparison for the conflict in Liberia.

General research literature about the relations between China and the Republic of Congo remains limited. Nathanaël T. Niambi provides an overview of the bilateral ties between the two countries and outlines that Congo-Brazzaville was one of the first African countries to start South–South cooperation (Niambi, 2018, p. 227). Beyond that, Congo's relations with China are mentioned in several reports that are, however, not dedicated to the bilateral relations between the two countries but rather cover the topic of China in Africa from a more general perspective or bilateral relations between China and neighbouring DR Congo (Bosshard, 2008; Molintas, 2013).

Nigeria 2009–ongoing
In 2009, the jihadist rebel group Boko Haram started violent attacks against the government of Nigeria (Rasheed, 2012, p. 21). The occasion on which the insurgency began was the group's refusal to follow the country's motorbike helmet law in three states of Nigeria and the subsequent police suppression, including the execution of the group's leader (ibid. p. 21). As a result, Boko Haram carried out a number of suicide bombings and other violent attacks mostly in northern Nigeria (ibid. 21). However, their superior objective was to introduce a so-called Islamic State in the region (ibid. 21). Until 2019, Boko Haram had killed more than 25,000 people and has become known for the kidnapping of over 250 schoolgirls in Chibok in 2014 (Apuke, 2016; Campbell, 2018). Insurgencies have also spilled over into neighbouring countries such as Cameroon, Niger and Chad (Campbell, 2018). The conflict in Nigeria is applied here as a synchronic control case for the conflict in Mali since both civil wars are in the same region and relate to Islamist terrorism.

In the research literature covering Chinese–Nigerian relations, a 2011 OECD report considers the two countries' bilateral ties a powerful South–South alliance and looks back at the first forty years of diplomatic relations between them (Egbula & Zheng, 2011, p. 4). Nevertheless, the report finds that, just like many other African countries, Nigeria has warmly welcomed China's approach as a new economic partner (ibid., p. 19). Additionally, Lemuel Ekedegwa Odeh adds an analysis on the dynamics of the bilateral relations between the two countries since 1971 (Odeh, 2014).

Odeh states that China's approach to Nigeria can be seen in contrast to Western imperialism, while both partners remain important to Nigerian institutional and economic development (ibid., p. 162). A 2018 report by the US Institute of Peace furthermore connects China's economic interests to the country's conflicting environment (Page, 2018). While Nigeria is seen as one of the most important export destinations for Chinese goods and, given its growing population and rise in consumption, it is also an important source of oil for China (ibid., p. 6). At the same time, Nigeria is one of the most critical and riskiest business environments when it comes to stability and security in Africa (ibid., p. 7). Finally, a special focus on trade relations between China and Nigeria is provided by Oke, Oshinfowokan and Okonda (2019). In their study, the authors find that Nigeria has been able to increase its gains from trading with China by avoiding imports of goods that can also be produced locally, increasing interactions between entrepreneurs and government officials on both sides and strengthening trade institutions (Oke, Oshinfowokan, & Okonoda, 2019, p. 77).

Annex 2: Background Information on Diachronic Control Cases

Morocco 1975
After the colonial power Spain had withdrawn from the "Spanish Sahara", Morocco and the Sahrawi indigenous POLISARIO Front entered into a violent conflict over the territory of today's Western Sahara (Theofilopoulou, 2006). First, Spain tried to hold a referendum that included the option of independence for the Sahrawi population (ibid., p.2). Yet, this was strongly opposed by King Hassan II of Morocco, who initiated a "Green March" with about 350,000 civilians who moved to Western Sahara to settle there and increase the Moroccan presence (ibid., p. 3). Due to large deposits of fish, oil and phosphates in the region, the conflict has been characterised by a dispute over natural resources (Leite, et al., 2006, p. 9). At first, King Hassan's initiative was met with little resistance. POLISARIO, however, soon started a period of guerrilla warfare, aiming at independence for the territory (Leite, et al., 2006). In 1979, an agreement was reached with Mauritania, which withdrew from the conflict (ibid., p.6). Only in 1991 did a ceasefire agreement with Morocco finally stop the violent fighting, even though a final resolution was not reached. As a result, the UN mission MINURSO was established (ibid.).

Annex 2: Background Information on Diachronic Control Cases

DR Congo 1998–2003
The Second Congo War in DR Congo began in 1998, only one year after the end of the First Congo War and lasted until 2003 (OHCHR, 2010, p. 153). Tribal disputes continued and the situation escalated when President Kabila was accused of systematically discriminating against Congolese members of the Tutsi clan and favouring his own Katanga clan (ibid. p. 153). In fear of a coup d'état, the president discharged a Tutsi general as his chief of staff. Tutsi soldiers revolted in an attempt to overthrow the president and gain control of the territory (ibid. p. 153). The country was split into two camps, one controlled by President Kabila supported by Zimbabwe, Angola and Sudan; the other supported by Rwanda, Uganda and Burundi (ibid.). During the war, alliances became more complex since Kabila tried to unite with the Hutu factions of these countries. Tutsis were systematically persecuted and killed with the help of propaganda calls through television and radio (ibid., pp. 155ff). Only in 2003, under intense diplomatic pressure, did the war officially end, and the Transitional Government of the Democratic Republic of the Congo then took power (ibid. pp. 155ff).

Liberia 1989–1997
In 1989, Charles Taylor, leader of the National Patriotic Front of Liberia (NPFL), led a revolt against President Samuel Doe, who was later executed (The Advocates for Human Rights, 2009, pp. 129-135). The invasion marked the beginning of a brutal seven-year long civil war. The conflict was characterised by violations of international human rights, many civilian victims and a large number of internally displaced people (ibid. pp. 129–135). The NPFL's attacks often resulted in local food shortages because farmers fled from their lands in fear of violence, leaving behind crops and unplanted fields (ibid.). Another characteristic of the conflict was the importance of spirituality among Taylor's followers. Sorcery, called "Juju" in Liberia, has been a crucial element of the country's political culture for a long time. Ritual killings, cannibalism or human sacrifice were seen as practices of those who seek power (Global Security, 2011). During the Liberian civil war, combatants would often wear costumes, camouflage paint or wigs to hide their identity or express magical powers which they believed they possessed. Some were marked with symbolic tattoos on their skin and wore masks. In traditional Liberian belief, it is believed that masks give spiritual powers to those who wear them. In practice, they hindered victims in identifying their attackers and frightened enemies (The Advocates for Human Rights, 2009, p. 114f). In 1997,

Charles Taylor was elected president. Yet, the fighting did not stop as rebel groups began to revolt against him (United Nations UNMIL, 2018, p. 17f).

Ivory Coast 2002–2007
In 2002, a political crisis in Ivory Coast turned into a violent civil war that only ended five years later (Kennedy, 2002). While rebels controlled northern areas of the country, the government remained in the country's south (ibid.). Violent conflict began shortly after the death of the former president Felix Houphouet Boigny in 1993 after 33 years in power. He left the economically prospering country with the challenge of dealing with competitive elections for the first time (ibid., p. 2). His successor Henri Konan Bedie, however, soon concentrated on the country's national identity and introduced the term "Ivorian-ness", which resulted in nationalist and xenophobic mobilisations. Bedie's intention may have been to discredit his political Muslim rival from the north (ibid. p. 2). Yet, the results were attacks on foreigners and immigrants, who represented about one quarter of Ivory Coast's population (ibid.). In 2004, the United Nations voted in favour of Resolution 1572, which introduced an arms embargo on the country (UNSCR, 2004). In 2006, the participation of Ivory Coast's national football team in the World Cup helped to initiate a truce between the two parties (Mehler, 2006). One year later, the government of Ivory Coast and the rival forces signed a peace agreement in Burkina Faso (Kennedy, 2002).

Lebanon 1975–1990
Between 1975 and 1990, the Lebanese Civil War broke out. The conflict was characterised by fighting between the different religious groups, which demanded more equality in political representation (Makdisi & Sadaka, 2003). In particular, this related to the Muslim community, who had grown in number due to the inflow of Palestinian refugees after the foundation of the state of Israel (ibid., pp.5–7). Despite increasing economic growth and per capita income, political confrontations caused the outbreak of the war (ibid., p.9). Mostly, disputes related to the sectarian system of power sharing which dated back to the French colonial power. Fighting between Christian Maronites and Palestinian Muslims began in 1975, while the latter rapidly received support from other Muslim forces. During the war, alliances often changed, as did external support from Israel or Syria. In 1989, the conflict ended with the Taif Agreement, which reformed the rules of the different religious groups' political representation. Religious tensions between Christians and Muslims as well

Annex 2: Background Information on Diachronic Control Cases

as between Sunni and Shia Muslims remained. Since 1978, the United Nations have established the United Nations Interim Force in Lebanon to survey a demilitarised zone on the border with Israel (Gurses, 2014).

Sudan 1983–2005
In 1983, nine years after the end of the First Sudanese Civil War (1955–1972), another violent North–South conflict broke out between the Sudanese government and the Southern People's Liberation Army (SPLA) (de Waal, 2016a, pp. 121-150). President Nimeiri had disobeyed a previous agreement which ensured the South a certain autonomy (ibid.). Yet, Nimeiri tried to impose Sharia Law in the whole country, which made the SPLA take up arms for another 20 years and made this civil war one of the longest worldwide (Ottaway & El-Sadany, 2012, p. 5). Even if the ruling party controlled both the North and South of the country, political stability was lacking and the ruling military or civilian governments each only held power for a very short period before it switched again to the opposite side (ibid., p. 5). Nevertheless, for a long time the North succeeded in exploiting the South, especially after the first oil wells were found in 1978 (ibid., p. 5). However, when President Jafaar Nimeiri came to power in 1969, he introduced Sharia law and reorganised the country into three provinces, which raised concerns among the non-Muslim population (ibid. p. 5f). From 1983, escalations re-emerged and after a coup d'état in 1993, Islamist leader Omar al-Bashir became president (ibid., p. 6). Violent clashes along tribal lines and the North–South divide continued. The conflict resulted in one to two million civil casualties and was only ended with a peace agreement in 2005 (ibid. p. 6). Six years after the termination of the war, a referendum was held that led to South Sudan's independence (ibid. p. 10).

Mali 1974–85
Between 1974 and 1985, Mali and Burkina Faso fought over a strip of land which is known for containing large amounts of natural resources such as gas and minerals (Salliot, 2010, pp. 22-24). The length of the strip varies between 160 and 275 km, depending on the source. The exact borders between the two countries, however, remain unclear (ibid. pp. 22–24). The conflict had been running for a long time but turned violent in the years 1974 and 1985, when it became known as the "Agacher Strip War" or "Christmas War" (ibid. pp. 22–24). On December 25, 1985, the Malian military attacked the border posts of Burkina Faso (ibid. p. 22). The latter responded with counterattacks, but Mali's government successfully

12. ANNEXES

captured several villages. However, only the third attempt at a ceasefire agreement ended the war on December 30, 1985 (ibid., p. 22). Since the border question remained unresolved, the case was handed to the International Court of Justice, whose ruling split the territory almost equally in 1986 (ibid. p. 22).

REFERENCES

Abbott, K. W., & Snidal, D. (1998). Why States Act Through Formal International Organizations. *The Journal of Conflict Resolution* (42 (1)), pp. 3–32.

Abdel-Latif, O. (2008). *Lebanon's Sunni Islamists—A Growing Force*. Washington D.C., Moscow, Beijing, Beirut, Brussels: Carnegie Endowment for International Peace.

Academy for Cultural Diplomacy. (2018). Retrieved June 21, 2018 from http://www.culturaldiplomacy.org/academy/index.php?chinese-diaspora

Acaps. (2017). *Republic of Congo, Conflict in Pool department*. Geneva: ACAPS.

Acemoğlu, D., & Robinson, J. A. (2013). *Warum Nationen Scheitern, Die Ursprünge von Macht, Wohlstand und Armut*. Frankfurt am Main: Fischer.

Acharya, A. (2016). Studying the Bandung conference from a Global IR perspective. *Australian Journal of International Affairs*(70 (4)), pp. 342–357.

Africa Research Bulletin. (2015). Morocco–China Trade Agreements. *Africa Research Bulletin: Economic, Financial and Technical Series* (51 (11)), pp. 20624C–20625A.

African Union. (2019). *Flagship Projects of Agenda 2063*. Retrieved May 01, 2019, from https://au.int/en/agenda2063/flagship-projects

Aftab Khan, S. (2007). Tackling Piracy in Somali Waters. *UN Chronicles online Edition*. Retrieved June 29, 2020, from https://web.archive.org/web/20080422072521/http://www.un.org/Pubs/chronicle/2007/webArticles/073107_somalia.htm

Ahmad, A. (2015). U.S. Africa Command: Military Operations or Good Governance. *IOSR Journal Of Humanities And Social Science* (20 (6)), pp. 57–67.

Ahmad, Y., Bosch, E., Carey, E., & Mc Donnell, I. (2020). *Six decades of ODA: insights and outlook in the COVID-19 crisis*. Paris: OECD.

Aiddata. (2018). *Mapping China's Global Development Footprint*. Retrieved May 01, 2019, from William & Mary: https://www.aiddata.org/china-project-locations

Aiddata. (2021). *William & Mary's Global Research Institute*. Retrieved May 24, 2021, from China's Global Development Footprint: https://www.aiddata.org/china-official-finance

Aidoo, R., & Hess, S. (2015). Non-Interference 2.0: China's Evolving Foreign Policy towards a Changing Africa. (G. G. Studies, ed.) *Journal of Current Chinese Affairs*, pp. 107–139.

Alaaldin, R., & Mezran, K. (2018). From Fragmentation to Decentralization: An Overview. In K. Mezran, & A. Varvelli, *The Arc of Crisis in the MENA Region, Fragmentation, Decentralization and Islamist Opposition* (pp. 23–35). Milano: Ledizioni LediPublishing.

Alagappa, M. (2011). International Relations Studies in Asia: Distinctive Trajectories. *International Relations of the Asia-Pacific* (11), pp. 193–230.

REFERENCES

Albert, E. (2017). China in Africa. *Council on Foreign Relations*.

Alden, C., & Alves, A. (2017). China's Regional Forum Diplomacy in the Developing World: Socialisation and the 'Sinosphere'. *Journal of Contemporary China*, pp. 151–165.

Alden, C., & Large, D. (2013). China's Evolving Policy towards Peace and Security in Africa: Constructing a new paradigm for peace building? In M. Berhe, & L. Hongwu, *China-Africa Relations, Governance, Peace and Security* (pp. 16–28). Ethiopia: Institute for Peace and Security Studies Addis Ababa University, Institute of African Studies Zhejiang Normal University.

Alijla, A., & Aghdam, M. (2017). Different Paths to Democracy in the MENA Region: A Configurational Comparative Analysis. *Journal of Political Sciences & Public Affairs* (5(2)). doi:10.4172/2332-0761.1000265

Allen, K. (2001). China's Foreign Military Relations with Asia-Pacific. *Journal of Contemporary China* (10), pp. 645–662.

Allen, K. (2015). What China hopes to achieve with first peacekeeping mission. Retrieved June 25, 2021 from https://www.bbc.com/news/world-africa-34976580

Allen, K., Saunders, P., & Chen, J. (2017). *China Strategic Perspectives No. 11, Chinese Military Diplomacy, 2003–2016: Trends and Implications*. Institute for National Strategic Studies (INSS). Washington, D.C.: National Defense University Press.

Al-Sharif, O. (2021). *Iran–China accord ushers in major geopolitical shift*. Retrieved May 26, 2021, from Arab News: https://www.arabnews.com/node/1834281/opinion

Altenburg, T., & Weikert, J. (2007). *Trilateral Development Cooperation with "New Donors"*. Bonn: Deutsches Institut für Entwicklungspolitik.

Alusala, N. (2004). The Democratic Republic of Congo 2003 in review. *African Security Review* (13), pp. 93–96.

Andersen, L. E., Lons, C., Peragovics, T., Rózsa, E., & Sidło, K. (2020). China–MENA Relations in the Context of Chinese Global Strategy. In K. W. Sidło, *The Role of China in the Middle East and North Africa (MENA). Beyond Economic Interests?* (pp. 10–31). Barcelona: European Institute of the Mediterranean.

Andersen, L. R., & Engedal, P. E. (2013). *Blue Helmets and Grey Zones: Do UN Multidimensional Peace Operations Work?* Copenhagen: Danish Institute for International Studies.

Anderson, J. (1998). The Devil They Know. *The New Yorker*. Retrieved April 01, 2020, from https://www.newyorker.com/magazine/1998/07/27/the-devil-they-know

Anderson, M., & Olson, L. (2003). *Confronting War: Critical Lessons for Peace Practitioners*. Cambridge, MA: The Collaborative for Development Action, Inc.

Anderson, S., Bennis, P., & Cavanagh, J. (2003). *Coalition of the Willing or Coalition of the Coerced? How the Bush Administration Influences Allies in its War on Iraq*. Washington D.C.: Institute for Policy Studies.

REFERENCES

Apuke, O. (2016). The evolution of boko haram, its attack on Chibok girls and the American amnesty intervention: A contextual analysis. *National Journal of Multidisciplinary Research and Development* (1 (3)), pp. 14–17.

Arduino, A. (2020). *The Footprint of Chinese Private Security Companies in Africa, Working Paper No. 2020/35.* Washington, DC: China Africa Research Initiative, School of Advanced International Studies, Johns Hopkins University. Retrieved September 26, 2020, from http://www.sais-cari.org/publications

Arend, A. (2003). International Law and the Preemptive Use of Military Force. *The Washington Quarterly*, pp. 89–103.

Arif, B. (2017). The Role of Soft Power in China's Foreign Policy in the 21st Century. International Journal of Social Sciences & Educational Studies 3.3.

Armstrong, A. (1981). The Political Consequences of Economic Dependence. *Journal of Conflict Resolution* (25 (3)), pp. 401–428.

Arteaga, F. (2008). *Global Policy Forum.* Retrieved August 11, 2018, from The Chad Conflict, United Nations (MINURCAT): https://www.globalpolicy.org/component/content/article/180-chad-car/33312-the-chad-conflict-united-nations-minurcat.html

Ashley, Jr, R. (2019). *China military power, modernizing a force to fight and win.* Washington: Defence Intelligence Agency. Retrieved 09 14, 2019, from https://www.dia.mil/Portals/27/Documents/News/Military%20Power%20Publications/China_Military_Power_FINAL_5MB_20190103.pdf

Asian–African Conference. (1955). *Final Communiqué of the Asian–African Conference.* Bandung.

Askary, H. (2018). Operation Felix, The Miracle of Yemen's Reconstruction and Connection to the New Silk Road. *Two World Systems*, pp. 20–29.

Atkinson, M. M., & Coleman, W. D. (1989). Strong States and Weak States: Sectoral Policy Networks in Advanced Capitalist Economies. *British Journal of Political Science* (19), pp. 47–67.

Atran, S., Axelrod, R., & Davis, R. (2007). Sacred barriers to conflict resolution. *Science American Association for the Advancement of Science* (317), pp. 1039–1040. doi: ijn_00505181

Attree, L. (2012). *China and conflict-affected states Between principle and pragmatism.* Saferworld.

Auregan, P. (2011). *La Chine en Côte d'Ivoire : le double jeu.* Vincennes: La Revue Politique.

Ayenagbo, K., Njobvu, T., Sossou, J., & Tozoun, B. (2012). China's peacekeeping operations in Africa: From unwilling participation to responsible contribution. *African Journal of Political Science and International Relations*, 6(2), pp. 22–32.

Azam, J.-P. (2001). The Redistributive State and Conflicts in Africa. (S. Publications, ed.) *Journal of Peace Research* (38 (4)), pp. 429–444.

Bachrach, P., & Baratz, S. (1962). Two Faces of Power. *The American Political Science Review* (56 (4)), pp. 1947-1952.

REFERENCES

Bader, J. (2015). China, Autocratic Patron? An Empirical Investigation of China as a Factor in Autocratic Survival. *International Studies Quarterly* (59 (1)), pp. 23–33.

Bader, J. (2015). Propping up dictators? Economic cooperation from China and its impact on authoritarian persistence in party and non-party regimes. *European Journal of Political Research* (54 (4)), pp. 655–672.

Badescu, C. (2007). Authorizing Humanitarian Intervention: Hard Choices in Saving Strangers. *Canadian Journal of Political Science / Revue canadienne de science politique* (40 (1)), pp. 51–78.

Bajwa, J. (2008). Defining Elements of Comprehensive National Power. *CLAWS Journal*, pp. 151–162.

Banerjee, A., & Duflo, E. (2019). *Poor Economics*. New York City: Perseus Books.

Baniela, S. I., & Ríos, J. V. (2012). Piracy in Somalia: A Challenge to The International Community. *The Journal of Navigation* (65), pp. 693–710.

Barnett, M., & Duval, R. (2005). Power in International Politics. *International Organization* (59 (1)), pp. 39–75.

Bass, G. J. (2008). *Freedom's Battle, The Origins of Humanitarian Interventions*. (A. A. House, ed.) New York: Borzoi Book.

Baumann, R., Rittberger, V., & Wagner, W. (1998). Macht und Machtpolitik: Neorealistische Außenpolitiktheorie und Prognosen für die deutsche Außenpolitik nach der Vereinigung. *Tübinger Arbeitspapiere zur Internationalen Politik und Friedensforschung*.

Bax, P. (2017). Concert Blast Shows Central African Republic Religious Rift. *Bloomberg*. Retrieved August 18, 2018, from https://www.bloomberg.com/news/articles/2017-11-22/blast-at-concert-shows-central-african-republic-s-religious-rift

Bayeh, E. (2014). The Current War on Gaza: A Challenge to the Principle of 'Responsibility to Protect'. (A. R. Journals, ed.) (9), pp. 205–210.

BBC News. (2012). *Q&A: DR Congo conflict*. Retrieved March 28, 2020, from https://www.bbc.com/news/world-africa-11108589

BBC News. (2014). *Hundreds of Chinese workers are evacuated from Libya*. Retrieved June 21, 2018, from https://www.bbc.com/news/world-africa-28684555

Beach, D., & Pedersen, R. (2013). *Process-Tracing Methods: Foundations and Guidelines*. University of Michigan Press. doi:10.3998/mpub.10072208

Beeson, M., & Li, F., (2016). China's Place in Regional and Global Governance: A New World Comes Into View. *Global Policy* (7 (4)), pp. 491–499.

Benabdallah, L. (2016). China's Peace and Security Strategies in Africa: Building Capacity is Building Peace? *African Studies Quarterly* (16 (3-4)), pp. 17–34.

Benabdallah, L., & Large, D. (2020). Development, Security, and China's Evolving Role in Mali. *China*Africa Research Initiative* (40).

Benner, T., & Blume, T. (2008). A Second Chance for Liberia, President Johnson-Sirleaf's quest to build a new Liberia. *Africa's Plight*, pp. 40-45.

REFERENCES

Bennett, D. S., & Stam, A. (1998). The Declining Advantages of Democracy: A Combined Model of War Outcomes and Duration. *The Journal of Conflict Resolution* (42 (3)), pp. 344–366.

Bennett, H. (2015). *Causes of Third Party Military Intervention in Intrastate Conflicts.* Senior Honors Project. Harrisonburg: James Madison University.

Bercovitch, J., & Rubin, J. Z. (1992). *Mediation in International Relations.* London: The Macmillan Press Ltd.

Bercovitch, J., & Schneider, G. (2000). Who Mediates? The Political Economy of International Conflict Management. *Journal of Peace Research* (37 (2)), pp. 145–165.

Berekovitch, J. (1991). International Mediation and Dispute Settlement: Evaluating the Conditions for Successful Mediation. (P. P. Corporation, ed.) *Negotiation Journal*, pp. 17–30.

Berg, P. (2008). *The Dynamics of Conflict in the Tri-Border Region of the Sudan, Chad and the Central African Republic.* Berlin: Friedrich Ebert Stiftung.

Besenjö, J. (2013). War at the Background of Europe: The Crisis of Mali. *AARMS, 12*(2), pp. 247–271.

Beswetherick, M., Astor, M., & Sanger, D. (2020). *Joseph R. Biden Jr.* Retrieved May 08, 2021, from The New York Times: https://www.nytimes.com/interactive/2020/us/politics/joe-biden-foreign-policy.html

Biden, J. (2019). *The Power of America's Example: The Biden Plan for Leading the Democratic World to Meet the Challenges of the 21st Century.* Retrieved June 30, 2021, from Biden Harris Democrats: https://joebiden.com/AmericanLeadership/

Biden, J. (2021). *Remarks by President Biden on America's Place in the World.* Retrieved May 28, 2021, from The White House Briefing Room: https://www.whitehouse.gov/briefing-room/speeches-remarks/2021/02/04/remarks-by-president-biden-on-americas-place-in-the-world/

Bishara, A. (2015). *Russian Intervention in Syria: Geostrategy is Paramount.* Doha: Arab Center for Research and Policy Studies.

Blainey, G. (1988). *Causes of War* (3rd ed.). New York: The Free Press.

Blanchard, B., & WU, J. (2016). China warns US officials not to meet Dalai Lama. *The Telegraph.* Retrieved June 30, 2021, from https://www.reuters.com/article/us-china-usa-diplomacy-idUSKCN0Z00VC

Blanchard, B., & Yimou, L. (2018). *Reuters.* Retrieved June 24, 2018, from https://www.reuters.com/article/us-china-parliament-taiwan/china-urges-taiwans-few-allies-to-follow-irresistible-trend-of-recognizing-beijing-idUSKCN1GK0KR

Blanchard, J.-M. (2021). China's MSRI in Africa and the Middle East: Political Economic Realities Continue to Shape Results and Ramifications. *China's Maritime Silk Road Initiative, Africa, and the Middle East*, pp. 1–51.

Blanchard, J.-M., & Lu, F. (2012). Thinking Hard About Soft Power: A Review and Critique of the Literature on China and Soft Power. *Asian Perspectiv* (36), pp. 565–589.

Blankson-Ocansey, K. (2009). *Looking East: China–Africa Engagements, Liberia Case Study.* Monrovia: African Center of Economic Transformation.

REFERENCES

Bleischwitz, R., Dittrich, M., & Pierdicca, C. (2012). *Coltan from Central Africa, International Trade and Implications for Any Certification, BEEP n° 23*. Bruges: Bruges European Economic Policy Briefings.

Boardman, R. (1974). Themes and Explanation in Sinology. In R. L. Dial, *Advancing and Contending Approaches to the Study of Chinese Foreign Policy* (pp. 3–50). Halifax, Nova Scotia: Centre for Foreign Policy Studies, Dalhousie University.

Bolton, J. (2018). *Remarks by National Security Advisor Ambassador John R. Bolton on the Trump Administration's New Africa Strategy*. Retrieved June 30, 2021, from Heritage Foundation, Washington D.C. The White House: https://trumpwhitehouse.archives.gov/briefings-statements/remarks-national-security-advisor-ambassador-john-r-bolton-trump-administrations-new-africa-strategy/

Bondurant, J. (1965). *Conquest of violence: The Gandhian philosophy of violence* (vol. 243). Univ. of California Press.

Boniface, P. (2003). What Justifies Regime Change? *The Washington Quarterly*, 26(3), pp. 61–71.

Boone, C., & Doshi, D. (2009). The China Model in Africa: A New Brand of Developmentalism. In R. Springborg, *Development Models in Muslim Contexts, Chinese, "Islamic" and Neo-Liberal Alternatives* (pp. 47–84). Edinburgh: Edinburgh University Press, The Aga Khan University.

Bosshard, P. (2008). *China's Environmental Footprint in Africa*. South Africa: SA Institute of International Affairs (SAIIA).

Boukhars, A. (2013). *Western Sahara: Beyond Complacency*. Carnegie Endowment for International Peace.

Boutros Ghali, B. (1992). *An agenda for peacepreventive diplomacy, peacemaking and peace-keeping. Report of the Secretary-General pursuant to the statement adopted by the Summit Meeting of the Security Council on 31 January 1992*. No. F/341.73 B6.

Bove, V., Ruffa, C., & Ruggeri, A. (2020). *Composing Peace: Mission Composition in UN Peacekeeping*. Oxford: Oxford University Press.

Bowen, J. (2017). *China File Viewpoint*. Retrieved June 30, 2021, from China, Global Peacemaker? Xi Jinping says One Belt, One Road will bring harmony and peace to the countries where China invests. Will it?: https://www.chinafile.com/reporting-opinion/viewpoint/china-global-peacemaker

bpb. (2007). *Bundeszentrale für Politische Bildung*. Retrieved April 05, 2020, from https://www.bpb.de/politik/hintergrund-aktuell/69901/un-mission-in-darfur-02-08-2007

bpb. (2017). *2. Februar 1982: Das Massaker von Hama in Syrien*. Retrieved April 11, 2020, from Bundeszentrale für politische Bildung: https://www.bpb.de/politik/hintergrund-aktuell/241689/massaker-von-hama

Bradsher, K., & Gettleman, J. (2012). Sudan Rebels Are Said to Hold Road Crew From China. *The New York Times*. Retrieved June 30, 2021, from https://www.nytimes.com/2012/01/30/world/asia/chinese-workers-are-reported-captured-by-sudan-rebels.html

Brautigam, D. (2009). *The Dragon's Gift: The Real Story of China in Africa*. Oxford: Oxford University Press.

REFERENCES

Brecher, M., & Wilkenfeld, J. (1997). *A Study of Crisis*. (U. o. Press, ed.)

Bree, F. (2014). Obama's 'Free Rider' Comment Draws Chinese Criticism. *Sinosphere*. Retrieved June 28, 2020, from https://onlinelibrary.wiley.com/doi/epdf/10.1111/mepo.12171

Breuer, J. (2017). *Two Belts, One Road? the role of Africa in China's Belt & Road initiative*. Köln: Stiftung Asienhaus.

Brodie, B. (1959). *Strategy in the Missile Age*. Santa Monica, California: Rand Corporation.

Broich, T. (2017). *Do authoritarian regimes receive more Chinese development finance than democratic ones? Empirical evidence for Africa*. Maastricht: Maastricht Economic and Social Research institute on Innovation and Technology, Maastricht Graduate School of Governance.

Bromley, S. (1998). Oil and the Middle East, The End of US Hegemony? *Middle East Report, US Foreign Policy in the Middle East: Critical Assessments* (208), pp. 19–22.

Brosché, J. (2008). *Darfur – Dimensions and Dilemmas of a Complex Situation*. Uppsala University: Department of Peace and Conflict Research.

Brown, K. (2013). Is China's non-interference policy sustainable? *BBC News*. Retrieved June 30, 2021, from https://www.bbc.com/news/world-asia-china-24100629

Brown, K. (2018). *The Diplomat*. Retrieved November 17, 2018, from China's Quest: To Be a Status Super Power: https://thediplomat.com/2018/03/chinas-quest-to-be-a-status-super-power/

Bruton, B. E. (2010). *Somalia A New Approach*. New York: Council on Foreign Relations.

Buche, J., & Siewert, M. B. (2015). Qualitative Comparative Analysis (QCA) in der Soziologie – Perspektiven, Potentiale und Anwendungsbereiche. *Zeitschrift für Soziologie, Jg. 44*(Heft 6), pp. 386–406.

Burton, J. (1990). *Conflict: Resolution and Prevention*. New York: St. Martin's Press.

Butler, D. M., & Wheeler, T. (2012). *China and conflict-affected states*. London: Saferworld.

Butler, M., & Wheeler, T. (2012). *China and conflict-affected states, Between principle and pragmatism*. London: Saferworld.

Butts, K., & Bankus, B. (2009). China's Pursuit of Africa's Natural Resources. *Collins Center Study* (1(9)), pp. 1–14.

Cai, P. (2017). *Understanding China's Belt and Road Initiative*. Sydney: Lowy Institute for International Policy.

Campbell, J. (2018). *Council on Foreign Relations*. Retrieved August 18, 2018, from Africa Program: https://www.cfr.org/nigeria/nigeria-security-tracker/p29483

Campbell, J. C. (1972). The Soviet Union and the United States in the Middle East. *The Annals of the American Academy of Political and Social Science*, pp. 126–135.

REFERENCES

Cantori, V. (2016). *Mediterranean Affairs*. Retrieved June 30, 2021, from http://mediterraneanaffairs.com/chinas-increasing-interests-in-mena-is-the-all-economy-solution-a-viable-path-for-stability/

Caramani, D. (2009). *Introduction to the Comparative Method With Boolean Algebra* (vol. 158). Zürich: SAGE Publications.

Carment, D., & James, P. (2004). Third-Party States in Ethnic Conflict: Identifying the Domestic Determinants of Intervention. In M. P. Lobell S.E., *Ethnic Conflict and International Politics: Explaining Diffusion and Escalation* (pp. 11–34). New York: Palgrave Macmillan.

Carr, E. H. (1939). *Twenty Years' Crisis, 1919–1939*.

Carrai, M., Defraigne, J.-C., & Wouters, J. (2020). The Belt and Road Initiative and global governance: by way of introduction. In M. A. Carrai, J.-C. Defraigne, & J. Wouters, *The Belt and Road Initiative and Global Governance* (pp. 1–19). Leuven Centre for Global Governance Studies: Edward Elgar Publishing.

CCICED. (2013). *China Council for International Cooperation on Environment and Development*. Retrieved November 17, 2018, from http://www.cciced.net/ccicedn/NEWSCENTER/LatestEnvironmentalandDevelopmentNews/201310/t20131030_82626.html

Chan, G., Lee, P. K., & Chan, L.-H. (2012). *China Engages Global Governance, A New World Order in the Making?* London: Routledge.

Chang, I.-w. (2018). *China and Yemen's Forgotten War*. Washington D.C.: United States Institute of Peace.

Chase, M. (2017). China's Assessment of the War in Iraq: America's "Deepest Quagmire" and the Implications for Chinese National Security. *China Brief* (7 (17)).

Chauzal, G., & van Damme, T. (2015). *The roots of Mali's conflict, moving beyond the 2012 crisis*. Netherlands Institute of International Relations. The Hague: Clingendael.

Chaziza, M. (2015). China's Middle East Foreign Policy and the Yemen Crisis: Challenges and Implications. *Middle East Review of International Affairs* (19 (2)), pp. 18–25.

Chaziza, M. (2016). China's Middle East Policy: The ISIS Factor. *Middle East Policy* (23 (1)), pp. 25–33.

Chaziza, M., & Goldman, O. (2016). What factors increase the probability of Chinese interventions in intrastate wars? *Asian Journal of Political Science* (1), pp. 1–20.

Chen, J. (2011). The Emergence of China in. (I. f. Studies, ed.) *Strategic Forum, National Defense University*.

Chen, L., Rogers, M., Moore, S., & Yankus, W. (2021). *U.S. China Policy Under the Biden Administration*. Brunswick Group.

Chen, Z. (2016). China Debates the Non-Interference. *The Chinese Journal of International Politics, vol. 9* (No. 3), pp. 349–374.

Chernoff, F. (2005). *The power of international theory: Reforging the link to foreign policy-making through scientific inquiry*. London: Routledge.

Cheung, G. (2008). International relations theory in flux in view of China's "Peaceful Rise". *Copenhagen Journal of Asian studies* (26 (1)), pp. 5–21.

China Daily. (2006). Israel was repeatedly warned before attack. *People's Daily*. Retrieved March 24, 2020, from http://en.people.cn/200607/28/eng20060728_287500.html

China Daily. (2015). *Full Text: China's second Africa policy paper*. Retrieved March 27, 2021, from Xinhua: https://www.chinadaily.com.cn/world/XiattendsPariscli mateconference/2015-12/05/content_22632874.htm

China Development Bank. (2015). *China– Africa Development Fund*. Retrieved May 23, 2021, from Comprehensive Finance Services: http://www.cdb.com.cn/Englis h/ywgl/zhjryw/zffzjjyxgs/

China Policy. (2017). *China Going Global: between ambition and capacity*. Beijing: China Policy. Retrieved 06 20, 2018, from https://policycn.com/wp-content/uplo ads/2017/05/2017-Chinas-going-global-strategy.pdf

ChinaMED. (2021). *ChinaMed INDEX*. Retrieved May 24, 2021, from Value of Chinese energy imports from Saudi Arabia: https://www.chinamed.it/chinamed -data/about-the-data

Cho, S. (2019). China's Participation in UN Peacekeeping Operations since the 2000s. *Journal of Contemporary China, 28* (117), pp. 482–498. doi:DOI:10.1080/10670564.2018.1542216

Chow, G. (2004). Economic Reform and Growth in China. (P. U. Department of Economics, ed.) *Annals of Economics and Finance*, pp. 127–152.

Christensen, T. (1996). *Useful adversaries: Grand strategy, domestic mobilization, and Sino-American conflict, 1947–1958*. Princeton: Princeton University Press.

Christensen, T. (2003). PRC Security Relations with the United States: Why Things Are Going So Well. *China Leadership Monitor* (8), pp. 1–10.

Churruca, C. (2015). EUFOR Chad/CAR Mission on the Protection of Civilians: A Distinctive EU Way to Peace Operations. In G. G. Maria, & M. R. Freire, *Managing Crises, Making Peace, Towards a Strategic EU Vision for Security and Defence* (pp. 216–235). Springer Verlag.

Chuwattananurak, W. (2016). China's Comprehensive national Power and its implications for the rise of China: reassessment and challenges. *CEEISA-ISA 2016 Joint International Conference* (pp. 1–39). Ljubljana, Slovenia: University of Ljubljana.

Clarke, M. (2010). China, Xinjiang and the internationalisation of the Uyghur issue. *Global Change Peace & Security* (2), pp. 213–229.

Claude, Jr., I. (1986). The Common Defense and Great-Power Responsibilities. (T. A. Science, ed.) *Political Science Quarterly* (101 (5)), pp. 719–732.

Cohen, R. (1996). Cultural aspects of international mediation. In J. Bercovitch, *Resolving international conflicts: The theory and practice of mediation* (pp. 107–128). London: Lynne Rienner Publishers.

Cold-Ravnkilde, S. M. (2013). *War and Peace in Mali, Background and Perspectives, Report 2013:33*. Danish Institute for International Studies (DIIS).

REFERENCES

Collier, P. (2011). *Undoing the Resource Curse* . Retrieved August 11, 2018, from International Monetary Fund: https://www.imf.org/en/News/Podcasts/All-Podcasts/2017/11/10/paul-collier-on-undoing-the-resource-curse

Collier, P., & Hoffler, A. (2004). Greed and grievance in civil war. *Oxford Economic Papers, 56*, pp. 63–595.

Collins, J. (2008). *Choosing War: The Decision to Invade Iraq and Its Aftermath.* Washington DC: Institute for National Strategic Studies, National Defense University Press.

Comtrade. (2021). *Trade Statistics.* Retrieved May 23, 2021, from UN Comtrade Database: https://comtrade.un.org/data/

Conflict Armament Research. (2015). *Non-State Armed Groups in the Central African Republic, Types and sources of documented arms and ammunition.* London: Conflict Armament Research Ltd.

Constituent and Legislative Assembly DR Congo. (2002). *Mining Law No. 007/2002.* DR Congo: Transition Parliament.

Convergne, E. (2015). Learning to Mediate? The Mediation Support Unit and the Production of Expertise by the UN. *Journal of Intervention and Statebuilding* (2), pp. 1–21.

Corkin, L. (2013). *Uncovering African Agency: Angola's Management of China's Credit Lines.* Oxon, New York: Routledge

Corbetta, R., & Dixon, W. (2005). Danger Beyond Dyads: Third-Party Participants in Militarized Interstate Disputes. *Conflict Management and Peace Science* (22), pp. 39–61.

Cortright, D. (2008). *Peace: A history of movements and ideas.* Cambridge: Cambridge University Press.

Council on Foreign Relations. (2020). *President-Elect Biden on Foreign Policy.* Retrieved May 08, 2021, from Council on Foreign Relations: https://www.cfr.org/election2020/candidate-tracker#defense

Crabtree, J. (2018). *CNBC.* Retrieved October 03, 2018, from https://www.cnbc.com/2018/01/04/china-president-xi-jinping-orders-military-not-to-fear-death.html

Cronqvist, L., & Berg-Schlosser, D. (2009). Multi-Value QCA (mvQCA). In C. C. Ragin, *Configuratonal Comparative Methods* (pp. 69–86). California: SAGE Publications.

Crook, R. C. (1997). The Failure of the Opposition in the 1990 and 1995 elections in Cote d'Ivoire. *African Affairs* (96), pp. 215–242.

Cusack, T., & Eberwein, W.-D. (1982). Prelude to war: Incidence, escalation and intervention in international disputes, 1900–1976. *International Interactions* (9(1)), pp. 9–28.

d'Hooghe, I. (2010). *The Limits of China's Soft Power in Europe Beijing's Public Diplomacy Puzzle.* The Hague: Netherland's Institute of International Relations 'Clingedael'.

Dados, N., & Connell, R. (2012). The Global South. (American Sociological Association, ed.) *Contexts* (11 (1)), pp. 12–13.

REFERENCES

Dag Hammarskjöld Library. (2021). *Dag Hammarskjöld Library;*. Retrieved 06 20, 2018, from Security Council: http://research.un.org/en/docs/sc/quick

Dagne, T. (2004). *Sudan: The Crisis in Darfur.* CRS Report for Congress.

Dahl, R. (1957). The Concept of Power. *Behavioral science* (2 (3)), pp. 201–215.

Danielová, V. (2014). Darfur Crisis of 2003: Analysis of the Darfur Conflict from the Times of First Clashes to the Present Day. *Ethnologia Actualis* (14 (1)), pp. 37–59.

Danju, I., Maasoglu, Y., & Maasoglu, N. (2013). The Reasons Behind U.S. Invasion Of Iraq. *Procedia—Social and Behavioral Science* (8), pp. 682–690.

Davidson, W., & Montville, J. (1981–1982). Foreign Policy According to Freud. (L. Slate Group, ed.) *Foreign Policy*, pp. 145–157.

Davidsson, S. (2020). Modeling the Impact of a Model: The (Non) Relationship between China's Economic Rise and African Democracy. *Politics & Policy* (48 (5)), pp. 859–886.

Davis, M., Dietrich, W., Scholdan, B., & Sepp, D. (2004). *International Intervention in the Post-Cold War World, Moral Responsibility and Power Politics.* Armonk, New York, London: M.E. Sharpe.

de Coning, C., & Osland, K. (2020). *China's Evolving Approach to UN Peacekeeping in Africa.* Oslo: Norwegian Institute of International Affairs.

De Soysa, I. (2002). Paradise Is a Bazaar? Greed, Creed, and Governance in Civil War, 1989-99. *Journal of Peace Research, 39* (4), pp. 395–416.

de Waal, A. (2016). (K. Noel, Interviewer) Retrieved August 11, 2018, from https://www.cfr.org/interview/understanding-roots-conflict-south-sudan

de Waal, A. (2016a). Sudan: Patterns of violence and imperfect endings. In B. Conley-Zilkic, *How Mass Atrocities End* (pp. 121–150). New York: Cambridge University Press.

Debiel, T., & Rinck, P. (2016). Rethinking the local in peacebuilding, Moving away from the liberal/post-liberal divide. In T. Debiel, T. Held, & U. Schneckener, *Peacebuilding in Crisis, Rethinking Paradigms and Practices of Transnational Cooperation* (pp. 240–256). Oxon, New York: Routledge.

Debiel, T., Held, T., & Schneckener, U. (2016). *Peacebuilding in Crisis, Rethinking Paradigms and Practices of Transnational Cooperation.* Oxon, New York: Routledge.

Debrix, F. (2003). *Rituals Of Mediation: International Politics And Social Meaning* (vol. 1). University of Minnesota Press.

Declaration of Principles, Oslo I. (1993). *Declaration of Principles on Interim Self-GovernmentArrangements.* Retrieved from Economic Cooperation Foundation (ECF): https://ecf.org.il/media_items/612

Declaration of Principles, Oslo II. (1995). *Israeli–Palestinian Interim Agreement on the West Bank and the Gaza Strip.* Retrieved from Economic Cooperation Foundation (ECF): http://ecf.org.il/media_items/624

REFERENCES

Defense Intelligence Agency. (2019). *China Military Power, Modernizing a Force to fight and win*. USA: US Defense Intelligence Agency. Retrieved April 13, 2020, from https://www.dia.mil/Portals/27/Documents/News/Military%20Power%20Publications/China_Military_Power_FINAL_5MB_20190103.pdf

Demmelhuber, T., & Zumbrägel, T. (2017). Legitimität und politische Herrschaft, Ein historischer Längsschnitt im Lichte der arabischen Umbrüche. In T. Demmelhuber, & M. Reinkowski, *Arabellion Vom Aufbruch zum Zerfall einer Region?* (pp. 47–65). Baden-Baden: Nomos.

Department of Defense. (2018). *Military Dictionary*. Retrieved June 30, 2021, from https://www.hsdl.org/?view&did=813130

DeRouen Jr, K., Bercovitch, J., & Pospieszna, P. (2011). Introducing the Civil Wars Mediation (CWM) dataset. *Journal of Peace Research* (48 (5)), pp. 663–672.

Dinstein, Y. (2017). *War, Aggression and Self-Defence*. Cambridge: Cambridge University Press.

Dirlik, A. (2015). The Bandung legacy and the People's Republic of China in the perspective of global modernity. *Inter-Asia Cultural Studies* (16 (4)), pp. 615–630.

Dollar, D. (2016). *China's Engagement with Africa, From Natural Resources to Human Resources*. Washington D.C.: John L. Thornton China Center at Brookings.

Dowty, A., & Gil, L. (1996). Refugee flows as grounds for international action. *International Security* (21 (1)), pp. 43–71.

Dukhan, N. (2016). *The Central African Republic Crisis*. University of Birmingham. Birmingham, UK: GSDRC.

Dumbaugh, K. (2009). *Taiwan's Political Status: Historical Background and its implications for US Policy*. Washington D.C.: Congressional Research Service.

Easterly, W. (2001). *The Elusive Quest for Growth: Economists' Adventures and Misadventures in the Tropics*. Massachusetts: MIT Press.

Egbula, M., & Zheng, Q. (2011). *China and Nigeria: a powerful south-south alliance*. Sahel and West Africa Club Secretariat (SWAC/OECD).

Ekanayake, E., & Ledgerwood, J. (2009). An Analysis of the Intra-Regional Trade in the Middle East and North Africa Region. *The International Journal of Business and Finance Research* (3 (1)), pp. 19–29.

Eksi, M. (2017). *The Syrian Crisis as a Proxy War and the Return of the Realist Great Power Politics*.

Elazar, G. (2017). *Moving Westward: The Chinese Rebuilding of Syria*. BESA Center Perspectives Paper.

Elgebeily, S. A. (2017). How China's foreign policy of non-intervention is all about selective action. *South China Morning Post*. Retrieved June 30, 2021, from http://www.scmp.com/comment/insight-opinion/article/2091502/how-chinas-foreign-policy-non-intervention-all-about

Elia, L., & Bove, V. (2011). *Supplying peace: Participation in and troop contribution to peacekeeping missions*. Essex, Calabria: University of Essex, Università della Calabria.

Erendor, M. (2017). Peacekeeping Operations and the United Nations. *Journals of Security Studies and Global Politics* (2), pp. 61–67.

Erickson, A., & Collins, G. (2012). China's New Challenge: Protecting Its Citizens Abroad. *The Wall Street Journal.* Retrieved June 21, 2018, from https://blogs.wsj.com/chinarealtime/2012/02/10/chinas-new-challenge-protecting-its-citizens-abroad/

Etzioni, A. (2013). The Devolution of American Power. *The Fletcher Forum of World Affairs* (37 (1)), pp. 13–34.

European Commission. (2019). *EU–China — A strategic outlook.* Strasbourg: European Commission, High Representative of the Union for Foreign Affairs and Security Policy.

Evron, Y. (2016). Israel's Response to China's Rise: A Dependent State's Dilemma. *Asian Survey* (56 (2)), pp. 392–414.

Eyler, B. (2014). *East by Southeast.* Retrieved May 26, 2021, from China's Maritime Silk Road is all about Africa: http://www.eastbysoutheast.com/chinas-maritime-silk-road-africa/

Fairbank, J. (1968). *The Chinese World Order.* Cambridge Mass.: Harvard University Press.

Fairbank, J. (1969). China's Foreign Policy in Historical Perspective. *Foreign Affairs* (47 (3)), pp. 449–463.

Fardella, E., & Ghiselli, A. (2019). *ChinaMed Report 2019,.* ChinaMed Project.

Farooq, M. S., Feroze, N., & Kai, Y. (2019). An Analysis of China and Africa Relations with Special Focus on 'One Belt and One Road'. *India Quarterly* (75(3)), pp. 366–379.

Fattah, H. M. (2007). Lebanon Pounds Refugee Camp,. *New York Times.* Retrieved March 23, 2020, from https://www.nytimes.com/2007/05/21/world/middleeast/21cnd-lebanon.html

Feltman, J. (2020). *China's expanding influence at the United Nations — and how the United States should react.* Washington D.C.: Brookings Institution.

Feng, C. (2015). Embracing Interdependence: The Dynamics of China. (B. D. Center, ed.) *Policy Briefing.*

Fergus, T. (2010). Democratic Republic of Congo Past. Present. Future? *Forced Migration Review* (36), pp. 50–51.

Filson, D., & Werner, S. (2004). Bargaining and Fighting: The Impact of Regime Type on War Onset, Duration and Outcomes. *American Journal of Political Science* (48 (2)), pp. 296–313.

Finkelstein, D. M. (2010). *The Military Dimensions of U.S. — China Security Cooperation: Retrospective and Future Prospects.* Alexandria: Center for Naval Analyses Corporation (CNA).

Finnemore, M. (1996). *National Interests in International Society.* London: Cornell University Press.

Finnemore, M. (2003). *The Purpose of Intervention: Changing Beliefs about the Use of Force.* Cornell: Cornell University Press.

REFERENCES

Fischer, H. (2016). *DW Afrika*. (D. Welle, ed.) Retrieved August 04, 2018, from UN-Mission in der Westsahara: Die Hüter des Status Quo: https://www.dw.com/de/un-mission-in-der-westsahara-die-h%C3%BCter-des-status-quo/a-19205987

Fischer, R., & Ury, W. (1981). *Getting to Yes* (2nd ed.). United Kingdom: Penguin.

Fleck, J., Walter, T., & Vogt, T. (2016). Alte Seidenstraße in neuem Gewand. (C.-P. d. Asienhaus, Hrsg.) *TAZ, Die Tageszeitung*. Retrieved June 30, 2021, from https://www.asienhaus.de/uploads/tx_news/Asienhaus_taz_4-Seiter_2016-10__Web.pdf

Follett, M. (1942). Power. In H. Metcalf, & L. Urwick, *Dynamic Administration* (pp. 72–95). USA, Canada: Routledge (2014).

Fontana, L. B. (2010). *Hezbollah vs. Israel: Confronting Information Strategies in the 2006 Lebanese War*.

Foster, V., Butterfield, W., Chen, C., & Pushak, N. (2008). *Building Bridges: China's Growing Role as Infrastructure Financier for Sub-Saharan Africa*. New York: The World Bank.

Fravel, M. (1996). China's Attitude toward U.N. Peacekeeping Operations since 1989. *Asian Survey* (36 (11)), pp. 1102–1121.

Fuchs, A., & Klann, N.-H. (2011). *Paying a Visit: The Dalai Lama Effect on International Trade*. Göttingen: Center for European Governance and Economic Development Research.

Fulton, J., Propper, E., & Fahmy, A. (2021). *US, Israel, and GCC perspectives on China–MENA relations*. Retrieved June 02, 2021, from Atlantic Council: https://www.atlanticcouncil.org/blogs/menasource/us-israel-and-gcc-perspectives-on-china-mena-relations/

Fung, C. (2016). *China and the Responsibility to Protect, From Opposition to Advocacy*. Washington D.C.: United States Institute of Peace.

Fung, C. J. (2016). *China's Troop Contributions to UN Peacekeeping*. Washington D.C.: United States Institute of Peace.

Gafarov, O. (2019). Rise of China's private armies. *The World Today*, pp. 41–43.

Galbraith, J. (2018). United States withdraws from the UN Human Rights Council, shortly after receiving criticism about its border policy. *American Journal of International Law* (112 (4)), pp. 745–751.

Gallaroti, G. (2011). *The Power Curse: The Paradox of Power in World Politics*. Division II Faculty Paper Publications, Paper 58.

Galtung, J. (1967). *Theories of Peace, A Synthetic Approach to Peace Thinking*. Oslo: International Peace Research Institute.

Gamassa, P., & Chen, Y. (2017). The Impact of China One Belt One Road on Abidjan Port Development Based on Gravity Model. *International Journal of Trade, Economics and Finance* (8 (3)).

Gambhir, H. (2016). *The Virtual Caliphate: ISIS's Information Warfare*. Washington: Instittue for the Study of War.

Garlick, J., & Havlova, R. (2000). China's "Belt and Road" Economic Diplomacy in the Persian Gulf: Strategic Hedging amidst Saudi–Iranian Regional Rivalry. *Journal of Current Chinese Affairs*, pp. 1–24.

REFERENCES

Garver, J. (2018). China and the Iran Nuclear Negotiations. *The Red Star and the Cresent; China and the Middle East*, pp. 123–148.

Gaub, F., & Popescu, N. (2018). The Soviet Union in the Middle East: an overview. *Russia's Return to the Middle East, Buidling Sandcastles?*, pp. 13–20.

Gelpi, C., & Grieco, J. (2001). Attracting Trouble: Democracy, Leadership Tenure, and the Targeting of Militarized Challenges, 1918–1992. *Journal of Conflict Resolution* (45 (6)), pp. 794–818.

Gerdes, F. (2013). *Civil War and State Formation, The Political Economy of War and Peace in Liberia.* Frankfurt am Main: Campus Verlag GmbH.

GFP Strength in Numbers. (2018). Retrieved October 03, 2018, from https://www.globalfirepower.com/countries-listing.asp

Ghafar, A., & Jacobs, A. (2019). *Beijing Calling: Assessing China's Growing Footprint in North Africa.* Brookings Doha Center.

Ghiasy, R. (2017). *China's Belt and Road Initiative, Security implications and ways forward for the European Union.* Friedrich Ebert Stiftung.

Gilbert, K. (2018). *World Atlas.* Retrieved June 24, 2018, from https://www.worldatlas.com/articles/which-countries-recognize-taiwan-as-a-country.html

Giles, K. (2013). *Russian Interests in Sub-Saharan Africa.* Carlisle, PA: US Army War College Press.

Gill, B. (1998). Chinese Arms Exports to Iran. *China Report* (34 (3–4)), pp. 355–379. Retrieved March 24, 2020, from https://journals.sagepub.com/doi/10.1177/000944559803400307

Gill, B., & Huang, C.-L. (2009). *China's Expanding Peacekeeping Role: Its Significance and the Policy Implications.* Solna, Sweden: Stockholm International Peace Research Institute.

Gill, B., & Reilly, J. (2000). Sovereignty, Intervention and Peacekeeping: The View from Beijing. (T. I. Studies, ed.) *Survival* (42 (3)), pp. 41–59.

Giovannetti, G., & Enrico, M. (2019). Trade Networks in the MENA Region. *Med. Mediterranean Yearbook, Strategic Sectors, Economy & Territory*, pp. 270–279.

Githaiga, N., Burimaso, A., Bing, W., & Mohammed Ahmed, S. (2019). The Belt and Road Initiative Opportunities and Risks for Africa's Connectivity. *China Quarterly of International Strategic Studies* (5 (1)), pp. 117–141.

Glaser, B., & Murphy, M. (2009). Soft Power with Chinese Characteristics, The Ongoing Debate. In C. McGiffert, *Chinese Soft Power and Its Implications for the United States, Competition and Cooperation in the Developing World, A Report of the CSIS Smart Power Initiative* (pp. 10–26). Washington, D.C.: Center for Strategic and International Studies.

Gleditsch, K., Salehyan, I., & Schultz, K. (2008). Fighting at Home, Fighting Abroad How Civil Wars Lead to International Disputes. *Journal of Conflict Resolution* (52(4)), pp. 479–506.

Global Center for the Responsibility to Protect. (2018). UN Security Council Resolutions and Presidential Statements Referencing R2P. Retrieved June 30, 2021 from https://www.globalr2p.org/resources/

REFERENCES

Global Coalition. (2014). *82 Partners United in enduring DAESH'S Enduring Defeat*. Retrieved from Global Coalition: https://theglobalcoalition.org/en/partners/

Global Security. (2002). *GlobalSecurity.org*. Retrieved March 31, 2020, from Ivory Coast Conflict: https://www.globalsecurity.org/military/world/war/ivory-coast-2002.htm

Global Security. (2011). *Liberian Conflict*. Retrieved August 11, 2018, from https://www.globalsecurity.org/military/world/war/liberia.htm

Global Security. (2016). *Chad–China Relations*. Retrieved June 30, 2021, from https://www.globalsecurity.org/military/world/africa/cd-forrel-prc.htm

Global Witness. (2010). *The Hill belongs to Them, The need for international action on Congo's conflict minerals trade*.

Global Witness. (2011). *China and Congo: Friends in Need*. Global Witness.

Godement, F., Rudolf, M., Julienne, M., Schwoob, M.-H., & Isenring-Szabó, K. (2018). *The United Nations of China: A Vision of the World Order*. Berlin: European Council on Foreign Relations.

Goethals, S., Okenda, J.-P., & Mbaya, R. (2009). *Chinese Mining Operations in Katanga Democratic Republic of the Congo*. United Kingdom: Rights & Accountability in Development (RAID).

Golann, D., & Folberg, J. (2011). *Mediation: The Roles of Advocate and Neutral*. New York: Wolters Kluwer.

Golden, S. (2011). China's perception of risk and the concept of comprehensive national power. *The Copenhagen Journal of Asian Studies* (29 (2)), pp. 79–109.

Gonzales-Vincente, R. (2015). The limits to China's non-interference foreign policy:pro-state interventionism and the rescaling of economic governance. *Australian Journal of International Affairs* (69 (2)), pp. 205–223.

Goodkind, D. (2019). *The Chinese Diaspora: Historical Legacies and Contemporary Trends*. Maryland, USA: United States Census Bureau.

Government of the DR Congo. (2003). *Mining Regulation Decree No. 038/2003*. DR Congo.

Government of the PRC. (2015). *China.org*. Retrieved from Xinhua: http://www.china.org.cn/world/2015-12/05/content_37241677.htm

Grayson, R. S. (2001). *Liberals International Relations and Appeasement*. New York: Routledge.

Greig, J. M., & Diehl, P. F. (2012). *International Mediation*. Cambridge: Polity Press.

Greig, J., & Regan, P. (2008). When do they say yes? An analysis of willingness to offer and accept mediation in civil wars. *International Studies Quarterly* (4), pp. 759–781.

Grieger, G. (2019). *China's growing role as a security actor in Africa*. Brussels: European Parliamentary Research Service.

Grimm, S. (2015). Militärische Interventionen. (W. M.-J. Raj Kollmorgen, ed.) *Handbuch Transformationsforschung*, pp. 625–633.

Guimarães, F., & Nasser de Carvalho, P. (2017). The United Nations Security Council Action in the Syrian Civil War: Conflicts of Interest and Impasses among the P5 and the consequent Lack of Resolution for the Question. *Brazilian Journal of Strategy & International Relation* (6 (12)), pp. 62–78.

Gurses, M. (2014). *The Lebanese Civil War 1975–1978.* Department of Political Science, University of North Texas. Research Gate.

Guzzini, S. (1993). Structural Power: The Limits of Neorealist Power Analysis. *International Organization* (47 (3)), pp. 443–478.

Guzzini, S. (2005). The Concept of Power: A Constructivist Analysis. *Millennium — Journal of International Studies*, pp. 495–521.

Haas, B. (2017). *The Guardian.* Retrieved October 02, 2018, from Xi Jinping speech: five things you need to know : https://www.theguardian.com/world/2017/oct/18/xi-jinping-speech-five-things-you-need-to-know

Haas, E. (1953). The Balance of Power: Prescription, Concept, or Propaganda. (C. U. Press, ed.) *World Politics* (5 (4)), pp. 442–477.

Haass, R. (1994). *Intervention: The Use of Military Force in the Post-Cold War World.* Carnegie Endowment for International Peace.

Haenle, P. (2013). China Misses a Golden Opportunity in Syria. *The Financial Times.*

Hakimi, M., & Katz Cogan, J. (2016). The Two Codes on the Use of Force. (O. U. o, ed.) *The European Journal of International Law* (27 (2)), pp. 257–291.

Halkort, M. (2013). *Rebuilding Nahr el Bared, Open Security Conflict and Peacebuilding.* London: Open Democracy.

Hammond, J. (2017). Morocco: China's Gateway to Africa? *The Diplomat.* Retrieved June 30, 2021, from https://thediplomat.com/2017/03/morocco-chinas-gateway-to-africa/

Hao, S. (2008). Harmonious world: the conceived international order in framework of China's foreign affairs. *Foreign Affairs* (87 (1)), pp. 29–55.

Harding, H. (1983). Change and Continuity in Chinese Foreign Policy. *Problems of Communism* (32), pp. 1–19.

Harnisch, S. (2003). Theorieorientierte Außenpolitikforschung in einer Ära des Wandels. In G. Hellmann, K. Wolf, & M. Zürn, *Die neuen Internationalen Beziehungen. Forschungsstand und Perspektiven in Deutschland* (pp. 313–360). Baden-Baden: Nomos.

Haroz, D. (2011). China in Africa: Symbiosis of Exploitation. (F. F. Affairs, ed.) *35*(2), pp. 65–88.

Hartmann, C. (2020). China's contribution to African governance, Some conceptual thoughts. In C. Hartmann, & N. Noesselt, *China's new role in African politics, from non-intervention towards stabilization?* (pp. 83–97). London, New York: Routledge.

Hartmann, C., & Noesselt, N. (2020). China's new role in African politics, From non-intervention towards stabilization? In C. Hartmann, & N. Noesselt, *China's new role in African politics, From non-intervention towards stabilization?* (pp. 1–14). Oxon, New York: Routledge.

REFERENCES

Hartnett, D. M. (2012). *China's First Deployment of Combat Forces to a UN Peacekeeping Mission—South Sudan.* Washington D.C.: U.S.–China Economic and Security Review Commission.

Hastrup, A. (2013). *The War in Darfur, Reclaiming Sudanese History.* London, New York: Routledge.

Hauss, C. (2003). *Beyond Intractability.* University of Colorado. Retrieved June 30, 2021 from https://www.beyondintractability.org/audiodisplay/hauss-c

He, Y. (2007). *China's Changing Policy on UN Peacekeeping Operations.* Institute for Security and Development Policy. Stockholm: Asia Paper.

He, Y. (2019). China Rising and Its Changing Policy on UN Peacekeeping. In C. de Coning, & M. Peter, *United Nations Peace Operations in a Changing Global Order* (pp. 253–276). Cham, Switzerland: Palgrave Macmillan.

Heraclides, A. (1990). Secessionist minorities and external involvement. *International Organizations*, pp. 341–378.

Hermann, M., & Kegley, C. (1996). *Ballets, a Barrier against the Use of Bullets and Bombs, Democratization and Military Intervention.* SAGE Publications Inc.

Herrmann, A., & Cronqvist, L. (2006). *Contradictions in Qualitative Comparative Analysis (QCA): Ways out of the Dilemma.* European University Insitute, Department of Political and Social Studies. San Domenico di Fiesole: European University Institute, Political and Social Science Department.

Hilpert, H. G. (2020). Trade, Economy and Finance: Rivalries,Conflicts, Escalation Risks. *Strategic Rivalry between United States and China*, pp. 25–29.

Hiltermann, J. (2017). *Tackling the MENA Region's Intersecting Conflicts.* Brussels: International Crisis Group.

Hinga, S., Jun, Y., & Yiguan, Q. (2013). China–Africa Cooperation—An outstanding relationship Built on Mutual Respect and Common Benefits: A Review. *International Research Journal of Social Sciences* (2(9)), pp. 26–32.

Hinton, H. C. (1994). China as an Asian Power. In T. W. Robinson, & D. Shambaugh, *Chinese Foreign Policy Theory and Practice* (pp. 348–401). Oxford: Clarendon Press.

HKTDC. (2019). *HKTDC Research.* Retrieved from http://china-trade-research.hktdc.com/business-news/article/The-Belt-and-Road-Initiative/The-Belt-and-Road-Initiative/obor/en/1/1X000000/1X0A36B7.htm

Holslag, J. (2008). China's Diplomatic Manoeuvring on the Question of Darfur. *Journal of Contemporary China* (17 (54)), pp. 71–84.

Holsti, O. R., Brody, R. A., & North, R. C. (1964). Measuring Affect and Action in International Reaction Models: Empirical Materials from the 1962 Cuban Crisis. *Journal of Peace Research* (1 (3/4)), pp. 170–190.

Hsieh, P. L. (2009). The Taiwan Question and the One-China Policy: Legal Challenges with Renewed Momentum. *Die Friedens-Warte: Journal of International Peace and Organization*, 84(3), pp. 59–81.

Hu, A., & Men, H. (2002). The Rising of Modern China: Comprehensive National Power and Grand Strategy. *Strategy and Management* (3), pp. 1–36.

REFERENCES

Huang, S. (1992). *Zhonghe guoli lun. Zhongguo shehui kexue chubanshe* . Beijing.
Hudson, V. (1997). Culture and foreign policy: Developing a research agenda. In V. M. Hudson, *Culture and foreign policy* (pp. 1–24). L. Rienner Publishers.
Hudson, V., & Vore, C. (1995). Foreign Policy Analysis Yesterday, Today, and Tomorrow. *Mershon International Studies Review* (39 (2)), pp. 209–238.
Human Rights Watch. (2007). *Darfur 2007 Chaos by Design, Peacekeeping Challenges for AMIS and UNAMID.* Human Rights Watch.
Human Rights Watch. (2017). *South Sudan.* Retrieved August 11, 2018, from https://www.hrw.org/world-report/2018/country-chapters/south-sudan
Human Security Baseline Assessment. (2007). *Small Arms Survey, Sudan Issue Brief No. 7.* Geneva: Human Security Baseline Assessment.
Humanitarian Response Plan Update. (2018). *Humanitarian Response Plan Congo 2017-2019.* UN Office for the Coordination of Humanitarian Affairs.
Humud, C., Blanchard, C., & Nikitin, M. (2018). *Armed Conflict in Syria: Overview and U.S. Response.* Congressional Research Service.
Hurst, C. (2006). *China's Oil Rush in Africa.* Washington: Institute for the Analysis of Global Security.
ICA Annual Report. (2012). *Infrastructure Financing Trends in Africa.* The Infrastructure Consortium for Africa.
ICISS. (2001). *The Responsibility to Protect.* International Commission on Intervention and State Sovereignty. Ottawa: International Commission on Intervention and State Sovereignty.
ICJ Reports. (1986). *Case Concerning Military and Paramilitary Activities in and against Nicaragua.* International Court of Justice.
IDE-JETRO. (2009). *China in Africa A Strategic Overview.* Chiba, Japan: Institute of Developing Economies Japan External Trade Organization.
Ikenberry, G. (2008). China and the Rest Are Only Joining the American-Built Order. *the Rise of the Rest* (25 (3)), pp. 18–21.
Ikenberry, J. G. (2003). Is American Multilateralism in Decline? *Perspectives on Politics* (1 (3)), pp. 533–550.
Infrastructure Consortium for Africa Secretariat. (2017). *Infrastructure Finance Trends in Africa — 2016.* Abijan, Côte d'Ivoire: African Development Bank.
Institute for Security and Development Policy. (2018). *China's Role in UN Peacekeeping.*
International Crisis Group . (2012). *Lebanon's Palestinian Dilemma: The Struggle over Nahr Al-Bared.* Middle East Report No. 117.
International Crisis Group (ICG). (2002). *Liberia: The Key To Ending Regional Stability, Africa Report N° 43.*
International Crisis Group. (2020). *Iraq: Fixing Security in Kirkuk, Middle East Report N° 215.* International Crisis Group.
International Monetary Fund. (2008). *Liberia: Poverty Reduction Strategy Paper.* Washington D.C.: International Monetary Fund Publication Services.

REFERENCES

IOM. (2020). *World Migration Report*. Geneva, Switzerland: International Organization for Migration.

Jackson, E. (1952). *Meeting of Minds*. New York: McGraw-Hill Book Company.

Jackson, P. T. (2011). *The Conduct of Inquiry in International Relations, Philosophy of Science and its Implications for the Study of World Politics*. London: Routledge.

Jacquemot, P. (2010). The dynamics of instability in eastern DRC. *Forced Migration Review* (36), pp. 6–7.

Jenkins, J., & Gottlieb, E. (2007). *Can Violence be Regulated?* New Brunswick, USA, London, UK: Transaction Publishers.

Jiang, W. (2009). Fuelling the Dragon: China's Rise and Its Energy and Resources Extraction in Africa. *The China Quarterly* (199), pp. 585–609.

Jiemian, Y., Gemayel, A., & Suleiman, M. (2016). Promoting a Community of Shared Future. *China Quarterly of International Strategic Studies* (2 (3)), pp. 421–429.

Johns Hopkins China–Africa Research Initiative. (2021). *China Exports to African Countries*. Retrieved May 23, 2021, from Data: China–Africa Trade: http://www.sais-cari.org/data-china-africa-trade

Johnson, D. H. (2014). Briefing: The Crisis in South Sudan. *African Affairs* (113 (451)), pp. 300–309.

Johnston, A. (2008). *Social States: China in International Institutions, 1980–2000*. Princeton: Princeton University Press.

Jordan, D., Kiras, J., Lonsdale, D., Speller, I., Tuck, C., & Walton, C. (2016). *Understanding modern warfare*. Cambridge: Cambridge University Press.

Josselin, D., & Wallace, W. (2001). Non-state Actors in World Politics: a Framework. In D. Josselin, & W. Wallace, *Non-state Actors in World Politics* (pp. 1–20). London: Palgrave Macmillan.

Joyce, K. A., & Braithwaite, A. (2013). Geographic proximity and third-party joiners in militarized interstate disputes. *Journal of Peace Research, 50*(5), pp. 595–608.

Kadidiatou, F., & Baolong, M. (2019). OBOR Economic Impact in Ivory Coast–China Agricultural Investment Prospect. *Proceedings of the 2019 10th International Conference on E-business, Management and Economics*, pp. 26–32.

Kadri, A. (2011). *Global Research*. Retrieved from Economic Development Performance: East Asia versus the Arab World: https://www.globalresearch.ca/economic-development-performance-east-asia-versus-the-arab-world/27239

Kahn, J. (2007). China Warns U.S. on Dalai Lama Trip. *The New York Times*. Retrieved June 30, 2021 from https://www.nytimes.com/2007/10/16/world/asia/16cnd-china.html

Kahneman, D., & Tversky, A. (1979). Prospect Theory: An Analysis of Decision under Risk. (T. E. Society, ed.) *Econometrica Journal of the Econometric Society* (47), pp. 263–291.

Kamara, T. S. (2003). *Liberia: Civil War and Regional Conflict, WriteNet Paper No. 17*. United Nations High Commissioner for Refugees.

Karemba, C. (2016). China–Democratic Republic of Congo Relations: From a Beneficial to a Developmental Cooperation. *African Studies Quarterly* (16 (3–4)), pp. 73–88.

Kathman, J. D. (2010). Civil War Contagion and Neighboring Interventions. *International Studies Quarterly, 54*(4), pp. 989–1012.

Kaufman, A. (2010). The "Century of Humiliation," Then and Now:Chinese Perceptions of the International Order. *Pacific Focus* (XXV (1)), pp. 1–33.

Kaufman, D. (2009). *China's Participation in Anti-Piracy Operations off the Horn of Africa: Drivers and Implications.* Arlington: CNA China Studies.

Kaure, A. (2006). Peacekeepers From China, With Love. *UNMIL FOCUS, 3,* (1), pp. 34–35.

Kãzemi, A. V., & Chen, X. (2014). China and the Middle East: More Than Oil. *The European Financial Review*, pp. 40–44.

Kennedy, E. (2002). *The Political Crisis and Civil War in Ivory Coast (2002–2007): ECOWAS Fourth Intervention at Conflict Resolution in West Africa.*

Keohane, R. (1988). International Institutions: Two Approaches. *International Studies Quarterly* (32 (4)), pp. 379–396.

Kernen, A. (2010). Small and Medium-sized Chinese Businesses in Mali and Senegal. *African and Asian Studies*(9), pp. 252–268.

Khosla, D. (1999). Third World States as Intervenors in Ethnic Conflicts: Implications for Regional and International Security. *Third World Quarterly, 20*(6), pp. 1143–1156.

Kim, S. (1979). *The United Nations and World Order.* Princeton: Princeton University Press.

Kim, S. (1984). Chinese Foreign Policy Behaviour. In S. S. Kim, *China And The World: Chinese Foreign Policy In The Post-mao Era* (2 ed., pp. 3–31). Boulder, Westview Pr.

Kim, S. K. (2012). *Third Party Intervention in Civil Wars: Motivation, War Outcomes, and Post-War Development.* Iowa: University of Iowa .

Kim, S. S. (2018). Chinese Foreign Policy in Theory and Practice. In S. S. Kim, *China and the World, Chinese Foreign Policy Faces the New Millenium* (pp. 3–33). New York, Oxon: Routledge.

King, G., Keohane, R., & Verba, S. (1994). *Designing Social Inquiry: Scientific Inference in Qualitative Research.* Princeton: Princeton University Press.

Kinzelbach, K. (2013). Chinas Menschenrechtspolitik in den UN, Beijings Normauslegung erfordert deutliche Antworten, auch von Deutschland. *Zeitschrift Vereinte Nationen*(2), pp. 57–62.

Kitano, N., & Miyabayashi, Y. (2020). *Estimating China's Foreign Aid: 2019–2020 Preliminary Figures.* Tokyo: Japan International Cooperation Agency, Ogata Sadako Research Institute for Peace and Development.

Kleiboer, M. (1996). Understanding Success and Failure of International Mediation. *The Journal of Conflict Resolution* (40 (2)), pp. 360–389.

REFERENCES

Koga, J. (2011). Where Do Third Parties Intervene? Third Parties' Domestic Institutions and Military Interventions in Civil Conflicts. *International Studies Quarterly*, pp. 1143–1166.

Kokoshin, A. A. (2016). *2015 Military Reform in the People's Republic of China, Defense, Foreign and Domestic Policy Issues*. Cambridge MA: Harvard Kennedy School, Belfer Center of Science and International Affairs.

Korinko, G., & Kirprop, C. J. (2014). China's Evolving Policy of Intervention in African Conflicts. *International Affairs and Global Strategy* (19), pp. 10–16.

Krain, M. (2005). International Intervention and the Severity of Genocides and Politicides. *International Studies Quarterly*, 49(3), pp. 363–387.

Kramer, R., Michalowski, R., & Rothe, D. (2005). "The Supreme International Crime": How the U.S. War in Iraq Threatens the Rule of Law. *Social Justice* (32 (2)), pp. 52–81.

Kressel, K., & Pruitt, D. G. (1989). *The Process and Effectiveness of Third-Party Intervention*. Jossey-Bass Inc. Pub. .

Kriesberg, L. (2015). *Realizing Peace: A Constructive Conflict Approach*. Great Britain: Oxford University Press.

Kumaraswamy, P. (2013). China, Israel and the US: The Problematic Triangle. *China Report* (49 (1)), pp. 143–159.

Kumsa, A. (2007). South Sudan Struggle for Independence, and its implication for Africa. *RUDN Journal of Sociology, 17*(4).

Kuo, S. (2012). Beijing's Understanding of African Security: Context and Limitations. *African Security* (5 (1)), pp. 24–43.

Kuo, S. (2015). Chinese Peace? An Emergent Norm in African Peace Operations. *China Quarterly of International Strategic Studies* (1 (1)), pp. 155–181.

Kuo, S. (2020). *Chinese Peace in Africa, from Peacekeeper to Peacemaker*. Oxon, New York: Routledge.

Kurlantzick, J. (2007). *Charm Offensive: How China's Soft Power is Transforming the World*. Yale: Yale University.

Lafarge, F. (2016). *The economic presence of China in the Maghreb: Ambitions and limits*. Paris: Fondation pour la Recherche Stratégique.

Lagon, M. P., & Lou, T. (2018). The Dragon in Turtle Bay: The Impact of China's Rise in the UN on the United States and Global Governance. *World Affairs* (181 (3)), pp. 239–255.

Lambach, D., Johais, E., & Bayer, M. (2016). *Warum Staaten zusammenbrechen*. Wiesbaden: Springer VS.

Lanegran, K. (2007). The Importance of Trying Charles Taylor. *Journal of Human Rights* (6), pp. 165–179.

Lange, M. (2010). Refugee return and root causes of conflict. *Forced Migration Review* (36), pp. 48–49.

Lanteigne, M. (2014). *China's Peacekeeping Policies in Mali: New Security Thinking or Balancing Europe?* Berlin: Freie Universität Berlin.

Lanteigne, M. (2014). Red and Blue: China's Evolving United Nations Peacekeeping Policies and Soft Power Development. In H. Y. Aoi C., *Asia-Pacific Nations in International Peace Support and Stability Operations. Asia Today* (pp. 113–140). New York: Palgrave Macmillan.

Lanteigne, M. (2015). *China's UN Peacekeeping in Mali: Strategies and Risks*. London: Oxford Research Group. Retrieved June 14, 2020, from https://www.oxfordresearchgroup.org.uk/blog/chinas-un-peacekeeping-in-mali-strategies-and-risks

Lanteigne, M. (2018). *The Role of UN Peacekeeping in China's Expanding Strategic Interests*. Washington DC: United States Institute of Peace.

Lanteigne, M. (2019). China's UN Peacekeeping in Mali and Comprehensive Diplomacy. *The China Quarterly* (239), pp. 635–655. doi:10.1017/S030574101800173X

Large, D. (2007, September). China and the Changing Context of Development in Sudan. *Development* (50 (3)), pp. 57–62.

Large, D. (2008). China & the Contradictions of 'Non-interference' in Sudan. *Review of African Political Economy* (35 Issue 115), pp. 93–106. doi:10.1080/03056240802011568

Large, D. (2008). *China's role in the mediation and resolution of conflict in Africa*. Oslo: Centre for Humanitarian Dialogue. Retrieved June 06, 2020, from https://pdfs.semanticscholar.org/c865/673edb1d67ba6cf7d89ec1cb9c25b24395ed.pdf

Large, D. (2009). China's Sudan Engagement: Changing Northern and Southern Political Trajectories in Peace and War. *The China Quarterly* (199), pp. 610–626.

Large, D. (2016). China and South Sudan's Civil War, 2013–2015. *African Studies Quarterly* (16 (3–4)), pp. 35–54.

Lasswell, H. D. (1935). *World politics and personal insecurity*. New York: McGraw-Hill Book Company, Inc.

Laub, Z. (2017). *Council on Foreign Relations*. Retrieved June 30, 2021 from https://www.cfr.org/backgrounder/whos-who-syrias-civil-war

Lavi, G., & Orion, A. (2019). *Israel–China Relations: Opportunities and Challenges*. The Institute for National Security Studies.

Law of the PRC on National Defence. (1997). *Database of Laws and Regulations*. Retrieved June 07, 2020, from http://www.npc.gov.cn/zgrdw/englishnpc/Law/2007-12/11/content_1383547.htm

Lee, F., Yuen, S., Tang, G., & Chen, E. (2019). Hong Kong's Summer of Uprising: From Anti-Extradition to Anti-Authoritarian Protests. *The China Review* (19 (4)), pp. 1–32.

Leeds, B. A., & Davis, D. (1999). Beneath the Surface: Regime Type and International Interaction, 1953–78. *Journal of Peace Research* (36 (1)), pp. 5–21.

Legarda, H., & Nouwens, M. (2018). *Guardians of the Belt and Road, The internationalization of China's private security companies*. Berlin: Mercator Institute for China Studies.

Leite, P., Olsson, C., Schöldtz, M., Shelley, T., Wrange, P., Corell, H., & Scheele, K. (2006). *The Western Sahara Conflict, The Role of Natural Resources in Decolonization*. Uppsala: Nordiska Afrikainstitutet.

REFERENCES

Levy, J. S. (1997). Prospect Theory, Rational Choice, and International Relations. *International Studies Quarterly* (41 (1)), pp. 87–112.

Li, S., & Rønning, H. (2013). *China in Africa: Soft power, media perceptions and a pan-developing identity.* Bergen: Chr. Michelsen Institut.

Lia, B. (2016). The Islamist Uprising in Syria, 1976–82: The History and Legacy of a Failed Revolt. *British Journal of Middle Eastern Studies, 43*(4), pp. 1–19.

Liang, S. (1997). Constructing an International Relations Theory with "Chinese Characteristics". *Political Science, 49*(1), pp. 23–39.

Lieberman, E. (2005). Nested Analysis as a Mixed-Method Strategy for Comparative Research. *American Political Science Review*, pp. 435–452.

Lintl, P. (2018). *Repercussions of the Unresolved Conflict on Israeli Power Constellations and Actor Perspectives.* Berlin: Stiftung Wissenschaft und Politik.

Lippert, B., & Perthes, V. (2020). *Strategic Rivalry between United States and China, Causes, Trajectories, and Implications for Europe.* Berlin: German Institute for International and Security Affairs.

Liu, H. (2019). (T. Walter, Interviewer) Berlin.

Liu, M. (2015). *China Dream: The Great Power Thinking and Strategic Positioing in the Post-American Age.* New York: CN Times Book.

Lons, C., Fulton, J., Sun, D., & Al-Tamimi, N. (2019). *China's Great Game in the Middle East.* London: European Council on Foreign Relations.

Loo, B. (2011). *Chinese military power : much less than meets the eye.* Nanyang: Nanyang Technological University.

Lukes, S. (2004). *Power. A Radical View (2nd Edition).* Palgrave Macmillan.

Lumumba-Kasongo, T. (2015). Rethinking the Bandung conference in an Era of 'unipolar liberal globalization' and movements toward a 'multipolar politics'. *Journal of the Global South* (2 (9)), pp. 1–17.

Lyall, G. (2017). *Rebellion and Conflict Minerals in North Kivu.* Retrieved August 11, 2018, from http://www.accord.org.za/conflict-trends/rebellion-conflict-minerals-north-kivu/

Lynch, C. (2016). *China Eyes Ending Western Grip on Top U.N. Jobs with Greater Control Over Blue Helmets.* Retrieved November 14, 2020, from Foreign Policy: https://foreignpolicy.com/2016/10/02/china-eyes-ending-western-grip-on-top-u-n-jobs-with-greater-control-over-blue-helmets/

Mabey, N., Schulz, S., Dimsdale, T., Bergamaschi, L., & Amin, A.-L. (2013). *Underpinning the MENA Democratic Transition.* London, Berlin, Brussels, Washington: E3G.

Mac Ginty, R. (2010). Hybrid Peace: The Interaction Between Top-Down and Bottom-Up Peace. *Security Dialogue* (41 (4)), pp. 391–412.

MacQueen, B. (2009). *Political Culture and Conflict Resolution in the Arab World.* Victoria, Australia: Melbourne University Press.

Maerk, J. (2012). Europe and the Middle East: Hegemony and Postcolonial Entanglements. *Ideaz* (10), pp. 53–63.

REFERENCES

Mahoney, J., & Goertz, G. (2004). The Possibility Principle: choosing negative cases in comparative research. (4), pp. 653–669.

Makdisi , S., & Sadaka, R. (2003). *The Lebanese Civil War, 1975–1990*. Beirut: American University of Beirut.

Malan, J. (1997). *Conflict Resolution Wisdom From Africa*. University of Durban-Westville, South Africa: African Centre for the Constructive Resolution of Disputes (ACCORD).

Mangi, L. (1987). US Military Bases in Africa. *Pakistan Horizon* (40 (2)), pp. 95–102.

Marafa, L. M. (2009). *Africa's Business and Development Relationship with China*. Uppsala: Norfiska Afrika Institutet.

Marfaing, L. (2010). Mali: Die andere chinesische Migration. (GIGA Institute, ed.) *Focus Afrika* (12), pp. 1–8.

Marigat, S., Nzomo, M., Kagwanja, P., & Kiamba, A. (2017, August). Power And Conflict Management: Is There A Relationship? *IOSR Journal of Humanities And Social Science* (22 (8)), pp. 08–15.

Matsuda, Y. (2006). *An Essay on China's Military Diplomacy: Examination of Intentions in Foreign Strategy*. National Institute for Defense Studies.

Mearsheimer, J. (2001). *The Tragedy of Great Power Politics*. Norton & Company.

Mehler, A. (2006). *Political Discourse in Football Coverage—The Cases of Côte d'Ivoire and Ghana, Working Paper No. 27*. Hamburg: GIGA Research Unit: Institute of African Affairs.

Melnykovska, I., Plamper, H., & Schweickert, R. (2012). Do Russia and China promote autocracy in Central Asia? *Asia Europe Journal* (10), pp. 75–89.

Melvin, N. (2019). *The Foreign Military Presence in the Horn of Africa Region*. Solna, Sweden: Stockholm International Peace Research Institute (Sipri).

Mendez, A., & Alden, C. (2019). China in Panama: from peripheral diplomacy to grand strategy. *Geopolitics*, pp. 1–23.

Mengjie. (2018). *Commentary: Xi demonstrates China's role as responsible country in New Year address* . Retrieved November 18, 2018, from Xinhua: http://www.xinhuanet.com/english/2018-01/01/c_136865307.htm

Miller, B. (1982). Colloqium: Women in Power. *Work in Progress Series 82-01, Stone Center for Development Services and Studies*, pp. 1–2.

Ministry of Commerce of the PRC. (2018, February 15). *MOFCOM Department of Outward Investment and Economic Cooperation Comments on China's Outward Investment Cooperation in January 2018*. (M. o. China, Editor) Retrieved June 21, 2018, from http://english.mofcom.gov.cn/article/newsrelease/policyreleasing/201802/20180202714358.shtml

Ministry of Energy, Russian Federation. (2009). *Energy Strategy of Russia* . Moscow: Government of the Russian Federation.

Ministry of External Affairs India. (2004). *Panchsheel*. India: External Publicity Division. Retrieved 06 20, 2018, from Ministry of External Affairs India;.

REFERENCES

Ministry of Foreign Affairs of the PRC. (2014). *The Five Principles of Peaceful Coexistence*. Retrieved 06 20, 2018, from http://www.fmprc.gov.cn/mfa_eng/wjb_663304/zwjg_665342/zwbd_665378/t1179045.shtml

Ministry of Foreign Affairs of the PRC. (2016). *Ministry of Foreign Affairs of the People's Republic of China*. Retrieved July 17, 2020, from China's Arab Policy Paper: https://www.fmprc.gov.cn/mfa_eng/zxxx_662805/t1331683.shtml

Ministry of Foreign Affairs PRC. (2013). *Ministry of Foreign Affairs of the People's Republic of China*. (M. o. Affairs, Editor) Retrieved November 17, 2018, from Xi Jinping Calls for the Building of New Type of International Relations with Win-Win Cooperation at the Core in a Speech at the Moscow State Institute of International Relations: https://www.fmprc.gov.cn/mfa_eng/topics_665678/xjpcf1_665694/t1024781.shtml

Ministry of Foreign Affairs PRC. (2013). *Ministry of Foreign Affairs of the People's Republic of China*. Retrieved November 17, 2018, from Xi Jinping: Let the Sense of Community of Common Destiny Take Deep Root in Neighbouring Countries: https://www.fmprc.gov.cn/mfa_eng/wjb_663304/wjbz_663308/activities_663312/t1093870.shtml

Ministry of Foreign Affairs PRC. (2015). *Ministry of Foreign Affairs of the People's Republic of China*. Retrieved from Speech by H.E. Xi Jinping President of the People's Republic of China At the Welcoming Dinner Hosted by Local Governments And Friendly Organizations in the United States: https://www.fmprc.gov.cn/mfa_eng/topics_665678/xjpdmgjxgsfwbcxlhgcl70znxlfh/t1305429.shtml

Ministry of National Defense, PRC. (2010). *China's National Defense White Paper*.

MINURCAT. (2010). *United Nations Peacekeeping*. Retrieved August 11, 2018, from https://minurcat.unmissions.org/

MINURSO Fact Sheet. (2020). *UN Peacekeeping*. (U. Nations, ed.) Retrieved August 04, 2018, from https://peacekeeping.un.org/en/mission/minurso

MINUSMA Factsheet. (2013). *UN Peacekeeping*. Retrieved August 11, 2018, from https://peacekeeping.un.org/en/mission/minusma

Minzer, C. (2011). *Countries at the Crossroad 2011: China*. Freedom House.

Mishra, P., & Shafak, E. (2014). *New Perspectives Quarterly*. Retrieved October 02, 2018, from http://www.digitalnpq.org/archive/2014_spring/06_brzezinski.html

Mitchell, C. (1970). Civil Strife and the Involvement of External Parties. *International Studies Quarterly* (14 (2)), pp. 166–194.

Moawia, A. (2018). China and The Conflict in South Sudan: Security and Engagement. *Journal of Economic* (2 (2)), pp. 111–128.

Molintas, D. (2013). *Impact of Globalisation on Rare Earth: China's co-optive conquest of Colongese coltan, Paper No. 96264*. Munich: Munich Personal RePEc Archive.

MONUC Peacekeeping. (2010). *United Nations Organization Mission in the Democratic Republic of the Congo, MONUC Background*. Retrieved March 28, 2020, from https://peacekeeping.un.org/mission/past/monuc/background.shtml

MONUSCO Fact Sheet. (2010). *UN Peacekeeping*. Retrieved August 11, 2018, from https://peacekeeping.un.org/en/mission/monusco

Moore, C. (2014). *The Mediation Process*. San Francisco: Jossey-Bass.

Moravcsik, A. (1988). *The Choice for Europe Social Purpose and State Power from Messina to Maastricht.* London: Routledge.

Moravcsik, A. (2010). Bipolar Order, Europe, the Second Superpower. *Current History, A Journal of Contemporary World Affairs*, pp. 91–98.

Morello, C. (2019). Trump shrugs as U.N. warns it's about to run out of money. *The Washington Post.* Retrieved November 14, 2020, from https://www.washingtonpost.com/national-security/trump-shrugs-as-un-warns-its-about-to-run-out-of-money/2019/10/09/568f8756-eac5-11e9-85c0-85a098e47b37_story.html

Morgenthau, H. (1948). *Politics among Nations—The struggle for power and peace.* New York.

Moro, L. (2012). China, Sudan and South Sudan Relations. *Global Review*, pp. 23–26.

Moumouni, G. (2014). *China and Liberia: Engagement in a Post-Conflict Country 2003-2013.* South Africa: South African Institute of International Affairs.

Mueller, H. (2013). *The Economic Costs of Conflict.* IAE (CSIC) and Barcelona GSE: IGC Working Paper.

Mullins, C., & Rothe, D. (2017). *The forgotten ones. The Darfuri genocide.* Springer Science Business Media B.V. 2007.

Murphy, E. (2009). Learning the Right Lessons from Beijing: A Model for the Arab World? In R. Springborg, *Development Models in Muslim Contexts, Chinese, "Islamic" and Neo-Liberal Alternatives* (pp. 85–114). Edinburgh: Edinburgh University Press, The Aga Khan University.

Muthanna, K. (2011). Military diplomacy. *Journal of Defence Studies* (5 (1)), pp. 1–15.

NABU. (2019). *Verflechtungen und Interessen des Deutschen Bauernverbandes.* Berlin: NABU (Naturschutzbund Deutschland) e.V.

Nantulya, P. (2019). *Chinese Hard Power Supports Its Growing Strategic Interests in Africa.* Washington: Africa Center for Strategic Studies. Retrieved June 15, 2019, from https://africacenter.org/spotlight/chinese-hard-power-supports-its-growing-strategic-interests-in-africa/

Neu, J., & Kriesberg, L. (2019). *Conflict Analysis and Resolution: Development of the Field.* Oxford: Oxford Research Encyclopedia of International Studies.

Newman, E. (2009). "Liberal" peacebuilding debates. In E. Newman, R. Paris, & O. Richmond, *New perspectives on liberal peacebuilding* (pp. 26–53). Tokyo, New York, Paris: United Nations University Press.

Ng-Quinn, M. (1983). the Analytic Study of Chinese Foreign Policy. *International Studies Quarterly* (27 (2)), pp. 203–224.

Niambi, N. (2018). Bilateral Cooperation between China and Congo-Brazzaville: The Other Side of the Ledger. *Open Journal of Political Science*, pp. 227–238.

Niu, Z. (2018). A Historical Overview of China–UN Relations. *Journal of Asia-Pacific Studies* (30), pp. 65–76.

Noesselt, N. (2010). *Alternative Weltordnungsmodelle?* Wiesbaden: VS Verlag.

Noesselt, N. (2012). *Is There a "Chinese School" of IR?* Hamburg: GIGA Institut.

Noesselt, N. (2014). *China and Socialist Countries: Role Change and Role Continuity.* Hamburg: GIGA Institute.

Noesselt, N. (2018). *Governance Innovation and Policy Change: Recalibrations of Chinese Politics under Xi Jinping.* Lanham: Rowman & Littlefield.

Noesselt, N. (2020). China's African dream, Assessing China's new strategy. In C. Hartmann, & N. Noesselt, *China's new role in African politics, from non-intervention towards stabilization?* (pp. 17–31). Oxon, New York: Routledge.

Northedge, F. S., & Donelan, M. D. (1971). *International Disputes: The Political Aspects.* London: Europa Publications.

Nye, J. S. (1990). Soft Power. *Washingtonpost.Newsweek Interactive, LLC,* pp. 153–171. Retrieved October 03, 2018, from https://www.wilsoncenter.org/sites/default/files/joseph_nye_soft_power_journal.pdf

Nye, J. S. (2004). *Soft Power, The Means to Success in World Politics.* New York: Public Affairs.

Nye, J. S. (2004). The Decline of America's Soft Power – Why Washington Should Worry. *Foreign Affairs* (83 (3)), pp. 16–20.

Nye, J. S. (2005). The Rise of China's Soft Power. *The Wall Street Journal.*

Nye, J. S. (2007). The Impressive-But Limited-Soft Power of the United Nations. *Daily Star.*

Nye, J. S. (2013). *Hard, soft, and smart power.* Oxford: The Oxford Handbook of Modern Diplomacy.

Obama, B. (2015). *Remarks by President Obama and President Xi of the People's Republic of China in Joint Press Conference.* Retrieved May 08, 2021, from The White House Office of the Press Secretary: https://obamawhitehouse.archives.gov/the-press-office/2015/09/25/remarks-president-obama-and-president-xi-peoples-republic-china-joint

OCHA. (2007). *Western Sahara.* Retrieved from Secretary-General appoints Major General Zhao Jingmin of China as Force Commander for Western Sahara Mission: https://reliefweb.int/report/western-sahara/secretary-general-appoints-major-general-zhao-jingmin-china-force-commander

OCHA. (2021). *Yemen Humanitarian Needs Overview 2021.* (Reliefweb, Editor) Retrieved June 19, 2021, from The United Nations Office for the Coordination of Humanitarian Affairs: https://reliefweb.int/report/yemen/yemen-humanitarian-needs-overview-2021-february-2021-enar

Odeh, L. (2014). Dynamics of China–Nigeria Economic Relations since 1971. *Journal of the Historical Society of Nigeria* (23), pp. 150–162.

OECD. (2018). *OECD Business and Finance Outlook, China's Belt and Road Initiative in the Global Trade, Investment and Finance Landscape.* Paris: Organisation for Economic Cooperation and Development.

OECD. (2021). *Official Development Assistance.* Retrieved April 16, 2021, from ODA 2020 preliminary data: https://www.oecd.org/dac/financing-sustainable-development/development-finance-standards/official-development-assistance.htm

Oertel, J. (2014). *China and the United Nations, Chinese UN Policy in the Areas of Peace and Development in the Era of Hu Jintao.* Nomos.

REFERENCES

Office of the Secretary of Defense. (2009). *Annual Report to Congress, Military Power of the People's Republic of China 2009*. Washington DC: Office of the Secretary of Defense.

Office of the Secretary of Defense. (2008). *Annual Report to Congress, Military Power of the People's Republic of China 2008*. Washington DC.: Office of the Secretary of Defense.

Ogwang, T. (2011). *The root Causes of the Conflict in Ivory Coast*. Ontario: Africa Portal.

OHCHR. (2010). *Democratic Republic of the Congo 1993–2003*. United Nations Human Rights, Office of the High Commissioner.

Oke, M., Oshinfowokan, O., & Okonoda, O. (2019). Nigeria–China Trade Relations: Projections for National Growth and Development. *International Journal of Business and Management* (14 (11)), pp. 77–89.

Oksamytna, K., Bove, V., & Lundgren, M. (2020). Leadership Selection in United Nations Peacekeeping. *International Studies Quarterly*, pp. 1–13.

Olimat, M. S. (2013). *China and the Middle East*. Routledge.

Olimat, M. S. (2014). *China and North Africa since World War II: A Bilateral Approach*. 16 Carlisle Street, London W1D 3BT, United Kingdom: Lexington Books.

Onyalo, P. (2020). Democracy or Liberal Autocracy; The Case of Africa. *International Journal of Humanities, Art and Social Studies* (5 (1)), pp. 9–17.

Operation ATALANTA. (2020). *EU Naval Force Somalia*. Retrieved June 29, 2020, from European Union External Action: https://eunavfor.eu/key-facts-and-figures/

Osgood, C. (1962). *An alternative to war or surrender*. Illinois: University of Illinois Press.

Osondu, A. (2013). Off and On: China's Principle of Non-Interference in Africa. *Mediterranean Journal of Social Sciences* (4 (3)), pp. 225–234.

Osondu-Oti, A. (2016). China and Africa:: Human Rights Perspective. *Africa Development / Afrique et Développement*(41 (1)), pp. 49–80.

Ottaway, M., & El-Sadany, M. (2012). *Sudan: From Conflict To Conflict*. Carnegie Papers. Carnegie Endowment For International Peace.

Pabst, M. (1999). The Western Sahara Conflict. *South African Journal of Military Studies*(29), pp. 71–79.

Page, M. (2018). *The Intersection of China's Commercial Interests and Nigeria's Conflict Landscape*. Washington DC: United States Institute of Peace.

Pajtinka, E. (2016). Military diplomacy and its present functions. *Security Dimensions. International and National Studies* (20), pp. 179–194.

Palik, J., Rustad, S., & Methi, F. (2020). *Conflict Trends: A Global Overview, 1946–2019*. Oslo: Peace Research Institute (PRIO).

Pan, E. (2006). *China's Soft Power Initiative*. Council on Foreign Relations. Retrieved June 14, 2020, from https://www.cfr.org/backgrounder/chinas-soft-power-initiative

REFERENCES

Panda, A. (2014). Reflecting on China's Five Principles, 60 Years Later. *The Diplomat*. Retrieved June 30, 2021 from https://thediplomat.com/2014/06/reflecting-on-chinas-five-principles-60-years-later/

Pang, Z. (2009). China's Non-Intervention Question. *Global Responsibility to Protect* (1), pp. 237–252.

Paris, R. (2004). *At War's End, Building Peace after Civil Conflict*. Cambridge, New York, Melbourne, Madrid, Cape Town: Cambridge University Press.

Paris, R. (2010). Saving liberal peacebuilding. *Review of International Studies* (36 (2)), pp. 337–365.

Patey, L. (2016). *Geopolitics and non-western intervention in Syria, China, the Syrian conflict and the threat of terrorism*. Danish Institute for International Studies.

Pauley, L. (2018). China Takes the Lead in UN Peacekeeping. *The Diplomat*. Retrieved June 22, 2018, from https://thediplomat.com/2018/04/china-takes-the-lead-in-un-peacekeeping/

Peace Research Institute Oslo. (2020). *Conflict Trends*. (P. a. Oslo, Editor) Retrieved June 23, 2018, from https://www.prio.org/Projects/Project/?x=1631

Peacekeeping, U. N. (2017). *Troop and Police Contributions*. Retrieved June 14, 2020, from UN Mission's summary detailed by country

Pearson, F. S. (1974). Geographic Proximity and Foreign Military Intervention. *The Journal of Conflict Resolution* (18 (3)), pp. 432–460.

People's Daily. (2006). *People's Daily Online*. Retrieved March 24, 2020, from http://en.people.cn/200607/24/eng20060724_286103.html

Perez-Des Rosiers, D. (2019). A Comparative Analysis of China's Relations with Lebanon and Syria. *Sociology of Islam*, 7(2–3), pp. 189–210.

Permanent Mission of the PRC to the UN. (2019). *Ambassador Zhang Jun Spoke on China's Position and Contribution on Yemen*. Retrieved November 13, 2020, from http://chnun.chinamission.org.cn/eng/chinaandun/securitycouncil/regionalhotspots/mideast/t1718194.htm

Peters, D. (2007). Ansätze und Methoden der Außenpolitikanalyse. In S. Schmidt, G. Hellmann, & R. Wolf, *Handbuch der Deutschen Außenpolitik* (pp. 815–835). Wiesbaden: GWV Fachverlage GmbH.

Petersen, K., Vasquez, J., & Wang, Y. (2004). Multiparty Disputes and the Probability of War, 1816–1992. *Conflict Management and Peace Science* (21), pp. 85–100.

Phillips, T. (2015). *The Guardian*. Retrieved November 17, 2018, from China military parade shows might as Xi Jinping pledges 300,000 cut in army : https://www.theguardian.com/world/2015/sep/03/xi-jinping-pledges-300000-cut-in-army-even-as-china-shows-military-might

Pichon, E. (2017). *Iraqi Kurdistan's independence referendum*. Brussels: European Parliament.

Pickering, J. (2002). War-weariness and Cumulative Effects: Victors, Vanquished, and Subsequent Interstate Intervention. *Journal of Peace Research* (39 (3)), pp. 313–337.

REFERENCES

Pickering, J., & Kisangan, E. (2006). Political, Economic, and Social Consequences of Foreign Military Intervention. *Political Research Quarterly* (59 (3)), pp. 363–376.

Pigato, M. (2008). *Strengthening MENA's trade and investments links with China and India.* The World Bank.

Pillsbury, M. (2000). *China Debates the Future Security Environment* . Washington DC: National Defense University Press.

Pohl, K.-H. (2012). Chinese and western values: reflections on the methodology of a cross-cultural dialogue. *Journal of globalization studies* (3(1)), pp. 95–103.

Polachek, S. W. (1980). Conflict and Trade. *Journal of Conflict Resolution* (24 (1)), pp. 55–78.

Polisario. (2020). *Representation of the Frente POLISARIO at the United Nations.* Retrieved March 25, 2020, from https://www.westernsahara-un.com/

Pollpeter, K. (2004). *US–China Security Management: Assessing the Military-to-Miltary Relationship.* Santa Monica CA: No. RAND/MG-143-USAF. RAND CORP .

Porter, M., Sachs, J., & Warner, A. (2000). Executive Summary: Current Competitiveness and Growth Competitiveness. In M. Porter, J. D. Sachs, A. M. Warner, P. Cornelius, M. Levinson, & K. Schwab, *The Global Competitiveness Report 2000* (pp. 14–17). New York, Oxford: Oxford University Press.

Poston, D., Mao, J., & Yu, M.-Y. (1994). The Global Distribution of the Overseas Chinese Around 1990. *Population and Development Review* (20 (3)), pp. 631–645.

Power, M., Mohan, G., & Tan-Mullins, M. (2012). *China's Resource Diplomacy in Africa, Powering Development?* New York: Palgrave Macmillan.

PRC State Council. (2009). *Law Info China.* Retrieved September 26, 2020, from Regulation on the Administration of Security and Guarding Services (保安服务管理条例, Baoan Fuwu Guanli Tiaoli): http://www.lawinfochina.com/display.aspx?lib=law&id=7779

Putnam, R. (1988). Diplomacy and Domestic Politics: The Logic of Two-Level Games. *International Organization* (42 (3)), pp. 427–460.

Putzel, L., Assembe-Mvondo, S., Bilogo Bi Ndong, L., Banioguila, R. P., Cerutti, P., Chupezi Tieguhong, J., Mala, W. (2011). *Chinese aid, trade and investment and the forests of the Democratic Republic of Congo.* Indonesia: Center for International Forestry Research.

Qin, Y. (2005). Theoretical Problematic of International Relationship Theory and Construction of a Chinese School. *Social Sciences in China*, pp. 62–72.

Ragin, C. (2000). *Fuzzy-Set Social Science.* Chicago: Chicago University Press.

Ragin, C. C. (1987). *The Comparative Method: Moving Beyond Qualitative and Quantitative Strategies.* (U. o. Press, ed.) Berkeley.

Rajagopalan, R. (2018). Understanding China's Military Strategy. *Strategic Analysis, 32*(6), pp. 1013–1046.

Rakhmat, M. Z. (2015). *China and Tunisia: A Quiet Partnership.* Retrieved June 20, 2018, from The Diplomat: https://thediplomat.com/2014/06/china-and-tunisia-a-quiet-partnership/

REFERENCES

Ramo, J. (2004). *The Beijing Consensus*. London: Foreign Policy Centre.

Ramsbotham, O., Woodhouse, T., & Miall, H. (2011). *Contemporary Conflict Resolution; the prevention, management and transformation of deadly conflicts* (vol. 3). Cambridge/Malden: Polity Press.

Rana, K. S. (2015). *Bilateral Diplomacy: A Practitioner Perspective*. Geneva: Diplo-Foundation Policy Papers and Briefs 15.

Ranke, L. (1955). *Die grossen Mächte – Politisches Gespräch*. Göttingen: Vandenhoeck & Ruprecht.

Rasheed, A. (2012). Boko Haram insurgency in Nigeria as a symptom of poverty and political alienation. *IOSR Journal Of Humanities And Social Science (JHSS)* (3 (5)), pp. 21–26.

Refugee Review Tribunal. (2009). *RRT Research Response Number LBN34442*. Australia: Refworld.

Regan, C. C. (2000). *Fuzzy-Set Social Science*. Chicago: Chicago University Press.

Regan, P. M. (2002). *Civil Wars and Foreign Powers, Outside Intervention in Intrastate Conflict*. Michigan: The University of Michigan.

Reiter, D., & Stam, A. (2002). *Democracies at War*. Princeton: Princeton University Press.

reliefweb. (2002). *Presidents of Uganda and DRC sign political accord*. Retrieved March 29, 2020, from reliefweb, OCHA Services: https://reliefweb.int/report/democratic-republic-congo/presidents-uganda-and-drc-sign-political-accord

Reuters. (2015). China Says Overseas Anti-Terror Missions must Respect Host Nation. *Reuters*. Retrieved June 28, 2020, from https://www.reuters.com/article/us-china-security-idUSKBN0UE0NE20151231

Reuters. (2017). Congo Republic signs peace accord with "Ninja" rebels. *Reuters*. Retrieved June 30, 2021, from https://af.reuters.com/article/africaTech/idAFKBN1EI07E-OZATP

Reuters. (2017). *Emerging Markets*. Retrieved October 03, 2018, from Promote peace, China's Xi tells soldiers at first overseas base: https://www.reuters.com/article/us-china-defence/promote-peace-chinas-xi-tells-soldiers-at-first-overseas-base-idUSKBN1D401U

Reuters. (2017). *Factbox: What Trump has said about the United Nations*. Retrieved May 08, 2021, from Thomson Reuters: https://www.reuters.com/article/us-un-assembly-trump-comments-factbox-idUSKCN1BU2J1

Rich, T. S., & Banerje, V. (2014). Running Out of Time? The Evolution of Taiwan's Relations in Africa. *Journal of Current Chinese Affairs* (44 (1)), pp. 141–146.

Richardson, N. (1978). *Foreign Policy and Economic Dependence*. Texas, USA: University of Texas Press.

Richmond, O. (2009). A Post-Liberal Peace: Eirenism and the Everyday. *Review of International Studies* (35 (3)), pp. 557–580.

Richmond, O., & Franks, J. (2007). Liberal Hubris? Virtual Peace in Cambodia. *Security Dialogue* (38 (1)), pp. 27–48.

Richter, C. (2003). Pre-emtive Self-Defence, International Law and US Policy. *Dialogue* (1 (2)), pp. 55–66.

Riffat, M. (2016). Theoretical Preliminaries of Military Intervention in Politics and its implications on Pakistan. *Journal of Indian Studies* (No. 2), pp. 90–105.

Rihoux, B. (2006). Qualitative Comparative Analysis (QCA) and Related Systematic Comparative Methods: Recent Advances and Remaining Challenges for Social Science Research. *International Sociology* (21 (5)), pp. 679–706. Retrieved 2020

Rihoux, B., & De Meur, G. (2009). Crisp-Set Qualitative Comparative Analysis. In C. C. Regan, *Configurational Comparative Methods* (pp. 33–68). California: SAGE Publications.

Rihoux, B., & Ragin, C. (2008). *Configurational Comparative Methods Qualitative Comparative Analysis (QCA) and Related Techniques.* SAGE Publications.

Rioux, J.-S. (2003). *Third Party Interventions in International Conflicts: Theory and Evidence.* Laval, Canada: Canada Research Chair in International Security, Institut québécois des hautes études internationales Université Laval.

Rittberger, V. (2001). German Foreign Policy Since Unification. In V. Rittberger, *German Foreign Policy Since Unification* (pp. 1–9). Manchester, New York, Vancouver: Manchester University Press.

Robinson, T. (1982). Restructuring Chinese Foreign Policy, 1959–76: Three Episodes. In K. Holsti, *Why Nations Realign: Foreign Policy Restructuring in the Postwar World* (pp. 134–171). London, New York: Routledge, Taylor and Francis Group.

Rolland, N. (2019). Securing the Belt and Road: Prospects for Chinese Military Engagement Along the Silk Roads. *The National Bureau of Asian Research, Special Report #80*, pp. 1–6.

Romano, G. (2020). *Changing Urban Renewal Policies in China.* Springer International Publishing.

Rosati, J. (2000). The Power of Human Cognition in the Study of World Politics. *International Studies Review* (2 (3)), pp. 45–75.

Rose, G. (1998). Review: Neoclassical Realism and Theories of Foreign Policy. (C. U. Press, ed.) *World Politics* (51 (1)), pp. 144–172.

Rosenau, J. (2006). *The Study of World Politics.* London, New York: Routledge Francis & Taylor.

Ross, W., & Coons, C. (2018). *Wilbur Ross and Chris Coons: China is 'pouring money into Africa.' Here's how the US can level the playing field.* Retrieved from CNBC, NBC Universal: https://www.cnbc.com/2018/08/02/china-is-pouring-money-into-in-africa-heres-why-the-us-must-compete.html

Rózsa, E. (2020). *Deciphering China in the Middle East.* Paris: European Union Institute for Security Studies.

Rózsa, E., & Peragovics, T. (2020). China's Political, Military and Cultural Engagement in the MENA Region. In K. Sidło, *The Role of China in the Middle East and NorthAfrica (MENA). Beyond Economic Interests?* (pp. 58–87). Barcelona: European Institute of the Mediterranean.

REFERENCES

Rudolf, P. (2020). The Sino-American World Conflict. *Strategic Rivalry between United States and China*, pp. 9–11.

Šabič, Z., & Pejič, N. (2019). The New Balance of Power in International Organisations: China in the Spotlight. *Teorija in Praksa* (56), pp. 372–513.

Sachs-Hombach, K., & Rehkämper, K. (2013). *Bild – Bildwahrnehmung – Bildverarbeitung, Interdisziplinäre Beiträge zur Bildwissenschaft* (vol. 15). Springer Verlag.

SADR. (1999). *Constitution of the Saharawi Arab Democratic Republic*. Congress of the Frente POLISARIO. Retrieved March 27, 2020, from http://www.arso.org/03-const.99.htm

Saferworld. (2013). *Managing risk in unstable countries: A conflict-sensitive approach*. London: Saferworld.

Sahui, M. (2018). An Analysis of China–Cote d'Ivoire Bilateral Trade. (S. R. Inc., ed.) *Open Journal of Business and Managemet* (6), pp. 923–937.

Saldinger, A. (2018). Congress again rejects steep cuts to US foreign assistance in new budget. *Devex*. Retrieved June 22, 2018, from https://www.devex.com/news/congress-again-rejects-steep-cuts-to-us-foreign-assistance-in-new-budget-92403

Salliot, E. (2010). *A review of past security events in the Sahel 1967– 2007*. OECD.

Sampathkumar, M. (2018). UN in deadlock after US and Russia vote against each other to investigate Syria chemical weapons attack. *Independent*. Retrieved June 30, 2021, from https://www.independent.co.uk/news/world/syria-chemical-attack-douma-latest-us-russia-un-deadlock-investigation-a8298671.html

Sarjoon, A., & Yusoff, M. A. (2019). The United Nations Peacekeeping Operations and Challenges. *Academic Journal of Interdisciplinary Studies* (8 (3)), pp. 202–211.

Sayin, Y., & Kilic, F. (2020). The Strait of Hormuz and Iran's International Relations. *Eurasian Research Journal* (2(1)), pp. 29–60.

SC/9089. (2007). *Security Council*. Retrieved April 05, 2020, from Meetings Coverage and Press Releases: https://www.un.org/press/en/2007/sc9089.doc.htm

Scharping, T. (2002). *Chinese Policy Interests in Sub-Saharan Africa*. Köln: Cologne China Studies Online.

Schirch, L. (2005). *Ritual and Symbol in Peacebuilding*. Bloomfield, USA: Kumarian Press Inc.

Schmidt, B., & Roy, N. (2013). Rising Powers: A Realist Analysis. In R. Friedman, K. Oskanian, & R. Pardo, *After Liberalism? The Future of Liberalism in International Relations* (pp. 67–87). London: Palgrave Macmillan.

Schmidt, M. G. (1995). *Wörterbuch zur Politik*. Stuttgart: Alfred Kröner Verlag.

Schneckener, U. (2006). Charakteristika und Dynamiken fragiler Staatlichkeit. Zur Auswertung der Fallstudien. In U. Schneckener, *Fragile Staatlichkeit: States at Risk, zwischen Stabilität und Scheitern* (pp. 358–359). Baden-Baden: Nomos.

Scot, J. (2007). Power, Domination and Stratification: Towards a conceptual synthesis. *Sociologia Problemas E Practicas*(55), pp. 25–39.

REFERENCES

Security Council 10987. (2013). *United Nations Meetings Coverage and Press Releases*. Retrieved November 05, 2020, from Security Council Establishes Peacekeeping Force for Mali Effective 1 July, Unanimously Adopting Resolution 2100 (2013): https://www.un.org/press/en/2013/sc10987.doc.htm

Security Council. (2018). *Security Council Report*. Retrieved 06 20, 2018, from http://www.securitycouncilreport.org/un-security-council-working-methods/the-veto.php

Security Degree Hub. (2020). *30 Most Powerful Private Security Companies in the World*. Retrieved September 26, 2020, from https://www.securitydegreehub.com/most-powerful-private-security-companies-in-the-world/

Seesaghur, H. (2015). Good Governance with Chinese characteristics: A perspective of China's Socialist Model. (M. Institute, ed.) *Journal of Public Administration and Governance* (5 (3)), pp. 36–45.

Seesaghur, H., & Ansong, R. (2014). An overview of China's expanding role in peacekeeping missions in Africa. *Science* (4 (11)), pp. 193–197.

Selim, G. (2019). The Sino-Russian strategic understanding on the Arab uprisings: Motivations and implications. *Journal of Contemporary Iraq & the Arab World* (13(2&3)), pp. 243-269.

Serebrov, S. (2017). *Yemen Crisis: Causes, Threats and Resolution Scenario*. Russia: Russian International Affairs Council.

Shambaugh, D. (1994). Patterns of Interaction in Sino-American Relations. In T. W. Robinson, & D. Shambaugh, *Chinese Foreign Policy Theory and Practice* (pp. 197–223). Oxford: Clarendon Press.

Shambaugh, D. (2005, Juli/August). China's Soft-Power Push. *Foreign Affairs* (94 (4)), pp. 99–107.

Sharp, G. (1973). *The politics of nonviolent action*. Boston: MA: Porter Sargent.

Sharp, M. J. (2018). *Yemen: Civil War and Regional Intervention*. Washington: Congressional Research Service.

Shen, G. (2001). *Statement by Ambassador Shen Guofang, Deputy Permanent Representative of China to UN at the Security Council on the Topic of "Peace-Building: towards a Comprehensive Approach"*. Retrieved October 07, 2020, from Statements and Documents: https://www.fmprc.gov.cn/ce/ceun/eng/smhwj/wangnian/fy01/t26857.htm

Shichor, Y. (1991). China and the Role of the United Nations in the Middle East: Revised Policy. *University of California Press* (31 (3)), pp. 255–269.

Shichor, Y. (2006). Silent Partner: China and the Lebanon Crisis. *China Brief* (6 (17)).

Shichor, Y. (2011). Speak Softly and Carry a Big Stick, Non-Traditional Chinese Threats and Middle Eastern Instability. In H. S. Yee (ed.), *China's Rise Threat or Opportunity?* (pp. 101–123). New York: Routledge.

Shichor, Y. (2013). Fundamentally Unacceptable yet Occasionally Unavoidable: China's Options on External Interference in the Middle East. *China Report* (1), pp. 25–41.

REFERENCES

Shirkey, Z. C. (2012). When and How Many: The Effects of Third Party Joining on Casualties and Duration in Interstate Wars. (C. U. Hunter College, ed.) *Journal of Peace Research* (49 (2)), pp. 321–334.

Shirkey, Z. C. (2016). Joining by Number: Military Intervention in Civil Wars. *Civil Wars* (18(4)), pp. 417–438.

Sid, R. (2013). Preventive diplomacy, mediation and the responsibility to protect in Libya: a missed opportunity for Canada? *Canadian Foreign Policy Journa l*(1), pp. 39–52.

Sidło, K. W. (2020). Foreword. In K. W. Sidło, *The Role of China in the Middle East and NorthAfrica (MENA). Beyond Economic Interests?* (pp. 6–9). Barcelona: European Institute of the Mediterranean.

Silverstone, S. A. (2016). *Intervention and Use of Force.* doi:10.1093/obo/9780199743292-0047

Singer, J. (1961). The Level-of-Analysis Problem in International Relations. *The International System: Theoretical Essays*, Cambridge University Press, pp. 77–92.

Siniver, A. (2006). Power, impartiality, and timing: three hypotheses on third party mediation in the Middle East. *Political Studies* (4), pp. 806–826.

Siradağ, A. (2016). Explaining the Conflict in Central African Republic: Causes and Dynamics. *Epiphany: Journal of Transdisciplinary Studies* (9 (3)), pp. 86–103.

Siverson, R. (1995). Democracies and War Participation: In Defense of the Institutional Constraints Argument. *European Journal of International Relations* (1 (4)), pp. 481–489.

Slaughter, A.-M. (2004). The use of force in Iraq: illegal and illegitimate. (C. U. Press, ed.) *Proceedings of the ASIL Annual Meeting* (98), pp. 262–263.

Snyder, J. (1991). *Myths of Empire, Domestic Politics and International Ambition.* Cornell: Cornell University Press.

Snyder, J. (2004). One World, Rival Theories. *Foreign Policy*, pp. 52–62.

Sofer, K. (2012). *China and the Collapse of its Noninterventionist Foreign Policy.* Washington D.C.: Center for American Progress.

Soper, T. (2015). Full text: China President Xi gives policy speech in Seattle, wants to fight cybercrime with the U.S. *GeekWire*. Retrieved October 04, 2018, from https://www.geekwire.com/2015/full-text-china-president-xi-gives-policy-speech-in-seattle-pledges-to-fight-cybercrime-with-u-s/

Sørensen, C. T. (2015). The Significance of Xi Jinping's "Chinese Dream" for Chinese Foreign Policy: From "Tao Guang Hui" to "Fen Fa You Wei". *Journal of China and International Relations* (3 (1)), pp. 52–73.

Sorokin, P. A. (1925). *The sociology of revolution.* Philadelphia: PA: J. B. Lippincott.

Spegele, B., & Bradley, M. (2013). Middle East Oil Fuels Fresh China–U.S. Tensions. *The Wall Street Journal*.

Sprangers, L., van der Putten, F.-P., & Forough, M. (2021). *The BRI and China's International Trade Map.* Retrieved April 17, 2021, from Belt and Road Research Platform: https://www.beltroadresearch.com/the-bri-and-chinas-international-trade-map/

Stacher, J. (2015). Fragmenting states, new regimes: militarized state violence andtransition in the Middle East. *Democratization* (22 (2)), pp. 259–275. doi:10.1080/13510347.2015.1010810

Stähle, S. (2008). China's Shifting Attitude Towards United Nations Peacekeeping Operations. *The China Quarterly* (195), pp. 631–655.

Starr, P. (2007). *Freedom's Power: The history and promise of liberalism*. New York: Basic Books.

State Council of the People's Republic of China. (2015). *China's Military Strategy*. Retrieved August 30, 2020, from White Paper: http://english.www.gov.cn/archive/white_paper/2015/05/27/content_281475115610833.htm

State Council PRC. (2020). *China's Armed Forces: 30 Years of UN Peacekeeping Operations*. Retrieved November 17, 2020, from White Paper: http://english.www.gov.cn/archive/whitepaper/202009/18/content_WS5f6449a8c6d0f7257693c323.html

Statistics Times. (2018). Retrieved October 03, 2018, from http://statisticstimes.com/economy/projected-world-gdp-ranking.php

Stearns, J. (2012). *North Kivu The background to conflict in North Kivu province of eastern Congo*. London: Rift Valley Institute.

Stowell, E. C. (1921). *Intervention in International Law*. Washington DC: John Byrne & Co.

Strachan, A. (2014). *Conflict analysis of Morocco*. Birmingham, UK: GSDRC, University of Birmingham.

Strüver, G. (2016). *International Alignment between Interests and Ideology: The Case of China's Partnership Diplomacy*. Hamburg: German Institute of Global and Area Studies (GIGA).

Sukhankin, S. (2020). Chinese Private Security Contractors: New Trends and Future Prospects. *China Brief* (20 (9)).

Sun Tzu. (2000). The Art of War. Leicester: Allandale Online Publishing.

Sun Tzu. (2020). *The Art of War, Weak Points and Strong*. Retrieved August 30, 2020, from Chinese Text Project: https://ctext.org/art-of-war/weak-points-and-strong

Sun, D. (2017). China and the Middle East security governance in the new era. *Contemporary Arab Affairs* (3), pp. 354–371.

Sun, D. (2017). China and the Middle East security governance in the new era. *Contemporary Arab Affairs*, 10 (3), pp. 354–371.

Sun, D. (2018). *China's Soft Military Presence in the Middle East*. Riyadh: King Faisal Center for Research and Islamic Studies.

Sun, D., & Zoubir, Y. (2018). China's Participation in Conflict Resolution in the Middle East and North Africa: A Case of Quasi-Mediation Diplomacy? *Journal of Contemporary China*, 27 (110), pp. 224–243.

Sun, D. (2019). China's Whole-of-Region Diplomacy in the Middle East, Opportunities and Challenges. *China Quarterly of International Strategic Studies* (5(1)), pp. 49–64.

REFERENCES

Susskind, L., & Babbit, E. (1992). Overcoming the Obstacles to Effective Mediation of International Disputes. In J. Bercovitch, & J. Rubin, *Mediation in international relations: Multiple approaches to conflict management* (pp. 30–51). London: The Macmillan Press Ltd.

Tang, X. (2019). (T. Walter, Interviewer) Berlin.

Taylor, I. (2010). *The International Relations of Sub-Saharan Africa*. USA: Bloomsbury Publishing.

Terhune, K. W. (1970). From National Character to National Behavior: A Reformulation. *The Journal of Conflict Resolution* (14 (2)), pp. 203–263.

The Advocates for Human Rights. (2009). *A House with Two Rooms*. Saint Paul, Minnesota: DRI Press.

The Guardian. (2000). Rebel paymaster loses EU aid. *The Guardian*. Retrieved April 02, 2020, from https://www.theguardian.com/world/2000/jun/14/sierraleone

The White House. (2002). *The National Security Strategy*. Retrieved July 21, 2018, from https://georgewbush-whitehouse.archives.gov/nsc/nss/2002/

The White House. (2012). *U.S. Strategy towards Sub-Saharan Africa*. Washington D.C.: The White House.

The White House. (2014). *Office of the Vice President*. Retrieved from Speeches and Remarks: https://obamawhitehouse.archives.gov/the-press-office/2014/09/26/opening-remarks-vice-president-un-summit-peacekeeping-operations%22

The White House. (2021). *Interim National Security Strategic Guidance*. Washington: The White House.

The World Bank. (2020). *China Data*. Retrieved October 02, 2018, from https://data.worldbank.org/country/china

The World Bank Data. (2019). *Military expenditure (% of GDP)*. Retrieved January 05, 2021, from All Countries and Economies: https://data.worldbank.org/indicator/MS.MIL.XPND.GD.ZS

The World Bank Group. (2018). *TCdata360*. Retrieved September 30, 2018, from https://tcdata360.worldbank.org/indicators/7bc4251b?country=BRA&indicator=28157&viz=choropleth&years=2017

Theofilopoulou, A. (2006). *The United Nations and Western Sahara, A Never-ending Affair*. Washington: United States Institute of Peace.

Theofilopoulou, A. (2012). Morocco's new constitution and the Western Sahara conflict — a missed opportunity? *The Journal of North African Studies* (17 (4)), pp. 687–696.

TRAC. (2020). *Terrorism Research & Analysis Consortium*. Retrieved March 24, 2020, from https://www.trackingterrorism.org/group/eastern-turkistan-islamic-movement-etim

Trenin, D. (2018). What drives Russia's policy in the Middle East? (E. U. Studies, ed.) *Russia's return to the Middle East, Building sandcastles?*(146), pp. 21–27.

Tsai, M.-Y. (2003). *From Adversaries to Partners, Chinese and Russian Military Cooperation after the Cold War*. Westport, Conneticut, London: Praeger.

REFERENCES

Tür, Ö. (2006). The Lebanese War of 2006: Reasons and Consequences. *Perceptions*, pp. 109–122.

U.S. Commercial Service. (2017). *China Country Commercial Guide*. Retrieved June 30, 2021, from https://www.export.gov/article?id=China-Oil-and-Gas

U.S. Department of State. (2014). *The Global Coalition To Defeat ISIS*. Retrieved from US Department of State: https://www.state.gov/bureaus-offices/bureaus-and-offices-reporting-directly-to-the-secretary/the-global-coalition-to-defeat-isis/

U.S. Energy Information Administration. (2020). *U.S. Energy Information Administration*. Retrieved June 19, 2020, from China's crude oil imports surpassed 10 million barrels per day in 2019: https://www.eia.gov/todayinenergy/detail.php?id=43216

U.S.–China Economic and Security Review Commission. (2006). *Report to Congress*. U.S.–China Economic and Security Review Commission.

UCDP. (2020). (U. C. Program, Herausgeber). Retrieved June 30, 2021, from http://ucdp.uu.se/#/encyclopedia

UCDP&PRIO. (2020). *UCDP Dataset Download Center*. Retrieved March 28, 2019, from https://ucdp.uu.se/downloads/#d1

Ulrichsen, K. (2013). *Qatar's Mediation Initiatives*. Norwege: Norwegian Peacebuilding Resource Center (NOREF).

UN Charter. (1945). *Charter of the United Nations*. San Francisco.

UN Comtrade Database. (2020). *United Nations, Department of Economic and Social Affairs, Statistic Division, Trade Statistics*. Retrieved April 10, 2020, from https://comtrade.un.org/data

UN Department for General Assembly. (2020). *United Nations Regional Groups of Member States*. Retrieved April 10, 2020, from https://www.un.org/depts/DGACM/RegionalGroups.shtml

UN Department of Economic and Social Affairs. (2017). *Population Division*. Retrieved September 19, 2020, from International Migration: https://www.un.org/en/development/desa/population/migration/data/estimates2/estimates17.asp

UN Department Political and Peacebuilding Affairs. (2019). *DPPA Around the World*. Retrieved from UNMHA, Hudaydah Agreement: https://dppa.un.org/en/mission/unmha-hudaydah-agreement

UN General Assembly. (1957). *Dag Hammarskjöld Library*. Retrieved from UN Documentation Research Guide : https://undocs.org/en/A/RES/1236(XII)

UN MONUC. (2010). *United Nations Organization Mission in the Democratic Republic of the Congo*. Retrieved March 28th, 2020, from https://peacekeeping.un.org/mission/past/monuc/

UN News. (2018). Global Perspective Human Strories. Retrieved June 30, 2021, from https://news.un.org/en/focus/syria

UN News. (2018). *UN News*. Retrieved from Security Council renews UN mission in Western Sahara: https://news.un.org/en/story/2018/04/1008532

UN OCHA. (2020). *Data on casualties*. Retrieved from UN OCHA Occupied Palestinian Territory: https://www.ochaopt.org/data/casualties

REFERENCES

UN Peacekeeping. (2019). *Troop and Police contributors*. Retrieved December 02, 2018, from Summary of Troops Contributing Countries by Ranking: Police, UN Military Experts on Mission, Staff Officers and Troops: https://peacekeeping.un.org/sites/default/files/02_country_ranking_28.pdf

UN Peacekeeping. (2020). *Troop and police contributors*. Retrieved February 20, 2021, from https://peacekeeping.un.org/en/troop-and-police-contributors

UN Peacekeeping. (2021). *Troop and Police Contributions*. Retrieved April 17, 2021, from Resources Data: https://peacekeeping.un.org/en/troop-and-police-contributors

UN Resolution 1701. (2006). *Adopted by the Security Council at its 5511th meeting*. New York: United Nations Security Council.

UN Security Council. (1948). *Resolution 50 (1948) of 29 May 1948*. New York.

UN Security Council. (1971). *United Nations Digital Library*. Retrieved April 16, 2021, from Restoration of the lawful rights of the People's Republic of China in the United Nations.: https://digitallibrary.un.org/record/192054

UN Security Council. (2015). *Meeting No. 7531*. Retrieved from Meeting Records: https://digitallibrary.un.org/record/806124?ln=en

UN Security Council. (2019). *Meeting No. 8484*. Retrieved from Meeting Records: https://digitallibrary.un.org/record/3795612?ln=en

UN Security Council. (2019). *Meeting No. 8556*. Retrieved from Meeting Records: https://digitallibrary.un.org/record/3810469?ln=en

UN Security Council. (2019). *Meeting No. 8610*. Retrieved from Meeting Records: https://digitallibrary.un.org/record/3825876?ln=en

UN Security Council Report 1027. (2003). *Final report of the Panel of Experts on the Illegal Exploitation of Natural Resources and Other Forms of Wealth of DR Congo (S/2003/1027)*. New York: UN Security Council.

UN Security Council Report. (2002). *Final report of the Panel of Experts on the Illegal Exploitation of Natural Resources and Other Forms of Wealth of the Democratic Republic of the Congo, S/2002/1146*. New York: UN Security Council.

UN Security Council Resolution 1457. (2003). *The situation concerning the Democratic Republic of the Congo*. New York: UN Security Council.

UNAMID. (2019). *United Nations Peacekeeping UNAMID*. (U. Nations, Producer) Retrieved December 19, 2019, from https://unamid.unmissions.org/about-unamid-0

UNAMID Fact Sheet. (2007). *UN Peacekeeping*. Retrieved August 18, 2018, from https://peacekeeping.un.org/en/mission/unamid

UNCTAD. (2010). *Economic Development in Africa South–South Cooperation: Africa and the New Forms of Development Partnerships*. New York and Geneva: UNCTAD.

UNEP. (2007). *Lebanon Post-Conflict Environment Assessment, United Nations Environment Programme*. UNEP.

UNIFIL. (2018). *United Nations Peacekeeping*. Retrieved July 22, 2018, from https://peacekeeping.un.org/en/mission/unifil

UNIFIL. (2019). *UNIFIL Mandate*. Retrieved March 23, 2020, from https://unifil.unmissions.org/unifil-mandate

United Nations. (2018). *UNMIL Factsheet*. United Nations Peacekeeping. Retrieved June 30, 2021, from https://peacekeeping.un.org/en/mission/unmil

United Nations Peacekeeping. (2018). *Military*. Retrieved June 30, 2021, from https://peacekeeping.un.org/en/military

United Nations Peacekeeping. (2020). Retrieved June 30, 2021, from https://peacekeeping.un.org/en/how-we-are-funded

United Nations Press Release. (2007). *Meetings Coverage and Press Releases*. Retrieved March 24, 2020, from https://www.un.org/press/en/2007/org1477.doc.htm

United Nations UNMIL. (2018). *UNMIL, UN Missions*. Retrieved August 11, 2018, from https://unmil.unmissions.org/The-story-of-UNMIL

UNMISS Fact Sheet. (2011). *UN Peacekeeping*. Retrieved June 30, 2021, from https://peacekeeping.un.org/en/mission/unmiss

UNOCI Fact Sheet. (2004). *UN Peacekeeping*. Retrieved August 13, 2018, from https://peacekeeping.un.org/en/mission/onuci

UNODA. (2020). *Treaty on the Non-Proliferation of Nuclear Weapons*. Retrieved August 30, 2020, from United Nations Office for Disarmament Affairs: http://disarmament.un.org/treaties/t/npt

UNSC Resolution 2170. (2014). *United Nations Security Council, Resolution 2170 (2014) on threats to international peace and security caused by terrorist acts by Al-Qaida*. New York: UN Security Council.

UNSC Resolution 2178. (2014). *United Nations Security Council, Resolution 2178 (2014) on threats to international peace and security caused by foreign terrorist fighters*. New York: UN Security Council.

UNSC Resolution 2199. (2015). *United Nations Security Council, Resolution 2199 (2015) on threats to international peace and security caused by terrorist acts by Al-Qaida and associated groups*. New York: UN Security Council.

UNSCR. (2004). *United Nations Security Council*. Retrieved August 19, 2018, from The situation in Côte d'Ivoire: http://unscr.com/en/resolutions/1572

UNSCR. (2020). *UNSCR Search engine for the United Nations Security Council Resolutions*. Retrieved April 03, 2020, from http://unscr.com/en/resolutions/1509

UNTSO. (2020). *United Nations Truce Supervision Organization*. Retrieved from UN Missions Background: https://untso.unmissions.org/background

Uppsala Conflict Data Program. (2020). *Number of Conflicts*. (D. o. Research, ed.) Retrieved 06 20, 2018, from Department of Peace and Conflict Research: http://ucdp.uu.se/

Ursu, A.-E., & van den Berg, W. (2018). *China and the EU in the Horn of Africa: competition and cooperation?* Den Haag: Clingendael—Netherlands Institute of International Relations.

REFERENCES

US Department of Defense. (2010). *Military and Security Developments Involving the People's Republic of China 2010.* Washington DC.: Office of the Secretary of Defense.

US Department of Defense. (2012). *Military and Security Developments Involving the People's Republic of China 2012.* Washington DC.: Office of the Secretary of Defense.

US Department of Defense. (2013). *Military and Security Developments Involving the People's Republic of China 2013.* Washington DC.: Office of the Secretary of Defense.

US Department of Defense. (2014). *Military and Security Developments Involving the People's Republic of China 2014.* Washington DC.: Office of the Secretary of Defense.

US Department of Defense. (2015). *Military and Security Developments Involving the People's Republic of China 2015.* Washington DC.: Office of the Secretary of Defense.

US Department of Defense. (2016). *Military and Security Developments Involving the People's Republic of China 2016.* Washington DC.: Office of the Secretary of Defense.

US Department of Defense. (2017). *Military and Security Developments Involving the People's Republic of China 2017.* Washington DC.: Office of the Secretary of Defense.

US Department of Defense. (2019). *Military and Security Developments Involving the People's Republic of China 2019.* Washington DC: Office of the Secretary of Defense.

US Department of Defense. (2020). *Military and Security Developments Involving the People's Republic of China 2020.* Washington D.C.: Office of the Secretary of Defense.

Usden, R., & Juergenliemk, H. (2014). *History of UN Peacekeeping Factsheet.* Brussels: Global Governance Institute.

Uvin, P. (1999). *The Influence of Aid in Situations of Violent Conflict, A synthesis and a commentary on the lessons learned from case studies on the limits and scope for the use of development assistance incentives and disincentives for influencing conflict situations.* Paris: OECD-DAC.

van der Putten, F. (2015). *China's Evolving Role in Peacekeeping and African Security.The Deployment of Chinese Troops for UN Force Protection in Mali.* Netherlands: Clingendael Report, Netherlands Institute of International Relations.

Van Eekelen, W. F. (1967). Five Principles of Peaceful Coexistence. In W. F. Van Eekelen, *Indian Foreign Policy and the Border Dispute with China* (pp. 38–49). Dordrecht, The Hague: Springer Science + Business Media.

Vanaga, N. (2004). *China's Military Rise: The Lack of Transparency and Internal Political Uncertainty, Strategic Review No. 08.* Latvia: National Defence Academy of Latvia.

Vasselier, A. (2016). *Chinese Foreign Policy in South Sudan: the View from the Ground.* Washington D.C.: The Jamestown Foundation.

REFERENCES

Vatanka, A. (2021, April 26). *Making sense of the Iran–China strategic agreement.* Retrieved May 26, 2021, from Middle East Institute: https://www.mei.edu/publications/making-sense-iran-china-strategic-agreement

Väyryne, R. (1985). Focus On: Is There a Role for the United Nations in Conflict Resolution. *Journal of Peace Research* (22 (3)), pp. 189–196.

Vertzberger, Y. (1990). *The World in Their Minds. Information Processing, Cognition, and Perception in Foreign Policy Decisionmaking.* Stanford: Stanford University Press.

Vincent, J. (1974). *Nonintervention and International Order.* (P. U. Press, ed.) New Jersey.

Vollmann, E., Bohn, M., Sturm, R., & Demmelhuber, T. (2020). Decentralisation as authoritarian upgrading? Evidence from Jordan and Morocco. *The Journal of North African Studies.* doi:0.1080/13629387.2020.1787837

von Hein, M. (2018). *Deutsche Welle Asia.* Retrieved November 17, 2018, from https://www.dw.com/en/xi-jinping-and-the-chinese-dream/a-43685630

Voss, J., & Dorsey, E. (1992). Perception and international relations: An overview. In E. S. Hudson, *Political psychology and foreign policy* (pp. 3–30). Westview Press.

Wacker, G. (2018). China und der Kampf gegen die »drei üblen Kräfte«. In F. Heiduk, *Das kommende Kalifat?* (pp. 49–57). Berlin: Stiftung Wissenschaft und Politik.

Waever, O., & Tickner, A. (2009). Introduction: Geocultural epistemologies. In O. Waever, & A. Tickner, *International Relations Scholarship Around the World* (pp. 1–31). London, New-York: Routledge.

Walter, T. (2020). Chinese Peacekeeping Forces: How China's new Commitment on the International Stage is Promoted by the Country's Film Industry. In N. Noesselt, *China's New Silk Road Dreams* (pp. 104–116). Wien: LIT Verlag GmbH & Co. KG.

Waltz, K. (1979). *Theory of International Politics.* University of California, Berkley: Addison-Wesley Publishing Company.

Waltz, K. (1996). International Politics is not Foreign Policy. *Security Studies* (6 (1)), pp. 54–57.

Wang Yi. (2017). *Permanent Mission of the Peoples Republic of China to the United Nations Office.* Retrieved from Fulfilling a Serious Commitment to a Future of Peace: http://www.china-un.ch/eng/zywjyjh/t1500174.htm

Wang, G. (1991). *China and the Chinese Overseas.* Singapore: Times Academic Press.

Wang, M. (2018). *China's Strategy in Djibouti: Mixing Commercial and Military Interests.* New York: Council on Foreign Relations.

Wang, S. (1996). *Shijie zhuyao guojia zonghe guoli bijiao yanjiu [Comparative studies of the comprehensive national power of the world's major nations].* Changsha: Hunan chubanshe.

Wang, Y. (2009). China: Between Copying and Constructing. In A. Tickner, & O. Waever, *International Relations Scholarship Around the World* (pp. 103–119). London, New York: Routledge.

REFERENCES

Wang, Y., & Tan, X. (2009). *Sixty Years of China Foreign Affairs*. (P. I. Ltd, ed.) China Social Science Press.

Weber, M. (1947). *The Theory of Social and Economic Organization*. New York: The Free Press.

Webster, D. (1837). *Yale Law School*. Retrieved June 30, 2021, from http://avalon.law.yale.edu/19th_century/br-1842d.asp#web1

Wee, S.-L. (2012). Chinese workers kidnapped in Egypt freed. *Reuters*. Retrieved June 21, 2018, from https://uk.reuters.com/article/china-workers-egypt-idINDEE8100CY20120201

Wehr, P. (1979). *Conflict Regulation*. New York: Westview Press.

Wehrey, F., Kaye, D. D., Watkins, J., Martini, J., & Guffey, R. A. (2010). *The Iraq Effect, The Middle East After the Iraq War*. Santa Monica, Arlington, Pittsburgh: RAND Corporation.

Weiss, T. G. (2014). Military Humanitarianism: Syria Hasn't killed it. *Washington Quarterly* (37 (1)), pp. 7–20.

Weitz, R. (2015). *China and Afghanistan After the NATO Withdrawal*. Jamestown: The Jamestown Foundation.

Wendt, A. (1992, March). Anarchy is what states make of it. *International Organizations* (46 (2)), pp. 391–425.

Wendt, A. (1999). *Social Theory of International Politics*. Cambridge: Cambridge University Press.

Werthmann, K. (2005). Wer sind die Dyula? Ethnizität und Bürgerkrieg in der Côte d'Ivoire. (I. f. Afrika-Kunde, ed.) *afrika spectrum* (40 (2)), pp. 221–240.

Weyns, Y., Hoex, L., Hilgert, F., & Spittaels, S. (2014). *Mapping Conflict Motives: The Central African Republic*. Brussels: International Peace Information Service (IPIS).

Williams, P. (2011). *War & Conflict in Africa*. Cambridge, Malden: Polity Press.

Wimmen, H. (2016). *Syria's Path from Civic Uprising to Civil War*. Washington DC: Carnegie Endowment for International Peace.

Woetzel, J., & et al. (2019). *China and the world: Inside the dynamics of a changing relationship*. Brussels, San Francisco, Shanghai: Mc Kinsey Global Institute.

Wolff, P. (2016). *China's 'Belt and Road' Initiative — Challenges and Opportunities*. Bonn: German Development Institute /Deutsches Institut für Entwicklungspolitik (DIE).

Woo, J.-Y. (2017). *Foreign Intervention in Civil Wars*. Newcastle upon Tyne,: Cambridge Scholars Publishing.

Workman, D. (2018). *World's top exports*. Retrieved November 01, 2020, from China's Top Trading Partners: http://www.worldstopexports.com/chinas-top-import-partners/

World Bank. (2018). *The World Bank Data Energy Use*. (W. Bank, ed.) Retrieved June 21, 2018, from https://data.worldbank.org/indicator/EG.USE.PCAP.KG.OE?locations=CN

World Bank. (2019). *GDP (current US$) — China*. Retrieved June 21, 2018, from World Bank national accounts data, and OECD National Accounts data files: https://data.worldbank.org/indicator/NY.GDP.MKTP.CD?locations=CN

World Bank. (2020). *Population, total — China*. Retrieved August 30, 2020, from The World Bank Data: https://data.worldbank.org/indicator/SP.POP.TOTL?locations=CN

World Bank Group. (2018). *IBRD — IDA Data*. Retrieved from Total natural resource rents: https://data.worldbank.org/indicator/ny.gdp.totl.rt.zs

World Integrated Trade Solution. (2018). *WITS*. (W. B. Group, ed.) Retrieved September 30, 2018, from https://wits.worldbank.org/CountryProfile/en/Country/CHN/Year/2013/TradeFlow/EXPIMP

World Peace Foundation. (2017). *Ivory Coast — United Nations Operation in Côte d'Ivoire (UNOCI)*. World Peace Foundation. Retrieved from African Politics, African Peace.

World Population Review. (2020). *Countries That Recognize Taiwan 2020*. Retrieved November 02, 2020, from https://worldpopulationreview.com/country-rankings/countries-that-recognize-taiwan

Worldometers. (2018). *Population by country*. Retrieved October 03, 2018, from http://www.worldometers.info/world-population/population-by-country/

Wright, Q. (1942). *A study of war*. Chicago, IL: University of Chicago Press.

WTO. (2018). *China and the WTO*. (WTO, Herausgeber) Retrieved June 30, 2021, from https://www.wto.org/english/thewto_e/countries_e/china_e.htm

Xi Jinping. (2017). Secure a Decisive Victory in Building a Moderately Prosperous Society in All Respects and Strive for the Great Success of Socialism with Chinese Characteristics for a New Era. *Full text of Xi Jinping's report at 19th CPC National Congress*. (C. Daily, ed., & Xinhua, Compiler) Beijing, China. Retrieved December 16, 2019, from https://www.chinadaily.com.cn/china/19thcpcnationalcongress/2017-11/04/content_34115212.htm

Xi Jinping. (2019). *China and the World in the New Era*. Xinhua. China Daily. Retrieved December 16, 2019, from https://www.chinadailyhk.com/articles/187/125/62/1569558431751.html

Xi quoted from Xinhua. (2017). *Xinhua*. Retrieved February 14, 2021, from Full text of President Xi's speech at opening of Belt and Road forum: http://www.xinhuanet.com//english/2017-05/14/c_136282982.htm

Xi, J. (2013). *China.org.cn*. Retrieved October 02, 2018, from http://www.china.org.cn/business/Boao_Forum_2013/2013-04/10/content_28501562.htm

Xi, J. (2015). *Xi Jinping Pays a State Visit to the US and Attends Summits Marking the 70th Anniversary of the UN*. Retrieved May 28, 2021, from Ministry of Foreign Affairs of the People's Republic of China: https://www.fmprc.gov.cn/mfa_eng/topics_665678/xjpdmgjxgsfwbcxlhgcl70znxlfh/t1304144.shtml

Xi, J. (2017). *Embassy of the People's Republic of China in the Republic of Iraq*. Retrieved October 03, 2018, from Work Together to Build a Community of Shared Future for Mankind: http://iq.chineseembassy.org/eng/zygx/t1432869.htm

REFERENCES

Xi, J. (2017). Secure a Decisive Victory in Building a Moderately Prosperous Society in all Respects and Strive for the Great Success of Socialism with Chinese Characteristics for a New Era. *Report*, (pp. 1–66). China. Retrieved November 18, 2018, from http://www.xinhuanet.com/english/download/Xi_Jinping's_report_at_19th_CPC_National_Congress.pdf

Xi, J. (2017). *Xinhua*. Retrieved October 03, 2018, from http://www.xinhuanet.com/english/2017-05/14/c_136282982.htm

Xi, J. (2018). *CGTN Politics*. Retrieved October 03, 2018, from Full text of President Xi's New Year address: https://news.cgtn.com/news/3063444d35637a6333566d54/share_p.html

Yahuda, M. (1991). Special Issue: Deng Xiaoping: An Assessment. *The China Quarterly* (135), pp. 551–572.

Yamamoto, Y., & Bremer, S. (1980). Wider Wars and Restless Nights: Major Power Intervention in Ongoing Wars, 1815–1965. In J. Singer, *The Correlates of War II: Testing Some Realpolitik Models* (pp. 199–229). New York: Free Press.

Yan, J. (2019). Managing Asymmetry: Reexamining China–South Sudan Relations. *China: An International Journal* (17 (3)), pp. 149–168.

Yan, X. (2014). From Keeping a Low Profile to Striving for Achievement. *The Chinese Journal of International Politics*, pp. 153–184.

Yang, H. (2018a). Time to up the game? Middle Eastern security and Chinese strategic involvement. *Asia Europe Journal* (16 (3)), pp. 283–296.

Yang, X. (2019). Theorizing the BRICS: Does the BRICS challenge the current global order? In L. Xing, *The International Political Economy of the BRICS* (pp. 37–56). New York: Routledge Taylor and Francis Group.

Yang, X. (2021). US–China Crossroads Ahead: Perils and Opportunities for Biden. *The Washington Quarterly* (44(1)), pp. 129–153.

Yang, Z. (2018b). *Securing China's Belt and Road Initiative*. Washington D.C.: United States Institute of Peace.

Yavuzaslan, K., & Cetin, M. (2016). *Soft Power Concept and Soft Power Indexes*. Istanbul: Aydin Adnan Menderes University; Istanbul University.

Yellinek, R. (2017). *Is China Intervening in the Israeli–Palestinian Conflict?* Ramat Gan, Israel: BESA Center Perspectives.

Yemen Data Project. (2021). Retrieved August 18, 2018, from https://yemendataproject.org/

Yilmaz, S. (2015). The Iranian Nuclear Dilemma: A Comparative Analysis of Chinese and US Strategy. *International Journal of China Studies* (6(1)), pp. 45–62.

Yom, S. (2020). US Foreign Policy in the Middle East: The Logic of Hegemonic Retreat. *Global Policy* (11 (1)), pp. 75–83.

Young, O. (1967). *Intermediaries: Third Parties in International Crises*. Princeton: Princeton University Press.

Young, O. (1972). Additional Thoughts on Third Parties. *The Journal of Conflict Resolution* (16 (1)), pp. 51–65.

REFERENCES

Yuan, J.-D. (2003). Sino–US Military Relations Since Tiananmen: Restoration, Progress, and Pitfalls. *Parameters: US Army War College Quarterly* (33 (1)), pp. 51–67.

Zaborowski, M. (2018). *EU–China security relations*. Paris: EU Institute for Security Studies.

Zaobao. (2018). Lu Chaomei, leader of the United Nations peacekeeping. *Zaobao*. Retrieved June 22, 2018, from https://www.zaobao.com.sg/wencui/politic/story20180127-830527

Zartman, I., & Touval, S. (1985). International Mediation: Conflict Resolution and Power Politics. *Journal of Social Issues* (41 (2)), pp. 27–45.

Zerba, S. H. (2014). China's Libya Evacuation Operation: anew diplomatic imperative—overseas citizen protection. *Journal of Contemporary China* (23 (90)), pp. 1093–1112.

Zhang, C. (2017). The Belt and Road Initiative and global governance in transition. *China Quarterly of International Strategic Studies* (3 (2)), pp. 175–191.

Zhao, S. (2010). The China Model: can it replace the Western model of modernization? (Routledge, ed.) *Journal of Contemporary China* (19 (65)), pp. 419–436.

Zhao, T. (2009). A Political World Philosophy in terms of All-under-heaven (Tianxia). (S. Publications, ed.) *Diogenes* (56 (5)), pp. 5–18.

Zheng, S. (2017). China completes registration of 8,000-strong UN peacekeeping force, defence ministry says. *South China Morning Post*. Retrieved June 30, 2021, from http://www.scmp.com/news/china/diplomacy-defence/article/2113436/china-completes-registration-8000-strong-un

Zheng, Y., & Zhang, C. (2021). 'Soft power' and Chinese soft power. In H. Lai, & Y. Lu, *China's Soft Power and International Relations* (pp. 21–38). Oxon, New York: Routledge.

Zhong, N. (2016). *China Daily*. Retrieved September 26, 2020, from Overseas security to get upgrade: http://www.chinadaily.com.cn/business/2016-04/22/content_24740448.htm

Zhou, E. (1955). *Main Speech by Premier Zhou Enlai, Head of the Delegation of the People's Republic of China, Distributed at the Plenary Session of the Asian–African Conference*. Washington D.C.: Wilson Center Digital Archive.

Zhou, L. (2016). Chinese firms evacuate 330 staff in South Sudan as deadly fighting escalates. *South China Morning Post*. Retrieved June 30, 2021, from http://www.scmp.com/news/china/diplomacy-defence/article/1989762/chinese-firms-evacuate-330-staff-south-sudan-deadly

Zhou, Z. (2015). China's Draft Counter-Terrorism Law. (J. Foundation, ed.) *China Brief* (15 (14)).

Zhu, L. (2010). *China's Foreign Policy Debates*. Institute for Security Studies European Union. Paris: Chaillot Papers.

Zhu, L. (2010). *China's Foreign Policy Debates*. Paris: Challiot Papers, Institute for Security Studies.

Zhu, W. (2011). Middle East Terrorism, Global Governance and China's Anti-terror Policy. *Journal of Middle Eastern and Islamic Studies (in Asia)* (5 (2)).

REFERENCES

Zhuo, C. (2018). *10 years of China's Gulf of Aden journey: A global player with more responsibility*. Retrieved from Ministry of National Defense of the People's Republic of China : http://eng.mod.gov.cn/news/2018-12/28/content_4833111.htm

ZiroMwatela, R., & Zhao, C. (2016, December). Africa in China's One Belt, 'One Road' Initiative: A Critical Analysis. *IOSR Journal Of Humanities And Social Science* (21(2)), pp. 10–21.

Zoubir, Y. (2020). *Expanding Sino–Maghreb Relations, Morocco and Tunisia*. Chatham House.

Zoubir, Y. H. (1996). The Western Sahara Conflict: A Case Study in Failure of Prenegotiation and Prolognation of Conflict. *California Western International Law Journal* (26 (2)), pp. 173–213.

Zürcher, C. (2019). *30 Years of Chinese Peacekeeping*. Ottawa: Center for International Policy Studies, University of Ottawa.